Making it Happen

Making it Happen

Student Involvement in Education Planning, Decision Making, and Instruction

edited by

Michael L. Wehmeyer, Ph.D.
The Arc National Headquarters
Arlington, Texas

and

Deanna J. Sands, Ed.D.
University of Colorado
Denver

·P A U L·H·
BROOKES
PUBLISHING C<u>O</u>

Baltimore • London • Toronto • Sydney

Paul H. Brookes Publishing Co.
Post Office Box 10624
Baltimore, Maryland 21285-0624

www.pbrookes.com

Typeset by Brushwood Graphics, Inc., Baltimore, Maryland.
Manufactured in the United States of America by
Versa Press, East Peoria, Illinois.

Some of the individuals and circumstances described in this book are real. Some names have been changed to protect identities. Selected case studies are composites based on the authors' experiences; these case studies do not represent the lives or experiences of specific individuals, and no implications should be inferred. Descriptions of real people or circumstances are presented herein with the individuals' written consent.

Library of Congress Cataloging-in-Publication Data

Making it happen : student involvement in education planning,
   decision making, and instruction / edited by Michael L. Wehmeyer and
   Deanna J. Sands.
      p.   cm.
   Includes bibliographical references and index.
   ISBN 1-55766-330-0
   1. Handicapped youth—Education—United States—Decision making.
   2. Autonomy (Psychology)—United States.   3. School-to-work
   transition—United States.   4. Postsecondary education—United
   States.   5. Student participation in curriculum planning—United
   States.   I. Wehmeyer, Michael L.   II. Sands, Deanna J.
   LC4031.M295   1998
   371.9—dc21
                                                            97-41736
                                                            CIP

British Library Cataloguing in Publication data are available from the British Library.

Contents

I   Involving Students with Disabilities in the Education Process: An Overview of the Impetus for Benefits from Student Involvement

II   Promoting Student Involvement in the Education-Planning and Decision-Making Process

About the Editors

Michael L. Wehmeyer, Ph.D., Assistant Director, Department of Research and Program Services, The Arc National Headquarters, 500 East Border Street, Suite 300, Arlington, Texas 76010. Dr. Wehmeyer received his doctoral degree in human development and communication sciences from the University of Texas and received master's and undergraduate degrees in special education. From 1987 to 1988, he was a Rotary Scholar at the University of Sussex, Brighton, England, where he read for the master's degree in experimental psychology. Dr. Wehmeyer taught students with mental retardation requiring extensive supports and multiple disabilities in public schools in Oklahoma and Texas for 7 years and also worked as an associate clinical psychologist for the Texas Department of Mental Health and Mental Retardation. He has directed numerous federally funded projects that involved conducting research, developing curricular and assessment materials, and disseminating model programs to promote students' self-determination and students' involvement. One such project resulted in the publication of *Whose Future Is it Anyway?* (The Arc National Headquarters, 1995), a student-directed transition-planning program, and another project resulted in the publication of The Arc's Self-Determination Scale (The Arc National Headquarters, 1995). Dr. Wehmeyer's research has been concentrated in the area of self-determination, focusing on theory construction, examining the degree to which students and adults with cognitive disabilities are self-determined, and developing curricular materials to promote students' self-determination and students' involvement. He has published more than 50 articles and chapters. His journal publications include articles in *American Journal on Mental Retardation, Educational and Psychological Measurement, Education and Training in Mental Retardation and Developmental Disabilities, Exceptional Children, Mental Retardation,* and *Psychological Reports.* In addition, Dr. Wehmeyer is co-editor of the book *Self-Determination Across the Life Span: Independence and Choice for People with Disabilities* (Paul H. Brookes Publishing Co., 1996) and is lead co-author of the book *Teaching Self-Determination to Students with Disabilities: Basic Skills for Successful Transition* (Paul H. Brookes Publishing Co., 1998).

Deanna J. Sands, Ed.D., Associate Professor, School of Education, University of Colorado, Campus Box 106, Post Office Box 173364, Denver, Colorado 80217-3364. Dr. Sands is Associate Professor and Coordinator, Division of Technology and Special Services, and Program Coordinator for the Division of Special Education in the School of Education at the University of Colorado at Denver. She is responsible for training graduate-level students who are pursuing master's degrees or endorsements in special education with a concentration in dealing with people with disabilities who have mild, moderate, and severe or profound needs. Her activities and responsibilities include ongoing recruitment, program monitoring, developing and teaching courses, advising students, developing professional development schools and internship sites, coordinating programs with professionals at those sites, and supervising practicum students, as well as maintaining an ongoing research agenda. Dr. Sands's research and publications have focused on the areas of curriculum, independent living skills, the quality of life of people with disabilities, self-determination, and transition services. Since 1994, she has served as Project Director of Best Practices: A Study to Understand Variables that Influence Student Participation in Transition Planning, a federally funded research project. She is co-editor of *Self-Determination Across the Life Span: Independence and Choice for People with Disabilities* (Paul H. Brookes Publishing Co., 1996). Dr. Sands has published widely in the areas of special education and curriculum, including journal articles in *Exceptional Children* and *Journal of Special Education*, and she served as Associate Editor of *Journal of Career Development for Exceptional Individuals*. She has worked closely with the Colorado Department of Education, Special Services Unit, on several task forces, including those dealing with transitions, deafblindness, independent living, and the mild/moderate needs consortium.

Contributors

Martin Agran, Ph.D.
Professor
Department of Special Education
Utah State University
2865 University Boulevard
Logan, Utah 84322-2865

Diane S. Bassett, Ph.D.
Associate Professor
Division of Special Education
University of Northern Colorado
McKee 29
Greeley, Colorado 80639

Anne Brown, B.S.
Portland Metro Regional Coordinator
Oregon COPE Project, Inc.
999 Locust Street, N.E.
Salem, Oregon 97303

Fredda Brown, Ph.D.
Professor
Special Education Program
School of Education
Queens College, City University
  of New York
65-30 Kissena Boulevard
Flushing, New York 11367

Winnelle D. Carpenter, M.A.
Director and Founder
Cognitive Learning Consultants
Post Office Box 202065
8105 13th Avenue South
Bloomington, Minnesota 55425

Emilee Curtis, B.S.
Executive Director
New Hats, Inc.
HC 64, Post Office Box 2509
Castle Valley, Utah 84532

Beth Doll, Ph.D.
Associate Professor
Division of Technology and Special
  Services
University of Colorado at Denver
Campus Box 106
Post Office Box 173364
Denver, Colorado 80217-3364

Ann Fullerton, Ph.D.
Associate Professor
Department of Special and Counselor
  Education
Portland State University
6th and Harrison, Room 204, 2nd Floor
Portland, Oregon 97207-0751

Carole R. Gothelf, Ed.D.
Director of Education
The Jewish Guild for the Blind
15 West 65th Street
New York, New York 10023

Andrew S. Halpern, Ph.D.
Professor of Education
University of Oregon
175 College of Education
Eugene, Oregon 97403

Carolyn Hughes, Ph.D.
Associate Professor
Department of Special Education
Peabody College
Vanderbilt University
Box 328
Nashville, Tennessee 37203

Jean Lehmann, Ph.D.
School of Education
Colorado State University
Fort Collins, Colorado 80523-1588

Constance Loesch, A.A.S.
Research Assistant
TAKE CHARGE
Center on Self-Determination
University Affiliated Program
Oregon Health Sciences University
3608 Southeast Powell Boulevard
Portland, Oregon 97202

Laura Huber Marshall, M.A.
Research Assistant
School of Education
Center for Self-Determination
University of Colorado at Colorado
  Springs
4059 Columbine Hall
1420 Austin Bluffs Parkway
Post Office Box 7150
Colorado Springs, Colorado 80933-7150

James E. Martin, Ph.D.
Professor and Coordinator
Special Education Program
School of Education
Center for Self-Determination
University of Colorado at Colorado
  Springs
4059 Columbine Hall
1420 Austin Bluffs Parkway
Post Office Box 7150
Colorado Springs, Colorado 80933-7150

Dennis E. Mithaug, Ph.D.
Professor of Education
Department of Health and Behavior
  Studies
Teachers College, Columbia University
525 West 120th Street
New York, New York 10027

Debra A. Neubert, Ph.D.
Associate Professor
Department of Special Education
College of Education
University of Maryland
1308 Benjamin Building
College Park, Maryland 20742

Susan Palmer, Ph.D.
Project Director
Self-Determination Research Project
Department of Research and Program
  Services
The Arc National Headquarters
500 East Border Street, Suite 300
Arlington, Texas 76010

Cecelia Ann Pauley
Student
Montgomery College
8740 Sleepy Hollow Lane
Potomac, Maryland 20854

Laurie E. Powers, Ph.D.
Associate Professor of Pediatrics
Center on Self-Determination
University Affiliated Program
Oregon Health Sciences University
3608 Southeast Powell Boulevard
Portland, Oregon 97202

Judith A. Presley, M.S.
Research Assistant
Department of Special Education
Peabody College
Vanderbilt University
Box 328
Nashville, Tennessee 37203

Charity Rowland, Ph.D.
Co-director
Center on Self-Determination
University Affiliated Program
Oregon Health Sciences University
3608 Southeast Powell Boulevard
Portland, Oregon 97202

Patricia L. Sitlington, Ph.D.
Professor
Department of Special Education
University of Northern Iowa
Cedar Falls, Iowa 50614-0601

Karen C. Spencer, Ph.D., OTR
Associate Professor
Department of Occupational Therapy
Colorado State University
Fort Collins, Colorado 80523-1573

Alison Turner, M.Ed.
Project Coordinator
TAKE CHARGE
31 Sheafe Street
Portsmouth, New Hampshire 03801

Anthony K. Van Reusen, Ph.D.
Associate Vice President for Academic
    Affairs
University of Texas at San Antonio
6900 North Loop #1604 West
San Antonio, Texas 78249-0603

Dean H. Westwood, B.S.
Outreach Coordinator
TAKE CHARGE
Center on Self-Determination
University Affiliated Program
Oregon Health Sciences University
3608 Southeast Powell Boulevard
Portland, Oregon 97202

Foreword

As discussed in Chapter 1 of this book, the Individuals with Disabilities Education Act (IDEA) of 1990 (PL 101-476) provided a federal focus for student involvement by defining *transition services* as

> A coordinated set of activities for a student, designed within an outcome-oriented process, which promotes movement from school to post-school activities, including post-secondary education, vocational training, integrated employment (including supported employment), continuing and adult education, adult services, independent living, or community participation. The coordinated set of activities shall be based upon the individual student's needs, taking into account the student's preferences and interests, and shall include instruction, community experiences, the development of employment and other post-school adult living objectives, and, when appropriate, acquisition of daily living skills and functional vocational evaluation. (20 U.S.C. § 1401 [a][19])

The requirement that the "coordinated set of activities shall be based upon the individual student's needs, taking into account the student's preferences and interests," implies that transition planning should not take place without input from the student regarding his or her needs, preferences, and interests. Therefore, the Office of Special Education Programs (OSEP) of the U.S. Department of Education, in developing regulations implementing this requirement, stated that "all students, beginning no later than age 16—and at a younger age, if determined appropriate—be invited to attend the Individualized Education Program (IEP) meeting at which a transition plan is to be developed" (34 C.F.R. § 300.344[c]).

However, the notion that the student should be invited to the IEP meeting did not originate with the IDEA regulations. The original federal regulations implementing Part B of the Education for All Handicapped Children Act of 1975 (PL 94-142), published in September 1977, permitted the child to attend the IEP meeting *when appropriate*. Although there were few studies done on students attending IEP meetings prior to the Individuals with Disabilities Education Act Amendments of 1991 (PL 102-119), anecdotal information indicated that most students did not attend their IEP meetings; therefore, one can assume that the other IEP committee members (i.e., parents, teachers, administrators) almost never considered the child's attendance to be appropriate.

At the same time that the new Part B regulations under the Individuals with Disabilities Education Act Amendments of 1991 pertaining to transition were being developed, OSEP was supporting several model demonstration projects to identify and teach skills necessary for self-determination. Many of the developers of these regulations strongly believed that it would be contradictory to the emerging body of knowledge on self-determination not to involve the student in any IEP meeting at which a statement of needed transition services is discussed. This belief was supported by many public comments and based on the concept that because many of these transition services would extend into adulthood, it was critical that students begin to have input and control over their lives. Therefore, the final regulations state that students *must* be invited to this meeting.

We must recognize that the emphasis on the involvement of students with disabilities in transition planning did *not* happen because of IDEA. It happened because it was a logical step within the context of the disability rights movement. It happened because the Education for All Handicapped Children Act of 1975 guaranteed all children with disabilities a free appropriate public education. It happened because more than 120 demonstrators took over the regional U.S. Department of Health, Education, and Welfare office in San Francisco for 25 days to force the signing and issuance of the final regulations for Section 504 of the Rehabilitation Act of 1973 (PL 93-112) (Shapiro, 1993). It happened because, for more than 20 years, groups such as ADAPT have chained themselves to buses, risking arrest to emphasize that accessible transportation is a critical key to independent living for millions of people with disabilities.

Student involvement should be viewed in the context of the disability rights movement. This movement has taken many successful steps toward actualizing the rights of Americans with disabilities, but there are more steps that need to be taken. For these future steps to be as successful, it is critical that students become part of the movement's leadership through the acquisition of a range of self-determination skills. For individual students, a critical initial skill must be their involvement in transition planning.

This book provides teachers and other practitioners a variety of procedures and materials to help students become involved in their transition planning to the maximum extent possible. These procedures and materials have been field-tested and validated with different populations at multiple sites. They work! Incorporate them into your curriculum. You could be teaching some of the much-needed future leaders of the disability rights movement.

Michael J. Ward, Ph.D.
Director
National Center for Self-Determination and 21st Century Leadership
Center on Self-Determination
University Affiliated Program
Oregon Health Sciences University
Portland, Oregon

REFERENCES

Education for All Handicapped Children Act of 1975, PL 94-142, 20 U.S.C. §§ 1400 *et seq.*

Individuals with Disabilities Education Act (IDEA) of 1990, PL 101-476, 20 U.S.C. §§ 1400 *et seq.*

Individuals with Disabilities Education Act Amendments of 1991, PL 102-119, 20 U.S.C. §§ 1400 *et seq.*

Rehabilitation Act of 1973, PL 93-112, 29 U.S.C. §§ 701 *et seq.*

Shapiro, J.P. (1993). *No pity: People with disabilities forging a new civil rights movement.* New York: Times Books.

Foreword

Much has been written about student involvement, decision making, and choice. Editors Michael L. Wehmeyer and Deanna J. Sands and their contributing authors have assembled an important book on these and related topics. This text marks an important benchmark in our collective understanding of the educational gains that have been made in relation to developing a secondary curriculum that promotes student involvement. Most important, this text is about power, choices, and self-determination.

The contributors to *Making it Happen: Student Involvement in Education Planning, Decision Making, and Instruction* introduce an impressive history of our understanding of student involvement. This understanding is compromised, though, by the realization that students with and *without* disabilities typically are not engaged in an education that values their active participation. These students are not actors in their own play; they are merely puppets in narrowly cast skits that are designed to fill the legal requirements of a school day and the expectations of unsuspecting parents.

Exceptions do exist, however. Wehmeyer and Sands introduce a select number of model programs and practices that have promoted student involvement in education planning, decision making, and instruction. These programs share certain characteristics that warrant explication, including planning, decision making, assessment, self-advocacy, and self-management. These education practices are important and deserve to be studied by current and future generations of high school teachers. Specifically, it must be recognized that the business of secondary education requires that the importance of students' being involved in their choices be inculcated and valued; that they learn self-discipline in relation to these choices; and, finally, that all students become informed about their actions. Personal strength is acquired through the incremental realization that actions influence intentions (i.e., being informed) and that intentions are linked to the power that one accumulates.

A number of ongoing debates will significantly influence the reception of *Making it Happen.* Most of these debates are longstanding and have generated more heat than light, most often as the result of armchair arguments. For example, argument continues about whether and when work-related opportunities should be introduced in the everyday curriculum of high schools *and* whether students with disabilities should continue to be segregated in special classrooms or schools. The importance of these debates should not be underestimated. They will influence the extent to which this text will affect the general population of students with disabilities. Because there is little or no consensus on educational goals, existing resources are being spent to support an outdated and ineffective education for students with disabilities.

Teachers must position themselves to offer a broad range of opportunities to students—choices from which students must select to begin to be self-determined. Ultimately, these choices empower students, just as others are empowered by the choices that they make every day of their lives. When people go out to eat, for example, their intentions are influenced by having eaten out before, by what they ordered, and by the company and topics of conversation at the table. People make choices about where to get their cars fixed, who cleans their houses, where they shop, what sporting events they attend, whether they will participate in planning their children's education, and so forth. They accumulate power based on their experiences.

Making it Happen is a welcome addition to the student involvement literature. A better understanding of how student involvement in education can be promoted can only lead to a stronger realization that youth must be prepared to make responsible choices, acquire a voice, and become intentioned.

Frank R. Rusch, Ph.D.
Transition Research Institute
University of Illinois at Urbana-Champaign

Preface

The Education for All Handicapped Children Act of 1975 (PL 94-142) required that parents be involved in the educational decision-making process and suggested that students be involved in planning meetings whenever appropriate. Unfortunately, in the past, this requirement was too frequently interpreted to mean that students were not an integral part of the planning process, and consequently students with disabilities were essentially left out of the education-planning and decision-making process. This circumstance developed in spite of growing evidence from the educational and psychological literature that student involvement had positive effects on student motivation, achievement, and education outcomes (see Chapter 1).

The Individuals with Disabilities Education Act (IDEA) of 1990 (PL 101-476) strengthened the language in the original legislation and mandated that the education-planning process for students with disabilities ages 16 and older include transition services based on students' needs and take into account students' interests and preferences. These mandates were maintained and strengthened in the Individuals with Disabilities Education Act Amendments of 1997 (PL 105-17). The student involvement mandate, in conjunction with the emergence of self-determination as a critical education outcome for learners with disabilities, has fueled a growing interest in and need for educational materials and instructional activities that promote students' involvement in all aspects of education-planning, decision-making, and instruction processes. This text provides information on such programs and strategies. It should be noted that although professionals in the field believe that student involvement should begin early in a student's educational career, most of the programmatic attention has focused on secondary education; as such, this text is most applicable for use with adolescents.

Section I provides an overview of student involvement. In Chapter 1, Michael L. Wehmeyer introduces and defines the term *student involvement* and discusses the relationship between student involvement and self-determination. In Chapter 2, Deanna J. Sands and colleagues report on the findings of a federally funded study of what predicts student involvement in transition planning. They describe how several school districts put these findings into action. The crux of student involvement is that students become involved in the goal-setting and decision-making processes. Beth Doll and Deanna J. Sands review the goal-setting and decision-making literature in Chapter 3 and provide 21 application principles that enable teachers to apply that research in the classroom. In Chapter 4, Patricia L. Sitlington and Debra A. Neubert provide information to enable educators to conduct assessments that provide information on student interests and preferences and that can promote student involvement. Carole R. Gothelf and Fredda Brown examine issues pertaining to student involvement for students with more significant disabilities in Chapter 5. The first section closes with Chapter 6, by a young woman with a disability, Cecelia Ann Pauley, who provides "the view from the student's side of the table" as she discusses the importance of student involvement to her.

Section II consists of chapters describing a variety of programmatic efforts to promote student involvement in education and transition planning. Many of these programs resulted from federally funded efforts to promote self-determination and student involvement. In Chapter 7, Anthony K. Van Reusen describes a program entitled *Self-Advocacy Strategy for Education and Transition Planning* that addresses motivational strategies to promote student self-advocacy and involvement. Michael L. Wehmeyer describes in Chapter 8 the *Whose Future Is it Anyway?* curriculum, a student-directed transition-planning program developed for students with cognitive disabilities. Chapter 9 introduces the *Next S.T.E.P.* curriculum developed by Andrew S. Halpern and discusses the key elements of any programmatic effort to promote student involvement in transition planning. In Chapter 10, Laurie E. Powers and colleagues describe *TAKE CHARGE for the Future*, a curriculum that youth with and without disabilities, including youth at risk for dropping out of school, have used to promote effective problem-solving, decision-making, and goal-setting skills. James E. Martin and Laura Huber Marshall, in Chapter 11, provide information on the *ChoiceMaker* framework, one of the earliest attempts to promote student involvement. In Chapter 12, Emilee Curtis describes *It's My Life*, a preference-based planning program incorporating innovative instruction strategies and materials. Winnelle D. Carpenter, in Chapter 13, describes *Become Your Own Expert!*, a curriculum designed for use with students with learning disabilities. In the final chapter in this section, Chapter 14, Ann Fullerton introduces *Putting Feet on My Dreams*, a student involvement and self-determination curriculum for students with autism.

Section III shifts the focus from student involvement in education planning and decision making to student-directed instruction strategies. Although most of the emphasis in the text is on the latter, if students are not involved in instruction activities arising from planning and decision-making activities, then it is unlikely that they will truly become involved in their education programs. In Chapter 15, Dennis E. Mithaug and colleagues introduce a model, the Self-Determined Learning Model of Instruction, that incorporates the principles of self-determination and problem solving and provides teachers a means by which to enable students to take control over all aspects of the instruction process. Chapters 16 and 17 introduce self-management and self-regulation strategies that can be employed to promote student-directed learning. In Chapter 16, Carolyn Hughes and Judith A. Presley overview self-instruction and antecedent cue regulation; in Chapter 17, Martin Agran discusses self-reinforcement, self-monitoring, and self-evaluation.

In the final chapter, Michael L. Wehmeyer and Deanna J. Sands identify additional factors needed to make student involvement a reality, including the importance of education- and transition-planning issues to school reform and general education.

REFERENCES

Education for All Handicapped Children Act of 1975, PL 94-142, 20 U.S.C. §§ 1400 *et seq.*

Individuals with Disabilities Education Act (IDEA) of 1990, PL 101-476, 20 U.S.C. §§ 1400 *et seq.*

Individuals with Disabilities Education Act Amendments of 1997, PL 105-17, 20 U.S.C. §§ 1400 *et seq.*

Acknowledgments

We would like to acknowledge the editorial and production staff at Paul H. Brookes Publishing Co., particularly Scott Beeler, who was the editor of this text. We appreciate their hard work; support; assistance; and, perhaps most important, their patience and forbearance! We also extend our thanks to Michael J. Ward and Frank R. Rusch for contributing forewords to the book. To the degree that this book achieves its purpose, much of the credit must go to our contributing authors, and to them we extend our thanks for their efforts. We would particularly like to recognize the work of James E. Martin and Laura Huber Marshall. Their federally funded work to gather and annotate self-determination curricula has been a valuable source of information in our efforts and those of others in the field. We would also like to acknowledge the contributions of the U.S. Department of Education, Office of Special Education Programs (OSEP), to the increased attention to student involvement. Many of the strategies described in this text were developed through grants funded by OSEP. Our research and programmatic efforts in the area of student involvement have benefited from our interactions with many colleagues, and we would like to acknowledge the ongoing contributions of the following individuals: Rick Berkobien, Sharon Davis, Sue Eades, Margaret Lawrence, Susan Palmer, and Michelle Schwartz (M.L.W.); Diane S. Bassett, Dan Boomer, Jeff Gliner, Jean Lehmann, Karen C. Spencer, Randall Swaim, and project staff from Fort Bragg High School (California), North High School (Denver), Thompson School District (Colorado), and Valley High School (Greeley, Colorado) (D.J.S.).

To our families . . .

To my parents, Leon and Dorothy; and my family, Kathy, Geoff, and Graham

M.L.W.

To my parents, Dean and Carol, and Taylor

D.J.S.

Making it Happen

INVOLVING STUDENTS WITH DISABILITIES IN THE EDUCATION PROCESS

An Overview of the Impetus for Benefits from Student Involvement

Student Involvement in Education Planning, Decision Making, and Instruction

An Idea Whose Time Has Arrived

Michael L. Wehmeyer

The educational experience of most students, particularly students with disabilities, can often be described as a one-way street. Students are recipients of instruction programs that are almost uniformly teacher delivered and based on plans and decisions made by others, including teachers, parents, administrators, school board members, and state legislators. There is no doubt in the minds of most students about who is in control when they are in school. Sarason described the typical classroom as such:

> Our usual imagery of the classroom contains an adult who is "in charge" and pupils who conform to the teacher's rules, regulations and standards. If students think and act in conformity to the teacher's wishes, they will learn what they are supposed to learn. (1990, p. 78)

3

The Education for All Handicapped Children Act of 1975 (PL 94-142), the landmark legislation that ensures the right of all children with disabilities to a free appropriate public education, reflects this instructional bias. In the Act, an *individualized education program* (IEP) is defined as

> a written statement for each handicapped child developed in any meeting by a representative of the local education agency or an intermediate educational unit . . . , the teacher, the parents or guardian of such child, and, *whenever appropriate*, such child. [Emphasis added] (Act § 4[a][19])

The premise of this book, and the bias of the editors and contributing authors, is that *whenever appropriate* is, in fact, *always*—from education planning and decision making to assessment and instruction. As Agran stated,

> A fundamental shift in focus is occurring in special education. Rather than continue to rely on an instructional model in which the teacher is given full responsibility for determining when, what, why, where, and how a student will learn, we are beginning to realize that there may be marked advantages in making the student more actively involved in educational decision making, as well as in the delivery of the instruction itself. (1997, p. 3)

Student involvement is an idea whose time has arrived. The chapters in this book introduce strategies, methods, and materials that will provide educators with the tools they need to enable students to become involved in education planning, decision making, and instruction. This chapter addresses some fundamental questions about student involvement, including what it is and what it is not; why the time for student involvement has arrived; and, perhaps most important, why we believe that *whenever appropriate* means *always*.

STUDENT INVOLVEMENT

What is meant when we say that we want to involve students in the education process? The term *involve* in this context is usually interpreted to mean "to draw in as a participant" (*The Merriam-Webster Dictionary*, 1978, p. 378). In other words, the student is to participate in his or her education program; however, there is more to student involvement than just participation. Although a participant shares in and takes part in an activity, there is no sense of ownership or control rooted in a participant's role. Student involvement is more than simply having students participate in the education process. The word *involve* also means "to connect closely" and "to influence or affect" (*The Merriam-Webster Dictionary*, 1978, p. 378). This takes us one step closer to the true intent. Student involvement connects the student with his or her education program and enables him or her to influence or affect this program. However, to capture the full intent of *involve*, one needs to look at the etymological roots of the word; it is derived from the Latin *involvere*, which means "to enwrap" or "to completely engross" (*The Merriam-Webster Dictionary*, 1978, p. 378). The Middle English form of the Latin *involvere* was *involven*, which meant "to wind or coil about" (*The Merriam-Webster Dictionary*, 1978, p. 378). Getting students involved in their education programs is more than having them participate; it is connecting students with their education, enabling them to influence and affect the program and, indeed, enabling them to become enwrapped and engrossed in their educational experiences.

Having students involved just as participants in education programming is relatively easy and too passive. Ask teachers what they really want from a student, and they almost unanimously say that they want students to be motivated to learn and to care about their education. The key to student involvement is for the student to be an active and not a passive partner in the totality of his or her education program. Unfortunately, many students are not motivated to learn or to participate, a fact frequently addressed in discussions on school reform.

Involvement in education planning, decision making, and instruction can take many forms, from students' generating their own IEP goals and objectives to students' tracking their progress on self-selected goals or objectives. It is important, however, not to equate independent performance of activities such as making decisions or setting goals with student involvement. Student involvement is not synonymous with independent performance. It is true that as students become actively involved in their education programs, they become more independent in many tasks. In fact, many of the programs described in this book teach students to become as independent as possible, and teaching students the skills that enable them to become more effective decision makers or communicators is critically important. However, it is not the independent performance of those skills but the degree to which the student is an equal partner in and, to the greatest extent, in control of his or her learning that constitutes student involvement. Students with severe disabilities can be involved in their IEPs every bit as much as students with mild disabilities are. Student involvement may look different in these cases, and students with severe disabilities may not be able to make independent decisions or to solve problems; but that is not the criteria by which student involvement should be judged. It is instead the degree to which the student is engrossed in his or her learning and education program that matters.

STUDENT INVOLVEMENT IN THE EDUCATION PROCESS

There are a number of reasons that student involvement is, as the title of this chapter suggests, an idea whose time has arrived. Research in education and psychology, highlighted in the next section, has begun to dispel some of the myths and stereotypes about students' capacities to participate in planning and decision making that have long served as barriers for them. Societal perceptions of disability and of individuals with disabilities have changed dramatically since the mid-1970s, and these changing perceptions have contributed to changes in expectations for people with disabilities. Research in education and vocational rehabilitation has shown that student-directed learning strategies are as successful as, if not more successful than, teacher-directed learning strategies, and that self-management strategies are an effective means by which to increase students' independence and productivity. Finally, as Agran noted, there are "marked advantages" (1997, p. 3) to making students more actively involved in education programming that move beyond issues of educational efficacy. This section examines the impetus to and benefits of promoting student involvement.

Importance to Transition and Self-Determination

Many of the model programs and research findings reported in this book emerged under the auspices of federal initiatives to promote self-determination for youth with disabilities and as a result of the transition services mandated in the Individuals with Disabilities Education Act (IDEA) of 1990 (PL 101-476). The Individuals with Disabilities Education Act Amendments of 1997 (PL 105-17) contain language requiring that the IEP include a statement of needed transition services for all students 14 years of age and older who are receiving special education services. IDEA also mandates student involvement in transition planning, stating that needed transition services must be based on students' preferences and interests. Although IDEA leaves intact the statutory language regarding student involvement in the IEP meeting "when appropriate," the federal regulations under IDEA regarding student involvement in transition planning are quite clear and unambiguous. These regulations state that if one of the purposes of the transition-planning meeting is to consider transition services, then the school must invite the student to the meeting (Assistance to States, 1992). The regulations then point out that "for all students who are 16 years or older, one of the purposes of the annual meeting will always be the planning of transition services, since transition services are a required component of the IEP for these students" (34 C.F.R. § 300.344, Note 2). As modified by the 1997 legislation (PL 105-17) cited previously, this regulation requires that schools invite all students ages 14 and older to planning meetings and that decisions made about students' transition services be based on students' preferences and interests.

Mithaug, Wolman, and Campeau suggested that the requirements in the IDEA transition services language "comprise a logical sequence or causal flow *beginning with* student-determined and defined needs, which lead to plans for coordinated services, which, in turn, result in community-based experiences that culminate in post-school adjustments" (1992, p. 7). Obviously, if the transition process begins with the student, then the student needs to be an equal partner in it.

Wehmeyer and Ward (1995) also emphasized the significance of the student involvement language in IDEA, arguing that this language places the intent and spirit of IDEA in line with efforts to promote student self-determination and consumer choice. Kochhar and Deschamps linked IDEA with other policy initiatives affecting the transition of youth from school to adulthood, including the Carl D. Perkins Vocational and Applied Technology Education Act Amendments of 1990 (PL 101-392) and the Americans with Disabilities Act (ADA) of 1990 (PL 101-336), stating that these acts "cross-reference each other and stand together to develop a broader, far-reaching mandate to include youth with special needs in the range of career/vocational and transition services options" (1992, p. 9). A key component of the broader mandate in each of these acts is the requirement of active consumer participation in service planning and delivery, referred to as *participatory planning.*

There are obvious links among the emergence of student involvement, the transition mandates, and the increased attention to promoting self-determination. As a result of federally funded initiatives to define and describe self-determination as an educational outcome (Ward, 1996; Ward & Kohler, 1996), a number of conceptualizations of self-determination to address educational needs have been forwarded (e.g., Field, 1996; Sands & Wehmeyer, 1996). Martin and Huber Marshall summarized the "evolving definition of self-determination in the special education literature" (1995, p. 147) as describing individuals who

> know how to choose—they know what they want and how to get it. From an awareness of personal needs, self-determined individuals choose goals, then doggedly pursue them. This involves asserting an individual's presence, making his or her needs known, evaluating progress toward meeting goals, adjusting performance and creating unique approaches to solve problems. (1995, p. 147)

As illustrated by this description, the actions of people who are self-determined enable them to fulfill roles typically associated with adulthood. A definitional framework of self-determination as an educational or adult outcome has been put forth (Wehmeyer, 1992, 1996; Wehmeyer, Agran, & Hughes, 1998; Wehmeyer, Kelchner, & Richards, 1996) wherein *self-determination* refers to "acting as the primary causal agent in one's life and making choices and decisions regarding one's quality of life free from undue external influence or interference" (Wehmeyer, 1996, p. 24). A causal agent is someone who makes or causes things to happen in his or her life. Within this definitional framework, *self-determined behavior* refers to actions that are identified by four *essential characteristics*:

1. The person acted autonomously.
2. The person's actions were self-regulated.

3. The person initiated and responded to the events in a "psychologically empowered" manner.
4. The person acted in a self-realizing manner.

These essential characteristics emerge as children, youth, and adults develop and acquire a set of component elements of self-determination (Doll, Sands, Wehmeyer, & Palmer, 1996), and it is this level at which instruction is focused. The component elements of self-determination include but are not limited to

1. Choice making
2. Decision making
3. Problem solving
4. Goal setting and attainment
5. Independence, risk taking, and safety
6. Self-observation, evaluation, and reinforcement
7. Self-instruction
8. Self-advocacy and leadership
9. Internal locus of control
10. Positive attributions of efficacy and outcome expectancy
11. Self-awareness
12. Self-knowledge

These component elements are similar to those introduced in other frameworks of self-determination (Abery, 1994; Field & Hoffman, 1994; Powers et al., 1996). It is obvious from scanning this list that many of these component elements, such as choice and decision making, goal setting, and self-awareness, are important to student involvement. Beginning with the work of Martin and colleagues (Martin & Huber Marshall, 1996; Martin, Huber Marshall, & Maxson, 1993), the focal point of several curricular efforts to promote self-determination has been the IEP meeting or the transition-planning meeting. The IEP meeting provides a unique and potentially powerful vehicle for teaching self-determination skills. First, to successfully take part in the meeting, students have to learn a host of self-determination skills, including how to evaluate their needs; set goals; communicate their wants, needs, and goals; make decisions; and solve problems. Second, the IEP meeting is the fulcrum for education programming and provides a unique opportunity to give students more control over their education programs. Thus, the IEP planning process and meeting are ideal circumstances in which to promote self-determination and achieve student involvement.

There is, however, a caveat that needs to be recognized, as described in greater detail in Chapter 2, which is that, although self-determination and student involvement in IEP planning meetings are clearly and logically linked, they are not synonymous. Students can be self-determined and not be actively involved in their IEP planning meetings. In far too many schools, the IEP meeting remains a bureaucratic requirement that bears little or no resemblance to a process in which students (and parents and teachers, for that matter) are viewed as equal partners. A self-determined student may take a look at such a meeting, weigh the costs and benefits of becoming involved, and reasonably decide that he or she would be better off directing his or her energy elsewhere. In such a situation, the student may decide to opt out of the process. In addition, students who are involved in their education-planning processes may not necessarily be self-determined, particularly if that involvement is strictly as participants. These issues are discussed further in Chapter 2; but suffice it to say that although student involvement in the IEP planning meeting presents a potentially valuable means of promoting student involvement and self-determination, this potential will not be achieved unless the system and the process reflect the belief that students are and should be equal partners in education planning, decision making, and instruction.

Educational Efficacy

A second reason to get students involved in the education process is that research findings from the fields of education and psychology have identified active student involvement as a means of improving educational and adult outcomes. That is, student involvement is an effective education strategy for students of all ages. There is increasing evidence that students who are involved in the education process perform better than their peers who are not involved. One body of evidence to support this comes from the literature on motivation. Research indicates that students who have the opportunity to choose school activities show enhanced motivation.

Koestner, Ryan, Bernieri, and Holt (1984) examined the role of teacher versus student control in school motivation activities and engagement in these activities. They constructed three conditions—controlling limits, informational limits, and no limits—in which elementary school students painted pictures. They found that students in the controlling condition reported less enjoyment from the activity and were less likely to select the activity during a free-choice period. Swann and Pittman (1977) found that elementary school students' persistence on an initially interesting activity declined when an adult selected the activity for them.

A similar line of research showed that opportunities to express preferences and make choices led to greater motivation and enhanced outcomes. In fact, Kohn, reviewing the evidence to support the view that choices lead to learning, concluded that this evidence is so compelling that "it is frankly difficult to understand how anyone can talk about school reform without immediately addressing the question of how students can be given more say about what goes on in their classes" (1993, p. 12). Numerous studies have documented the positive impact of expressing preferences and making choices on educational and behavioral outcomes (Dattilo & Rusch, 1985; Dunlap et al., 1994; Kennedy & Haring, 1993; Mithaug & Mar, 1980; Newton, Ard, & Horner, 1993; Realon, Favell, & Lowerre, 1990).

Dunlap and colleagues (1994) found that the opportunity to choose from a menu of academic tasks, rather than simply having access to preferred tasks, resulted in increased task engagement and decreased disruptive behavior for students with emotional and behavioral disorders. In addition, choice making has been related to increased motivation (Foster-Johnson, Ferro, & Dunlap, 1994), academic gains (Cooper et al., 1992), increases in productivity (Mithaug & Mar, 1980), and decreases in aggressive behavior (Dyer, Dunlap, & Winterling, 1990). At the same time, providing access to selected or preferred items, events, or situations has been shown to have positive effects on individuals' performances (Dyer et al., 1990; Fisher et al., 1992; Kennedy & Haring, 1993; Parsons, Reid, Reynolds, & Bumgarner, 1990). For example, Parsons and colleagues (1990) showed that when people with severe disabilities were assigned preferred rather than nonpreferred tasks, their productivity and on-task behavior increased.

Additional evidence for the educational efficacy of student involvement comes from research examining student participation in goal setting. This research shows that such participation leads to more positive outcomes. This is a finding that has strong face validity because one assumes, as Schunk (1985) pointed out, that participation in goal setting can result in higher commitment to a goal and, consequently, increased performance. This assumption has also been borne out by research. Schunk (1985) found that children with learning disabilities who participated in setting goals related to mathematics activities showed greater improvement than did students who participated in the same instruction but either had goals selected for them or had no goals identified.

Similar findings permeate the research in students' self-directed and self-regulated learning. This research typically examines components of individual self-monitoring, self-instruction, self-evaluation, and self-reinforcement. (See Martin, Burger, Elias-Burger, & Mithaug, 1988, for a comprehensive overview of the research literature prior to 1986.) Self-monitoring and self-recording procedures have been shown to improve the motivation and performance of students with disabilities. Malone and Mastropieri (1992) determined that, under a self-monitoring condition, middle school students with learning disabilities performed better on reading comprehension transfer tasks than peers who did not self-monitor. McCarl, Svobodny, and Beare (1991) found that teaching three students with mental retardation to record progress on classroom assignments improved on-task behavior for all students and showed an increase in productivity for two of the three students.

Kapadia and Fantuzzo (1988) used self-monitoring procedures to increase attention to academic tasks for students with developmental disabilities and behavior problems. Lovett and Haring (1989) showed that self-recording activities enabled adults with mental retardation to improve task completion of daily living activities. Chiron and Gerken (1983) found that students with mental retardation who charted progress on school reading activities showed significant increases in their reading levels. Trammel, Schloss, and Alper (1994) found that self-recording (graphing) and student-directed goal setting enabled students with learning disabilities to increase the number of assignments that they completed successfully.

The use of self-instruction strategies has also proved to be beneficial for individuals with disabilities. *Self-instruction* refers to "verbalizations an individual emits to cue, direct or maintain his or her own behavior" (Agran, Fodor-Davis, & Moore, 1986, p. 273), although several authors (Hughes, Harmer, Killian, & Niarhos, 1995; Rusch, McKee, Chadsey-Rusch, & Renzaglia, 1988) reported self-instruction strategies in which students thought through the strategies instead of verbalizing them. A number of studies have found that self-instruction training is a useful technique for increasing job-related skills of individuals with mental retardation (Agran et al., 1986; Hughes & Petersen, 1989; Rusch, McKee, Chadsey-Rusch, & Renzaglia, 1988; Salend, Ellis, & Reynolds, 1989). Graham and Harris (1989) found that a self-instruction strategy improved the essay composition skills of students with learning disabilities. Agran, Salzberg, and Stowitschek (1987) found that self-instruction strategies increased the percentages of initiations with a work supervisor when employees, five individuals with mental retardation, ran out of work materials or needed assistance.

The third common component of self-directed learning is self-evaluation or self-judgment. Schunk (1981) showed that students who verbalized cognitive strategies related to evaluating their study and work habits had increased math achievement scores. Brownell, Colletti, Ersner-Hershfield, Hershfield, and Wilson (1977) found that students who determined their performance standards demonstrated increased on-task time when compared with students operating under imposed standards.

A fourth component of self-regulated learning, self-reinforcement, also leads to increased performance. Lagomarcino and Rusch (1989) used a combination of self-reinforcement and self-monitoring procedures to improve the work performance of a student with mental retardation in a community setting. Moore, Agran, and Fodor-Davis (1989) used a combination of student-directed activities, including self-instruction, goal setting, and self-reinforcement, to improve the production rates of workers with mental retardation.

Other Benefits of Student Involvement

Agran (1997) listed several other benefits to active student involvement in learning. One practical benefit is that enabling students to direct their own learning provides teachers with more time to teach other skills. Teachers spend less time monitoring, evaluating, and reinforcing student activities and are able to attend to other activities. A second benefit is that student involvement, particularly student-directed learning, promotes the generalization of learned skills. Students who apply self-directed learning strategies acquire the skills to do likewise in any situation. Finally, as most disability advocates have noted, student involvement is beneficial because it levels the playing field for students with disabilities. Although students without disabilities are making decisions to varying degrees about their school careers by choosing to take a specific class or opting to participate in an extracurricular activity, they are also learning the problem-solving and decision-making skills that will enable them to succeed. Students with disabilities too often are not afforded the same opportunity.

In summary, the answer to the question "Why involve students in education planning, decision making, and instruction?" is that it is a valuable instruction strategy that enhances students' motivation to learn, results in positive outcomes, and provides students with the skills that they need to succeed as adults. Given that this is indeed a good idea whose time has arrived, what barriers exist to student involvement?

BARRIERS TO STUDENT INVOLVEMENT

There are a number of factors that have served as barriers to student involvement. The following sections examine some of these factors.

Student Competence to Make Decisions

One belief that many educators hold that limits student involvement is that minors do not have the capacity to make informed choices and decisions. This assumption is also frequently made about individuals with disabilities, so that the overwhelming assumption about adolescents with disabilities is that they are incapable of participating in the decision-making process. However, changing perceptions of the capacity of individuals with disabilities and research in student competence to make decisions have shown that minors, including minors with disabilities, are competent at making important decisions (see Chapter 3).

Changing Perceptions of Disability   The way in which disability is conceptualized in a society directly influences the opportunities available to individuals with disabilities within that society. Such conceptualizations influence how other members of society perceive people with disabilities, what they expect from people with disabilities, and how people with disabilities perceive themselves and what they expect from themselves. Disability has been conceptualized within a number of theoretical perspectives, including medical, educational, sociopolitical, and religious models. The common theme across these conceptualizations, however, has been that disability is outside of typical or accepted human behavior and functioning. Disability has been seen as pathological, aberrant, atypical, and dysfunctional. The stereotypes of people with disabilities built from these conceptualizations, and subsequent expectations of people with disabilities based on those stereotypes, are often as debilitating as the disability itself. This is evident in reviewing the way in which people with disabilities have been seen by the general public since the turn of the 20th century.

During the late 19th century and the early 20th century, people with disabilities were viewed as menaces and were linked with crime, poverty, promiscuity, and the general decline of civilization. They were seen as subhuman (e.g., as vegetables, as being animal-like) or as objects to be feared or dreaded. After World War II, advances in science and medicine changed the way that disability was perceived and greatly increased the life spans of people with disabilities. These advances were influenced by the large number of veterans who were disabled in the war. As a result, rehabilitation and training were emphasized, and success was achieved in developing vaccines for diseases such as polio, giving hope of greater cures for disabling conditions. The earlier stereotypes of disability were replaced by more humane, though in many ways still debilitating, stereotypes. People with disabilities were viewed as objects to be fixed, needing to be cured and rehabilitated and, at the same time, pitied.

Within this stereotype, people with disabilities were viewed as "holy innocents" (e.g., special messengers, children of God) and thus were considered incapable of sin and not responsible for their own actions. Because of this stereotype and the increase in the use of mental age as calculated by using IQ scores, people with disabilities came to be perceived as "eternal children." No longer feared and blamed for society's ills, people with disabilities were then perceived as children to be protected, pitied, and cared for. Obviously, these perceptions were antithetical to the portrayal of students with disabilities as being capable of being involved in their IEPs. Adolescents with "the minds of 3-year-olds" were not expected to hold a job, make decisions, or solve problems.

Since the mid-1970s, a different perception of disability has emerged, first within the disability rights and advocacy movements, then within the disability services field, and increasingly among the general public. There are many factors that contributed to this shift, including 1) the introduction of the normalization principle; 2) the rise of the independent living, self-help, and self-advocacy movements; 3) the shift from institutional to community-based services; 4) civil rights legislation, such as Section 504 of the Rehabilitation Act of 1973 (PL 93-112), IDEA, and the ADA; and 5) access to education and community life. As a result of these forces, there has been a significant change in the way in which disability is defined or described and, consequently, in the way in which people with disabilities are perceived. This change is perhaps best represented in language from the Rehabilitation Act Amendments of 1992 (PL 102-569). The rationale of the U.S. Congress for that legislation is as follows:

1) Millions of Americans have one or more physical or mental disability and the number of Americans with disabilities is increasing;
2) Individuals with disabilities constitute one of the most disadvantaged groups in society;
3) Disability is a natural part of the human experience and in no way diminishes the right of individuals to:
   a) Live independently;
   b) Enjoy self-determination;
   c) Make choices;
   d) Contribute to society;
   e) Pursue meaningful careers; and
   f) Enjoy full inclusion and integration in the economic, political, social, cultural and educational mainstream of American society; and
6) The goals of the nation properly include the goal of providing individuals with disabilities the tools necessary to:
   a) Make informed choices and decisions; and
   b) Achieve equality of opportunity, full inclusion and integration into society, employment, independent living and economic and social self-sufficiency, for such individuals. (Act § 2 [29 U.S.C. § 701])

The significant change that is reflected in this conceptualization is that disability is no longer seen as aberrant, outside the "norm," or pathological but instead is seen as part of being human. Within this conceptualization, all human abilities and experiences exist on a continuum, and disability is a part of, not outside of, that continuum. The history of education and the stereotypes held within education settings share a similar historical path. Even a cursory review of articles written since the mid-1970s that are related to the education of students with disabilities shows that expectations for students with disabilities have changed substantially in a relatively short period of time. Although most educators do not retain perceptions about disability that reflect beliefs held early in the 20th century, vestiges of later perceptions remain and have an impact on the education setting. The well-known self-fulfilling prophecy is still alive and well. Cutler (1993) listed several myths about children with disabilities that still exist in schools, including the beliefs that a child's disability is the source of all of his or her problems and that children with disabilities can learn only by rote, cannot handle a full school day, and would be better off in a caregiving situation. In addition, the language still used by too many educators reflects long-held assumptions of pathology and dysfunction. One hardly expects a trainable student to take control of his or her learning.

The conceptualization of people with disabilities as competent is relatively new and has influenced how others think about and what they expect from people with disabilities. In addition, it has changed how people with disabilities think about themselves and what they expect from themselves. Student involvement both contributes to and benefits from these changing perceptions and expectations.

Competence of Minors to Make Decisions   Adelman and colleagues (Adelman, Lusk, Alvarez, & Acosta, 1985; Kaser-Boyd, Adelman, & Taylor, 1985; Taylor, Adelman, & Kaser-Boyd, 1983, 1985) conducted a series of studies showing that students with and without disabilities demonstrate the ability to make competent decisions. Taylor and colleagues (1983) found that the majority of adolescents referred for special support services wanted to participate in a decision-making meeting regarding those services, knew what outcomes they wanted, believed that they were capable of participating in the meeting, followed through on actions agreed to at the meeting, and subsequently rated their involvement in the meeting as effective. Taylor and colleagues (1985) replicated these findings with students identified as having a learning disability or a severe emotional disorder and also found that these students were interested in improving the skills that they would need to participate more effectively. Adelman and colleagues (1985) found that youth with school-related problems were competent to understand, evaluate, and communicate their psychoeducational problems.

Other researchers have determined that, when provided the opportunity to participate in educational decision making, students with disabilities do as well as other team members. Salend (1983) found considerable congruence between students' self-selected IEP objectives and those selected by the interdisciplinary team. Phillips (1990) and Van Reusen and Bos (1994) found that students with learning disabilities were able to participate in the decision-making process, a finding confirmed by Wehmeyer and Lawrence (1995) with students who have mental retardation.

Contributing heavily to the misperception of minors as being incapable of making competent decisions is the perception that minors and students with disabilities cannot take into account the degree of risk involved with various options. However, this assumption is not supported by research in developmental psychology. Grisso and Vierling (1978) reviewed the cognitive and behavioral characteristics of minors in relation to the question of competence to consent to treatment. They concluded that "there [are] no psychological grounds for maintaining the general legal assumption that minors age 15 and above cannot provide competent consent, taking into account risk-related factors" (Grisso & Vierling, 1978, p. 423). In fact, these researchers contended that there are "circumstances that would justify the sanction of independent consent" (p. 424; emphasis added) by minors between the ages of 11 and 14. It should be reiterated that Grisso and Vierling were interested only in the degree to which adolescents should be allowed to independently consent to treatment. Their review provides guidelines for the degree to which students with disabilities should be allowed to make independent decisions and, if taken a step further, suggests that students could become involved in and part of, though not solely responsible for, such decisions as team members at a much earlier age.

Kaser-Boyd and colleagues (1985) confirmed this suggestion. Students ages 10–20 who were identified as having a learning or behavior problem in school were asked to list potential risks and benefits of entering psychoeducational therapy. As expected, there was a relationship between age and efficacy in this task. However, even young students were able to identify relevant concerns that were appropriate to their situation and their developmental needs.

In summary, the belief that students cannot make competent decisions and take risks into account is one that is not supported in the literature. Certainly, students who have had very few opportunities to learn and practice decision-making, problem-solving, or choice-making skills need considerable support to become involved. Nonetheless, there should not be an a priori assumption of incompetence; to the contrary, as discussed in detail in Chapter 3, there should be an assumption of competence.

Student Motivation

Another frequently cited barrier to student involvement is the perceived lack of motivation on behalf of the students to participate in meetings and education programs. Although it is true that student motivation to participate has been linked to participation in the educational decision-making process (Adelman, MacDonald, Nelson, Smith, & Taylor, 1990), the assumption that students should not or cannot participate in planning meetings because they lack the motivation to do so seems incongruous with the previously described findings that student involvement in all aspects of the education process increases motivation. The reality is that the lack of motivation to participate is often a direct result of the students' lack of control over the process, and, as such, student involvement is one solution to the problem. Kohn, discussing the state of education, concluded,

> Much of what is disturbing about students' attitudes and behavior may be a function of the fact that they have little to say about what happens to them all day. They are compelled to follow someone else's rules, study someone else's curriculum and submit continually to someone else's evaluation. The mystery, really, is not that so many students are indifferent about what they have to do in school, but that any of them are not. (1993, p. 10)

Complexity of Education Process

A third barrier to student involvement is the assertion that the transition process is too complex for students with disabilities. Although this barrier does have some face validity, given the complexity of most school processes and the often-emphasized paperwork associated with education planning, the fact is that students can and do participate in all aspects of their individualized transition plans (ITPs) with considerable success. The assumption that the transition process is too complex for students to be involved rests on the related and incorrect assumptions that student involvement means independently performing all activities and that students are not competent to make decisions. Both assumptions, discussed previously, have been shown to be erroneous. Perhaps the strongest evidence to the contrary is that a number of researchers have shown that students can be involved effectively in either planning and decision making (Martin & Huber Marshall, 1995; Van Reusen & Bos, 1994; Wehmeyer & Lawrence, 1995) or, as highlighted previously, in student-directed instructional activities.

Severity of Disability

One final factor that has too often led to the assumption that student involvement is not appropriate is the presence of a severe disabling condition. Until the mid-1990s, issues of student choice and preference for students with severe multiple disabilities were largely ignored by most educators (Guess, Benson, & Siegel-Causey, 1985). For example, in a study of students with severe disabilities, Houghton, Bronicki, and Guess (1987) determined that classroom staff seldom responded to student-initiated expressions of preference or choice during the school day.

The assumption that students with severe disabilities cannot be involved in education planning and decision making is not consistent with findings from the student-directed learning literature, which shows that students with severe disabilities can self-direct their learning. Many of the studies highlighted previously showed that students and adults with severe disabilities can self-regulate all or a portion of the learning process. The primary barrier for students with severe disabilities is the assumption, once again, that student involvement is equated with independent performance.

Turnbull and colleagues (1996) showed that students with severe cognitive and multiple disabilities could be involved in transition planning and decision making. Their method succeeds because they actively involve students to maximally participate in their transition programs. In many cases, maximal participation is achieved by use of the principle of partial participation (Baumgart et al., 1982). This principle was originally forwarded in relationship to the participation of students with severe disabilities in education programs and, simply put, suggests that most students can be at least partially involved in virtually any activity.

In summary, there seems to be clear evidence that student involvement in education planning, decision making, and instruction can have multiple benefits and that students can become effectively involved. If this is so, how involved are students in their education programs?

LEVEL OF STUDENT
INVOLVEMENT IN EDUCATION PROGRAMS

The consensus of student involvement proponents has been that students are basically not involved in education planning or decision making (Gillespie & Turnbull, 1983; Van Reusen & Bos, 1990, 1994; Wehmeyer & Lawrence, 1995). Unfortunately, there has been little empirical evidence concerning the degree to which students with disabilities are involved. The U.S. Department of Education has funded projects involving research regarding issues of student involvement, and the findings from one of these efforts are presented in Chapter 2. Field, Hoffman, and Sawilowsky (1994) conducted a pilot study of student involvement in transition planning. They interviewed 41 students who were classified as having a disability and as being eligible for special education services regarding their involvement in their last IEP meetings. The majority (71%) of these students indicated that they attended their last IEP meetings. However, 56% said that they had not been told the purpose of the meeting; 63% indicated that they had not been given issues to think about prior to the meetings; 76% said they had not prepared for the meetings; and only 41% indicated that they had helped to identify goals that were included in their IEPs.

Although there is also limited documentation of the degree to which teachers use student-directed strategies, there is a general agreement that such strategies are underutilized in special education (Agran, 1997). A comprehensive reading of the literature leads to several conclusions. Self-directed learning techniques are most likely to be used with low-incidence populations, such as students with mental retardation. Student-directed learning seems to be a treatment of last resort in that it is frequently applied in circumstances in which traditional teaching models have failed. For example, self-management procedures are frequently used to address challenging or problematic behaviors. In essence, despite evidence that student-directed learning strategies have the potential to benefit students with and without disabilities across a broad range of subjects and settings, these procedures are marginalized and frequently employed only with low-incidence populations or in circumstances in which all else has failed.

CONCLUSIONS

Despite evidence to suggest that student involvement is an effective instruction strategy, students with disabilities largely appear to remain outsiders with regard to their IEPs. If students with disabilities are to leave school and become self-sufficient, satisfied, and independent young adults, it is critical that this trend be reversed and that students become truly engaged in their IEPs. The chapters that follow provide both the impetus and the means by which to achieve this end. The time has come to reverse the historical trend of students' lack of involvement in education planning, decision making, and instruction and to interpret *whenever appropriate* as meaning *always*.

REFERENCES

Abery, B.H. (1994). A conceptual framework for enhancing self-determination. In M.F. Hayden & B.H. Abery (Eds.), *Challenges for a service system in transition: Ensuring quality community experiences for persons with developmental disabilities* (pp. 345–380). Baltimore: Paul H. Brookes Publishing Co.

Adelman, H.S., Lusk, R., Alvarez, V., & Acosta, N.K. (1985). Competence of minors to understand, evaluate and communicate about their psychoeducational problems. *Professional Psychology: Research and Practice, 16,* 426–434.

Adelman, H.S., MacDonald, V.M., Nelson, P., Smith, D.C., & Taylor, L. (1990). Motivational readiness of children with learning and behavior problems in psychoeducational decision making. *Journal of Learning Disabilities, 23,* 171–176.

Agran, M. (1997). *Student-directed learning: Teaching self-determination skills.* Pacific Grove, CA: Brooks/Cole.

Agran, M., Fodor-Davis, J., & Moore, S. (1986). The effects of self-instructional training on job-task sequencing: Suggesting a problem-solving strategy. *Education and Training of the Mentally Retarded, 21,* 273–281.

Agran, M., Salzberg, C.L., & Stowitschek, J.J. (1987). An analysis of the effects of a social skills training program using self-instructions on the acquisition and generalization of two social behaviors in a work setting. *Journal of The Association for Persons with Severe Handicaps, 12,* 131–139.

Americans with Disabilities Act (ADA) of 1990, PL 101-336, 42 U.S.C. §§ 12101 *et seq.*

Assistance to States for Education of Children with Disabilities, 34 C.F.R. § 300 (1992).

Baumgart, D., Brown, L., Pumpian, I., Nisbet, J., Ford, A., Sweet, M., Messina, R., & Schroeder, J. (1982). Principle of partial participation and individualized adaptations in educational programs for severely handicapped students. *Journal of The Association for Persons with Severe Handicaps, 7,* 17–27.

Brownell, K.D., Colletti, G., Ersner-Hershfield, R., Hershfield, S.M., & Wilson, G.T. (1977). Self-control in school children: Stringency and leniency in self-determined and externally imposed performance standards. *Behavior Therapy, 8,* 442–455.

Carl D. Perkins Vocational and Applied Technology Education Act Amendments of 1990, PL 101-392, 104 *Statutes at Large* 753–804, 806–834.

Chiron, R., & Gerken, K. (1983). The effects of a self-monitoring technique on the locus of control orientation of educable mentally retarded children. *School Psychology Review, 3,* 87–92.

Cooper, L.J., Wacker, D.P., Thursby, D., Plagmann, L.A., Harding, J., Millard, T., & Derby, M. (1992). Analysis of the effects of task preferences, task demands, and adult attention on child behavior in outpatient and classroom settings. *Journal of Applied Behavior Analysis, 25,* 823–840.

Cutler, B.C. (1993). *You, your child, and "special" education: A guide to making the system work.* Baltimore: Paul H. Brookes Publishing Co.

Dattilo, J., & Rusch, F.R. (1985). Effects of choice on leisure participation for persons with severe handicaps. *Journal of The Association for Persons with Severe Handicaps, 10,* 194–199.

Doll, B., Sands, D.J., Wehmeyer, M.L., & Palmer, S. (1996). Promoting the development and acquisition of self-determined behavior. In D.J. Sands & M.L. Wehmeyer

(Eds.), *Self-determination across the life span: Independence and choice for people with disabilities* (pp. 65–90). Baltimore: Paul H. Brookes Publishing Co.

Dunlap, G., DePerczel, M., Clarke, S., Wilson, D., Wright, S., White, R., & Gomez, A. (1994). Choice making to promote adaptive behavior for students with emotional and behavioral challenges. *Journal of Applied Behavior Analysis, 27,* 505–518.

Dyer, K., Dunlap, G., & Winterling, V. (1990). Effects of choice making on the serious problem behaviors of students with severe handicaps. *Journal of Applied Behavior Analysis, 23,* 515–524.

Education for All Handicapped Children Act of 1975, PL 94-142, 20 U.S.C. §§ 1400 *et seq.*

Field, S. (1996). Self-determination instructional strategies for youth with learning disabilities. *Journal of Learning Disabilities, 29,* 40–52.

Field, S., & Hoffman, A. (1994). Development of a model for self-determination. *Career Development for Exceptional Individuals, 17,* 159–169.

Field, S., Hoffman, A., & Sawilowsky, S. (1994). *Student involvement in transition planning: A proposal submitted to the U.S. Department of Education* [Unfunded grant proposal]. Detroit: Wayne State University.

Fisher, W., Piazza, C., Bowman, L., Hagopian, L., Owens, J., & Slevin, I. (1992). A comparison of two approaches for identifying reinforcers for persons with severe and profound disabilities. *Journal of Applied Behavior Analysis, 25,* 491–498.

Foster-Johnson, L., Ferro, J., & Dunlap, G. (1994). Preferred curricular activities and reduced problem behaviors in students with intellectual disabilities. *Journal of Applied Behavior Analysis, 27,* 493–504.

Gillespie, E.B., & Turnbull, A.P. (1983). It's my IEP! Involving students in the planning process. *Teaching Exceptional Children, 29,* 27–29.

Graham, S., & Harris, K.R. (1989). Improving learning disabled students' skills at composing essays: Self-instructional strategy training. *Exceptional Children, 56,* 231–214.

Grisso, T., & Vierling, L. (1978). Minors' consent to treatment: A developmental perspective. *Professional Psychology, 9,* 412–427.

Guess, D., Benson, H.A., & Siegel-Causey, E. (1985). Concepts and issues related to choice-making and autonomy among persons with severe disabilities. *Journal of The Association for Persons with Severe Handicaps, 10,* 79–86.

Houghton, J., Bronicki, G.J.B., & Guess, D. (1987). Opportunities to express preferences and make choices among students with severe disabilities in classroom settings. *Journal of The Association for Persons with Severe Handicaps, 10,* 87–95.

Hughes, C., Harmer, M.L., Killian, D.J., & Niarhos, F. (1995). The effects of multiple-exemplar self-instructional training on high school students' generalized conversational interactions. *Journal of Applied Behavior Analysis, 28,* 201–218.

Hughes, C.A., & Petersen, D.L. (1989). Utilizing a self-instructional training package to increase on-task behavior and work performance. *Education and Training in Mental Retardation, 24,* 114–120.

Individuals with Disabilities Education Act (IDEA) of 1990, PL 101-476, 20 U.S.C. §§ 1400 *et seq.*

Individuals with Disabilities Education Act Amendments of 1997, PL 105-17, 20 U.S.C. §§ 1400 *et seq.*

Kapadia, S., & Fantuzzo, J.W. (1988). Training children with developmental disabilities and severe behavior problems to use self-management procedures to sustain attention to preacademic/academic tasks. *Education and Training in Mental Retardation, 23,* 59–69.

Kaser-Boyd, N., Adelman, H.S., & Taylor, L. (1985). Minors' ability to identify risks and benefits of therapy. *Professional Psychology: Research and Practice, 16,* 411–417.

Kennedy, C., & Haring, T. (1993). Teaching choice making during social interactions to students with profound multiple disabilities. *Journal of Applied Behavior Analysis, 26,* 63–76.

Kochhar, C.A., & Deschamps, A.B. (1992). Policy crossroads in preserving the right of passage to independence for learners with special needs. *Journal for Vocational Special Needs Education, 14,* 9–19.

Koestner, R., Ryan, R.M., Bernieri, F., & Holt, K. (1984). The effects of controlling versus informational limit-setting styles on children's intrinsic motivation and creativity. *Journal of Personality, 52,* 233–248.

Kohn, A. (1993). Choices for children: Why and how to let students decide. *Phi Delta Kappan, 75*(1), 8–20.

Lagomarcino, T.R., & Rusch, F.R. (1989). Utilizing self-management procedures to teach independent performance. *Education and Training in Mental Retardation, 24,* 297–305.

Lovett, D.L., & Haring, K.A. (1989). The effects of self-management training on the daily living of adults with mental retardation. *Education and Training in Mental Retardation, 24,* 306–307.

Malone, L.D., & Mastropieri, M.A. (1992). Reading comprehension instruction: Summarization and self-monitoring training for students with learning disabilities. *Exceptional Children, 58,* 270–279.

Martin, J.E., Burger, D.L., Elias-Burger, S., & Mithaug, D. (1988). Application of self-control strategies to facilitate independence in vocational and instructional settings. In N.W. Bray (Ed.), *International review of research in mental retardation* (Vol. 15, pp. 155–193). San Diego: Academic Press.

Martin, J.E., & Huber Marshall, L. (1995). ChoiceMaker: A comprehensive self-determination transition program. *Intervention in School and Clinic, 30,* 147–156.

Martin, J.E., & Huber Marshall, L. (1996). ChoiceMaker: Infusing self-determination instruction into the IEP and transition process. In D.J. Sands & M.L. Wehmeyer (Eds.), *Self-determination across the life span: Independence and choice for people with disabilities* (pp. 215–236). Baltimore: Paul H. Brookes Publishing Co.

Martin, J.E., Huber Marshall, L., & Maxson, L. (1993). Transition policy: Infusing self-determination and self-advocacy into transition programs. *Career Development for Exceptional Individuals, 16,* 53–61.

McCarl, J.J., Svobodny, L., & Beare, P.L. (1991). Self-recording in a classroom for students with mild to moderate mental handicaps: Effects on productivity and on-task behavior. *Education and Training in Mental Retardation, 26,* 79–88.

Mithaug, D., & Mar, D. (1980). The relation between choosing and working prevocational tasks in two severely retarded young adults. *Journal of Applied Behavior Analysis, 13,* 177–182.

Mithaug, D.E., Wolman, J., & Campeau, P. (1992). *Research in self-determination in individuals with disabilities: Technical proposal.* Palo Alto, CA: American Institutes for Research.

Moore, S.C., Agran, M., & Fodor-Davis, J. (1989). Using self-management strategies to increase the production rates of workers with severe handicaps. *Education and Training in Mental Retardation, 24,* 324–332.

Newton, J., Ard, W., & Horner, R. (1993). Validating predicted activity preferences of individuals with severe disabilities. *Journal of Applied Behavior Analysis, 26,* 239–245.

Parsons, R., Reid, D., Reynolds, J., & Bumgarner, M. (1990). Effects of chosen versus assigned jobs on the work performance of persons with severe handicaps. *Journal of Applied Behavior Analysis, 23,* 253–258.

Phillips, P. (1990). A self-advocacy plan for high school students with learning disabilities: A comparative case study analysis of students', teachers', and parents' perceptions of program effects. *Journal of Learning Disabilities, 23,* 466–471.

Powers, L.E., Sowers, J.-A., Turner, A., Nesbitt, M., Knowles, E., & Ellison, R. (1996). *TAKE CHARGE:* A model for promoting self-determination among adolescents with challenges. In L.E. Powers, G.H.S. Singer, & J.-A. Sowers (Eds.), *On the road to autonomy: Promoting self-competence in children and youth with disabilities* (pp. 291–322). Baltimore: Paul H. Brookes Publishing Co.

Realon, R., Favell, J., & Lowerre, A. (1990). The effects of making choices on engagement levels with persons who are profoundly multiply handicapped. *Education and Training in Mental Retardation, 25,* 299–305.

Rehabilitation Act of 1973, PL 93-112, 29 U.S.C. §§ 701 *et seq.*

Rehabilitation Act Amendments of 1992, PL 102-569, 29 U.S.C. §§ 701 *et seq.*

Rusch, F.R., McKee, M., Chadsey-Rusch, J., & Renzaglia, A. (1988). Teaching a student with severe handicaps to self-instruct: A brief report. *Education and Training in Mental Retardation, 23,* 51–58.

Salend, S.J. (1983). Self-assessment: A model for involving students in the formulation of their IEPs. *Journal of School Psychology, 21,* 65–70.

Salend, S.J., Ellis, L.L., & Reynolds, C.J. (1989). Using self-instruction to teach vocational skills to individuals who are severely retarded. *Education and Training in Mental Retardation, 24,* 248–254.

Sands, D.J., & Wehmeyer, M.L. (Eds.). (1996). *Self-determination across the life span: Independence and choice for people with disabilities.* Baltimore: Paul H. Brookes Publishing Co.

Sarason, S.B. (1990). *The predictable failure of educational reform: Can we change course before it's too late?* San Francisco: Jossey-Bass.

Schunk, D.H. (1981). Modeling and attributional effects on children's achievement: A self-efficacy analysis. *Journal of Educational Psychology, 73,* 93–105.

Schunk, D.H. (1985). Participation in goal setting: Effects on self-efficacy and skills of learning-disabled children. *Journal of Special Education, 19,* 307–316.

Swann, W.B., & Pittman, T.S. (1977). Initiating play activity of children: The moderating influence of verbal cues on intrinsic motivation. *Child Development, 48,* 1128–1132.

Taylor, L., Adelman, H.S., & Kaser-Boyd, N. (1983). Perspectives of children regarding their participation in psychoeducational decisions. *Professional Psychology: Research and Practice, 14,* 882–894.

Taylor, L., Adelman, H.S., & Kaser-Boyd, N. (1985). Minors' attitudes and competence toward participation in psychoeducational decisions. *Professional Psychology: Research and Practice, 16,* 226–235.

The Merriam-Webster Dictionary. (1978). New York: Simon & Schuster.

Trammel, D.L., Schloss, P.J., & Alper, S. (1994). Using self-recording, evaluation, and graphing to increase completion of homework assignments. *Journal of Learning Disabilities, 27,* 75–81.

Turnbull, A.P., Blue-Banning, M.J., Anderson, E.L., Turnbull, H.R., Seaton, K.A., & Dinas, P.A. (1996). Enhancing self-determination through Group Action Planning: A holistic emphasis. In D.J. Sands & M.L. Wehmeyer (Eds.), *Self-determination across the life span: Independence and choice for people with disabilities* (pp. 237–256). Baltimore: Paul H. Brookes Publishing Co.

Van Reusen, A.K., & Bos, C.S. (1990). I PLAN: Helping students communicate in planning conferences. *Teaching Exceptional Children, 22*(4), 30–32.

Van Reusen, A.K., & Bos, C.S. (1994). Facilitating student participation in individualized education programs through motivation strategy instruction. *Exceptional Children, 60,* 466–475.

Ward, M.J. (1996). Coming of age in the age of self-determination: A historical and personal perspective. In D.J. Sands & M.L. Wehmeyer (Eds.), *Self-determination across the life span: Independence and choice for people with disabilities* (pp. 3–16). Baltimore: Paul H. Brookes Publishing Co.

Ward, M.J., & Kohler, P.D. (1996). Teaching self-determination: Content and process. In L.E. Powers, G.H.S. Singer, & J.-A. Sowers (Eds.), *On the road to autonomy: Promoting self-competence in children and youth with disabilities* (pp. 275–290). Baltimore: Paul H. Brookes Publishing Co.

Wehmeyer, M.L. (1992). Self-determination and the education of students with mental retardation. *Education and Training in Mental Retardation, 27,* 302–314.

Wehmeyer, M.L. (1996). Self-determination as an educational outcome: Why is it important to children, youth, and adults with disabilities? In D.J. Sands & M.L. Wehmeyer (Eds.), *Self-determination across the life span: Independence and choice for people with disabilities* (pp. 17–36). Baltimore: Paul H. Brookes Publishing Co.

Wehmeyer, M.L., Agran, M., & Hughes, C. (1998). *Teaching self-determination to students with disabilities: Basic skills for successful transition.* Baltimore: Paul H. Brookes Publishing Co.

Wehmeyer, M.L., Kelchner, K., & Richards, S. (1996). Essential characteristics of self-determined behaviors of adults with mental retardation and developmental disabilities. *American Journal on Mental Retardation, 100,* 632–642.

Wehmeyer, M.L., & Lawrence, M. (1995). Whose future is it anyway? Promoting student involvement in transition planning. *Career Development for Exceptional Individuals, 18,* 69–83.

Wehmeyer, M.L., & Ward, M.J. (1995). The spirit of the IDEA mandate: Student involvement in transition planning. *Journal for Vocational Special Needs Education, 17,* 108–111.

2

Factors Contributing to and Implications for Student Involvement in Transition-Related Planning, Decision Making, and Instruction

Deanna J. Sands, Diane S. Bassett,
Jean Lehmann, and Karen C. Spencer

Chapter 1 sets the context for understanding why it is important to move toward a system that encourages students to be more involved in their own educational experiences. Specifically, the chapter reviews the academic and social benefits of promoting students to become independent and self-directed learn-

The project described in this chapter, Best Practices: A Study to Understand and Support Student Participation in Transition Planning, was supported by Grant H158U40013 from the U.S. Department of Education, Office of Special Education Programs, awarded to the University of Colorado at Denver. The contents of this chapter do not necessarily represent the policies of the U.S. Department of Education, and endorsement by the federal government should not be inferred.

ers. During the late 1980s, the Office of Special Education and Rehabilitative Services (OSERS), U.S. Department of Education, began an initiative to support systemwide efforts to increase the degree to which students with disabilities participate in decisions that affect their lives (Ward, 1996). The construct of self-determination served as an underlying catalyst and frame for this initiative. From 26 funded projects, a series of assessments and curricula emerged that could be used to assess students with regard to, and teach students to learn, skills such as self-evaluation and analysis, decision making, goal setting, self-advocacy, and self-regulation. The outcomes of these projects are well documented (see, e.g., Martin & Huber Marshall, 1996; Powers et al., 1996; Serna, 1996). One of the lessons learned from those projects, as well as from thorough analyses of the construct of self-determination, is the complexity of the processes necessary to promote and support active student involvement and self-determined actions (Abery & Stancliffe, 1996; Doll, Sands, Wehmeyer, & Palmer, 1996). Just as students need to develop and be able to use the skills and attitudes associated with self-determined behavior (Wehmeyer, 1996), their home, school, and community environments play an important role in providing the support and opportunities needed to refine and generalize those skills across many life settings and circumstances (Abery & Stancliffe, 1996; Mithaug, 1996a, 1996b).

Understanding how the education system can support student involvement and self-determination requires that we investigate the many variables that facilitate or obstruct active student participation. The value for active student involvement has legal and regulatory protection. With the passage of the Individuals with Disabilities Education Act (IDEA) of 1990 (PL 101-476), student involvement is required within the context of transition services. In a broad sense, *transition services* are defined as a coordinated set of activities that support the student as he or she moves from school to postschool activities. Planning for transition usually occurs in conjunction with the individualized education program (IEP) planning process. Starting in 1990, under the requirements set forth in IDEA, students 16 years of age and older had to be invited to their IEP meetings. Then, in 1997, with the passage of the Individuals with Disabilities Education Act Amendments of 1997 (PL 105-17), this requirement was extended to cover students ages 14 and older. In addition, the goals, objectives, and activities developed for the IEP must take into account the students' self-perceived needs, preferences, and interests (Martin & Huber Marshall, 1996).

This chapter reports the results of a series of research studies that were conducted to better understand school, student, and family variables that predict or relate to high levels of student involvement in transition-related activities. This research was part of a federally funded research project entitled Best Practices: A Study to Understand and Support Student Participation in Transition Planning. The aim of the research was to use information about critical variables to develop and implement school, student, and family interventions that would increase student involvement in transition-related activities. Ultimately, it was hoped that education communities, parent and advocacy organizations, and community support systems could be informed and guided in their attempts to support student participation not only in the context of transition services but also in other important life arenas. In the first half of this chapter, an overview of the research and results is provided. The second half of the chapter discusses how four school sites used this information to enhance their services and supports to facilitate active student involvement in transition-related activities.

RESEARCH OVERVIEW

The research presented here was conceptualized from years of work in the areas of learning, transition services, and self-determination. To fully understand student involvement in transition services, one must look inward to the student as well as examine the influences of students' home and school environments. The present studies were guided by this overarching question: What are the relative contributions of personal, environmental, and systemic variables that relate to high levels of student participation in transition-related activities?

Two types of studies, quantitative and qualitative, were conducted to identify variables important to student involvement in transition-related activities. Both types of studies were used because quantitative and qualitative research methodologies stem from different philosophical orientations regarding the nature and conduct of research. Quantitative research is based on the notion that phenomena should be studied and measured numerically. It is often used to determine relationships between two or more variables. In contrast, qualitative research is based on the idea that the most valuable information is obtained from a relatively small group of people who are significantly involved in the topic or issue in which the researcher is interested. This information provides an understanding of the phenomenon being studied. Because the development of self-determined behaviors is so complex, both types of research were incorporated to capture a broad understanding of what variables might be important to active student participation in transition-related activities. Once the two main studies were completed, a series of follow-up analyses and studies were conducted to further explain the variables that emerged initially. In this section, an overview of the research methods, procedures, and analyses for each type of study is presented. A more comprehensive discussion of this research can be found in Lehmann, Bassett, and Sands (1997); Sands, Spencer, Gliner, and Swaim (1997); and Spencer and Sands (1996).

Quantitative Study

For the quantitative portion of our study, data were collected on 237 students with disabilities, their families, and their teachers. Students were between 14 and 21 years of age and attended middle school or high school in one of three participating school districts. The districts represented urban, rural, and suburban settings. A total of nine disability categories were used to classify the students, with a majority (60.8%) classified as having specific learning disabilities. The second most common type of disability was serious emotional disturbance (8.8%), followed by mental retardation (7.9%), speech and language impairment (7.5%), health impairment (3.3%), multiple disabilities (2.1%), vision and hearing impairments (.8%), and traumatic brain injury (.4%).

The students and their families were from diverse ethnic and socioeconomic backgrounds. Although approximately 40% of the families chose not to identify their ethnic heritage, information received revealed that a majority of students were Caucasian (39.2%), followed by students who were Hispanic (24.2%), Native American (4.6%), or African American (2.1%).

Data for the quantitative study were collected by using 10 instruments. The student variables represented information about the student's locus of control; autonomy; self-regulation; psychological empowerment; self-realization; and job, social, and scholastic competence. Many of these measures included both students' perceptions and teachers' perceptions. The cluster of family variables included information about parental expectations for student performance, family climate, and adults' perceptions of their parenting competence. School variables consisted of data on school climate, the nature of students' IEPs, and transition-related opportunities. These data were analyzed using multiple regression and structural equation modeling techniques. Details of these analyses can be reviewed in Sands et al. (1997) and Spencer and Sands (1996).

Qualitative Study

The qualitative component of the study was designed to enable understanding of the perceptions of teachers, students, and mothers regarding student involvement in the transition process. Special education teachers from three school sites assisted in the selection of students and families to participate in the study. Teachers were asked to select students and their respective families, representing a variety of ages, ethnic backgrounds, and socioeconomic statuses (SESs) who also had upcoming individualized transition plan (ITP) meetings scheduled. Twelve students, four from each district, were the focus of data collection. More than 300 hours of observations were conducted in students' classes and during their IEP meetings. Information from the observations was initially used to develop the interview questions and later to substantiate the data obtained from the interviews. A total of 31 people (teachers, students, and mothers) took part in participant observations and interviews.

The three questions guiding the inquiry were

1. What transition-related activities are occurring?
2. How are teachers, students, and mothers involved in this process?
3. What are the perceptions of teachers and mothers regarding the barriers to student involvement?

The interview questions for each group were similar but were modified to more adequately reflect the role of the group questioned. For example, the first statement directed to students was "Tell me about school," whereas teachers were directed to "Tell me about your work." Finally, mothers were asked to describe their families. The basis of the question remained the same, with the context being changed according to the type of respondent.

Once the observations and interviews were completed, the information from each set of research activities was coded and analyzed. Observation data were captured through a set of detailed field notes written on site or immediately after the observation period. Interviews were audiotaped and transcribed. To analyze the qualitative data, the researchers immersed themselves in the written documentation to look for patterns, redundancies, and explanations tied to the guiding questions. They were looking for information that could illuminate participants' beliefs about transition services, roles and responsibilities, and student involvement.

Summary and Implications of Research Results

Individually and collectively, the studies revealed that school, student (or personal), and family variables are all important predictors of student involvement in transition-related services. A summary of results is given in Figure 1. A brief explanation of these variables is provided in the following section.

School Variables   The school environment is particularly important in facilitating active student involvement in transition-related activities. The first of the quantitative analyses revealed two strong school environment conditions that related highly to active student involvement. When students 1) received their special education services in general education classrooms and 2) participated in higher numbers of general education classes, they were more actively involved in their own transition-planning services. Secondary analyses revealed a third critical school variable: Students are ultimately more involved in transition-related activities when they are provided with overt, ongoing opportunities to plan, express, and actively pursue their own goals as well as to evaluate their progress and adjust their activities accordingly. The qualitative study of teachers and mothers revealed the importance of holding a positive value for student involvement in transition-related activities. Both groups discussed the need for solid communication among the IEP and ITP members and the need for administrative support for focused transition-planning meetings at the building level.

Student (or Personal) Variables   Four variables emerged from the quantitative studies as significant predictors of active student participation in transition-related activities: 1) the student's job-related competence as perceived by the teacher; 2) the student's ability to self-regulate his or her own behaviors; 3) the student's social skills; and 4) the student's engagement in transition-related social, work, and educational opportunities. The first variable suggests that there is a relationship between teachers' positive beliefs about students' job competencies and students' involvement in transition-related services. The present authors are not in a position to definitively speculate about the nature of this relationship, but it might be related to variables entailing teacher expectations and student performance. The second student variable, that of self-regulation, suggests that students who are able to activate and maintain thinking and behavior directed toward goals are more likely to demonstrate self-determined participation in their ITP processes. The third variable, students' social skills, remains an enigma. The formal analyses indicated that social skills were important to active student involvement; however, these analyses could not authoritatively indicate which aspect of the social domain may be important. The social domain is complex and includes components such as social cognition, motivation, social skills, self-efficacy, and social control. From the research conducted, it could not be concluded which

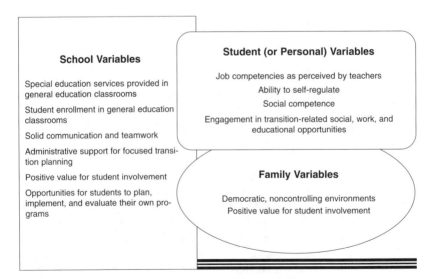

Figure 1.   Factors critical to student involvement in transition planning.

component or combination of components was most crucial to student involvement. Until further studies are completed, it can only be suggested that students' social competence plays an important part in active transition-related activities. The fourth variable, opportunities for students, mirrors and thus further confirms a school variable that emerged from the qualitative study and was discussed previously; that is, it is important for students to have available and to engage in ongoing overt opportunities to participate in transition-related planning, implementation, and evaluation in many different contexts.

Family Variables   A student's home environment emerged as an important variable. It appears that children in families that are not overly rule bound (and directive) are more likely to demonstrate active participation in transition-related activities. This conclusion is consistent with a previously reported finding (Spencer & Sands, 1996) that higher levels of involvement occur among students who are able to self-regulate (i.e., they operate from an internal versus an external set of rules or principles). It was also found that when families hold a positive value for student involvement, participation of the student is realized more successfully through school-based planning processes.

Nonsignificant Variables   Often, it is only the positive or significant relationships discovered through research that receive attention. However, in addition to the variables that were positively linked to active student involvement, there were variables that did not predict or correlate highly to student involvement. For example, data were collected on student academic achievement in areas such as reading and math. Scholastic competence was not a predictor of active student involvement. This is important because it suggests that support for active involvement should not be directed solely toward those students perceived as academically more capable. All students have the right to supports and services that are targeted to develop their abilities to act in self-determined ways.

Students were also rated for their overall levels of self-determination. Intuitively, it seems that students who are more self-determined are more likely to be involved actively in transition-related activities. In fact, the analyses revealed that there was not a strong relationship between a measure of self-determination and the measure used in this research for active student involvement. Thus, the constructs of self-determination and active involvement may not be synonymous. As pointed out in Chapter 1, self-determined students may choose not to engage in transition-related activities, and students who are considered active participants in fact may not appear to be fully self-determined. These nuances are important to keep in mind while striving for more active participation by students (within the context of transition services) and while building on their attitudes, skills, and dispositions toward more self-determined behaviors.

The findings of the studies are significant because they reveal that to truly achieve active student involvement in transition-related services, a multipronged approach to realizing that outcome must be adopted. One cannot just assume that, by teaching students the skills associated with self-determined behavior, students will become active participants in the transition process. In fact, the research suggests that students' actual skills may not be as important as the opportunities they have, the expectations of others, and the environmental conditions that are directly linked to and support their ultimate ability to actively participate in transition-related services. The next section provides details of how four school sites responded to the results of this research by designing and implementing interventions targeted to key variables.

TRANSLATING RESEARCH INTO PRACTICE

As noted in the previous sections, the results of these studies have led us in many directions. On the one hand, it is important to recognize that placing students with special needs in general education classrooms is a critical variable to enhance student involvement. On the other hand, it is clear that teachers' perceptions of students' job competence are related to self-determined behavior, as are family systems that rely on a strong and consistent set of parenting principles. Students play a part in their journey toward active involvement through their use of self-regulation strategies. Indeed, there is much to consider in planning for successful self-determination practices in schools.

It is also evident that these variables cannot be artificially separated from each other, but rather work in an intricate and complicated assemblage of interactions that ultimately composes a system in which students live, study, work, and develop relationships. For example, the need for positive values for student involvement emerged in both the school and family variables, and overt opportunities were identified as important school and student variables. It is necessary, therefore, to actively attend to variables across all three contexts.

A second phase of the Best Practices Project was to translate these findings into practice. To meet this objective, four school sites in two different states agreed to participate during a 2-year period to design, implement, and evaluate interventions that were targeted to the critical research variables. The four sites provided great contrasts in location, student population, SES, and community values and culture. Furthermore, there was a wide variance in the developmental nature of transition services across the school systems. For example, whereas one site had a fairly sophisticated transition services program in place, another site was struggling with basic issues such as student schedules and finding a common planning time for the transition services team to meet. A brief demographic description of the four project sites follows.

Demography

Washington High School   Washington High School is located in a densely populated urban environment in a city of 2 million people. Approximately 70% of its 1,700 students are Hispanic, and many are from lower socioeconomic backgrounds. The school is one of the oldest in the city and in need of major repair. The dropout rate is extremely high—more than 60% of the student population drop out between ninth grade and graduation. Teachers at Washington High School are overwhelmed by the transience of the students, the lack of support from the school district's central administration, and their own difficulties in attempting to connect the school to the community at large. They have experienced difficulties such as finding a common meeting time for members of the special education department and providing special education services in general education classrooms. Prior to the Best Practices Project, formal transition services for students at Washington High School were limited.

Lincoln High School   Situated in a valley amid three communities, Lincoln High School draws rural students within a 25-mile radius. Most of the 500 students come from families involved in agriculture. Almost 30% of the total school population are Hispanic; many are recent immigrants to the region from Mexico and speak only Spanish. Teachers at Lincoln feel compelled to provide the few educational opportunities that the region has to offer. Family support for the school community is mixed, ranging from strong support provided by multigenerational families raised in the area to support provided by those families new to the region and unfamiliar with the culture. Most teachers seem to have close relationships with their students. To these teachers, seeking active student involvement in transition services seemed valuable but hard to achieve in the face of so many other demands.

Roosevelt High School   Roosevelt High School is located in an isolated coastal community of approximately 6,500 people. The community is under heavy social and economic stress caused in part by the closure of a commercial fishing season, the decline of the lumber industry, and the loss of jobs in construction. The present unemployment rate is 16.8%, and the number of social services applicants increased by 50% during the previous year. Roosevelt High School has a dropout rate of 10%, and 20% of the student population are Hispanic. The school district experiences severe difficulties in serving an increasing number of students in the English as a Second Language (ESL) program, meeting the rising demand for alternative programs, and restructuring current programs to serve the middle 60% of the student population who are at risk of school failure and dropping out. The special education teachers experience great difficulties in finding appropriate general education placements for students with disabilities. Both overcrowded classrooms in an insufficient physical plant and lack of sufficient resources to direct personal support in general education classrooms contribute to their dilemma. In addition, few of their efforts have been directed toward systematic transition services.

Jefferson School District   The Jefferson School District site is based centrally within a district, as opposed to being a high school site. It is located in a rapidly growing suburban community of approximately 60,000 people. The vast majority of its residents are Caucasian. This district has been designated by the Colorado Department of Education as a model for transition and school-to-work practices. The district has a transition team that works with each of its four high schools. Unlike the other sites, this team is responsible for making district-level decisions about the delivery of transition services and programs. The district transition coordinators believe strongly in the concept of active student involvement, but they are also tied to the determinants of district policy and decision-making procedures.

To initiate the intervention phase of the project, each site constituted a project team. These teams were responsible for reflecting on the results of the research and for designing a set of interventions targeted toward one or more of the critical student, school, or family variables. Given what was learned from the results, paired with the overt differences in school cultures, it was clear that each school site should design its own set of interventions. This strategy for individualizing interventions also fit with the project research teams' philosophical beliefs for site-based empowerment. Thus, each site team, with the support of the research team, identified interventions best suited to their own needs and goals. The Best Practices Project provided an equal funding source to each site to support implementation of their action plans. The action plans of each school site are summarized in the section that follows.

Action Plans

Washington High School   Washington High School special educators entered into the Best Practices Project with trepidation. Once funded, the school administration adopted a stance of "out of sight, out of mind" toward the project. The Best Practices Project core team at Washington consisted of only the special education staff. The staff strongly believed that they needed to concentrate on their own skills and needs before they could work successfully with other school community members, such as their general education colleagues. Accordingly, the Washington team targeted their first intervention efforts toward the school variable that addressed strong communication among team members. This team believed it was imperative to provide the opportunity for self-reflection, to articulate strengths and problems, and to develop a framework for successful implementation of transition procedures. At two 2-day workshops held away from the school campus, a professional facilitator led the team through team-building exercises. The concept of transition services was used as the context for moving the team's work forward in that regard. Goals were established for the core team and included objectives for school–staff collaboration, developing a mission and vision statement to drive its work, and formulating a framework for providing transition services to students in Grades 9–12. Issues such as finding a consistent meeting time, managing paperwork, maintaining adequate contact with students, and working more closely with families were also discussed. The two workshops provided both the time and a safe environment in which to work on personal and professional problems; this was considered to be the breakthrough that the teachers needed to solidify their team and move ahead on specific goals.

Once the core team was better able to define its goals, it looked to strengthen contacts with families within the system as a second intervention goal. An advisory group of parents was solicited to help develop a parent and student handbook on transition services. The handbook included IEP planning guides for each student, along with information on school and community resources, including names and telephone numbers. The handbooks were initially distributed to every family of incoming ninth-grade students with disabilities during an on-site registration process. Washington High School special educators were amazed at the success of the handbook. Family members called to thank them for preparing the information. Teachers even received requests for the handbook from families at other schools. Development of the handbook proved to be a valuable first step in reclaiming communication among teachers, students, and their families.

In addition to the handbook, the Parent Advisory Committee assisted the core team in modifying a traditional family-focused school activity. At Washington High School, a family member must come to school to pick up the child's report card. Previously, the special education faculty had supplemented this evening with activities directed toward providing parents with transition-related information. For example, speakers from community-based agencies such as rehabilitation services, developmental disabilities service providers, and potential employers had provided information booths and materials throughout the evening. Parent attendance, however, was traditionally low. Through the Parent Advisory Committee, several changes were made to the scheduled events. First, dinner was offered; second, members of the Parent Advisory Committee made telephone contact with the parents of every student served by the special education services unit and personally invited them to come to the report card pick-up evening. As a result of these two changes, parents' attendance increased by more than 50%.

As a third intervention strategy, the core team at Washington High School believed it was necessary to develop a transition curriculum designed for the unique needs of their Grades 9–12 students. This effort was directed toward several of the research variables, including the provision of opportunities for students to be involved and to target students' skill development. The intent of the curriculum was to increase students' skills and knowledge in disability awareness, IEP and ITP planning participation, goal setting, and self-advocacy. The Best Practices Project team hoped that use of the curriculum would support students to graduate from Washington High School. In addition to curriculum development and implementation, the team decided that each student would develop and possess a transition portfolio. The portfolio would contain a student's current IEP/ITP, a summation of his or her personal learning style, an individualized listing of accommodations for school or job situations, a list of appropriate agencies and telephone numbers, letters of recommendation, a description of the student's legal rights, and a plan for achieving the student's self-determined long-term goals.

A fourth overall intervention strategy implemented by Washington's core team was aimed at giving students more opportunities to express choices and have a voice in their education planning. The Student Advisory Committee was formed with representatives from all grade levels. The students agreed to meet during their lunch hour on a monthly basis. The core project team also decided to provide nominal financial compensation to students for the duration of the project as an extra incentive for them to give their time. Through the Student Advisory Committee, several activities took place. For example, a volunteer from the Colorado Department of Education and the Project Director guided the entire student body of the special education department through a series of planning sessions. The purpose of these sessions was to allow students who received special education services to provide direction and feedback to the department. Through these sessions, students ranked two activities for the Student Advisory Committee to pursue: 1) changing the name of the department from special education and 2) sponsoring a series of off-campus learning experiences. While these activities were in progress, the Student Advisory Committee took action on these goals and utilized a student survey to guide the direction of their activities. Students requested a department name change by sending a formal letter to the district's secondary education curriculum department. Two field-based learning experiences were scheduled, and a third was in progress at the time of this writing.

The morale changes and professional growth of Washington's core team over the course of the project were significant. Their strong efforts at self-reflection and planned action resulted in a more cohesive team that shared positive goals for their students and themselves. Although support from the administration was not strong, the core team synthesized their energies to provide themselves with strong leadership and a renewed sense of purpose.

Lincoln High School   Lincoln High School participants who were planning for active student involvement in transition-related services included special education teachers, general education teachers, students with disabilities, and parents. This Best Practices Project core team decided to work on activities related to school, student, and family variables. The team divided itself into subgroups to address each area. Each subgroup worked regularly with its members and then met together at least once per month or more often for training or other team-building activities. Lincoln High School team activities were facilitated by one or more of the grant research coordinators; other project activities were implemented with assistance provided by project-supported graduate students.

Because the research findings recognized the importance of family values and support for active student participation, family goals centered around attempts to engage more families in school-based activities during the transition process. This proved to be more difficult to achieve than previously believed. Although a large library of resources was purchased for family use, several scheduled meetings were unattended. A welcome dinner at a local restaurant was well attended, but there was sporadic attendance at subsequent meetings. Best Practices Project team members realized that to target only families of high school–age students was limiting. They therefore targeted families from the middle grades as well, and attendance improved. A number of family members were funded to attend a national conference on inclusive school practices as well as a regional training program for families on transition and self-determination issues.

School variables related to a variety of different goals. All team members were interested in improving the inclusive practices in the school, from scheduled collaborative planning meetings to team teaching and the use of curricula across content areas. Training was provided at the school using the curriculum Learning with a PURPOSE (Serna & Lau-Smith, 1995) during a 2-year period. Teachers devised a matrix showing where different components of the curriculum would be taught across content areas to students in both the general and special education programs. The special education team was also trained in the Self-Advocacy Strategy for Education and Transition Planning (Van Reusen, Bos, Schumaker, & Deshler, 1994; see Chapter 7) and the Self-Directed IEP (Martin & Huber Marshall, 1996; see Chapter 11), with the intention of providing students with disabilities with the skills they needed to set goals and participate in their own IEP meetings.

The core team was interested in using team-building activities to improve their communication. Team-building activities were highlighted by a day of a variety of events, with each being coordinated by a different team member. Finally, a fund was established to allow teachers and related staff to attend conferences related to self-determination. At the time of this writing, seven teachers have taken advantage of this funding.

Student variables included the formation of a student club with the purpose of promoting advocacy with and for students with disabilities. The student group, People Redefining Independence through Disability Education (PRIDE), was kicked off with a party that included about 30 students with and without disabilities. It meets regularly and is an integral part of formal school club meeting times. Students also wanted to start a school store in their newly renovated cafeteria. The school clubs of PRIDE, Future Business Leaders of America, and Family and Consumer Leaders of America met to plan the store's operation. Inventory was ordered, along with a computerized inventory program. Students also worked together to write a $5,000 grant to support the early months of the store's operation. The store is up and running, with new inventory being ordered regularly.

Additional activities targeted the student variable of job competence. The team sought to link with community-based organizations such as the Chamber of Commerce and the Family Support Council. It also used students to provide community service as well as to develop, conduct, and analyze a survey of local business opportunities in the region. Because Lincoln is located in a rural area, job opportunities are limited and scarce. Project funding has provided the school with a part-time job developer/coach to help with this problem. A wide range of students were involved in a daylong Go to Work Day alongside employees from a local department store. Both students and employers were excited about the day; several students later completed job applications for employment at the store.

Through this process, the morale of the Best Practices Project team was high. For the first time, special and general educators found value in working together. The students on the team were respected and given a voice. The parents, too, were feeling more a part of the community. It seems evident that self-determination can occur, but only if it is implemented in a holistic way that is respectful of all parts of the system. Progress was slow but meaningful. There was also strong support from the principal, who attended meetings and participated when possible.

Roosevelt High School   The core project team at Roosevelt High School was made up of two special education teachers, a guidance counselor, a Title I reading aide, and a service coordinator from a local developmental disabilities service agency. The project team placed emphasis on the following two variables: 1) providing increased opportunities for students to plan, implement, and evaluate their own programs; and 2) developing a strong interagency team approach to support focused transition planning for all high school students, including students with and without disabilities. A multipronged effort was initiated for the first variable. The core team was not satisfied that their existing assessment procedures placed a value on or invited student participation. The team decided that if they were to build education programs that incorporated the students' interests and goals, a different set of procedures would need to be implemented. Therefore, Roosevelt's first project activity was an in-service day on the Personal Futures Planning (Mount & Zwernik, 1988) approach to education planning. This student-centered approach is qualitatively different from traditional educational diagnostic and standardized assessments. Personal Futures Planning places the student at the center of all discussions, and it is the student's hopes and dreams, along with those of his or her family members and friends, that focus and direct his or her impending education program and supports.

The second action taken by the Roosevelt team (with regard to the first variable) was to examine how a self-determination curriculum could be implemented within the high school program so that all students with and without disabilities would have access to and the opportunity to develop the attitudes, skills, and habits associated with self-determined behavior. This objective was consistent with a school policy that all students would contribute to and hold to an IEP that would direct their high school experiences. At this point, the core team expanded to include two of the high school health teachers. These teachers were responsible for teaching a health curriculum to all incoming freshmen. The core team decided that if they were to ensure that all students were to have equal access to opportunities to learn and apply skills associated with self-determined behaviors, this freshman health class would serve as the most consistent place to offer such access. Furthermore, the skills and habits associated with self-determination were consistent with many of the underlying concepts and skills in the health curriculum. While activities on this objective continued, the team was reviewing myriad existing self-determination curricula and was in the process of selecting which curricula to use as a guide and of making decisions about how to infuse the content into the health class.

To expand opportunities for both students and teachers to deepen their understanding of and ability to increase student involvement, a second major curriculum initiative was implemented. The project team planned an outdoor experiential retreat at a local challenge course to facilitate a cultural and attitudinal change among students and teachers within the context of self-determination. The opportunity to attend the retreat was extended first to juniors and then to other students, and an interview process was used to select participants. The activities were designed to focus on and strengthen student goal setting, decision making, and self-advocacy. Emphasis was placed on how those skills might generalize to other life experiences. The retreat was also designed with a follow-up component. Once back from the experiential retreat, all student and teacher participants agreed to meet 1 hour per week for 4 weeks during lunch to continue discussions on how the skills and attitudes experienced at the retreat could be used on a daily basis. An additional action strategy was targeted to students with severe disabilities. Six students with significant support needs and their teachers attended a statewide supported living conference. The workshops and sessions during this 2-day conference provided many experiences for students and their teachers to learn how to plan, implement, and evaluate students' long-term transition goals.

The second variable targeted by the Roosevelt team had to do with creating a strong interagency transition-planning team from which to conduct focused transition-planning activities. Several initiatives supported their objective. An existing interagency team was brought to the school to provide an overview of the project goals and objectives. In addition, this team participated in an in-service day on developing a more student-focused planning process. The interagency team is currently planning a 2-day retreat to focus their planning efforts on designing a comprehensive, focused transition process especially targeted toward students ages 18–21 years. The goal of this process is to provide students with the supports and services they need in community-based living, work, education, and recreational or leisure environments.

Jefferson School District   The Best Practices Project team was made up of the existing district transition team whose members included a parent; representatives from four high schools, the community college, and a business school partnership program; and a school social worker. The interventions designed by this team related most closely to the student and school variables identified by the research study. The Jefferson District team identified two main interventions—one designed to increase students' opportunities to achieve their desired futures and the other aimed at increasing the skills of general education teachers in working with students with disabilities.

The first intervention targeted the student variables of job competence and increasing opportunities in which students could be involved. This intervention was aimed at helping those students who were completing school and who were perceived by educators as being ready to work. The team discussed the fact that frequently these students have little motivation for planning for their future because they have no resources with which to achieve this goal. For example, many students and their families do not have the financial means needed to enroll in postsecondary training programs that would lead the students to the career in which they are interested. These students may not be eligible for adult services support, because they have been labeled as having disabilities. Also, given their low high school grade point averages, they are usually not candidates for scholarships or education loan packages. These students, then, may consider planning to be moot or at least not in the realm of possibilities.

The Jefferson District team developed a procedure for identifying students caught in this predicament as well as a process for providing these students with the support they needed to attain their goals. All special education secondary teachers in the district and families of students were informed about this intervention and asked to recommend students who might benefit from such an approach. The Jefferson District team designed an intervention application form to be completed collaboratively by interested students and their special education teachers. The application form documented whether students matched specific criteria established by the team for identifying students. Selection criteria required that students

- Were high school juniors or seniors and still in school
- Demonstrated a strong commitment to a personal employment goal
- Had no other resources available to achieve that goal

- Had a school sponsor who would vouch for the potential success of the student
- Received special education services
- Were willing to participate in a person-centered planning meeting
- Completed the application form

Thus, teachers and families were invited to identify students who they believed were ready to advance into a career but did not have the resources to do so. Teachers who acted as student sponsors were required to conduct two planning meetings with students, using a person-centered approach. Briefly, *person-centered planning* is the generic name for a group of meeting strategies described in the literature under various names such as *Personal Futures Planning*; *Making Action Plans (MAPs)* (Forest & Pearpoint, 1992; Pearpoint, Forest, & O'Brien, 1996); and *Group Action Planning* (Turnbull et al., 1996). All of these planning processes are characterized by their emphases on people's capacities and the development of opportunities to support people's full rights to citizenship in the community. During this meeting, the individual and family, friends, and supporters identify their hopes and dreams for the individual's future.

Students in the Jefferson School District who were participating in the intervention identified going to cosmetology school, living in an apartment, and becoming a hunting guide, for example, as hopes for their futures. A second meeting of team members and interested parties was held to determine whether there were any financial resources to support the students' goals. The district transition team reviewed every possible avenue, including vocational rehabilitation, state grants, and district projects, before offering support to the students. Examples of student support that was provided using the funds allotted for this intervention include expenditures for tuition, textbooks, supplies, rent, and driving school.

The intent of this intervention approach was to increase students' participation in their planning meetings by using a strategy that, unlike many traditional IEP planning sessions, promoted the student's view of his or her future and then helped students implement their plans by providing the necessary resources for them to attain their goals. Thus, opportunities for students were expanded because students had a reason to be involved in their planning meetings. Resources identified during the meeting could be provided, and tasks resulting from goals could be accomplished instead of ignored. The meeting itself garnered credibility for the students. As the IEP planning session became more than a perfunctory school exercise, it became a way for the students to achieve their goals.

The second intervention that the Jefferson School District implemented was a strategy to increase the knowledge and confidence of general education teachers to work more effectively with students with disabilities in their general education classrooms. This intervention was derived from the research variable that found that when students received their special education services in general education classrooms, they were more likely to be actively involved in their own transition-related services. The focus of this intervention was entirely different from the beginning. That is, this intervention was devised to help all secondary students with disabilities in the district by creating a mechanism for better communication between special education and general education staff.

The Jefferson School District team arranged a series of three workshops. The agenda of the first workshop (attended by 9 special educators, 12 general education teachers, and 1 building custodian) was to provide participants with an overview of the grant project, discuss the need to foster students' empowerment, describe the need for the project, and review possible classroom modifications. The general education teachers were given the assignment to select one or two students in their classrooms with whom they wanted to collaborate in becoming more proficient educators. The teachers were then responsible for devising a plan that outlined their strategies for improving the students' performance. The strategies typically involved meeting with the students and identifying ways in which both parties could change or redirect their efforts to ensure the students' success in the classroom. The purpose of the two remaining workshops was to encourage networking among participants and to report progress of the teachers' plans.

The role of the special educators was to follow up at least three times during the semester to ascertain what type of assistance teachers needed. Two outcomes of those follow-up meetings have been that special education teachers have greater contact with general educators and have become more aware of the issues faced by these teachers in their classes. This increased communication between general and special education is leading to changes by the special education personnel in how they provide information to general educators about modifications that students need in their classrooms. General educators have indicated that they have needed this level of dialogue with all of their colleagues, as well as the support from special educators, to better address students' needs in their classrooms.

CONCLUSIONS

As the Best Practices Project headed into its final year, project staff were confident that it had greatly contributed to understanding variables important to goals for active student involvement in transition-related services. Furthermore, the four school sites that participated in the intervention phase of the project illustrated the many ways in which schools can respond to those variables. Although there was much variety among the sites in terms of the interventions employed, there were also important commonalities. For example, it was critical for each site to identify a team responsible for implementing activities to increase student involvement in the context of transition-related services. Also, most sites determined that engaging general educators in this process was a worthwhile strategy, either by directly targeting interventions with and for general educators or by including them as site team members. In addition, acquiring curricular materials and resources was necessary at most school sites to systematically increase the overt opportunities of students to plan, implement, evaluate, and adjust their transition-related activities. It is important to note that curricular efforts at most school sites have been infused within their existing programming. Active student involvement has been approached as integral to students' education and not simply as an "add-on."

Finally, although this project was conducted within the context of transition services, the findings presented here have some bearing on active student involvement across multiple contexts. To involve students takes a combination of attitude and effort across multiple contexts and environments to give them the skills, opportunities, and support required.

REFERENCES

Abery, B., & Stancliffe, R. (1996). The ecology of self-determination. In D.J. Sands & M.L. Wehmeyer (Eds.), *Self-determination across the life span: Independence and choice for people with disabilities* (pp. 111–145). Baltimore: Paul H. Brookes Publishing Co.

Doll, B., Sands, D.J., Wehmeyer, M.L., & Palmer, S. (1996). Promoting the development and acquisition of self-determined behavior. In D.J. Sands & M.L. Wehmeyer (Eds.), *Self-determination across the life span: Independence and choice for people with disabilities* (pp. 65–90). Baltimore: Paul H. Brookes Publishing Co.

Forest, M., & Pearpoint, J. (1992). MAPS: Action planning. In J. Pearpoint, M. Forest, & J. Snow (Eds.), *The inclusion papers: Strategies to make inclusion work* (pp. 52–56). Toronto: Inclusion Press.

Individuals with Disabilities Education Act (IDEA) of 1990, PL 101-476, 20 U.S.C. §§ 1400 *et seq.*

Individuals with Disabilities Education Act Amendments of 1997, PL 105-17, 20 U.S.C. §§ 1400 *et seq.*

Lehmann, J., Bassett, D., & Sands, D.J. (1997). *Understanding students', mothers', and teachers' perceptions of active student involvement in transition-related actions.* Unpublished manuscript, Colorado State University, Fort Collins.

Martin, J.E., & Huber Marshall, L. (1996). ChoiceMaker: Infusing self-determination instruction into the IEP and transition process. In D.J. Sands & M.L. Wehmeyer (Eds.), *Self-determination across the life span: Independence and choice for people with disabilities* (pp. 215–236). Baltimore: Paul H. Brookes Publishing Co.

Mithaug, D.E. (1996a). *Equal opportunity theory.* Thousand Oaks, CA: Sage.

Mithaug, D.E. (1996b). The optimal prospects principle: A theoretical basis for rethinking instructional practices for self-determination. In D.J. Sands & M.L. Wehmeyer (Eds.), *Self-determination across the life span: Independence and choice for people with disabilities* (pp. 147–165). Baltimore: Paul H. Brookes Publishing Co.

Mount, B., & Zwernik, K. (1988). *It's never too early, it's never too late: A booklet about Personal Futures Planning* (Pub. No. 421-88-109). St. Paul, MN: Governor's Planning Council on Developmental Disabilities.

Pearpoint, J., Forest, M., & O'Brien, J. (1996). MAPs, Circles of Friends, and PATH: Powerful tools to help build caring communities. In S. Stainback & W. Stainback (Eds.), *Inclusion: A guide for educators* (pp. 67–86). Baltimore: Paul H. Brookes Publishing Co.

Powers, L.E., Wilson, R., Matuszewski, J., Phillips, A., Rein, C., Schumacher, D., & Gensert, J. (1996). Facilitating adolescent self-determination: What does it take? In D.J. Sands & M.L. Wehmeyer (Eds.), *Self-determination across the life span: Independence and choice for people with disabilities* (pp. 257–284). Baltimore: Paul H. Brookes Publishing Co.

Sands, D.J., Spencer, K., Gliner, J., & Swaim, R. (1997). *Structural equation modeling of student involvement in transition-related actions: The path of least resistance.* Unpublished manuscript, University of Colorado at Denver.

Serna, L.A. (1996). Learning with PURPOSE: A lifelong learning approach using self-determination skills. In D.J. Sands & M.L. Wehmeyer (Eds.), *Self-determination across the life span: Independence and choice for people with disabilities* (pp. 285–309). Baltimore: Paul H. Brookes Publishing Co.

Serna, L.A., & Lau-Smith, J. (1995). Learning with a PURPOSE: Self-determination skills for students who are at risk for school and community failure. *Intervention in School and Clinic, 30,* 142–146.

Spencer, K., & Sands, D.J. (1996). *Prediction of student participation in transition-related actions.* Unpublished manuscript, Colorado State University, Fort Collins.

Turnbull, A.P., Blue-Banning, M.J., Anderson, E.L., Turnbull, H.R., Seaton, K.A., & Dinas, P.A. (1996). Enhancing self-determination through Group Action Planning: A holistic emphasis. In D.J. Sands & M.L. Wehmeyer (Eds.), *Self-determination across the life span: Independence and choice for people with disabilities* (pp. 237–256). Baltimore: Paul H. Brookes Publishing Co.

Van Reusen, A.K., Bos, C.S., Schumaker, J.B., & Deshler, D.D. (1994). *The Self-Advocacy Strategy for Education and Transition Planning.* Lawrence, KS: Edge Enterprises.

Ward, M.J. (1996). Coming of age in the age of self-determination: A historical and personal perspective. In D.J. Sands & M.L. Wehmeyer (Eds.), *Self-determination across the life span: Independence and choice for people with disabilities* (pp. 3–16). Baltimore: Paul H. Brookes Publishing Co.

Wehmeyer, M.L. (1996). Self-determination as an educational outcome: Why is it important to children, youth, and adults with disabilities? In D.J. Sands & M.L. Wehmeyer (Eds.), *Self-determination across the life span: Independence and choice for people with disabilities* (pp. 17–36). Baltimore: Paul H. Brookes Publishing Co.

Student Involvement in Goal Setting and Educational Decision Making

Foundations for Effective Instruction

Beth Doll and Deanna J. Sands

Chapter 1 describes the benefits of active student participation in education planning, decision making, and instruction and the barriers that to a large extent have excluded students from such involvement. Chapter 2 describes how transition services can serve as a context in which students with disabilities can learn, practice, and apply involvement skills. In addition, Chapter 2 explains the variables that predict or facilitate students' involvement in their education programming. In particular, if students are ultimately to develop into active, self-determined individuals, they must be provided with frequent opportunities in which to practice and use skills associated with planning, implementing, and evaluating their own individualized education programs (IEPs).

In this chapter, two skills associated with education planning are examined: goal setting and decision making. This chapter 1) defines and discusses the processes of goal setting and decision making as well as their developmental precursors; 2) recommends education practices that foster the development, use, and refinement of goal-setting and decision-making skills; and 3) reviews the positive benefits of student engagement in goal setting and decision making for student motivation, achievement, and life adjustment.

The discussion here is limited to some degree by the nature of the research in goal setting and decision making. Although purposeful behavior is evident in early infancy (Butterworth & Hopkins, 1988; Crain, 1992; Willats, 1990), the importance of young children's goals and decisions is not widely acknowledged in research. There is considerable research on intentional behaviors of infants and toddlers that focuses on their changing abilities to represent their goals through gestures and language and to devise strategies to meet those goals (Ellis & Siegler, 1994). For example, if a young child's goal is physical proximity to his or her parent, research has demonstrated that "the child will use any and all means at his or her disposal to achieve this goal" (Crain, 1992, p. 44). However, goals of school-age children have not yet been widely studied, although there is research on children's responses to goals set for them by adults (Ellis & Siegler, 1994; Siegler & Jenkins, 1989) and on children's abilities to self-evaluate their progress toward those goals (Pomerantz, Ruble, Frey, & Greulich, 1995; Ruble & Flett, 1988). Research on decision-making abilities tends to focus on adolescents or on adults (Beyth-Marom, Fischhoff, Quadrel, & Furby, 1991), with relatively few investigations of the decision-making abilities of young children (Weithorn & Campbell, 1982).

This chapter takes the unconventional tack of advocating for goal-setting and decision-making opportunities for all students, beginning in the earliest grades. In describing this approach, it has not always been possible to identify research that directly addresses the larger skills of goal setting and decision making, so support is also sought in investigations of school-age children's self-directed behaviors in relation to self-evaluative processes (Pomerantz et al., 1995), motivational attributes (Ames, 1992; Deci & Ryan, 1992; Wentzel, 1992), expectancy outcomes (Schunk, 1991, 1996), problem solving (Ellis & Siegler, 1994; Spivack, Platt, & Shure, 1976), and goal orientations (Brown & Cohen, 1996; Umbreit & Blair, 1996). Although a thorough review of this literature is beyond the scope of this chapter, these studies provide some of the foundation for the discussion of education practices that foster the emergence of goal setting and decision making in children and adolescents.

GOAL SETTING

Goal setting is one of the most basic skills associated with self-directed, motivated, independent behavior (Watson & Tharp, 1993; Wentzel, 1992). Goals are an a priori specification of what students intend to accomplish through their own actions. More than a good intention to do well, a goal defines an end result with sufficient clarity to make it self-evident when that result is or is not reached. In education settings, goal setting has occurred, for example, when a student determines in advance that he or she intends to complete 90% of the problems on his or her math worksheet correctly, when a work-study student decides that he or she intends to arrive at work on time every day, or when an athlete determines that he or she intends to run the mile in less than 6 minutes. Setting a goal creates tension within the student because it represents a discrepancy between "where I am" and "where I want to be." In this sense, goal setting nourishes the self-sufficiency of students by linking their present behavior with their possible futures. Locke and Latham (1990) defined the purposefulness of goal-setting behavior as quintessentially human. The premise of their goal-setting theory and of this chapter is that when students set goals and personal standards, they increase their chances of acting in self-determined, self-regulated ways.

Latham and his colleagues conducted seminal research on goal setting in the logging industry of the 1970s (Latham & Baldes, 1975; Latham & Yukl, 1976; Locke & Latham, 1990). Latham and his colleagues examined the impact of supervisor-assigned goals on worker productivity and attendance during a period in the industry when the work force was inconsistent and absenteeism rates were high. A series of studies established that worker productivity increased significantly and workers described the work as more meaningful when supervisors assigned goals representing the amount of work that they expected workers to complete in a workday. From this and subsequent research, Locke and Latham (1990) derived their theory of goal setting to specify the factors that affect goals and their relationship to action and performance. Distinctions between Latham's logging industry and public education blurs when it is noted that the issues that he addressed—work productivity, work quality, and attendance—mirror the issues that most concern many educators. Thus, Locke and Latham's (1990) descriptions of why some people work harder and perform better than others, independent of their ability and knowledge, hold striking relevance for education.

The first and primary principle of Locke and Latham's (1990) goal-setting theory is that more difficult goals lead to more productive work. This finding—that difficult goals are essentially more motivating than easy ones—seems almost counterintuitive. Common sense would suggest that work is most rewarding if goals are believed to be easy to achieve. Consequently, this principle was tested repeatedly in subsequent goal-setting research. Locke and Latham (1990) cited four separate meta-analyses of more than 210 studies, with 90% of these verifying that more difficult goals lead to greater effort and persistence than easier goals. Indeed, individuals who were working toward easier goals were often observed to set new, more difficult goals to guide their work once their easier goals had been achieved. The only instances in which difficult goals did not have this dominant impact were when the goals were clearly outside the competence of the person, in which cases work performance leveled off at the upper limits of workers' abilities. Goal-setting research explains this universal preference for difficult goals by suggesting that more difficult goals prompt greater effort and more persistence than easier goals. Perhaps easier goals impose an artificial upper limit on a person's work productivity, whereas difficult goals do not prevent people from performing in line with their capabilities (Locke & Latham, 1990).

The second principle of goal-setting theory is that goals are most influential when they are clear, specific, and even quantifiable. Early goal-setting research compared specific goals with instructions to do one's best, and later studies contrasted clear with ambiguous or vague goals (Latham, 1996; Locke & Latham, 1990; Mento, Steel, & Karren, 1987; Tubbs, 1986; Wood, Mento, & Locke, 1987). In either case, the superiority of specific goals was evident. Furthermore, goal-setting theory explains the importance of goal specificity by suggesting that goals become tools for guiding self-evaluation during work. By monitoring their performance relative to their goals, workers determine whether to persist with their current work strategies or to revise their efforts to be more diligent, strenuous, or efficient. Ambiguous goals make it difficult for workers to monitor whether they have met them. Indeed, studies of goal setting in work environments (Latham, 1996; Locke & Latham, 1990) showed that the effects of goals are enhanced further when workers are provided with ongoing feedback describing their progress in relation to those goals.

One of the most provocative findings of goal-setting theory was that worker-set goals are no more effective than supervisor-set goals in raising work quality or productivity. This finding is contrary to the natural expectation that providing workers with choices over their goals fosters goal ownership and consequently enhances their commitment to the goals and their efforts to reach them. As long as both were equally difficult, workers strove to meet assigned goals with the same diligence as goals they set for themselves.

The first and second principles of goal-setting theory clearly operate in education settings and serve as the basis for Application Principles 1–3. Student goals that "incorporate specific performance standards, are short term, and are moderately difficult are more likely to enhance performance than goals that are general, long term, or are perceived as overly easy or difficult" (Schunk, 1996, p. 360). Clear goals accompanied by specific performance standards provide students with the tools that they need to monitor, adjust, and guide their own progress. When these goals span shorter time intervals such that students receive more frequent feedback on their progress, students tend to view their work as being more manageable. However, the ultimate aim of schools is to gradually prepare students to work toward goals that enhance their futures. The degree to which students work toward longer-term goals is influenced by their ability levels, self-efficacy, and interest in the goals (Deci & Ryan, 1992; Harackiewicz, Manderlink, & Sansone, 1992). Schools need to enhance these factors to direct students toward longer-term aspirations. Also, the superiority of difficult goals is not altogether absolute for students in schools. If students see the goals as being so difficult as to be impossible to achieve, their motivation and persistence diminish rapidly. The challenge facing educators is to set goals high enough to truly enhance performance but not so high as to discourage students' efforts (Schunk, 1991).

Application Principle 1

At all grades, help students work toward goals that are so specific that the students know immediately whether the goals have been met.

Application Principle 2

At all grades, assist students to set manageable goals that they are likely to reach within a defined time interval, such as one class period, day, week, month, or semester.

Application Principle 3

At all grades, set or help students set goals that are somewhat more challenging than what the students are expected to achieve.

Application Principle 4 is based on education research that has established that the meaningfulness of goals is of special importance in education settings (Ellis & Siegler, 1994; Siegler & Jenkins, 1989). Education goals are more effective when they provide students with a rationale for the learning task and an understanding of the many purposes of what they learn in the classroom. Too often, students in schools find themselves learning new procedures and skills without ever understanding their ultimate purpose. When teachers' goals describe the relevant purpose of student learning, students are better able to monitor and select strategies that will help them achieve those goals and to use their understanding to reject potential strategies that take them off course (Ellis & Siegler, 1994; Siegler & Jenkins, 1989).

Application Principle 5 is based on education research that has identified an extremely important distinction between process goals and performance goals. Performance goals focus students' attention on completing a particular

---

Application Principle 4

Set or help students set goals that make meaningful connections among their learning and their home and community lives.

---

task. Process goals, in contrast, direct students' attention to how they are learning—that is, the strategies and problem-solving procedures they are using. Research in education settings has shown that when instruction is guided by process goals, instead of or in addition to performance goals, students' self-efficacy and achievement are improved (Schunk, 1991, 1996; Schunk & Swartz, 1993). One possibility is that process goals force students to connect their own actions with their learning such that they learn more and, more important, their beliefs about themselves as learners are enhanced.

Although goal-setting theory establishes that worker- and supervisor-set goals are equally effective supports for vocational performance (Locke & Latham, 1990), education research has not definitively established a similar equivalence between student- and teacher-set goals for student performance (Schunk & Rice, 1988; Weinberg, Fowler, Jackson, Bagnall, & Bruya, 1991). In studies involving goal setting and physical activities, Hall and Byrne (1988) and Wraith and Biddle (1989) found that students in both experimenter- and self-set goal conditions performed equally well. Yet, other researchers found that students performed at higher levels and had higher perceptions of self-efficacy when working toward goals that they had set themselves (Harackiewicz et al., 1992; Schuldt & Bonge, 1979). Some researchers speculate that as long as a student values or has an interest in a goal, it may not matter if the goal is teacher set; students tend to set and to persist in working toward goals that they value positively (Meece & Courtney, 1992). Pending further research on effects of student- versus teacher-set goals, sufficient evidence exists to support the use of teacher-set goals in those instances in which student-set goals are not practical, as recommended in Application Principle 6.

Application Principle 5

Set or assist students in setting goals that describe the processes or strategies that they will use to accomplish a task or create a product.

Application Principle 6

When students cannot set goals for their own learning, providing them with teacher-set goals is an effective substitute.

Still, enhanced student performance is only one of many outcomes that educators attempt to achieve. When the impact of goal setting on student self-efficacy is considered, working toward goals that students set for themselves is categorically different from working toward teacher-set goals (Harackiewicz et al., 1992; Schuldt & Bonge, 1979; Schunk, 1985). When tasks are structured in a way that students are involved in setting their own goals, they are more likely to experience a sense of self-efficacy (Ames, 1992) and to be intrinsically motivated (Deci & Ryan, 1992). Application Principle 7 represents a value for both.

DECISION MAKING

As they strive to reach their goals, students use decision-making skills to choose from competing courses of action (Beyth-Marom et al., 1991). When they face decisions because obstacles prevent them from reaching their goals, their decision making can also be described as problem solving, and they might focus either on changing their goals or on identifying ways around the obstacles. However, not all decisions are problem focused. Students may struggle to choose between alternative opportunities for growth and learning, or they may attempt to choose the course of action that will move them more efficiently toward their goals.

Defining student competence in decision making is not as simple as it first appears. Initially, it seems reasonable to judge the adequacy of their decision making by the correctness of student decisions and to judge correctness by the degree to which student decisions match adult decisions (Mann, Harmoni, & Power, 1989). This standard fails to account for the fact that there are

Application Principle 7

Plan classroom activities to provide students with opportunities to set their own goals for learning at least some of the time.

multiple paths that can lead to a single goal and more than one choice that can lead, in time, to the same place. Moreover, closer examination shows several reasons why adult decisions are a poor measure against which to judge students' decisions. First, not all adult decisions are sound. Indeed, much of the research on errors in reasoning has been conducted by studying adults rather than children. Second, the correctness of a decision changes depending on the information that is available and the goals of the person making it (Furby & Beyth-Marom, 1992; Mann et al., 1989). Because students often have access to information that is different from that which adults have when making decisions, and because students and adults have different goals, their decisions differ. Third, students may use effective decision-making skills to pursue goals that are socially unacceptable, leading them to make decisions that adults consider maladaptive (Beyth-Marom et al., 1991). Finally, as becomes clearer later in this chapter, decision making is a value-laden process and students' values differ in important ways from those of adults. Respect for the self-determination of students dictates that students' values be the ones to guide student decisions.

Rather than promoting correct decisions, Mann et al. (1989) suggested that we seek to foster vigilant decision makers. Such a student

> thoroughly canvasses a wide range of alternative courses of action, surveys a full range of objectives and values implicated by the choice, carefully weighs the positive and negative consequences that could flow from each alternative, intensively searches for new information, incorporates new information even when it is unpleasant, and plans for the implementation of the decision. (Mann et al., 1989, pp. 266–267)

Thus, in its ideal form, vigilant decision making is a systematic, step-by-step process. Fortunately, there is consensus among researchers regarding the nature and sequence of these steps. Once they have established a goal, competent decision makers

1. Envision multiple alternative courses of action to take
2. Actively seek accurate information about the decision and each alternative
3. Use this information to anticipate probable consequences of each alternative
4. Select one alternative rather than the others as being the most reasonable
5. Make the decision and implement it (Beyth-Marom et al., 1991; Furby & Beyth-Marom, 1992; Mann et al., 1989)

These are the steps that schools and families can foster in their attempts to strengthen children's decision-making competencies. Table 1 illustrates two

Table 1. Two students' decisions

Erin's decision	Decision-making step	Salvio's decision
Seven-year-old Erin wants to achieve 100% mastery of her spelling list every week. She has been following her parents' suggestions until now—she studied every night, Monday through Friday, using a different strategy each night. On Monday, she wrote each word several times. On Tuesday, she wrote the words in a sentence. On Wednesday, she figured out a mnemonic trick for the words she was having trouble learning. On Thursday, she looked for patterns in the words' spellings and selectively studied the hard words.		Seventeen-year-old Salvio desperately wants a car of his own. A car would serve as convenient transportation to and from his after-school job. The family car is not always available when he needs it, and buying his own car would solve that problem. Also, having a car might make it possible for him to find a cheaper place to live when he moves away from home the following year. Salvio's friend has offered to sell him a reconditioned sports car that had been used to race at a local speedway.
Finding this regimen a bit tedious, Erin began to experiment with different ways of studying. She studied as usual on Monday, skipped Tuesday, wrote the word several times on Wednesday, and quickly looked over her list on Friday morning before school.		The car is 20 years old, but it looks shiny and new. More important, the engine and transmission were replaced within the past 6 months. His friend wants only $2,500 for the car—the cost of the parts used in reconditioning it. Although Salvio does not have much in the way of savings, he does earn about $300 per month, so he thinks he can afford the car. If he had not needed his parents' signature to cosign a loan, Salvio might not have realized that he had a decision to make. He might have simply put down the money and picked up the key. Asking for his parents' help made him slow down. He put his decision into these words: Should I buy the sports car?
That Friday, Erin earned a 50% on the spelling test, much lower than her usual 90%. She considered her decision this way: Do I have to go back to studying my old way?		

(continued)

Table 1. (continued)

Erin's decision	Decision-making step	Salvio's decision
When she first showed her spelling test to her parents, Erin saw two choices: 1. Go back to studying her parents' way (the old way). 2. Study less often, as she tried this week. Then her parents suggested that she try some different ways of studying: 1. Study every day but for less time. 2. Change her strategy on some nights.	Envision multiple alternative courses of action.	When he first approached his parents, Salvio saw two choices: 1. Buy the sports car. 2. Do not buy a car. Then his parents added two more choices to the list: 3. Shop around town for a different car. 4. Assume payments on the family's second car and take it as his own.
Erin wanted to know how other students in her class studied their spelling. She asked them how long they studied each night and what they did to learn their words.	Actively seek out new information about the decision and the alternatives.	Salvio was looking for more information before he ever spoke with his parents. He wanted to know 1. The payments on a $2,500 loan 2. Whether his parents would cosign the loan Then his parents suggested that he also find out 3. The monthly cost of car insurance 4. The license and registration fees 5. How much money would he have left each month after making his car payment and paying for insurance? 6. Could he do without the things on which he was spending that money now? 7. How much did repairs cost for the 20-year-old car?

54

Erin's questions helped her figure out the consequences of studying less. Of the 10 children she asked, the ones earning high scores on the test were studying as much as she had been. The children who studied less were earning lower scores on the test.

Use that information to identify probable consequences of each alternative.

With the additional information, Salvio analyzed each alternative:

1. Purchasing the sports car would cost $140 monthly for payments and $112 for car insurance. He would have $48 left over each month. Registration fees would be $96 annually. The loan would be repaid in 2 years.
2. Other used cars cost as much as the sports car and needed some important repairs.
3. Payments on the family car would be $120 a month for 15 months plus insurance payments of $112. The family car had an extended warranty for repairs.
4. Salvio could assume payments on the family's second car later or save to buy the car with cash.

Erin did not want to give up her strong test scores. She did not think she could keep them high without studying so much, so she decided to return to her old way of studying.

Select one alternative as being the one that maximizes benefits and minimizes negative consequences.

Salvio eliminated Options 1 and 2 because he did not know if he could cover repairs and maintenance on his budget. Option 3 was still possible; but he did not want to limit his monthly spending to $68, so he chose not to purchase a car at this time.

Erin told her parents that she would go back to studying her spelling list as before and began that night.

Act on the selection.

Salvio told his friend to sell the car to his other buyer. Then he began to put $20 of every paycheck into his car fund.

decisions as a product of these five steps. The first is made by a 7-year-old, and the second is made by a 17-year-old. These examples are referred to throughout the following examination of decision making.

The complexity of the decision-making steps and their hierarchical interdependence mark this ideal of systematic decision making as a higher-order mental ability (Furby & Beyth-Marom, 1992). Because of this complexity, it is not until middle adolescence, paralleling the onset of Piagetian formal operations, that most students have the potential to be reasonably vigilant decision makers (Furby & Beyth-Marom, 1992; Grisso & Vierling, 1978; Mann et al., 1989; Melton, 1981, 1983; Weithorn & Campbell, 1982). Still, the components that compose this vigilance emerge gradually as students grow in age and experience such that approximations to mature decision making can be seen in much younger children. Thus, a comprehensive examination of student decision making must consider the process as it occurs at earlier ages and in less-than-perfect forms. A child's growing ability to make decisions in a systematic, step-by-step fashion is one way in which decision-making skills develop with age.

Although ideal decision making is systematic and step-by-step, evidence exists that individuals of all ages make many of their decisions intuitively, short-cutting the systematic process in ways that improve its efficiency and occasionally diminish its rationality (Furby & Beyth-Marom, 1992). Refer to Table 1. If Salvio had had $2,500 in his savings account, he might have immediately purchased the sports car without systematically considering his alternatives. Similarly, Erin decided to abandon her effective study strategies without carefully considering her options. Such intuitive decision making can emerge even at very early ages and with mixed effects. Although some research (Furby & Beyth-Marom, 1992; Greenberg, 1983; Weithorn & Campbell, 1982) on young children's intuitive decisions shows a reassuring competence in their ability to make sound, adultlike decisions, other research (Fischhoff & Quadrel, 1991; Lewis, 1981; Siegler, 1976) has uncovered distortions that occur when young children omit critical decision-making steps. The ability to use heuristic shortcuts without distorting or biasing the decision-making process is a second way in which children's decision-making skills develop with age. Both systematic and heuristic strategies are examined in this discussion of decision making.

Envisioning Multiple Alternative Courses of Action

When students make decisions about how to best achieve their goals, their responses are bound by the optional responses they can envision. If their list of options is limited in number, or if the alternatives they envision are of dubious effectiveness, then the course of action they select from these options is likely to be less beneficial. An illustration of this can be seen in Salvio's example. Salvio's overriding goal was to solve his transportation problem. At first, he limited his choices to two alternatives—buying the sports car or not buying it. Extending this list of options, both in its length and in its quality, is an essential first step toward enhancing student decisions. In Salvio's case, his parents wisely chose to add two choices to his list of options—namely, buy a different car or assume payments on the family's second car.

Empirical studies conducted at all ages have repeatedly shown that the number of options a student envisions is a critical feature of his or her list. The earliest evidence of this can be found in Spivack et al.'s (1976) seminal research on problem solving, in which these researchers showed that preschoolers who can list more solutions to a social problem are also those who are more socially competent. Subsequent studies replicated this finding with older students (Mann et al., 1989). When results are combined across diverse studies, a clear developmental trend is evident, with older students generating more alternatives than younger students (i.e., preschool age through early adolescence) (Lewis, 1981; Mann et al., 1989; Rowe, 1984). Moreover, an awareness of the importance of generating multiple options before making decisions emerges only in late adolescence (Mann et al., 1989). These results provide ample support for Application Principle 8 for decision making.

Application Principle 8

At all grades, enhance students' decision making by extending the list of options that students consider before making their choices.

This ability to imagine multiple hypothetical actions and multiple consequences for each action is essentially a formal operational task (Gordon, 1990). To be successful, students must be able to separate themselves from the "here and now" and enter into an imaginary world of the possible. For students who are still unable to envision such a hypothetical future or whose vision of that future is incomplete, adults frequently support decision making (as both Salvio's and Erin's parents did) by providing additional alternatives for consideration. For example, Weithorn and Campbell (1982) provided a list of optional choices when investigating children's abilities to make legally competent decisions about psychotherapy; with this support, children as young as age 9 were able to make decisions comparable to those of a mature adult. Their research demonstrates the value of Application Principle 9 for decision-making support.

Application Principle 9

When students' own lists of decision options are too meager even with teacher assistance, provide them with additional options that they have not considered.

Actively Seeking Information
About the Decision and Alternatives

Although they may not always exercise it, students have considerable control over the amount and quality of information that they use to make their decisions. Industrious students seek additional information about the choices that they are making, with a cautionary eye toward securing information that is most likely to be unbiased and accurate (Mann et al., 1989). Indeed, Wang and Peverly (1987) suggested that motivated students demonstrate a strong sense of personal control over their own lives. Alternatively, students who passively accept readily available knowledge without seeking to extend or evaluate it are easily persuaded to make decisions that may not further their own goals. Application Principle 10 emphasizes the importance of such an information search.

Application Principle 10

Before students make their decisions, prompt them to think about what other information they might need to know—that is, information about the decision itself or about the different courses of action under consideration.

Having access to accurate information is not always sufficient to reach a decision; information to support a decision must be not only available but also understandable and detailed enough to avert misinterpretations. This became evident when adolescents in Fischhoff and Quadrel's (1991) study misunderstood information given to them about critical health decisions. For example, some of the individuals studied believed that advertisements telling them not to drink and drive applied only if they drank 10 glasses of beer, drank until they blacked out, or drank until they could no longer stand. Application Principle 11 stresses the importance of information accuracy.

Application Principle 11

Ask students to think aloud when analyzing their decisions to monitor their understanding of key information relevant to the decisions.

As decisions become more complex, with multiple alternatives and numerous hypothetical consequences for each alternative, the amount of information that is relevant to the decision increases exponentially and can quickly surpass the student's capacity to attend to it. Consequently, skilled decision makers need to be able to select only the most important information for use in a decision (Payne, 1976). Competent decision makers decline opportunities to gather more information under certain conditions—for example, if securing the information requires an effort or expense that is out of proportion to the goal's importance or if the information is unlikely to be acted on. Emerging sensitivity to the costs and benefits of information searches has been demonstrated even in preschoolers and appears to be enhanced with age (Davidson & Hudson, 1988; Gregson-Paxton & John, 1995). When gathering information to support a decision, early elementary school students tend to be exhaustive and unconcerned with relevance. By the late elementary grades, students learn to seek less information and selectively search for information that is directly relevant to the decisions that they are making (Davidson, 1991). Thus, adapting one's information search to the importance of the decision, the cost of the search, and the value of the information is the purpose underlying Application Principle 12.

Application Principle 12

Encourage students to examine the relevance of information for their decisions and to disregard information that is irrelevant or unimportant or both.

The source of decision information may be a good indicator of its reliability. Competent decision makers make more use of information from sources they know to be knowledgeable and are cautious about using information from sources having a vested interest in their decision. Salvio struggled with such source issues when he considered the seller's reassurances that the sports car was in excellent mechanical condition. That is, although the seller was an expert mechanic and a trusted friend, he was also the person seeking a buyer for his car. Sensitivity to the vested interests of information sources has been demonstrated in students as young as 12 years old but is far more pronounced in high school students than in middle school students (Lewis, 1981). For this reason, Application Principle 13 applies mainly to secondary students.

Application Principle 13

Beginning in middle school, coach students to consider the reliability of their information sources, including the accuracy of sources' information and the degree to which sources might have a vested interest in influencing students' choices.

A common adult concern is that, once they reach adolescence, students use their peers as information sources for making decisions and disregard more reliable adult sources of information. The belief that teenage students are overpowered by peer influence and peer pressure, however, has not been supported by empirical research (Furby & Beyth-Marom, 1992). Instead, in two independent surveys of adolescent decision making, students reported that they rely relatively little on peer information when making important life decisions and trust their parents' advice to a far greater degree (Benthin, 1988, as cited in Furby & Beyth-Marom, 1992; Poole & Gelder, 1985). Because these results are limited to student self-reports, Furby and Beyth-Marom (1992) concluded that empirical research has not clarified the degree to which adolescents rely on peers rather than on other sources of information about risky behaviors.

Anticipating the Probable Consequences of Alternatives

Quality decisions are those that maximize the favorable consequences and minimize the negative consequences for the student (Fischhoff & Quadrel, 1991). This would be a simple task if a course of action had only one consequence and if that consequence's impact were clearly positive or clearly negative for the student. Of course, real-life decisions never present themselves in such simple forms. Any course of action has multiple consequences, some of which are certain to occur and others that are less probable. Positive and negative consequences can emerge simultaneously from a single decision, and some of these consequences are immediate, whereas others may occur months or even years later. Salvio's decision is a prime example: If he had bought the sports car, he almost certainly would have been low on spending money (a negative consequence) but undoubtedly would have had more convenient transportation to his job (a positive consequence). It is also possible that he would have been hit with a major repair bill that, if he could not pay it, would render the car unusable even while he was making loan payments (a very negative but not certain consequence). Thus, anticipating multiple consequences of different courses of action is another example of complex hypothetical reasoning that emerges developmentally and that is strengthened by the emergence of formal operations (Gordon, 1990; Mann et al., 1989; Walesa, 1975).

Adults and older adolescents are surprisingly similar in the number and types of consequences that they can envision for different courses of action (Beyth-Marom et al., 1991). Until late adolescence, however, older students are generally more adept at consequential thinking than younger students. For example, twelfth graders were more adept than seventh, eighth, or tenth graders at anticipating the risks and consequences of medical decisions (Lewis, 1981), and students 14 years of age and older identified more risks and benefits of psychotherapy than students 13 years of age and younger (Kaser-Boyd, Adelman, & Taylor, 1985). Indeed, differences in the ability to anticipate consequences explain much of the variance between a child's and an adult's decisions: When consequences were completely explained to students in advance, 14-year-olds did not differ significantly from adults in their ability to make reasonable choices for medical care (Weithorn & Campbell, 1982) or custody decisions (Greenberg, 1983). Thus, Application Principle 14 is especially relevant to children in the elementary grades.

Application Principle 14

Provide students at all ages with assistance in anticipating the multiple risks and benefits of different courses of actions.

Given its complexity and its hypothetical nature, it is not surprising that limitations in students' consequential thinking underlie many of their decision-making errors. First, immediate consequences are more easily envisioned than those that could occur several years later (Lewis, 1981; Marecek, 1986). Indeed, both adolescents and adults often adopt courses of action because of the positive immediate consequences and despite the long-term negative consequences (Barnes, 1981; Bauman, 1980). Elements of this can be seen in Erin's decision when she abandoned her studying regimen out of convenience despite the end-of-the-week drop in her grade. Second, consequences are more easily anticipated if they are certain to occur rather than being merely probable or possible (Cvetkovitch, Grote, Bjorseth, & Sarkissian, 1975). Again, Salvio's decision was eased because he could be certain of the payments he would need to make. The ability to judge and make allowances for differing levels of uncertainty is so central to effective decision making that Beyth-Marom and her colleagues (1991) declared it to be a necessary component of any decision-making curriculum. Third, decision making is sometimes impaired because students have difficulties in differentiating between high-probability and low-probability consequences and in distinguishing between chance events and those under their direct control (Gordon, 1990). In Salvio's decision, repair costs were difficult to factor into his choice because they might not occur and because their size was difficult to estimate. Fourth, both adolescents and adults tend to grossly overestimate their ability to compensate for risks posed by different consequences or to underestimate the risks to themselves (Fischhoff & Quadrel, 1991; Lewis, 1981). This, too, was evident in Erin's decision when she initially assumed that she could do as well on the test despite studying less. Application Principle 15 stresses the need to alert students to such common errors in thinking.

Application Principle 15

Engage high school students in sophisticated analyses of bias or errors in their own thinking about consequences of decisions.

For adolescents in particular, poor decision making is often given as an explanation for students' tendencies to take unnecessary risks (Beyth-Marom et al., 1991). The extremely deleterious long-term consequences of smoking cigarettes, using controlled substances, engaging in unprotected sexual intercourse, and other adolescent behaviors do not appear to stem the prevalence of these behaviors among adolescents. Although this discrepancy often is used as evidence of poor adolescent decision-making skills, Beyth-Marom and her colleagues instead suggested that these trends show how the same consequences are valued differently by teenagers and adults (Beyth-Marom et al., 1991; Furby & Beyth-Marom, 1992). In particular, these trends suggest that adolescents may place a higher value than adults on peer approval or might see the excitement of risk taking as a positive rather than a negative consequence. Application Principle 16 suggests that possible value differences be considered whenever adolescents engage in risky behaviors.

Application Principle 16

When students endorse decisions that are unnecessarily risky, explore the values that they attach to the anticipated risks, being open to the possibility that their beliefs about risks may be inconsistent with your own adult beliefs.

Selecting One Alternative as Most Reasonable

As the list of alternative choices lengthens and probable consequences become less certain, picking the most reasonable decision from among the alternatives becomes complex. Identifying choices that maximize students' benefits while minimizing risks requires a complex comparison that considers both the relative value of each possible consequence and the likelihood that each might occur (Fischhoff & Quadrel, 1991; Furby & Beyth-Marom, 1992). Many decision-making curricula explain this balancing of gain and loss in quasimathematical terms. Students are taught to assign numerical values to each possible consequence of a course of action, with positive values assigned to good outcomes and negative values assigned to poor ones. To allow for the likelihood of different outcomes, they might be taught to multiply an outcome's value by its probability. Comparisons of different alternatives are then made quantitatively by comparing their respective sums (Fischhoff & Quadrel, 1991; Furby & Beyth-Marom, 1992). One example of this mathematical modeling can be found in Shanteau, Grier, Johnson, and Berner (1991).

The pragmatic utility of these quasimathematical models has been challenged by several researchers who pointed out that expert adult decision makers rarely use complex mathematical manipulations (Davidson, 1991; Payne, 1982). Furby and Beyth-Marom (1992) took this position one step further, arguing that mathematical modeling is a disservice to students because the procedures that mathematical modeling teaches are unlikely to be able to be generalized to the intuitive decisions made in the real world. They asserted that, as a result, "It's hard to know whether any of these programs actually change the way adolescents make decisions (and if so, whether the change is for the better)" (Furby & Beyth-Marom, 1992, p. 38). Together, these researchers agree that decision-making curricula should instead teach heuristic strategies like those that adults use to bring overwhelmingly complex decision analyses into line with the capacity of their cognitive abilities (Davidson, 1991; Furby & Beyth-Marom, 1992; Payne, 1982). For example, one heuristic that adults employ is to systematically rule out some alternatives as unacceptable and then analyze the remaining options to make a decision. Salvio appeared to be using such a strategy when deciding whether to buy his sports car, ruling out any alternative that would cost most of his monthly income. Once he had applied this rule, he was left to consider only two of the four alternatives—waiting to buy a car or assuming payments on the family car—representing a reduction of 50% of the necessary decision information. Another heuristic is to focus on a single dimension of the decision—for example, the likelihood of financial loss—as the most important dimension to consider. Alternatively, decision makers can seek certainty over risk, choosing the option that provides more guarantees. Each of these strategies represents a compromise between the ideal step-by-step analysis of consequences and the intuitive decision that bypasses analysis—each is a deliberate choice to focus on certain aspects of the decision to reduce its complexity. Application Principle 17 emphasizes students' needs for direct instruction in the best of these heuristics.

Application Principle 17

Teach students heuristic rules to simplify decisions in reasonable ways.

Left to their own devices, children also simplify their decision reasoning but in less cautious ways. For example, children younger than 6 or 7 years of age generally fail to consider multiple dimensions in problem solving and may or may not select the best dimension to which to attend (Siegler, 1976). Early elementary school–age students can successfully juggle multiple dimensions in simple decisions but revert to selection by intuition if decisions become too complex (Gregson-Paxton & John, 1995). Until they reach late adolescence, students find it difficult to hold in mind both positive and potential negative consequences of a decision simultaneously and thus tend to attend to either one or the other (Walesa, 1975). For example, students might choose risky alternatives because "they focus on the potential gain and pay little attention to the potential loss" (Furby & Beyth-Marom, 1992, p. 32; see also Lewis, 1981). Without effective heuristics, children and adolescents sometimes make expedient decisions that reflect some but not all of the important information they have about a decision. The acquisition of more reasoned heuristics emerges gradually as children mature, so that they can successfully reason by gist without overlooking critical information (Reyna & Ellis, 1994).

Comparing risks of varying magnitudes for different options presents a special challenge to students making decisions. Preschool and early elementary school students have not yet mastered the ability to differentiate between risks of different magnitude and thus do not figure the amount of risk into their decisions at all (Reyna & Ellis, 1994). By early adolescence, students can compare risks of different sizes but do not necessarily do so when making decisions. Instead, Marecek (1987) determined that some teenagers choose one course over another out of fear of the immediate consequences, such as when they choose abortion out of the fear of labor or when they choose childbirth out of the fear of abortion. To complicate decisions further, students struggle when comparing disparate types of risks. For example, how might Salvio compare the risk of diminished leisure time without a car to the risk of less money as a result of purchasing a sports car? Such difficult decisions are more likely to be made ineffectively and to frustrate the decision maker (Fischhoff & Quadrel, 1991). Application Principle 18 applies primarily to secondary students because they are most ready to compare hypothetical probabilities.

Application Principle 18

Assist middle and high school students in comparing the likelihood of different consequences of decisions when choosing among options.

Competent analysis of decision choices may also be disrupted during emotion-laden times. In particular, Gordon (1990) noted that students' capacities to engage in higher-order thinking may diminish in the face of anxiety or stress. Adler and Dolcini (1986) suggested that this may be because in times of crisis, adolescents avoid adult authority. Alternatively, Furby and Beyth-Marom (1992) examined the possibility that adolescents might make hurried, emotion-driven decisions without first weighing all of the alternatives and their consequences. However, they concluded that there was not yet empirical evidence that adolescents make more frequent emotional decisions than do adults. Application Principle 19 alerts educators at all levels to the potential impact of emotions on decisions.

Application Principle 19

Be sensitive to the ways in which emotions can influence students' decision making and, when this occurs, slow down the students' decision making so that they can avoid decisions that are hasty or biased.

Making and Implementing a Decision

Once a decision and its choices are clarified, investigated, weighed, and compared, students must select and implement one choice. The willingness to make such a choice has been called *decision control* (Mann et al., 1989). First, research suggests that students with a strong internal locus of control select and implement choices more readily, whereas students who believe that critical events are outside of their control often neglect decisions that they could otherwise make easily. Second, Mann and his colleagues (1989) noted that some adolescents are not accepting of the need to compromise. They may be incapacitated by situations in which their own goals conflict with those of peers or family members, thus requiring that they negotiate a mutually acceptable decision and perhaps sacrifice some of what they want. To some extent, this may be a developmental phenomenon, because compromising in the interest of another requires important role-taking abilities (Mann et al., 1989). An inability to compromise can stop some students from taking any action at all, thus leading them to surrender control over their important life decisions to others. Third, students differ in their recognition that making a decision can be binding and can entail commitment to future action (Mann et al., 1989). In this case, it is not making the decision that is disrupted but the implementation of the decision, once made. In part, such commitment may be developmental. Among students with learning disabilities, one study found that students 16 years of age and older were more likely to follow through on their decisions than students who were 15 years of age and younger. Application Principles 20 and 21 stress the need for adults to monitor this final stage in decision making.

Application Principle 20

Ensure that even reluctant students make decisions by asking them to commit to their decisions in writing or to make public proclamations of their decisions.

Application Principle 21

Remind students to monitor the impact of their decisions and make changes as appropriate when decisions are found to be ineffective.

EFFECTS OF GOAL SETTING AND DECISION MAKING ON MOTIVATION AND ACHIEVEMENT

The previous discussion indicates that goal setting and decision making are essential components of any program meant to foster active, ongoing student involvement in purposeful behaviors. The rewards of autonomy-oriented classrooms are impressive: Students are more curious, demonstrate preferences for more challenging tasks, display higher independent mastery attempts, and indicate higher self-efficacy and perceived competence (Deci & Ryan, 1992; Pintrich, Roeser, & DeGroot, 1994). Increasing student autonomy has been shown to be positively related to high self-determination (Grolnick & Ryan, 1990), quality engagement in learning activities, higher levels of conceptual learning, and increased retention (Ames, 1992). Other studies suggested that when students are involved in designing, evaluating, and modifying goals, they demonstrate higher levels of self-efficacy and fewer behavior problems (Schunk, 1996; Sisco, 1992).

Opportunities for autonomy-oriented behaviors have the potential to result in rapid and extensive improvements in student behavior. For example, Umbreit and Blair (1996) reported the results of a study involving preferences of an elementary school–age student with mental retardation who exhibited a variety of disruptive behaviors. When provided with an education program based on the student's preferred activities and when given choices among those activities, virtually all behavior problems were eliminated immediately. This effect lasted several months, and the behavioral improvements generalized to three additional environments. In a similar study, an adult who had significant behavior problems was able to hold a job and move from a restrictive to an independent living environment when given a program in which he made decisions about his daily schedule and the reinforcements that he would earn and recorded the consequences of his behavior (Jackson & Altman, 1996). Owings and Follo (1992) found that math students who designed their own math evaluation portfolios were more aware of their strengths and weaknesses. Moreover, portfolio designers set realistic goals that were more detailed and better targeted their weaknesses than those of the control group. Middle school students were more focused on learning and mastery, used cognitive strategies, and regulated their own thinking and effort when classes provided them with some choice of task and allowed them to work with others (Pintrich et al., 1994).

STRUCTURING CLASSROOMS TO FACILITATE GOAL-SETTING AND DECISION-MAKING OPPORTUNITIES

Purposeful behaviors do not merge effortlessly into all classroom routines and procedures. With mounting evidence of the significant contributions that goal-setting and decision-making behaviors have on students' personal and academic achievements, it becomes important that school professionals structure students' educational experiences to support these opportunities. Wentzel (1992) maintained that classroom environments have the potential to provide many opportunities for students to pursue both academic and social goals. Even more important, she argued, academic achievement can best be explained when the degree to which social and academic goals are rewarded and valued is understood, as well as how these goals interact and influence academic outcomes.

Education environments facilitate and support students' purposeful behavior in two ways. First, goal-setting and decision-making skills need to be taught overtly because many students do not naturally acquire these in efficient ways when left to their own devices (Nickerson, 1994). A comprehensive review of 11 different curricula to teach decision making is available in Baron and Brown (1991). Additional curricula that promote active student involvement in setting goals and making decisions are described in Sands and Wehmeyer (1996). Although these curricula are uniformly targeted toward secondary school–age students, they are easily adapted to younger grades using the application principles described throughout this chapter.

Skills learned through direct instruction will not persist or be used in students' natural environments unless they are given frequent and varied opportunities to set goals and make decisions (Mithaug, 1996). Thus, it is just as important for education environments to be structured in a way that promotes students' use of purposeful behaviors (Lindsey, 1996). Several authors have identified key classroom features that positively affect and support student participation and mastery of self-directed, goal-oriented behaviors (Abery & Zajac, 1996; Ames, 1992; Deci & Ryan, 1992; Doll, Sands, Wehmeyer, & Palmer, 1996; King, 1991; Lutkenhaus & Bullock, 1991). Features that they have identified as important include learning activities, ways of sharing control with students, procedures for giving students feedback, ways of grouping students for instruction, procedures for evaluating students' work, and scheduling routines. Specific examples of ways to structure these features into classrooms are listed in Table 2.

CONCLUSIONS

Turning the control of decisions and goals over to students is a radical step for many educators. Indeed, many education systems and procedures place primary responsibility for student learning on teachers. For example, the notion that teachers in some school systems are being threatened with losing their jobs because their students do not meet specified standards appears to shift accountability for learning from students to teachers. Learning will be effective only when both teachers and students share responsibility for the learning that occurs in classrooms. Furthermore, students will never truly share that responsibility unless they also share in the authority governing their educational experiences. Students' goal setting and decision making are essential procedures to include students in this authority.

Table 2. Suggestions for structuring classrooms for fostering autonomous student behaviors

Learning activities	Sharing control with students	Giving feedback	Grouping for instruction	Evaluating student work	Scheduling and routines
Structure tasks that connect learning to students' lives.	Provide many opportunities for students to participate in learning through leadership roles, choices, and decision making.	Give feedback that addresses students' progress toward their targeted goals.	Use cooperative, heterogeneous, and varied groupings.	Evaluate for individual progress, improvement, and mastery.	Allow flexibility in the time students need to complete their work.
Help students see the purpose or reason for learning new skills or knowledge.	Provide real choices with equally desirable options, and avoid motivating students by failure avoidance.	Make sure that all students have opportunities to receive rewards and recognition.	Give choices to students about with whom, when, where, or how an activity will occur.	Provide multiple opportunities for students to improve their performance.	Give students opportunities to map out their own schedules for completing tasks and products.
Involve students in setting their own goals.	Avoid competitive structures, which can decrease motivation.	Give recognition privately.	Capitalize on incidental teaching opportunities.	Vary methods of evaluation and make evaluation private.	Teach organizational and time management skills.
Make goals specific and short term.	Solicit student input on how to run your class and how well they believe the class is run.	Prior to tasks, present clear, concrete standards for performance expectations. (What am I trying to accomplish? How will I know	Help students identify their preferences for doing their work. Do they prefer to work alone or in small or large groups? Vary groupings for	The goal of evaluation should be to help students identify what they need to do in order to progress toward mastery of their goals.	

(continued)

Table 2. (continued)

Learning activities	Sharing control with students	Giving feedback	Grouping for instruction	Evaluating student work	Scheduling and routines
		when I have done a good job?)	instruction to balance their needs.	Allow students opportunities to evaluate their own learning performance capabilities and progress toward skill acquisition.	
Focus tasks on the opportunities they provide for students to learn and expand their skills, not on tests and grades.	Solicit student input as to what consequences should be implemented when rules are broken.	Recognize effort, improvement, and accomplishments.		Let students choose what products or tasks will be used to evaluate their progress and achievement.	
Combine goals that focus on process and product.		Avoid depending on and having a preponderance of external rewards.			
State goals and objectives in a manner that promotes student choice and preference.					

REFERENCES

Abery, B., & Zajac, R. (1996). Self-determination as a goal of early childhood and elementary education. In D.J. Sands & M.L. Wehmeyer (Eds.), *Self-determination across the life span: Independence and choice for people with disabilities* (pp. 169–196). Baltimore: Paul H. Brookes Publishing Co.

Adler, N., & Dolcini, P. (1986). Psychological issues in abortion for adolescents. In G.B. Melton (Ed.), *Adolescent abortion: Psychological and legal issues* (pp. 74–95). Lincoln: University of Nebraska Press.

Ames, C. (1992). Achievement goals and the classroom motivational climate. In D.H. Schunk & J.L. Meece (Eds.), *Student perceptions in the classroom* (pp. 327–348). Hillsdale, NJ: Lawrence Erlbaum Associates.

Barnes, G.M. (1981). Drinking among adolescents: A subculture phenomenon or a model of adult behaviors. *Adolescents, 16,* 211–229.

Baron, J., & Brown, R.V. (1991). *Teaching decision-making to adolescents.* Hillsdale, NJ: Lawrence Erlbaum Associates.

Bauman, K.E. (1980). *Predicting adolescent drug use: Utility structure and marijuana.* New York: Praeger.

Benthin, A. (1988). *A psychometric study of adolescent risk perception.* Unpublished master's thesis, University of Oregon, Eugene.

Beyth-Marom, R., Fischhoff, B., Quadrel, M.J., & Furby, L. (1991). Teaching decision-making to adolescents: A critical review. In J. Baron & R.V. Brown (Eds.), *Teaching decision-making to adolescents* (pp. 19–59). Hillsdale, NJ: Lawrence Erlbaum Associates.

Brown, F., & Cohen, S. (1996). Self-determination and young children. *Journal of The Association for Persons with Severe Handicaps, 21*(1), 22–30.

Butterworth, G., & Hopkins, B. (1988). Hand–mouth coordination in the newborn baby. *British Journal of Developmental Psychology, 6,* 303–314.

Crain, W. (1992). *Theories of development: Concepts and applications* (3rd ed.). Englewood Cliffs, NJ: Prentice-Hall.

Cvetkovitch, G., Grote, B., Bjorseth, A., & Sarkissian, J. (1975). On the psychology of adolescents' use of contraception. *Journal of Sexual Research, 11,* 256–270.

Davidson, D. (1991). Children's decision-making examined with an information-board procedure. *Cognitive Development, 6,* 77–90.

Davidson, D., & Hudson, J. (1988). The effects of decision reversibility and decision importance on children's decision-making. *Journal of Experimental Child Psychology, 46,* 35–40.

Deci, E.L., & Ryan, R.M. (1992). The initiation and regulation of intrinsically motivated learning and achievement. In A.K. Boggiano & T.S. Pittman (Eds.), *Achievement and motivation: A social-developmental perspective* (pp. 9–36). New York: Cambridge University Press.

Doll, B., Sands, D.J., Wehmeyer, M.L., & Palmer, S. (1996). Promoting the development and acquisition of self-determined behavior. In D.J. Sands & M.L. Wehmeyer (Eds.), *Self-determination across the life span: Independence and choice for people with disabilities* (pp. 65–90). Baltimore: Paul H. Brookes Publishing Co.

Ellis, S., & Siegler, R.S. (1994). Development of problem-solving. In R.J. Sternberg (Ed.), *Thinking and problem solving: Handbook of perception and cognition* (2nd ed., pp. 333–367). San Diego: Academic Press.

Fischhoff, B., & Quadrel, M.J. (1991). Adolescent alcohol decisions. *Alcohol Health and Research World, 15,* 43–51.

Furby, L., & Beyth-Marom, R. (1992). Risk taking in adolescence: A decision-making perspective. *Developmental Review, 12,* 1–44.

Gordon, D.E. (1990). Formal operational thinking: The role of cognitive-developmental processes in adolescent decision-making about pregnancy and contraception. *American Journal of Orthopsychiatry, 60,* 346–356.

Greenberg, E.F. (1983). An empirical determination of the competence of children to participate in child custody decision-making (Doctoral dissertation, University of Illinois, 1983). *Dissertation Abstracts International, 45*(0–1), 350-B.

Gregson-Paxton, J., & John, D.R. (1995). Are young children adaptive decision-makers? A study of age differences in information search behavior. *Journal of Consumer Research, 21,* 567–580.

Grisso, T., & Vierling, L. (1978). Minors' consent to treatment: A developmental perspective. *Professional Psychology, 9,* 412–427.

Grolnick, W.S., & Ryan, R.M. (1990). Self-perceptions, motivation, and adjustment in children with learning disabilities. *Journal of Learning Disabilities, 23,* 117–184.

Hall, H., & Byrne, T. (1988). Goal setting in sport: Clarifying anomalies. *Journal of Sport and Exercise Psychology, 10,* 189–192.

Harackiewicz, J.M., Manderlink, G., & Sansone, C. (1992). Competence processes and achievement motivation: Implications for intrinsic motivation. In A.K. Boggiano & T.S. Pittman (Eds.), *Achievement and motivation: A social-developmental perspective* (pp. 115–137). Cambridge, England: Cambridge University Press.

Jackson, T.L., & Altman, R. (1996). Self-management of aggression in an adult male with mental retardation and severe behavior disorders. *Education and Training in Mental Retardation and Developmental Disabilities, 31,* 55–65.

Kaser-Boyd, N., Adelman, H., & Taylor, L. (1985). Minors' ability to identify risks and benefits of therapy. *Professional Psychology, 16,* 411–417.

King, A. (1991). Effects of training in strategic questioning on children's problem solving performance. *Journal of Educational Psychology, 83,* 307–317.

Latham, G.P. (1996, August). *Critical issues in goal setting theory and research: Moving beyond 1990.* Paper presented at the 104th annual convention of the American Psychological Association, Toronto, Ontario, Canada.

Latham, G.P., & Baldes, J.J. (1975). The "practical significance" of Locke's theory of goal setting. *Journal of Applied Psychology, 60,* 122–124.

Latham, G.P., & Yukl, G.A. (1976). Effects of assigned and participative goal setting on performance and job satisfaction. *Journal of Applied Psychology, 61,* 166–171.

Lewis, C.C. (1981). How adolescents approach decisions: Changes over grades seven to twelve and policy implications. *Child Development, 52,* 538–544.

Lindsey, P. (1996). The right to choose: Informed consent in the lives of adults with mental retardation and developmental disabilities. *Education and Training in Mental Retardation and Developmental Disabilities, 31,* 171–187.

Locke, E.A., & Latham, G.P. (1990). *A theory of goal setting and task performance.* Englewood Cliffs, NJ: Prentice-Hall.

Lutkenhaus, P., & Bullock, M. (1991). The development of volitional skills. In D. Kuhn (Series Ed.) & M. Bullock (Ed.), *Human development series: Vol. 22. The development of intentional action: Cognitive, motivational, and interactive processes* (pp. 14–23). New York: Karger.

Mann, L., Harmoni, R., & Power, C. (1989). Adolescent decision-making: The development of competence. *Journal of Adolescence, 12,* 265–278.

Marecek, J. (1986). Consequences of adolescent child-bearing and abortion. In G.B. Melton (Ed.), *Adolescent abortion: Psychological and legal issues* (pp. 74–95). Lincoln: University of Nebraska Press.

Marecek, J. (1987). Counseling adolescents with problem pregnancies. *American Psychologist, 42,* 89–93.

Meece, L.J., & Courtney, D.P. (1992). Gender differences in students' perceptions: Consequences for achievement-related choices. In D.H. Schunk & J.L. Meece (Eds.), *Student perceptions in the classroom* (pp. 209–228). Hillsdale, NJ: Lawrence Erlbaum Associates.

Melton, G.B. (1981). Effects of state law permitting minors to consent to psychotherapy. *Professional Psychology, 12,* 647–654.

Melton, G.B. (1983). Toward "personhood" for adolescents. *American Psychologist, 38,* 99–103.

Mento, A.J., Steel, R.P., & Karren, R.J. (1987). A meta-analytic study of the effects of goal setting on task performance: 1966–1984. *Organizational Behavior and Human Decision Processes, 39,* 52–83.

Mithaug, D.E. (1996). *Equal opportunity theory.* Thousand Oaks, CA: Sage.

Nickerson, R.S. (1994). The teaching of thinking and problem solving. In R.J. Sternberg (Ed.), *Handbook of perception and cognition* (2nd ed., pp. 409–449). San Diego: Academic Press.

Owings, C.A., & Follo, E. (1992). *Effects of portfolio assessment on students' attitudes and goal setting abilities in mathematics.* Washington, DC: ERIC Clearinghouse. (ERIC Document Reproduction Service No. ED 352 394)

Payne, J.W. (1976). Task complexity and contingent processing in decision-making: An information search analysis. *Organizational Behavior and Human Performance, 16,* 366–387.

Payne, J.W. (1982). Contingent decision behavior. *Psychological Bulletin, 92,* 382–402.

Pintrich, P.R., Roeser, R.W., & DeGroot, E.A.M. (1994). Classroom and individual differences in early adolescents' motivation and self-regulated learning. *Journal of Early Adolescence, 14,* 139–161.

Pomerantz, E.M., Ruble, D.N., Frey, K., & Greulich, F. (1995). Meeting goals and confronting conflict: Children's changing perceptions of social comparison. *Child Development, 66,* 723–738.

Poole, M.E., & Gelder, A.J. (1985). Family cohesiveness and adolescent autonomy in decision making. *Australian Journal of Sex, Marriage, and Family, 5,* 65–75.

Reyna, V.F., & Ellis, S.C. (1994). Fuzzy-trace theory and framing effects in children's risky decision-making. *Psychological Science, 5,* 275–279.

Rowe, K.L. (1984, August). *Adolescent contraceptive use: The role of cognitive factors.* Paper presented at the meeting of the American Psychological Association, Toronto, Ontario, Canada.

Ruble, D.N., & Flett, G.L. (1988). Conflicting goals in self-evaluative information seeking: Developmental ability level analysis. *Child Development, 59,* 97–106.

Sands, D.J., & Wehmeyer, M.L. (Eds.). (1996). *Self-determination across the life span: Independence and choice for people with disabilities.* Baltimore: Paul H. Brookes Publishing Co.

Schuldt, W.J., & Bonge, D. (1979). Effects of self-imposition and experimenter imposition of achievement standards on performance. *Psychological Reports, 45,* 119–122.

Schunk, D.H. (1985). Participation in goal setting: Effects of self-efficacy and skills of learning-disabled children. *Journal of Special Education, 19,* 307–317.

Schunk, D.H. (1991). Goal setting and self-evaluation: A social cognitive perspective on self-regulation. In M.L. Maehr & P.R. Pintrich (Eds.), *Advances in motivation and achievement* (Vol. 7, pp. 85–113). Greenwich, CT: JAI Press.

Schunk, D.H. (1996). Goal and self-evaluative influences during children's cognitive skill learning. *American Educational Research Journal, 33,* 359–382.

Schunk, D., & Rice, J.M. (1988, August). *Learning goals during reading comprehension instruction.* Paper presented at the annual meeting of the American Psychological Association, Atlanta, GA. (ERIC Document Reproduction Service No. ED 296 294)

Schunk, D., & Swartz, C.W. (1993, April). *Goals and progress feedback: Effects on self-efficacy and writing achievement.* Paper presented at the 16th annual convention of the American Educational Research Association, Atlanta, GA. (ERIC Document Reproduction Service No. ED 359 216)

Shanteau, J., Grier, M., Johnson, J., & Berner, E. (1991). Teaching decision-making skills to student nurses. In J. Baron & R.V. Brown (Eds.), *Teaching decision-making to adolescents* (pp. 185–206). Hillsdale, NJ: Lawrence Erlbaum Associates.

Siegler, R.S. (1976). Three aspects of cognitive development. *Cognitive Psychology, 8,* 481–520.

Siegler, R.S., & Jenkins, E. (1989). *How children discover new strategies.* Hillsdale, NJ: Lawrence Erlbaum Associates.

Sisco, S.S. (1992). *Using goal setting to enhance self-esteem and create an internal locus of control in the at-risk elementary student.* Unpublished master's thesis, Nova University, Fort Lauderdale, FL. (ERIC Document Reproduction Service No. ED 355 017)

Spivack, G., Platt, J., & Shure, M. (1976). *The problem-solving approach to adjustment.* San Francisco: Jossey-Bass.

Tubbs, M.E. (1986). Goal setting: A meta-analytic examination of the empirical evidence. *Journal of Applied Psychology, 71,* 474–483.

Umbreit, J., & Blair, K.S. (1996). The effects of preference, choice, and attention on problem behavior at school. *Education and Training in Mental Retardation and Developmental Disabilities, 2,* 151–161.

Walesa, C. (1975). Children's approaches to chance and skill-dependent risk. *Polish Psychological Bulletin, 6,* 131–138.

Wang, M.C., & Peverly, S.T. (1987). The role of the learner: An individual difference in school learning and functioning. In M.C. Wang, M.C. Reynolds, & H.J. Walberg (Eds.), *Handbook of special education: Research and practice: Vol. 1. Learner characteristics and adaptive education* (pp. 59–92). Oxford, England: Pergamon Press.

Watson, D.L., & Tharp, R.G. (1993). *Self-directed behavior: Self-modification for personal adjustment.* Pacific Grove, CA: Brooks/Cole.

Weinberg, R., Fowler, C., Jackson, A., Bagnall, J., & Bruya, L. (1991). Effect of goal difficulty on motor performance: A replication across tasks and subjects. *Journal of Sport and Exercise Psychology, 13,* 160–173.

Weithorn, L.A., & Campbell, S.B. (1982). The competency of children and adolescents to make informed decisions. *Child Development, 53,* 1589–1598.

Wentzel, K.R. (1992). Motivation and achievement in adolescence: A multiple goals perspective. In D.H. Schunk & J.L. Meece (Eds.), *Student perceptions in the classroom* (pp. 287–305). Hillsdale, NJ: Lawrence Erlbaum Associates.

Willats, P. (1990). Development of problem solving strategies in infancy. In D. Bjorklund (Ed.), *Children's strategies: Contemporary views of cognitive development* (pp. 23–66). Hillsdale, NJ: Lawrence Erlbaum Associates.

Wood, R.E., Mento, A.J., & Locke, E.A. (1987). Task complexity as a moderator of goal effects: A meta-analysis. *Journal of Applied Psychology, 72,* 416–425.

Wraith, S.C., & Biddle, S.J. (1989). Goal setting in children's sport: An exploratory analysis of goal participation, ability and effort, instructions, and post-event constructions. *International Journal of Sports Psychology, 20,* 79–92.

Transition Assessment

Methods and Processes to Determine
Student Needs, Preferences, and Interests

Patricia L. Sitlington and Debra A. Neubert

One of the most important ongoing activities in which a student should be involved is planning for his or her transition from school to adult life. This planning should start when the student is no older than age 14, and families in particular advocate that transition planning should begin at a much earlier age. Many schools are beginning this process as the student enters middle or junior high school. If transition planning is to be effective, it must be based on assessment of the student's needs, preferences, and interests, using a variety of methods. Such assessment should be an ongoing process that assists students with disabilities and their families to define goals, monitor progress toward those goals, and make appropriate program adjustments while preparing for future adult roles. These roles are implemented in employment, in postsecondary education or training program settings, in the community, and through personal and social relationships.

Practitioners, students with disabilities, and the students' families need to understand what types of assessment data are most useful at different life junctures, who is in the best position to collect the assessment data, and how the results of the assessments will ultimately be used in the transition-planning and service delivery processes. Students with disabilities must be encouraged to assume a greater role in the assessment process. For example, students with moderate disabilities can be involved in determining the assessment activities in which they will participate and how they can use these activities to identify their strengths and preferences as they prepare for adult roles. Students with severe disabilities can be involved, along with their family members, in planning vocational, community, and domestic experiences that will help to identify preferences, strengths, and accommodations needed in various environments. The following section describes transition and transition assessment, with a focus on assessment and student involvement.

TRANSITION AND TRANSITION ASSESSMENT

The need for transition processes to facilitate better postsecondary outcomes for individuals with disabilities has received increased attention in the field of special education since the early 1980s. For the purposes of this chapter, the term *transition* is defined as follows:

> Transition refers to a change in status from behaving primarily as a student to assuming emergent roles in the community. These roles include employment, participating in postsecondary education, maintaining a home, becoming actively involved in the community and experiencing satisfactory personal and social relationships. The process of enhancing transition involves the participation and coordination of school programs, adult agency services and natural supports within the community. The foundation for transition should be laid during the elementary and middle school years, guided by the broad concept of career development. Transition planning should begin no later than age 14, and students should be encouraged, to the full extent of their capabilities, to assume a maximum amount of responsibility for such planning. (Halpern, 1994, p. 117)

The Division on Career Development and Transition of the Council for Exceptional Children has defined *transition assessment* as follows:

> Transition assessment is the ongoing process of collecting data on the individual's needs, preferences, and interests as they relate to the demands of current and future working, education, living, and personal and social environments. Assessment data serve as the common thread in the transition process and form the basis for defining goals and services to be included in the Individualized Education Program (IEP). (Sitlington, Neubert, & Leconte, 1997, pp. 70–71)

Although the purposes of transition assessment vary depending on the individual and the setting, the broad purposes include

1. To determine and facilitate the student's self-determination skills
2. To determine the student's current level of career development so that appropriate transition activities can be planned
3. To assist the student in identifying postsecondary goals based on his or her interests, preferences, strengths, and abilities; goal areas include employment opportunities, postsecondary education and training opportunities, independent living situations, community involvement, and personal and social skills
4. To determine appropriate placements within educational, vocational, and community settings that assist in the attainment of these postsecondary goals
5. To determine the accommodations, supports, and services that the student will need to gain access to and maintain his or her postsecondary goals

The next section of this chapter presents methods of gathering information both on the individual and on future living, working, and education environments. The section following that one discusses the transition assessment process, including developing an assessment plan and using the information gathered to make the best possible match between the student's needs, preferences, and interests and future adult living, working, and educational environments.

METHODS OF GATHERING INFORMATION

This section provides an overview of methods that practitioners can use to collect assessment data throughout the transition-planning process. These methods fall into two categories: 1) methods of assessing individuals and 2) methods of assessing future living, working, and educational environments identified by the student. There is a wealth of information in the general education, special education, rehabilitation, and vocational education literature on methods and models of assessment that identify instructional, vocational, community, independent living, and personal and social strengths and needs of individuals with disabilities. New methods and models of assessment are not needed to identify postsecondary goals and facilitate transition planning. The task is to determine what methods of assessment are needed at various transition points for individuals with disabilities to make appropriate decisions regarding their futures.

Transition assessment requires students, families, and professionals to think beyond commonly used assessment practices (i.e., paper-and-pencil tests) and to move toward conducting assessments in actual life contexts such as jobsites, the community, and independent living situations. This move toward more authentic assessment is also evident in education settings in terms of performance-based assessment and outcomes-based measurement. The transition assessment process should focus on deciding what type of assessment data to collect, who will collect the data, and how the results will be used. Assessment data must come from many sources and must be updated frequently to ensure that the student's transition goals are appropriate and realistic. Most important, the results of the assessment process must be used to develop a match between the student's transition goals and the program plan identified through the individualized education program (IEP) process. Transition assessment and planning should drive the IEP process.

Transition assessment is an ongoing process that takes place during the middle and high school years. This process may need to start earlier and be continued throughout the adult years for some individuals with disabilities. Data should be collected that identify student goals and lead to appropriate programming in the areas of employment, community involvement, independent living, postsecondary education, and personal and social relationships. There are several principles that can be used to guide the selection of methods and how the information gathered during the assessment process is used. These principles are adapted from the Interdisciplinary Council on Vocational Evaluation and Assessment (Smith et al., 1994) and include the following:

- A variety of methods should be used to provide accurate assessment. A broad range of questions must be posed to determine what makes an individual's abilities and needs unique.
- Assessment information should be verified by using different methods.
- Behavioral observation is essential in the assessment process. Behavioral observation (e.g., observing physical performance, social characteristics, and interactions with people and other aspects of the environment) occurs throughout the assessment process. The observation process can be informal or formal, can occur in a variety of environments, and should be completed by a variety of people.
- Assessment requires a collaborative approach to data collection and decision making. This entails the collection of input from a variety of individuals and an understanding of how to use the results of the assessment process. Individuals with disabilities and their families; special, general, and vocational educators; guidance counselors; and other personnel already possess much of this vital information.

Each information-gathering method is briefly described and presented along with a discussion of the types of information that can be collected by using the method. First, methods for assessing individuals are presented, including review of background information, interviews, psychometric tests, work samples, curriculum-based assessment techniques, behavioral observation, and situational assessment. Second, methods of assessing environments are presented, including community, job, and program analysis. Much of the information included in this section is taken from *Assess for Success: Handbook on Transition Assessment* (Sitlington, Neubert, Begun, Lombard, & Leconte, 1996). This handbook provides more information on each of these assessment methods and discusses the strengths and weaknesses of each approach, and examples of each method are also given.

Methods of Gathering Student Information

This section presents an overview of basic methods of gathering information about the student that can be used as you assist him or her in planning for the transition from school to adult life. The methods covered are 1) analysis of background information, 2) interviews, 3) psychometric tests, 4) work samples, 5) curriculum-based assessment techniques, 6) behavioral observation, and 7) situational assessment.

Analysis of Background Information   One of the first sources of information about the student should be existing records, which contain observations of previous teachers, support staff, and staff from other agencies (i.e., mental health, vocational rehabilitation) who have worked with the student. In addition to the cumulative folder, there are often other records kept by teachers or other support staff who have worked with the student. Often these other records have more useful information than the official student files. Be sure that you also review past IEPs, with particular emphasis on transition-related objectives and activities contained within these IEPs. In addition, ask for any additional formal and informal student assessments that have been conducted. Although all of this information should be in the student's official file, this is often not the case. If other youth and adult services agencies have been working with the student, ask whether you can also review their information after receiving appropriate releases of information from the family or the student.

Student portfolios provide valuable information that has been selected by the student and staff as representative of his or her interests, goals, and finest work. In fact, a transition portfolio is an excellent means of organizing and summarizing all of the transition assessment and transition-planning activities in which the student has participated. These and other existing records often contain a wealth of information on the student's strengths and interests, as well as on the areas in which the student needs to focus instructional activities. This information may be in the form of comments of previous teachers, guidance counselors, and other support staff and adult services providers; formal and informal assessment results; and records of IEP meetings. These records may also contain information on the experiences that the student has had in the community related to living and employment, and the techniques and approaches that have or have not worked with the student in the past. They may also contain information on health-related issues. If transition-planning activities have been conducted with the student in previous years, it is very helpful to review the trends in the student's expressed interests and preferences during those years.

In reviewing records, however, it is important to remember that students may react differently to new education, living, or work environments and personnel. Thus, although previous information should be considered, time should be taken to form opinions based on observations and experiences with the student as well as on his or her self-reports.

Interviews   Interviews with the student, family members, former teachers, friends, counselors, other support staff, and former employers may be one of the best sources of information on how the student functions in the real world and what he or she wants to do as an adult. The importance of including student perspectives in this process is discussed throughout this book. Interviews of people who know a student well may also uncover valuable information. Frequently, brothers and sisters of students have more realistic and accurate information than their parents about their siblings' long-term goals, their social and personal aspirations, and their abilities. Siblings are major stakeholders in these students' transitions because they may one day assume responsibility for their brothers and sisters with disabilities.

Psychometric Tests   *Psychometric tests* (often called paper-and-pencil tests) are often standardized tests that are available from commercial publishers. They are further removed from tasks required in the real world than most of the other techniques presented in this section. Many of these tests have been formally field tested with sample groups and often include a norm group with which the individual is compared. Some psychometric tests are criterion referenced and provide information on how the individual has performed relative to specific content areas of the test, such as budgeting, health, or job-seeking skills. Examples of these tests include tests of academic achievement, vocational interest, functional living skills, self-concept, learning styles, and vocational aptitude. Although some of these tests must be administered by evaluators formally trained in test administration and interpretation, there are a number of tests that can be administered by the classroom teacher. Consult other sources (Clark, 1996, in press; Corbey, Miller, Severson, & Enderle, 1993) for information on the major psychometric tests related to the major areas of transition.

When many people think of assessment, they think mainly of these formal instruments. The advantage of this approach is that it provides an "official looking" score and a standardized method of gathering specific information. Like any of the techniques described in this chapter, psychometric tests should not be used as the *only* method of gathering the information needed to assist the student and his or her family in transition planning. These tests, however, can provide information on the academic functioning level of the student, including the areas of strength and areas in need of improvement. Many professionals use these instruments as starting points to plan other assessment activities or to engage in discussions with students.

These tests can also provide information on the knowledge level of the student related to functional living areas (i.e., managing money, maintaining a home, shopping) and to specific occupations or occupational clusters. These instruments, however, do *not* provide information on how well the individual applies this knowledge in real-life situations. The ability of the student to perform well on these instruments depends not only on knowledge but also on the amount of experience the student has had with the situations presented in the test.

Work Samples   *Work sampling* is defined as a "work activity involving tasks, materials, and tools which are identical or similar to those in an actual job or cluster of jobs" (Fry & Botterbusch, cited in Dowd, 1993, p. 12). Work samples can be used to assess an individual's interests, abilities, work habits, and personal and social skills. The key to administering work samples is that the practitioner observes and documents information concerning level of interest, attention to task, and requests for assistance or clarification, in addition to an individual's actual task performance. Work samples often provide a direct link to occupational information because they simulate specific aspects of vocational training or employment. Daily living activities can also be simulated in a type of community living sample.

Work samples generally fall into two categories: 1) commercial and 2) locally developed or homemade. Commercial work samples are generally found in vocational evaluation units in school systems or rehabilitation facilities. Information on commercial work samples and the advantages and disadvantages of using them with individuals with disabilities is presented in Brown, McDaniel, and Couch (1994) and Pruitt (1986).

Locally developed or homemade work samples are generally developed by a teacher or a vocational evaluator and are more often used in the transition assessment process. These work samples can be developed on the basis of local job analyses and tasks in vocational training programs or as part of the classroom career exploration process.

A teacher could develop a work sample for students to operate a cash register (without a scanner) in a retail store. A used cash register might be obtained from a local retailer. Students would enter the price of a set of items, compute the tax (if not done by the machine), and state the total amount of the sale. Students would then enter the amount of the check or cash provided and state and count the change. Key behaviors and skills the teacher might observe include attention to detail, ability to operate the cash register, ability to compute tax (if not done by the machine), and ability to compute and/or count appropriate change. Additional behaviors observed might include attention to detail, ability to stay on task, student interest, and personal and social skills.

Follow-up activities might include a visit to selected retail stores and to a distributive education program within the school. Information concerning job opportunities, pay, and training needed could be obtained from the state occupational information system.

Work samples generally have a standard set of directions, tasks, materials, and key behaviors to observe. Homemade work samples can also be found within vocational evaluation units and tend to sample tasks found in vocational programs or jobs specific to the local community. These samples tend to have high face validity because students can see and think about actual work.

Curriculum-Based Assessment Techniques   *Curriculum-based assessment* (CBA) is a major assessment and evaluation thrust in the field of education. This is assessment based on what a student has been taught within a curriculum. Salvia and Hughes (1990) listed eight steps in the CBA approach: 1) specify reasons for assessment, 2) analyze curriculum, 3) formulate behavioral objectives, 4) develop appropriate assessment procedures, 5) collect data, 6) summarize data, 7) display data, and 8) interpret data and make decisions.

CBA is really an approach rather than one specific method. This approach is included here, however, because it is often viewed as a specific assessment technique and is being used increasingly in content area classes, such as math and English, as well as in vocational education programs. CBA instruments can be developed by the teacher or other staff and can focus specifically on the content being taught. These instruments can include any of the methods already discussed in this chapter, such as behavioral observations or paper-and-pencil tests. Examples of CBA techniques include criterion-referenced testing, curriculum-based measurement, portfolio assessment, and curriculum-based vocational assessment. These approaches are discussed in the following subsections. They can be used to gather information related to planning for future living, working, or education environments.

Criterion-Referenced Testing   The *criterion-referenced testing* approach compares the individual's performance with a preestablished level of performance (i.e., 80%) rather than to the performance of others or to a set of norms. In this approach, the emphasis is on the knowledge or skills needed for a specific content area and on whether the individual has demonstrated mastery of this knowledge. Results of the assessment would indicate that the student scored 70% on two-digit by one-digit multiplication problems and 40% on two-digit by two-digit multiplication problems. The criterion-referenced testing approach is used primarily in academic areas but can be used in any content area in which skills can be broken down into specific subareas.

Curriculum-Based Measurement   *Curriculum-based measurement* is an ongoing assessment approach that was developed by individuals at the University of Minnesota. It consists of a specific set of assessment techniques for the areas of reading, written expression, spelling, and math. This approach uses the concept of units correct per minute to measure the student's performance in the specific content area. Initial probes are taken from the beginning, middle, and end of the instructional content, and additional probes of the student's performance area are taken at least twice weekly throughout the instructional period. The student's performance is graphed on an ongoing basis, and instruction is modified based on the student's progress toward established goals. For more information on curriculum-based measurement, consult Marston and Magnusson (1985) and Shinn (1989).

Portfolio Assessment   The concept of *portfolio assessment* has been in use in the fine arts for a number of years as well as in vocational programs such as architecture, drafting, and graphic arts. As the emphasis in assessment moves toward the concept of *authentic assessment,* portfolios are being developed in and across a number of content areas. The major steps in portfolio assessment are to 1) describe the curricular area; 2) identify the overall goals of the portfolio; 3) delineate the portfolio format and the type of materials to be included; 4) describe procedures for evaluating the work in the portfolio, such as student conferences or teacher review of material; and 5) describe how the contents of the portfolio will be summarized.

The types of materials to be included in the portfolio can range from the results of vocational interest tests to essays written by the student concerning his or her goals to samples of projects from a social studies class or an architectural drafting class. This approach is an excellent method of compiling and summarizing all of the student's transition assessment activities. In using this method, it is critical that the student have input into the types of materials to be included in the portfolio and that guidelines be established and followed for including materials in the portfolio. It is also important that the material in the portfolio be evaluated on an ongoing basis by both the student and the teacher.

Curriculum-Based Vocational Assessment   One of the most recognized applications of the CBA approach is *curriculum-based vocational assessment* (CBVA). This is a process for determining the student's career development, vocational, and transition-related needs based on his or her ongoing performance within existing course content. For the specific application of CBVA, the target is usually performance in vocational education courses or in work experience sites in the school or community, although important information can also be gathered from performance in academic classes. This process allows not only collection of information on the student's performance in a setting close to real life but also determination of the support that the student will need to succeed in vocational education classes or on the job. Albright and Cobb (1988b) identified three general phases in the CBVA process:

1. *Assessment during program placement and planning:* This assessment includes activities that occur prior to and during the first few weeks of stu-

dent participation in a vocational program. Information gathered during this phase assists in program selection, placement, and planning.

2. *Assessment during participation in a vocational program:* These activities monitor student progress, determine the appropriateness of the program and service delivery plan, and evaluate the success of the student's program.

3. *Assessment during program exiting:* Assessment activities in this phase occur near the end of, and immediately following completion of, the student's program. Information gathered in this phase assists the team in identifying the services needed to enable the student's transition into employment or postsecondary education, and the best programs for the student.

For more information on CBVA, consult Albright and Cobb (1988a, 1988b) and Stodden, Ianacone, Boone, and Bisconer (1987). If the student is in vocational education classes or is working in the community, information can be gathered on how well the individual actually performs tasks related to specific occupations. The student can also determine whether he or she is interested in the specific vocational area. Information can also be gathered on how well the individual relates to others, including peers and supervisors, and in such areas as working independently, staying on task, and asking for assistance when needed.

Behavioral Observation　　Observing and recording individual behavior in different work and community settings over time provides the foundation for transition assessment. Observing individual behavior is a key component of the methods described in this section. Dowd defined an *observation procedure* as "an organized method of observing and objectively recording the behavior of an individual for the purpose of documenting this behavior. The emphasis is usually upon productivity, behavior patterns, expressed interest, and interpersonal interaction" (1993, p. 20).

For information to be useful, behavioral observation should be systematic and should take place in a variety of settings. It is also helpful to have different team members observe the same individual in various situations to make sure the information gathered is valid and reliable. There are a number of different techniques that practitioners can use to observe and record behavior, including narrative recording, time sampling, event recording, and rating scales.

Situational Assessment　　*Situational assessment* is the systematic observation process for evaluating behaviors in environments as close as possible to the individual's future living, working, or education environment. The demands of the environment (i.e., work tasks, independent living tasks, community functioning skills) can be varied while recording student behaviors such as his or her interests, actual skill levels, use of materials, and social interactions. Situational assessments can be valid and reliable sources of data if the sites are systematically developed (i.e., uniform tasks a student will do, amount of time spent there, supervision responsibilities) and if practitioners systematically record behaviors during the assessment process. The data collected then can be used in planning and placement decisions concerning further situational assessment sites, types of programs to consider for placement, and instructional or social accommodations needed in specific situations.

Situational assessments can be conducted at recreation sites, community sites (e.g., a bank), and simulated or real sites that require independent living skills (e.g., home economics lab, family home, supervised apartment). For example, a student plays on an intramural volleyball team. The teacher observes the student's interactions with teammates and the coach. Also noted is the student's interest in the game and ability to follow directions. The teacher, student, and family can explore additional recreation opportunities in the community based on this initial assessment data.

Situational assessment also can be used to collect data on students' interests; abilities; interpersonal and social skills; and accommodations and needs in school-based worksites, community-based worksites, and vocational training programs. The following example illustrates a situational assessment site. A tenth-grade student has repeatedly expressed an interest in enrolling in a drafting program. The teacher arranges for the student to spend a week in a vocational education drafting program to determine her interest level, ability to follow safety rules, ability to use the equipment and tools required in the program, interactions with the instructor and other students, and what (if any) instructional or equipment accommodations are needed. Both the drafting instructor and the special education teacher agree to collect narrative data on a daily basis in addition to using a competency-based checklist of tasks that the student completes while in the program. At the end of the assessment, the instructor, teacher, and student discuss whether this is a realistic placement option or postsecondary employment goal for the student.

In arranging situational assessments in worksites, educators should keep in mind that guidelines have been developed by the U.S. Departments of Labor and of Education for the purpose of placing students in unpaid jobs. (For a complete listing of the guidelines, see Inge, Simon, Halloran, & Moon, 1993; Simon, Cobb, Norman, & Bourexia, 1994.)

Methods of Assessing Potential Environments

The first part of this section presents information on a number of methods that can be used to gather information about a student. To determine the training and support a student needs to succeed in his or her preferred future living, working, and education environments, it is critical that the instructor or someone in the program systematically look at the demands of these environments. In general, the bigger the gap between a student's abilities and the demands of the environment, the more detailed the analysis should be. This allows the needed training and supports required for student success to be identified. It is important to remember that the environment, situations, and circumstances can be adapted, adjusted, or realigned so that minimal supports are needed. The following section presents basic information on analyzing community settings, jobs, and postsecondary training programs. Again, much of this information is taken from Sitlington et al. (1996). This handbook contains more information on each of these techniques and provides sample forms for conducting such analyses.

Analysis of Community Environments   The concept of *environmental analysis*, particularly as related to community-based living settings, was first introduced by professionals working with individuals with moderate and severe disabilities. In terms of future living environments, it is important to identify the demands of both the home environment in which the individual will be living and the immediate and broader community in which the individual will be shopping, banking, and pursuing leisure activities.

McDonnell, Wilcox, and Hardman (1991) indicated that the following must be determined: 1) where the individual will perform the activity, 2) what tasks he or she will complete at each site, 3) how the individual will complete difficult steps of the activity, and 4) what level of performance will be expected to terminate the training program. If the specific community-based environments are known, the task becomes one of analyzing the demands of these specific environments (i.e., apartment, grocery store, bank). Often, however, the specific location in which an individual will live is unknown. In addition, a person will want to frequent a number of locations within a given community, such as different restaurants. For this reason, McDonnell and colleagues (1991) recommended a general case procedures analysis in which the variations in performance demands across all of the settings in which the individual will be expected to complete each activity are identified. For more information on completing an analysis of community environments, consult McDonnell et al. (1991) or Moon, Inge, Wehman, Brooke, and Barcus (1990).

Job Analysis   The process of analyzing the demands of working environments is called *job analysis*. In essence, it is a task analysis of the job and the demands of the job. This process involves systematically gathering information on what the worker does and how the work is done. It includes other areas such as amount of supervision, production requirements, and so forth. Information should also be gathered on other demands of the workplace, including activities during breaks and transportation to and from work. The job analysis process is time consuming and must be done on site to observe the *essential functions* of the job as that term is defined in the Americans with Disabilities Act (ADA) of 1990 (PL 101-336). McDonnell et al. (1991) identified five basic steps in conducting a job analysis. The example of a respiratory therapist is used here:

1. Identify the specific responses required to complete each job assigned. These responses should be both observable and measurable. (Identify the basic tasks that the respiratory therapist must complete. Be very specific. Identify the tasks you have observed and other tasks completed at a time you were not observing.)

2. Identify the environmental cues that control the completion of the task. These cues tell the individual to perform certain tasks or parts of the task. (Identify the commands of the doctor in charge, the patient's requests, and the requests of other office staff that prompt the specific tasks.)

3. Identify the speed requirements of the job in terms of average time required to complete a response or task, or number of products to be completed within a given time period. Identify how important this speed requirement is to the employer. (Identify how quickly the respiratory therapist must respond to the requests of the patient and other staff. Indicate the importance of speed.)

4. Specify the quality requirements for each job task. The accuracy of the supervisor's expectations should be cross-checked by discussing them with other co-workers who perform the same job. (Identify what criteria will be used to evaluate the quality of the respiratory therapist's performance.)

5. Identify exceptions to the normal routine. These exceptions may include changes in the job routine or unpredictable situations that may arise during the course of the workday. (Identify tasks that the respiratory therapist does not perform daily but that are important to completion of the job, such as procedures to be performed in an emergency.)

Analysis of Postsecondary Training Environments   If one of the goals of the student is postsecondary education, the instructor, the student, or the family should visit the targeted education program to determine the demands of specific courses and of the total education environment. This process involves gathering information on the specific courses in which the student will be enrolled and determining the demands of these courses in terms of daily assignments, amount of reading required, major tests, and so forth. Information should also be gathered on the requirements of any field experiences or laboratories related to the class. Also identify the support services and accommodations that are available.

Information should be gathered on the following aspects of the training program: 1) application procedures, 2) admission requirements, 3) support services, 4) willingness of individual faculty members to provide accommodations, 5) career or personal counseling services, 6) academically and vocationally related training programs, 7) existing fee structure, and 8) availability of financial support.

As in the job analysis, it is important to identify the types of information that are to be gathered on postsecondary programs and to adopt, adapt, or develop a program analysis form that provides this information. The form should allow you to record information on a specific program and then refer to this information later. The form should also be one that all staff members can use and one that allows the results of a specific program analysis to be shared with other staff as well as with the individual.

An analysis of the demands of future living, working, and education environments the individual has chosen is a major help in determining the training he or she needs to succeed in these programs. This training could involve enrollment in general education courses in high school, participation in work experiences in the community, instruction in learning strategies or study skills, or training in self-determination. If the training involves enrolling in general education classes, such as vocational education, math, or English classes, it is helpful to conduct an analysis of the demands of these training environments so that the support the student needs to learn from these programs can be determined. The steps involved in this program analysis are identical to those discussed in analyzing postsecondary education environments, although most of the programs being analyzed are in the high school.

Summary

The preceding sections identify a number of methods of gathering information on the individual and on potential living, working, and education environments. The best way to determine which methods would be useful is to determine the questions that need to be answered regarding the student as well as the information needed to answer these questions. In cooperation with the student, his or her family, and others on the planning team, the methods that can provide the needed information can be chosen. The portfolio approach presented previously in this chapter offers an ideal vehicle for the student, family, and other members of the transition-planning team to select and compile the most relevant transition assessment information that has been collected. This transition assessment portfolio can then be used in making the match between the student's needs, interests, and preferences and the future environments in which the student will function as an adult.

THE TRANSITION ASSESSMENT PROCESS

The Individuals with Disabilities Education Act (IDEA) of 1990 (PL 101-476) heightened educators' awareness of the transition process and the importance of collecting information on students' needs, preferences, and interests. The IDEA Amendments of 1997 (PL 105-17) define *transition* as "a coordinated set of activities for a student with a disability that are designed within an outcome-oriented process, which promotes movement from school to postschool activities" (IDEA Amendments § 602). Postschool activities include postsecondary education, vocational training, integrated employment (including supported employment), continuing and adult education, adult services, independent living, and community participation (IDEA Amendments § 602).

In terms of the transition assessment process, it is important to note that activities must be based on the individual student's needs, taking into account the student's preferences and interests. Such activities include instruction; related services; community experiences; development of employment and other postschool adult living objectives; and, when appropriate, acquisition of daily living skills, and functional vocational evaluation.

To plan appropriate postsecondary goals and identify individual needs, preferences, and interests, educators must have a systematic approach to the transition assessment process. This section of the chapter provides information on 1) how to develop an assessment plan for all students with disabilities to ensure that appropriate methods are selected for the assessment process and 2) how to use transition assessment data in matching the student to appropriate education, vocational, and community environments.

Developing an Assessment Plan

The first section of this chapter provides an overview of methods that can be used in the transition assessment process. Selecting methods to gather information about the student and potential living, working, and education environments means that the assessment process must be individualized for each student. An obvious challenge to practitioners is to find time to individualize the assessment process and decide which methods are appropriate to use at different stages of transition planning for students with disabilities. The development of an assessment plan, which can be updated each year, can facilitate an individualized assessment process. The assessment plan should be developed as soon as transition planning begins for students, which may be in elementary or middle school. However, all students should have an assessment plan in place by the time they are 14 years of age to comply with the IDEA Amendments of 1997, which require,

> (I) beginning at 14, and updated annually, a statement of the transition service needs of the child under the applicable components of the child's IEP that focuses on the child's courses of study (such as participation in advanced-placement courses or a vocational education program); [and]
> (II) beginning at 16 (or younger, if determined appropriate by the IEP team), a statement of needed transition services for the child, including, when appropriate, a statement of the interagency responsibilities or any needed linkages. (IDEA Amendments of 1997 § 614[d][1][A][vii])

The assessment plan should be developed through a team approach, with the student included as an integral team member. In addition, the following personnel may also compose the assessment team: family members, special and general education teachers, work-study staff, school guidance personnel, school psychologists, career and technology teachers, community college personnel, adult services providers, employers, job coaches, and other support services personnel. The assessment team members will change over time as the student develops clearer postsecondary outcomes and as the needed transition services and activities are identified. The assessment team should be coordinated by one individual or case manager to ensure that the assessment plan is implemented and that the team uses the assessment data in transition planning. An obvious choice for the service coordinator is the secondary special education teacher or the transition specialist. The assessment plan should be updated at least once per year when the IEP committee reviews the plan's transition needs and services or if the student is experiencing difficulty in a specific placement.

Initiating and maintaining active student involvement is one challenge to developing an assessment plan. Halpern indicated that students often have little voice in determining the types of assessment activities in which they participate or in reviewing assessment data to make informed choices about postsecondary goals:

> Because traditional assessment practices in special education have often treated the subject of assessment as an object of assessment, there have not been very many opportunities for people with disabilities to take charge and ownership of their own evaluation within the context of customary assessment activities. In response to this disenfranchisement, students with disabilities and their families often feel intimidated by the assessment process and its outcomes, which then defeats the very possibility of using assessment information as a foundation for transition planning. (1994, p. 118)

Halpern urges students (see Chapter 9) to engage in self-evaluation, which includes teaching students a process for examining and evaluating academic, vocational, independent living, and personal and social skills and goals. Many of the self-determination curricula (e.g., Field & Hoffman, 1996; Wehmeyer & Kelchner, 1997) provide teachers and parents with a structured approach to teach self-evaluation, goal-setting, and advocacy skills to students with disabilities. Halpern (1994) recommended that the locus of control be transferred to the family when a student's cognitive disability significantly limits active planning in the assessment and transition processes. Many of the Personal Futures Planning processes (e.g., Making Action Plans [MAPs], Forest & Pearpoint, 1992; Vandercook, York, & Forest, 1989; *Choosing Outcomes and Accommodations for Children: A Guide to Educational Planning for Students with Disabilities* [COACH] (Second Edition), Giangreco, Cloninger, & Iverson, 1998; Lifestyles Planning Process, O'Brien & Lyle, 1987) can provide teachers and families with a structured approach to plan and develop services and activities that lead to positive postsecondary choices for the student (see Chapter 5).

Steps in Assessment Plan Development   There are four steps in the development of an assessment plan. These steps are outlined in the following paragraphs.

Step 1   The first step in developing the assessment plan is to determine what information about the student is available. This is an important and often overlooked step in the assessment process. The assessment team must determine what information already exists about the student and compile the information in a manner that allows the assessment team to use the data and to begin the transition profile. In addition, this step involves seeking information about postsecondary goals and dreams from the student and his or her family (see Chapter 12). Step 1 incorporates methods such as background review (e.g., medical, academic, vocational), student and family interviews, interviews with pertinent school personnel, or Personal Futures Planning activities. Table 1 provides guidelines for collecting information during the first step of the assessment plan.

It is important that students be active partners in Step 1 of the assessment plan. They should provide input about their postsecondary goals and the types of assessment activities in which they would like to participate. For students who have difficulty verbally expressing their needs, preferences, and interests, family members can be asked to provide information on their son's or daughter's or sibling's interests, preferences, and hobbies.

Steps 2 and 3   Step 2 of the assessment plan requires the assessment team to determine what additional information is needed about the student (e.g., Do we have enough information on this student's vocational interests and skills to match him or her to a work environment? Do we have enough information about the student's recreational and social interests to match to community activities?) and what methods will provide this information. Step 3 involves determining which environments need to be analyzed (e.g., community college program, high school vocational-technical program, service sector jobs, community recreation facilities). Data on both the student and the potential environments to which he or she may gain access are needed to determine if a good fit can be obtained among the student's needs, interests, and preferences and the environment.

Sitlington et al. (1996) compiled a list of sample questions related to employment, postsecondary education, community involvement, personal and social skills, and independent living outcomes that can be asked during these steps of the assessment plan along with the methods that solicit the information. The methods described in the first part of this chapter (i.e., psychometrics, work samples, situational assessments, job analyses, community analyses) may all be used to provide the needed information. Other references also

Table 1.　Guidelines for developing an assessment plan: Step 1

Conduct a background review of the student—look for information on

- Previous assessments
- Previous career and vocational experiences and work history
- Medical background
- Academic achievement
- Attendance
- Participation in IEP meetings

Interview the student—Focus on his or her

- Interests and goals for future, including work, postsecondary education, independent living, community functioning, and social and recreation activities
- Knowledge of academic and vocational options in high school
- Knowledge of academic and vocational options in postsecondary settings
- Knowledge of community services and recreational activities
- Knowledge of independent living opportunities after high school
- Level of career awareness
- Level of self-determination and advocacy skills
- Acknowledgment of strengths and needs in various environments
- Expressions of assessment activities (methods) in which he or she would like to participate

Interview the family—Focus on their

- Goals for son or daughter in terms of employment, independent living, recreational/social activities, and community functioning
- Types of supports they view important for son or daughter to reach postsecondary goals
- Knowledge of school or community programs and services needed to reach these goals
- Assessment activities that they believe would help their son or daughter determine whether the chosen postsecondary goals are feasible
- Level of advocacy, service coordination skills (to support the student in transition process)

provide examples of specific commercial instruments or methods to consider in the transition assessment process (see Clark, 1996, in press; Corbey et al., 1993). The importance of conducting situational assessments in actual job or community environments, especially for students with more significant disabilities, has also been discussed in the literature and should assist practitioners in planning the assessment process (e.g., Moon et al., 1990; Parker, Szymanski, & Hanley-Maxwell, 1989). Information on interests, preferences, skills, and needs can be collected while the student is actually engaged in assessment activities such as situational assessment. For further information about identifying preferences for individuals with severe disabilities who do not have functional communications skills, see Winkling, O'Reilly, and Moon (1993).

Step 4　Step 4 in the assessment plan requires the assessment team to make decisions about how data will be collected and what formats will be used to organize and present assessment data for use in IEP planning. During this step, the assessment team should discuss the following points:

- Who will collect assessment data in various environments?
- What data collection forms and techniques will be used?
- How will the information be compiled to review with the student and his or her family?
- How will the student be taught to summarize assessment data or express preferences, interests, and needs at the IEP meeting?
- How will the assessment data be compiled to review at the IEP meeting?
- How will the assessment data be stored and updated for future IEP meetings?

This step deserves careful consideration because IDEA and the IDEA Amendments of 1997 made it clear that secondary special educators are responsible for inviting students and their families to their IEP meetings when transition goals are discussed. Thus, IDEA and its amendments reinforce self-determination and choice for students with disabilities to the greatest extent possible (see Chapter 1).

Another important issue to consider during this part of the assessment plan is how to present the data to the student so that he or she can self-evaluate needs, preferences, and interests in relation to potential environments. Students must then be taught a strategy, or practice summarizing these data, to present at their IEP conference. Students should be able to describe their interests, postsecondary goals, programs they are interested in attending, and community references to which they believe they need to gain access. If a student is not able to present this information, the family should be encouraged to assume responsibility for presenting these assessment data at the IEP meeting. There are a number of strategies and curricula that can assist students to participate in the IEP process and learn to express their needs, interests, and preferences (e.g., see Martin, Huber Marshall, Maxson, & Jerman, 1993; Sitlington et al., 1996).

Organizing Assessment Results   One issue that has remained consistent in both the special education and rehabilitation literature is the lack of use of vocational and assessment data and/or recommendations generated through these assessment processes in planning individual programs (e.g., Adami & Neubert, 1991; Leconte, 1994). It is important that the assessment team give time and thought to how assessment data are displayed and used in the IEP process to avoid problems in transition assessment. Formats for collecting and organizing assessment data vary depending on the setting, the skill level of the practitioners, compliance with state and local school system forms, and the methods that are used to collect the assessment data. Formats that should be considered for organizing transition assessment data include profiles or portfolios. For example, Sarkees-Wircenski and Scott (1995) recommended organizing information into a learner profile that includes the following main areas: educational, academic, and psychological; physical and medical; social and interpersonal relations; and vocational information.

Sarkees-Wircenski and Wircenski (1994) also presented a method for organizing a career portfolio for students to facilitate transition planning. Five major areas of transition competencies are included in the portfolio: employment skills, work-related social skills, self-help and independent living skills, generalizable skills, and job-specific skills. For transition assessment, practitioners would also have to include a section for the analyses of potential environments such as job analyses, postsecondary program analyses, and community analyses. Once a profile or portfolio is developed, it can be updated yearly or as needed. Some students' portfolios should include videotapes that document their performance on jobsites and in the community. This is especially important for students with moderate and severe disabilities; the use of videotapes can demonstrate tasks performed in the workplace and in the community along with supports that a student needs to succeed in a specific environment. This information can then be passed to adult services providers or to other relevant parties to plan for the transition from school to the next environment.

The Rehabilitation Act Amendments of 1992 (PL 102-569) mandated that eligibility determinations must first focus on the use of existing data, particularly on information provided by the individual with a disability, the family, or advocates. Other sources of information may include education agencies, the individual's personal physician, current or previous employers, Social Security agencies, community organizations, and any organization or person referring the individual (Virginia Commonwealth University, 1993). A transition profile or portfolio can facilitate referrals to rehabilitation and other adult programs as well as serve as the basis for transition planning in the schools. The information contained in the profile or portfolio can be used to make planning and placement decisions concerning transition needs and goals at the IEP meeting.

Making the Match: Transition Assessment

Figure 1 presents a process for collecting assessment data to be used in the transition-planning process and for integrating that information into a statement of needed transition services on the student's IEP (Sitlington et al., 1996). There are three components to this process. First, the student's interests, preferences, strengths, and needs should be identified through a variety of assessment methods. The methods reviewed in the first section of this chapter should be tailored to the student, keeping in mind the student's age, severity of disability, and level of career development. Second, potential living, working, and education environments to which the student will have access should be identified and then analyzed through methods such as job analysis,

Making the match

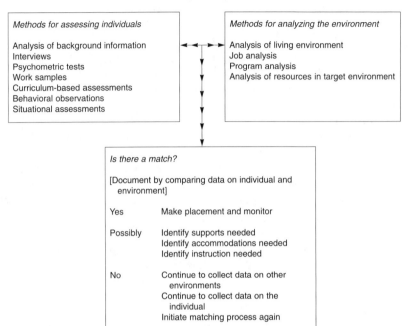

Figure 1. Making the match. (From Sitlington, P.L., Neubert, D.A., Begun, W., Lombard, R.C., & Leconte, P.J. [1996]. *Assess for success: Handbook on transition assessment* [p. 99]. Reston, VA: Council for Exceptional Children; reprinted by permission. Copyright © 1996 by the Council for Exceptional Children.)

community resource analysis, and vocational program analysis. This component of the assessment process can also include an identification of formal and natural supports found in each environment. In addition, assistive technology devices or services that might enhance the student's placement in the environment can also be tried out and analyzed. Finally, the third component requires the assessment team to review all of the assessment data and to determine if there is a match between the student and the potential environments that were analyzed. The process allows the assessment team to consider a broad range of transition goals and outcomes when developing the IEP that enables practitioners to comply with the requirements of the IDEA Amendments of 1997 and address quality-of-life issues for the student.

If the assessment team determines that there is a confluence of the student's interests, abilities, and needs and the potential environment, a number of activities should then be carried out, including 1) the development of transition goals and corresponding activities to reach the goal to be included in the IEP, 2) the identification of supports and accommodations (if needed) to reach the goals, 3) the identification of personnel who will assist the student in obtaining placement and provide support in specific environments, and 4) the time frame for reviewing placement decisions and for collecting additional assessment data in specific environments.

If the assessment team determines that there are not appropriate matches between the student's needs, interests, and preferences and the environments that were analyzed, then the assessment team needs to go back to Step 2 of the assessment plan and continue to collect data on the individual through various assessment methods and on other environments (e.g., different jobsites or community sites) that might provide better matches for the student. Again, practitioners should consider the use of assistive technology and other support services to enhance a match between the individual and potential environments. Finally, the assessment team should document the need to collect additional assessment data on the student's IEP before determining specific transition needs or placements.

In summary, the use of an assessment plan and the matching process depicted in Figure 1 provides students, families, and practitioners with a comprehensive process to conduct transition assessment. Students' assessment plans should be updated yearly to prepare for the IEP meeting when transition services and goals are discussed. In addition, the assessment plan can assist members who are added to the assessment team over time to understand what assessment data have already been collected. This helps the team in determining when to update dreams and goals with students and their families and how to monitor students' progress in meeting their transition goals.

REFERENCES

Adami, H., & Neubert, D.A. (1991). A follow-up of vocational assessment recommendations and placement in secondary vocational education programs for students with disabilities. *Vocational Evaluation and Work Adjustment Bulletin, 23*(1), 101–107.

Albright, L., & Cobb, R.B. (1988a). *Assessment of students with handicaps in vocational education: A curriculum-based approach.* Alexandria, VA: American Vocational Association.

Albright, L., & Cobb, R.B. (1988b). Curriculum-based vocational assessment: A concept whose time has come. *Journal of Vocational Special Needs Education, 10,* 13–16.

Americans with Disabilities Act (ADA) of 1990, PL 101-336, 42 U.S.C. §§ 12101 *et seq.*

Brown, C.D., McDaniel, R., & Couch, R. (1994). *Vocational evaluation systems and software: A consumer's guide.* Menomonie, WI: Rehabilitation Resource, Stout Vocational Rehabilitation Institute.

Clark, G.M. (1996). Transition planning assessment for secondary-level students with learning disabilities. *Journal of Learning Disabilities, 29,* 91–92.

Clark, G.M. (in press). *Assessment for transitions planning.* Austin, TX: PRO-ED.

Corbey, S., Miller, R., Severson, S., & Enderle, J. (1993). *Identifying individual transition needs: A resource guide for special educators working with students in their transition from school to adult life.* St. Paul: Minnesota Department of Education.

Dowd, L.R. (Ed.). (1993). *Glossary of terminology for vocational assessment, evaluation and work adjustment.* Menomonie, WI: Rehabilitation Resource, Stout Vocational Rehabilitation Institute.

Field, S., & Hoffman, A. (1996). *Steps to self-determination.* Austin, TX: PRO-ED.

Forest, M., & Pearpoint, J. (1992). MAPS: Action planning. In J. Pearpoint, M. Forest, & J. Snow, *The inclusion papers: Strategies to make inclusion work* (pp. 52–56). Toronto: Inclusion Press.

Giangreco, M.F., Cloninger, C.J., & Iverson, V.S. (1998). *Choosing outcomes and accommodations for children (COACH): A guide to educational planning for students with disabilities* (2nd ed.). Baltimore: Paul H. Brookes Publishing Co.

Halpern, A.S. (1994). The transition of youth with disabilities to adult life: A position statement of the Division on Career Development and Transition. *Career Development for Exceptional Individuals, 17,* 115–124.

Individuals with Disabilities Education Act (IDEA) of 1990, PL 101-476, 20 U.S.C. §§ 1400 *et seq.*

Individuals with Disabilities Education Act (IDEA) Amendments of 1997, PL 105-17, 20 U.S.C. §§ 1400 *et seq.*

Inge, K.J., Simon, M., Halloran, W., & Moon, M.S. (1993). Community-based vocational instruction and the labor laws: A 1993 update. In K.J. Inge & P. Wehman (Eds.), *Designing community-based vocational programs for students with severe disabilities* (pp. 51–80). Richmond: Virginia Commonwealth University, Rehabilitation Research and Training Center on Supported Employment.

Leconte, P.J. (1994). *A perspective on vocational appraisal: Beliefs, practices, and paradigms.* Unpublished doctoral dissertation, George Washington University, Washington, DC.

Marston, E., & Magnusson, D. (1985). Implementing curriculum-based measurement in special and regular education settings. *Exceptional Children, 52,* 266–276.

Martin, J.E., Huber Marshall, L., Maxson, L., & Jerman, P.A. (1993). *Self-directed IEP.* Colorado Springs: University of Colorado, Center for Educational Leadership.

McDonnell, J., Wilcox, B., & Hardman, M. (1991). *Secondary programs for students with developmental disabilities.* Needham Heights, MA: Allyn & Bacon.

Moon, M.S., Inge, K.J., Wehman, P., Brooke, V., & Barcus, J.M. (1990). *Helping persons with severe mental retardation get and keep employment: Supported employment strategies and outcomes.* Baltimore: Paul H. Brookes Publishing Co.

O'Brien, J., & Lyle, C. (1987). *Framework for accomplishment.* Decatur, GA: Responsive Systems Associates.

Parker, R.M., Szymanski, E.M., & Hanley-Maxwell, C. (1989). Ecological assessment in supported employment. *Journal of Applied Rehabilitation Counseling, 20*(3), 26–33.

Pruitt, W. (1986). *Vocational (work) evaluation* (2nd ed.). Menomonie, WI: Walt Pruitt Associates.

Rehabilitation Act Amendments of 1992, PL 102-569, 29 U.S.C. §§ 701 *et seq.*

Salvia, J., & Hughes, C. (1990). *Curriculum-based assessment: Testing what is taught.* New York: Macmillan.

Sarkees-Wircenski, M., & Scott, J.L. (1995). *Vocational special needs.* Homewood, IL: American Technical Publishers.

Sarkees-Wircenski, M., & Wircenski, J.L. (1994). Transition planning: Developing a career portfolio for students with disabilities. *Career Development for Exceptional Individuals, 17,* 204–214.

Shinn, M.R. (Ed.). (1989). *Curriculum-based measurement: Assessing special children.* New York: Guilford Press.

Simon, M., Cobb, B., Norman, M., & Bourexia, P. (1994). *Meeting the needs of youth with disabilities: Handbook for implementing community-based vocational education programs according to the Fair Labor Standards Act.* Fort Collins: Colorado State University.

Sitlington, P.L., Neubert, D.A., Begun, W., Lombard, R.C., & Leconte, P.J. (1996). *Assess for success: Handbook on transition assessment.* Reston, VA: Council for Exceptional Children.

Sitlington, P.L., Neubert, D.A., & Leconte, P.J. (1997). Transition assessment: The position of the Division on Career Development and Transition. *Career Development for Exceptional Individuals, 20,* 69–79.

Smith, F., Lombard, R., Neubert, D., Leconte, P., Rothenbacher, C., & Sitlington, P. (1994). The position statement of the Interdisciplinary Council on Vocational Evaluation and Assessment. *Journal for Vocational Special Needs Education, 17,* 41–42.

Stodden, R., Ianacone, R.N., Boone, M.R., & Bisconer, W.S. (1987). *Curriculum-based vocational assessment: A guide for addressing youth with special needs.* Honolulu, HI: Centre Publications, International Education Corp.

Vandercook, T., York, J., & Forest, M. (1989). MAPS: A strategy for building the vision. *Journal of The Association for Persons with Severe Handicaps, 14*(3), 205–215.

Virginia Commonwealth University. (1993). *P.L. 102-569: The Rehabilitation Act Amendments of 1992.* Richmond: Author.

Wehmeyer, M., & Kelchner, K. (1997). *Whose Future Is it Anyway? A student directed transition planning process.* Reston, VA: Council for Exceptional Children.

Winkling, D.L., O'Reilly, B., & Moon, M.S. (1993). Individual preference: The missing link in the job match process of individuals with severe disabilities who do not have functional communication skills. *Journal of Vocational Rehabilitation, 3*(3), 27–42.

Participation in the Education Process

Students with Severe Disabilities

Carole R. Gothelf and Fredda Brown

Trends in educating students with disabilities emphasize the involvement of each student in critical elements of the education process (Abery, 1994; Brown & Cohen, 1996; Doll, Sands, Wehmeyer, & Palmer, 1996; Wehmeyer, 1996), including education planning and decision making. Students with severe disabilities represent a challenge to achieving this goal because many strategies to increase participation in these types of activities require skills that individuals with severe disabilities often do not have. Participation in programmatic efforts to increase student involvement and self-determination in the education process often requires levels of expressive and receptive communication that are difficult for individuals with severe, multiple disabilities.

This chapter suggests approaches and strategies appropriate for students who have severe, multiple disabilities and behavior problems. These strategies are designed to enable them to participate in planning, goal development, and design and evaluation of the education process. The chapter also discusses how administrative systems can support self-determination in both staff and students. Before discussing *how* students with severe disabilities can partic- ipate in the education process, it is critical to first review *who* these students are and *why* these students should participate in the education process along with their peers with less severe disabilities.

STUDENTS WITH SEVERE DISABILITIES

Individuals with severe disabilities have been defined and described in many ways, and these definitions have evolved over time (Brown & Snell, 1993; Cipani & Spooner, 1994). Historically, individuals with severe or profound disabilities have been classified according to IQ score (i.e., an IQ score of 20–34 indicates mental retardation requiring extensive supports, an IQ score of less than 20 indicates mental retardation requiring pervasive supports). Heward and Orlansky (1992) pointed out that definitions were based on nega- tive behavioral descriptors. These definitions usually were divided into a list of "nonskills" such as nonverbal, nonambulatory, and lack of social skills, and into a list of possible problem behaviors, such as tantrums, self-stimulatory behavior, aggression, and self-injury. These descriptors reinforced a negative and incompetent view of individuals with severe disabilities and thus had a di- rect impact on the kinds of educational and community opportunities that were made available for them (Meyer, Peck, & Brown, 1991). These expecta- tions, or the lack thereof, were also evidenced by referring to individuals as "trainable" or "educable." These types of descriptions also shed light on how the field viewed potential outcomes and expectations for individuals with the most severe disabilities.

In 1959, the American Association on Mental Deficiency (Heber, 1959) revised earlier definitions of mental retardation to include a measure of the person's adaptive behavior in addition to the IQ score construct. This addition of adaptive behavior was an important initial attempt to look at the functional skills of an individual in relation to his or her everyday environments. In the 1990s, definitions of disability have moved away from the IQ score construct to focus on the level of support that the individual needs to participate in the community. For example, the American Association on Mental Retardation (AAMR) no longer uses modifiers such as *mild, moderate, severe,* or *profound* to describe levels of mental retardation (Luckasson et al., 1992). Instead, AAMR classifies individuals by the level of supports that they need (i.e., *in- termittent, limited, extensive, pervasive*) across the various adaptive skill areas (i.e., communication, self-care, social skills, home living, community use, self-direction, health and safety, functional academics, leisure, work). Individ- uals with severe disabilities often need extensive or pervasive supports across many of these skill domains. This strategy acknowledges that an individual may need pervasive supports in one or more life domains (e.g., home living, self-care) and need a less intensive level of support in other areas (e.g., self-direction, communication, social skills).

The inclusion of self-direction as a category of adaptive skills in the revised AAMR definition is a promising direction in the field of disabilities. The AAMR defines *self-direction* as

> skills related to making choices; learning and following a schedule; initiating activities appropriate to the setting, conditions, schedule, and personal interests; completing necessary or required tasks; seeking assistance when needed; resolving problems confronted in familiar and novel situations; and demonstrating appropriate assertiveness and self-advocacy skills. (Luckasson et al., 1992, p. 40)

The Association for Persons with Severe Handicaps (TASH) has also begun describing individuals with severe disabilities in relation to the supports they need to meaningfully participate in the community. TASH defines these individuals as those "who require extensive ongoing support in more than one major life activity in order to participate in integrated community settings and to enjoy a quality of life that is available to citizens with fewer or no disabilities" (Meyer et al., 1991, p. 19).

The definition of *mental retardation* has thus moved first from reliance on the construct of IQ score, to a focus on measurement of the individual's relationship to his or her environment (i.e., adaptive behavior), and then to a focus on the supports needed to meaningfully participate in integrated community environments. The critical variable to consider in this evolution is the focus on the individual's participation in integrated environments, as opposed to measures of pathology and deviance from what is typical as measured by constructs such as IQ score. This reflects an important paradigm shift. Wehmeyer (1996) pointed out that the self-determination initiative has emerged as the logical extension of a changing view of disability in our society (see also Chapter 1). According to Bradley (1994), there have been three paradigms in the field of developmental disabilities: the era of institutionalization, dependence, and segregation (ending in the mid-1970s); the era of deinstitutionalization and community development with a focus on specialized services; and the era of community membership, which is characterized by functional supports and quality of life. These evolutionary processes and paradigm shifts have created a different vision of outcomes for individuals with the most severe disabilities, one in which each individual is empowered to pursue a self-determined, satisfying quality of life.

IMPORTANCE OF CHOICE

The students discussed in this chapter have the most severe disabilities. Although the authors are reluctant to focus on the disabilities rather than on the multitude of abilities of students with the most severe disabilities, the intent is to convince the reader that there is no student with disabilities that are so severe as to prevent meaningful participation in making the types of choices that will positively influence his or her life. Brown and Gothelf (1996) pointed out that there are many misconceptions and concerns about the application of self-determination processes to individuals with profound disabilities and/or challenging behavior, and they offered counterpoints to each misconception to dispel these unfounded beliefs (Table 1). All that is required is consideration of each person's abilities to determine how best to facilitate, support, and teach an individual how to become actively involved in his or her own life, and how to teach others to acknowledge the value of and encourage self-determination.

Table 1.   Misconceptions about self-determination

Myth	Counterpoint
Some individuals have disabilities that are too profound for them to be self-determining.	Research has shown that individuals with even the most profound disabilities have definite preferences and seek to control their environment.
The presence of disruptive behavior requires increased control of the individual, not self-determination.	Behavior problems are often a way of communicating protest about lack of control. Supporting the individual to have more control over his or her environment, rather than less, may serve to reduce some problem behaviors.
If given the opportunity to be self-determining, some individuals would make inappropriate choices or choose to do nothing.	All individuals, regardless of presence or level of disability, have the right to make "bad" decisions. If an individual frequently chooses to do nothing, ways of creating a more stimulating and personally meaningful environment should be explored.
Some individuals cannot be self-determining because they need a highly structured environment with planned and systematic instructional opportunities.	If extensive physical and cognitive support is needed across many areas of daily life, it should not be assumed that such assistance is also necessary for the individual to make decisions and take control over many elements of life.
Program standards and regulations concerning habilitation prohibit self-determination.	There are no regulations that prohibit individuals from taking control of their lives. Increasingly, regulations are requiring procedures that promote self-determination.

From Brown, F., & Gothelf, C.R. (1996). Self-determination for all individuals. In D.H. Lehr & F. Brown (Eds.), *People with disabilities who challenge the system* (p. 337). Baltimore: Paul H. Brookes Publishing Co.; reprinted by permission.

Understanding a person's disabilities is an important element, not for the purpose of judging or restricting an individual's participation, but to design an educationally effective strategy of support for the individual.

Because of the severity of some disabilities, the strategies that are developed to teach and support the development of self-determination and student involvement skills are often basic and concrete, even though the concept of self-determination is as complex as human behavior and far from concrete. Thus, educators or families are sometimes in the position of interpreting, guessing, or hypothesizing what the individual is attempting to communicate. However, the more skills the individual with disabilities has and the greater the expectations of the supporters, the more effective educators will be in facilitating self-determination and meaning in that individual's life.

PHILOSOPHICAL ASSUMPTIONS

> We can never improve our understanding unless we examine and reformulate our assumptions. (Douglas, cited in Johnson, Baumgart, Helmstetter, & Curry, 1996, p. 3)

Self-determination is one of the most important, and often one of the most difficult, areas of instruction for teachers of students with severe special education needs. In a field that has undergone nonstop transformations since the early 1970s, the question remains, How can we support the structures and skills that enable individuals with severe disabilities to achieve self-determination, cope with options and choices, and control their lives? The shift to instructional paradigms that emphasize autonomy, choice, and empowerment as opposed to obedience, compliance, and conformity represents one of the most radical and promising changes to date.

The following assumptions provide a philosophical foundation that enables us to stop thinking and teaching mechanistically and to stop acting as if a professionally structured system of control is a rational and just response to students with severe disabilities (Skrtic, 1991). The types of choices presented by much of the current methodology tend to give students choices that are extremely constrained or even illusory. The reengineering of curricula to support self-determination and student involvement is an approach that extends beyond the current strategies and methodologies by recognizing that if students are to learn how to choose, they must be presented with opportunities to make real and meaningful choices (Kohn, 1993; Mithaug, 1996; Schloss, Alper, & Jayne, 1993).

The goal of this chapter is to present implications of the research in ways that are beneficial and available to instructional staff and administrators of programs in which students with severe special education needs are included. This, in turn, should serve as the basis for promoting student involvement in all phases of the education process. Four philosophical assumptions are fundamental to those everyday instruction practices that support self-determination. The process of reviewing these axioms should aid the reader in clarifying his or her own personal assumptions as well as illuminating why certain strategies are recommended in the design of curriculum that supports active involvement.

Assumption 1

The development of communicative competence goes hand in hand with the development of self-determination (Williams, 1991). Individuals with severe disabilities may respond appropriately when others give them directives to follow, but they may also have significant difficulty in developing a conventional means by which to communicate their own needs and desires to others (Siegel-Causey & Downing, 1987). Ineffective communication often becomes apparent when the communication partner or the receiver of the intended message (e.g., teacher, parent, peer) does not respond appropriately to the individual's conveyance. Gothelf and Brown (1996) pointed out that continued unsuccessful attempts to send or transmit a message impede the development of the communication processes by which an individual exerts control over his or her situation.

Attention must be focused on the *beliefs, attitudes, responsiveness, flexibility*, and *motivation* of communication partners and not just the skills and deficits of the message sender (Johnson et al., 1996). Communication partners must recognize that behavior is simultaneously a bid for attention, a message that begs a response, an attempt to influence a situation, an expression of self-determination, and an acknowledgment that both partners share in the responsibility for the exchange.

Assumption 2

When self-determination is the focus of instruction, chances for students to use their own initiative, indicate choices, and influence daily routines are enhanced. Activities, objects, and people who spark an individual's interest, desire, or dislike represent natural opportunities for instructional staff to support students' self-determined actions and consequent involvement. Sometimes what appears to be a relatively minor feature of an instructional routine may present an opportunity for a student to influence what occurs (Brown, Belz, Corsi, & Wenig, 1993; Gothelf & Brown, 1996).

Assessment procedures must consider the environmental opportunities for self-determined behavior across the variety of daily experiences. Opportunities to support active student involvement and self-determination are available in all activities across the curriculum and should not be limited to isolated programs designed for the rehearsal of skills considered to be components of self-determination.

Assumption 3

Acts of self-determination must be consistently and enthusiastically reinforced. The pairing of specific behaviors with particular desired outcomes increases the probability that the behavior will be performed again when the individual finds him- or herself in a similar situation (Reichle, 1991). It is well established that contingent relationships between events and corresponding behaviors are naturally established and maintained in the context of daily routines (Reichle & Wacker, 1993; Skinner, 1957). For example, a student who pushes away materials when a teacher presents a nonpreferred activity may be communicating, "I don't like this activity, and I don't want to do this." Because the activity represents an individualized education program (IEP) objective, the teacher persists in his or her attempt to engage the student, and the student drops to the floor. The teacher attempts to get the student up from the floor, and the student runs out of the room. The student is corralled by the teacher and the assistant and escorted to the time-out room. When the student returns, the time scheduled for the nonpreferred activity has passed. In this scenario, the student has learned that inappropriate behavior resulted in successfully avoiding a task in which he did not want to participate.

Respecting a student's right to self-determination would result in radically different teacher behavior. For example, when the student pushed away the materials, the teacher could have paused and then modeled how to indicate, "I don't want to do this now" (e.g., point to communication board, sign), demonstrating that there are appropriate ways to avoid an activity. The student could then have put the materials away and chosen another preferred activity. The teacher would then reflect on and reevaluate the type of activities that are being presented to the student, explore more preferred means that could be used to teach the objective, or perhaps postpone teaching the objective.

Assumption 4

Because problem behaviors are effective in influencing what happens, they may be counted as acts or expressions of self-determination. Many programs continue to treat inappropriate behavior as random acts to be decelerated. However, Wehmeyer described self-determination as "the attitudes and abilities necessary to act as the causal agent in one's life" (1992, p. 305). Systems that respond to such expressions by attempting to enforce control (Figure 1) may, in fact, limit self-determination. Being responsive to the sometimes unconventional modes of communication used by students with severe disabilities and reflective in one's teaching practices (Schön, 1983) is the first step in supporting self-determined behavior in students.

Teaching functional communication skills is the essential component in reducing students' dependence on behavior problems as expressions of self-determination (Durand, 1990; Reichle & Wacker, 1993). Gothelf and Brown

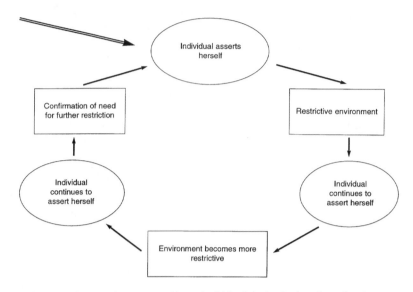

Figure 1.   Some systems respond to an individual's behavior by attempting to enforce control.

(1996) pointed out that the tools necessary to achieve communicative competence for self-determination and decrease behavior problems are 1) a vocabulary that corresponds to the individual's personal preferences and desires and 2) an appropriate mode of communicating through which this vocabulary can be effectively employed.

INCREASING STUDENT INVOLVEMENT

Recommended practices for educating individuals with severe disabilities suggest that systematic instructional technology is the methodology of choice (e.g., Cipani & Spooner, 1994; Snell & Brown, 1993). It thus becomes critical to consider the potential impact of these instruction strategies on the opportunity to develop and practice skills related to self-determination (Brown & Cohen, 1996) and to become involved in education programming. Because of severe levels of cognitive impairment and the possible presence of physical disabilities, many students require extensive and ongoing support to participate in daily activities and routines. To support attainment of functional goals and objectives, discrete and planned opportunities for practice are scheduled and systematic strategies are designed to teach the objectives. Furthermore, if the student displays any type of problem behavior, the teacher develops a support plan to address behavioral needs. At each level of support in this instructional and behavioral methodology comes the danger of inhibiting the development of self-determination and minimizing student involvement. At each level, the teacher has the opportunity to either support the student to be involved or prohibit such participation. The teacher must be challenged to provide the necessary support to the student to acquire functional skills and participate as independently and competently as possible while respecting the student's right to control the direction of daily events and situations.

Scheduling Instructional Activities

Brown and Gothelf (1996) noted that self-determination is demonstrated when an individual recognizes his or her own choices and preferences, effectively communicates them, and takes charge of obtaining them. The degree and quality of the acts of self-determination are governed, in part, by the opportunities available in the setting and by what is permitted, prohibited, or encouraged within each environment. This section identifies ways to begin to actively shape and restructure fundamental features of the teaching and learning environment so that students with severe disabilities have opportunities to learn to make good choices and express them effectively.

Most teaching and learning environments have some structural framework in the form of a schedule. Schedules provide teachers and staff with the means to know where they are supposed to be at a certain time and provide administrators with a mechanism for accountability (e.g., ensuring that Johnny gets his mandated speech therapy three times per week). For students, schedules can add to the predictability and security of the environment (Devault, Turnbull, & Horner, 1994). However, schedules can also restrict the freedom of students with respect to what they do; when they do it; for how long they do it; with whom they do it; and, in the most restrictive interpretation, how they do it (Bannerman, Sheldon, Sherman, & Harchik, 1990; Brown et al., 1993; Brown & Gothelf, 1996).

To foster self-determination, emphasis must be placed on developing structures that do not give administrators, teachers, and staff all the responsibility and authority (and hence students have none) for determining when, with whom, and where activities and events will occur (Abery & Zajac, 1996; Brown, 1991). Emphasis must be placed on restructuring the practice of the classroom schedule so that it is a source of motivation for students with severe disabilities, providing meaningful opportunities for them to develop control over their daily activities.

The schedule must be reinvented to structure routines to promote choice making, and it must be reconceptualized so that it is flexible and supports the recognition of naturally occurring opportunities for choice making. The value of communicating one's choice and having it respected is essential for the development of a student's capacity for self-initiated and self-directed learning (see Chapters 16 and 17), skill building, and experiencing the consequences of one's decisions (Gothelf & Brown, 1996; Hanline & Fox, 1993; Kohn, 1993).

The quality of an individual's life may be judged by the frequency with which the individual has the chance to exercise his or her own initiative and make choices as a matter of routine (Gothelf, Crimmins, Mercer, & Finocchiaro, 1994). Maccoby (1984) pointed out that as children mature, they begin to share moment-to-moment control of events with adults; a process described as *coregulation* (Abery & Zajac, 1996). Students wield primary control over events while adults support students' choices and facilitate, monitor, and endorse students from a distance. Teachers are compelled by their own sense of values, the process of implementing age-appropriate curriculum, and intervention research to fundamentally restructure the way in which they use classroom schedules to support the development of self-determination in students with disabilities.

Enhancing Choice-Making Skills   Educators are faced with the paradox of how to build predictability and security into the environment through the use of a consistent schedule while promoting the development of a flexible milieu with opportunities for choice. In other words, how can the environment be organized in a way that gives students a sense of control and pleasure and also supports active student involvement?

In 1993, Brown et al. developed a procedure for uncovering the many unseen opportunities to make relevant choices within the context of one's daily routine (see also Gothelf & Brown, 1996). In this model, individuals typically have an array of choices concurrently available within the context of most activities and routines. The model is used to help us discover the diverse range of unnoticed choices that are available in the natural course of the day, such as

- Choosing within an activity (e.g., choosing between a muffin and toast for breakfast)
- Choosing between two or more activities (e.g., choosing to go to computer class or to help clean the classroom)
- Choosing when or where to do an activity (e.g., exercise either in the morning or after lunch, in the gym or outside in the schoolyard)
- Selecting the individual with whom to participate in an activity (e.g., choosing to go to the copy center with Andrew, not with Ian)
- Refusing to participate in a planned activity
- Choosing to terminate an activity at a self-selected time

This model can also be used to evaluate a student's current level of choice making. This allows one to focus on specific kinds of choices that are not being made and then to judge whether a student is being encouraged and instructed to expand his or her ability to make a range of diverse choices.

As we search for ways to increase an individual's ability to wield control over his or her environment, let us look at an application of this functional procedure. For example, during the scheduled time for his school-based work program, Billy, a 15-year-old student with severe disabilities, is given the opportunity to choose between two activities—recycling cans or setting out condiments in the cafeteria. He could choose when to do these jobs (it is possible to recycle cans in the afternoon as well as in the morning), choose with whom he will do these jobs (he could choose peers and/or staff to do it with him), refuse to do one or both of the jobs, or partially complete the can-recycling chore and terminate the cafeteria job at a self-selected time.

Using this choice assessment procedure to determine the range of choices that Billy makes, we learn that Billy always works alone and that he completes both jobs, one right after the other. One way of looking at him is to say that Billy is a model employee, so "if it's not broken, don't fix it." However, we know the value of being able to appropriately terminate an activity (instead of using inappropriate behavior to terminate the activity), to expand one's social circles, and to schedule the events in one's life to vary the routine (Brown, 1991; Crimmins & Berotti, 1996). We can use this situation to teach Billy choice-making skills that he does not demonstrate by embedding these fundamental skills (i.e., to terminate the activity, to choose with whom he would like to work, to choose when he wants to do an activity) in a routine that Billy enjoys and in which he is competent. Once he has learned these new choice-making skills, he can make an "informed choice" that he does indeed want to work alone. Skill building through elaborating functional routines related to preferred activities provides students who have severe disabilities with a variety of appropriate means to control their environment and increased opportunities for student involvement.

Flexible Scheduling: Responding to Student Expressions of Self-Determination   Taking student involvement and self-determination seriously requires a further examination of the controlling nature of schedules. By their very nature, the context of a static schedule that supports the teacher's control and authority over what students do throughout the day does not have sufficient flexibility to allow instructional staff to be responsive to students' communications of choice frequently enough to stimulate the development of self-determination (Abery & Zajac, 1996; Gothelf & Brown, 1996; Kohn, 1993). Flexible classroom management strategies based on developing and maintaining teacher–student relationships through reciprocal interaction and shared control promote self-determination. Fellowship of this nature provides students with ongoing opportunities for their communications to be heard and, in turn, to influence the environment.

There is an important relationship among schedules, functional communication, and self-determination. Calculator and Jorgensen stated that "in order to be functional, language must influence others' behavior and bring about effects that are appropriate and natural in a given social context" (1991, p. 204). According to Rowland and Schweigert, functional communication 1) occurs in the natural course of events throughout the day; 2) results in real consequences in that the communication prompts or elicits a response from the listener in accordance with its intent; and 3) is spontaneous—that is, "communication skills are not functional if the communicator is incapable of using them except when prompted to do so" (1993, p. 161).

Rowland (1990) demonstrated that students with severe disabilities have few opportunities to communicate and do so infrequently. Gothelf and Brown (1996) added that individuals with severe disabilities may not be able to communicate their desires or choices clearly or appropriately, even when provided with opportunities to do so. These individuals may, in fact, use idiosyncratic, inconsistent, or self-selected modes to communicate (e.g., actions, vocalizations, gestures) that may be ineffective, problematic, and/or disruptive. Halle (1987) pointed out that spontaneity is the most significant function of language because spontaneous communication is the means by which individuals transmit messages to appropriately exert control over what is happening to them. Therefore, it becomes essential that these individuals be provided with the opportunities, training, and support necessary for them to develop the ability to effectively and appropriately communicate personal choice so that they can begin to exert control over their lives, including their school lives.

When student involvement and self-determination are the foci of instruction, opportunities for individuals with severe disabilities to exercise their own initiative, indicate choices, and shape their daily routines are revealed (Gothelf & Brown, 1996; Siegel-Causey & Ernst, 1989). Objects, people, and activities that are reflected in students' daily schedules and that spark their interests, desires, dislikes, or avoidance represent natural opportunities for students to learn to spontaneously, effectively, and appropriately communicate their needs and wants as expressions of self-determination.

According to Rowland and Schweigert, "the ideal communicative interaction is an entirely natural one that is prompted by the demands of the moment" (1993, p. 173), as well as being one that has real consequences in that the interaction influences the environment, "which, in turn, responds in accordance with the intent of the communication" (p. 161). Teachers must balance the need to follow scheduled instruction with the need to respond positively and appropriately to the intent of a student's communication and to focus on supporting self-determination.

Systematic Instruction

Educators know that "students with severe disabilities often learn skills and grasp concepts more slowly than do their peers, forget their learning more quickly, and are less likely to generalize their learning from one situation to the next" (Snell & Brown, 1993, p. 99). We have learned a great deal about how to teach students with these challenges and have developed a variety of instruction strategies that have been demonstrated to be effective in promoting the learning of functional skills. These strategies require the teacher to task analyze activities into small steps and to provide various levels of verbal and physical prompting. These same strategies that are so effective in helping students acquire skills must be carefully analyzed to ensure that each student's right to be self-determining is not compromised.

Task Analysis   A *task analysis* is the process of breaking down a complex behavior, skill, or activity into its component parts. In this process, a teacher identifies those components that he or she feels are critical for the individual to perform to participate in that activity or routine. Traditionally, task analyses are conducted by observing the individual steps that are physically required to complete performance of the activity. These steps are then used to determine how the student will participate in the activity and to evaluate progress on the skill. Although this widespread methodology can be effective in teaching concrete participation in an activity, there has been much criticism.

Neel and Billingsley (1989) discussed the need for routines and activities to begin with a natural cue for the skill, to end with a behavior that elicits a natural reinforcer, and to accomplish some function. For example, dirty hands serve as the student's natural cue for washing his or her hands. Having a teacher give a verbal or signed cue ("wash hands") is not a natural cue. If the student learns to respond to the natural cue, the student is more likely to gain independence in the future and make informed decisions about when he or she should wash his or her hands, thus promoting self-determination. Continued dependence on a verbal cue from the teacher is not likely to lead to independence but rather fosters continued reliance on others (Snell & Brown, 1993).

Brown and colleagues (Brown, Evans, Weed, & Owen, 1987; Brown & Lehr, 1993; Gothelf & Brown, 1996) pointed out that when task analyses are lists of motor skills, students with severe and multiple disabilities have little opportunity for meaningful participation and control of the activity. For students with severe physical disabilities, partial participation in motor skills often results in meaningless participation (e.g., brushing the left side of one's hair). Brown et al. (1987) suggested that task analysis should not focus solely on motor skills but should include components that allow the student to have control of the activity. This becomes a critical issue for individuals who must frequently rely on others to accomplish the function of the routines in which they participate (e.g., eating, dressing, showering, moving about). For example, a student who only partially participates in the motor elements of eating a snack can participate in that activity in other ways that are more meaningful to him or her and that provide him or her with control over the activity even if he or she cannot physically perform most of the skill. He or she can *initiate* (e.g., pointing on his or her communication board that he or she is hungry), *choose* (e.g., what type of snack he or she would like to eat), *monitor quality* (e.g., indicate that he or she likes his or her yogurt stirred), *problem solve* (e.g., let the teacher know that he or she is uncomfortable in his or her wheelchair), and *terminate* (e.g., let the person who is helping him or her eat know that he or she does not want any more). These forms of participation allow the student meaningful control over an activity in which he or she had participated mostly with full physical assistance from a teacher.

Prompting   Students with severe and multiple disabilities frequently rely on others to participate in activities. Snell and Brown (1993) pointed out that the extensive reliance on physical prompting and manipulation that is used to facilitate participation in instructional activities is likely to foster excessive dependence on teachers and others who support the student. Although this level of physical prompting can be decreased to some extent, the focus on participation in the motor components of activities perpetuates this problem. Brown and Cohen (1996) found that many IEP objectives of young children with severe disabilities include partial and physical prompts. Although physical prompting may be necessary to achieve independence for some individuals, the virtually exclusive identification of objectives that involve prompted behavior is questionable (Brown & Gothelf, 1996). Certainly a different quality of goal and objective must be designed to allow the student some level of independent achievement.

Behavioral Support

Behavior problems are socially distancing, often resulting in increased isolation of the student and limited access to options that define effective education and quality lifestyles (Gothelf & Mercer, 1996). There has been much controversy about the provision of behavioral supports for individuals with severe disabilities. Historically, behavioral approaches used with students with severe disabilities and challenging behavior relied heavily on such strategies as time-out, extinction, overcorrection, and response cost (Brown & Cohen, 1996; Brown & Gothelf, 1996). These types of behavioral procedures that could be considered intrusive or aversive are contrasted with procedures that use positive strategies.

Methods that were considered intrusive often focused on the reduction of the problem behavior, with behavior support and analysis focusing on manipulation of both negative (e.g., time-out, overcorrection, response cost) and positive (e.g., increase schedule of reinforcement, change reinforcer) consequences. Positive supports, however, have led us away from reliance on such strategies and placed greater emphasis on how antecedent events and lifestyle variables contribute to the development of problem behaviors (Brown & Cohen, 1996; Brown & Gothelf, 1996). Koegel, Koegel, and Dunlap described positive behavioral supports as methods that would be effective in "changing undesirable patterns of behavior; [would be] respectful of a person's dignity; and [would be] successful in promoting a person's capabilities, expanding a person's opportunities, and enhancing the quality of a person's lifestyle" (1996, p. xiii). Furthermore, the foundations of positive supports are based on "a grounding in person-centered values; a commitment to outcomes that are meaningful from the perspective of a person's preferred lifestyle" (Koegel et al., 1996, p. xiii). Thus, positive behavior supports focus on dimensions that are attributed to the development of self-determination and that have an impact on the assessment, intervention, and evaluation phases of behavior change.

Assessment   The process of functional assessment helps the educator to determine the variables that may be associated with problem behavior, to identify the function of the problem behavior, and to examine the consequences of the behavior that may be contributing to its maintenance. This process guides us to examine a range of possible variables that may contribute to the presence of the problem behavior. Many of these variables are related to the individual's lifestyle and lead to an examination of issues related to self-determination (Brown, 1996). For example, are problem behaviors found to be associated with the student's mandated participation in activities that he or she finds boring, meaningless, or difficult? Is the student prevented from doing a preferred activity? Does the student determine the activities in which he or she participates, or the order in which they will occur? Does the teacher respect the student's efforts to end a task at a self-selected time, or does the teacher require the student to work on the task regardless of the student's request?

Intervention   An effective intervention plan is based on the results of functional assessment and typically includes multiple components (Lucyshyn, Horner, & Ben, 1996). It is no longer acceptable to design a behavior support plan that merely focuses on reinforcing appropriate behavior and extinguishing the problem behavior. Based on results of the functional assessment, the support plan must include variables related to changing an individual's lifestyle, arranging the environment to allow the student more control of daily events, and teaching the individual skills that would support this growing control over daily and long-term events.

In school settings, changes are often needed in the curriculum. Many researchers have demonstrated that greater student choice in the selection of learning activities may foster characteristics such as initiative, independence, decision-making ability, and a sense of control over one's environment (Dyer, Dunlap, & Winterling, 1990; Meyer & Evans, 1989; Munk & Repp, 1994). For example, students can participate in the development of daily schedules of school activities, curriculum changes can be made to present materials that are of great interest to the student and of the appropriate difficulty level, and a student's desire to spend 15 minutes rather than 30 minutes working in his or her seat can be respected (see Chapters 16 and 17 for additional strategies).

Evaluation of Outcomes   Professionals are now increasingly looking at qualitative outcomes of behavior change rather than at narrow quantitative measures of a single target behavior (e.g., instances of noncompliance, rate of self-injury, frequency of aggression) (Haring & Breen, 1989; Meyer & Evans, 1993; Meyer & Janney, 1989). The literature is replete with examples of how severe problem behaviors have been reduced. Meyer and Evans pointed out that clear and objective descriptions of behavior in precisely measurable terms very often led to reports of what could be characterized as trivial outcomes. In order to specify behavior change in objective terms that could be reliably monitored by observers, researchers have often been reduced to reporting relatively minor motor topographies of behavior such as hand movements to head. (1993, p. 409)

Changes in problem behaviors are obviously of great significance. A person who was hurting him- or herself or others, and no longer does, has indeed progressed. Family members, neighbors, and educators would all celebrate this outcome. However, it cannot be assumed that just because the problem behavior has been reduced that collateral changes in the individual's life are improved.

Researchers continue to discover that the quality of a person's life and lack of control may be a major contributor to the problem behavior. Thus, reducing the problem behavior without changing the quality of life makes maintenance of behavior change difficult if not impossible. Meyer and Evans (1993) described a broader set of outcome criteria for judging behavioral intervention outcomes. Included in their delineation of successful outcomes are those related to self-determination and quality of life—acquisition of general self-control strategies to support generalized and durable behavior change; less restrictive placements and greater participation in integrated school experiences; subjective quality-of-life improvements, such as happiness, satisfaction, choices, and control; improvements perceived by teachers, family, and significant others; and expanded social relationships and informal support networks.

For example, Jonathan is a young man who lived at a facility where he received contingent electric shock for the self-injurious behavior of scratching himself. He wore a shock device 24 hours per day at his school program and in his group home. After he had received many thousands of shocks, his self-injurious behavior was significantly reduced, although not entirely. Using only reduction of the problem behavior as a measure of success, it could be concluded that the strategy, although aversive, was effective for Jonathan. However, the following list demonstrates that the outcomes of this program were far from effective:

- Wearing a shock device 24 hours per day
- Inability to self-manage behavior without shock device
- Living in a group home with other individuals who have severe behavior problems
- Having no control over daily activities
- Going to school with only individuals who have severe problem behaviors
- Limited social interaction with individuals without disabilities
- Limited social interaction with nonpaid individuals
- Reports of being unhappy
- No control over future place of residence

- No control of future vocation
- Living far from family

Broader outcomes that reflect quality of life and self-determination and are based on principles of active involvement must be identified for each individual to help determine if indeed behavioral interventions are effective.

ENABLING SYSTEMS TO SUPPORT STUDENT INVOLVEMENT

Despite the fact that self-determination is a concept that has come of age, it will not magically become part of the pedagogy simply because everyone agrees that it is a good idea. Although it may be ingrained in people's consciousness and codified in law, there is still a gap between the acceptance of the concept and its implementation in schools and service systems. The execution of this concept requires that service providers "walk the walk" by modifying their practices on a daily basis through the process of organizational restructuring and not just "talk the talk" of choice and empowerment.

Implementing self-determination to achieve student involvement cannot be done simply by adding it to the traditional service paradigm through the regulatory process or by writing a few more chapters in curriculum planning guides. It requires a complete restructuring of service delivery systems because it changes the whole notion of who is in control.

A system focused on student involvement and self-determination differs from the traditional model in several fundamental ways (see also Chapter 1). The traditional model is hierarchical and impersonal, with decision making flowing downward from a central bureaucracy with no participation by citizens (Van de Ven, 1980). The new model is more relational and individualized, with decision making being shared among those people who are involved with and affected by the outcome of the process: teachers; service providers; family; and, most important, the individuals themselves (Mount, 1988).

The prescript of shared decision making is a marker of school restructuring and is tied to research on effective schools (Barrett, 1991; Field & Hoffman, 1996; Sailor, Gee, & Karasoff, 1993). The process of teacher empowerment in school governance results in the people who are directly involved with students having decision-making authority and the autonomy needed to implement school programs. To improve the prospects for self-determination in students and the potential for student involvement, the practices of shared responsibility for planning and decision making must be reflected in the organization of a school as a whole. Whether focused on youth or on adults, empowerment and autonomy undergird all efforts to promote self-determination (Sands & Wehmeyer, 1996).

Bradley pointed out that "organizations don't like to change and will fend off change in subtle and not so subtle ways in order to maintain equilibrium and the status quo" (1997, p. 7). For organizations to promote self-determination, they must demonstrate a steadfast resolution to change on all levels and a commitment to reinvent themselves. They must establish organizational policy and patterns of support that give staff and consumers the knowledge and the influence that enable them to determine their own paths and outcomes (Mount, 1988; Shumway & Nerney, 1996).

Organizational change in support of individualized, self-determined paths begins with the assumption that people with disabilities (and their families and friends) are competent and committed and should be key players in determining the shape and processes of education and related services and not just act as passive recipients of someone else's bright ideas (Glatthorn, 1992). Self-determination is a principle that can provide a foundation for school improvement, IEPs, and curriculum development (Field & Hoffman, 1996). Following are five supportive elements in recognition of the difficult job faced by those consumers, professionals, and organizations determined to reinvent themselves and to lay the groundwork for restructuring services to support self-determination throughout the system.

1. Administrative support   Administrators must continually support self-determination for teachers and staff as well as for students. Unempowered staff are in no position to support the empowerment of their students. Decision making must be relational and participatory, not hierarchical and unilateral. Rules should be viewed critically and challenged as part of a comprehensive plan to restructure classrooms in support of self-determination (Gothelf & Mercer, 1996). Implementing these supportive elements is a complex undertaking that takes time. "Changing a schedule will take a few weeks, changing the culture will require years" (Glatthorn, 1992, p. 160).

2. Teacher and staff empowerment   Providing teachers and staff with meaningful autonomy about the curriculum of their class and supporting their involvement in decision making and school management empowers them. Teachers cannot support the development of self-determination in their students if they are confronted by education policies based on schoolwide prescriptions and dependent on universal compliance. Self-determination for students begins by empowering teachers and staff. Teachers can develop individualized curricula because they have flexibility and access to resources. The content of the curriculum is based on the individualized goals and education outcomes necessary for living independently, developing personal and social relationships, and obtaining a job in the community (Sage & Burrello, 1994).

3. School-level collaboration   Collaboration is directed toward supporting students to achieve meaningful outcomes through the development and practice of self-determination. Administrators, teachers, students, and parents work together collaboratively to achieve the goals of the organization. A spirit of cooperation pervades the classroom, the school organization, and home–school relationships. Power is shared with all those involved, within the limits of each person's maturity. All those affected by decisions have a voice in making those decisions (Glatthorn, 1992).

4. *Collegial relationships*   Adult learning becomes energized when there is a schoolwide commitment to increasing the capacity of staff to respond to the unique expressions of self-determination of all students. Teachers become informed and aware of the specific skills and behaviors that are necessary for self-determination in an environment that promotes the development of supportive relationships among colleagues and peers. In such a collegial environment, school staff members talk about practice regularly; observe each other in the practice of teaching and in the administration of learning settings; actively engage in planning and designing curriculum, structures, processes, and systems that they will implement according to the evolving needs of their students; and are always teaching each other what they know about teaching, learning, and leading (Sage & Burrello, 1994).

5. *Team-building and problem-solving structures*   The practice of self-determination is supported by having systems in place for collaborative problem solving. Teams adopt a problem-solving approach and regularly meet and reflect on the outcomes and instructional practice. All participants share in generating solutions and responses, building consensus, and ensuring that minority views are heard. Teams plan staff development as their needs for information, reflection, and evaluation emerge (Sage & Burrello, 1994).

These five elements of school restructuring are in harmony with the concept of self-determination and "take into account the perceptions, needs, and concerns of individuals within [the school] and provide for a large degree of control by those who will be . . . affected by the decisions that are made" (Field & Hoffman, 1996, p. 198). They provide the architecture for the self-determination of a school as a whole.

CONCLUSIONS

The question with which this chapter begins is, How can we support the structures and skills that enable individuals with severe disabilities to achieve self-determination, cope with options and choices, and control their lives? Asking this question is also a fitting way to end the chapter. It is a question on which all educators and administrators should focus, because it serves to keep us on track.

This chapter has outlined some core education practices that the authors believe support self-determination in students with severe disabilities through their participation in the education process. The focus has not been on fixing students so that they fit in or on sanctioning exclusion if they do not, but rather on prioritizing classroom and administrative strategies to reflect the value of self-determination and on the organization necessary to provide teachers and administrators with the opportunity and structure to find broader insight. This chapter concludes with one last thought—the capacity to question one's long-standing way of thinking and acting (and to reconsider one's approach to teaching students with severe disabilities and directing education programs) belongs at the top of any good teacher's or administrator's list of priorities.

REFERENCES

Abery, B.H. (1994). A conceptual framework for enhancing self-determination. In M.F. Hayden & B.H. Abery (Eds.), *Challenges for a service system in transition: Ensuring quality community experiences for persons with developmental disabilities* (pp. 345–380). Baltimore: Paul H. Brookes Publishing Co.

Abery, B.H., & Zajac, R. (1996). Self-determination as a goal of early childhood and elementary education. In D.J. Sands & M.L. Wehmeyer (Eds.), *Self-determination across the life span: Independence and choice for people with disabilities* (pp. 169–196). Baltimore: Paul H. Brookes Publishing Co.

Bannerman, D.J., Sheldon, J.B., Sherman, J.A., & Harchik, A.E. (1990). Balancing the right to habilitation with the right to personal liberties: The right of people with developmental disabilities to eat too many donuts and take a nap. *Journal of Applied Behavior Analysis, 23,* 79–89.

Barrett, P.A. (Ed.). (1991). *Doubts and certainties: Working together to restructure schools.* Washington, DC: National Education Association.

Bradley, V.J. (1994). Evolution of a new service paradigm. In V.J. Bradley, J.W. Ashbaugh, & B.C. Blaney (Eds.), *Creating individual supports for people with developmental disabilities: A mandate for change at many levels* (pp. 11–32). Baltimore: Paul H. Brookes Publishing Co.

Bradley, V.J. (1997). Implementing person-centered approaches: Now the hard part. *Spotlight, 2*(1), 7.

Brown, F. (1991). Creative daily scheduling: A non-intrusive approach to challenging behaviors in community residences. *Journal of The Association for Persons with Severe Handicaps, 16,* 75–84.

Brown, F. (1996). Variables to consider in the assessment of problem behaviors. *TASH Newsletter, 22*(7), 20–21.

Brown, F., Belz, P., Corsi, L., & Wenig, B. (1993). Choice diversity for people with severe disabilities. *Education and Training in Mental Retardation, 28,* 318–326.

Brown, F., & Cohen, S. (1996). Self-determination and young children. *Journal of The Association for Persons with Severe Handicaps, 21,* 22–30.

Brown, F., Evans, I.M., Weed, K.A., & Owen, V. (1987). Delineating functional competencies: A component model. *Journal of The Association for Persons with Severe Handicaps, 12,* 117–124.

Brown, F., & Gothelf, C.R. (1996). Self-determination for all individuals. In D.H. Lehr & F. Brown (Eds.), *People with disabilities who challenge the system* (pp. 335–353). Baltimore: Paul H. Brookes Publishing Co.

Brown, F., & Lehr, D. (1993). Making activities meaningful for students with severe multiple disabilities. *Teaching Exceptional Children, 25,* 12–16.

Brown, F., & Snell, M.E. (1993). Meaningful assessment. In M.E. Snell (Ed.), *Instruction of students with severe disabilities* (4th ed., pp. 61–98). New York: Merrill Education.

Calculator, S.N., & Jorgensen, C.M. (1991). Integrating augmentative communication instruction into regular education settings: Expounding on best practices. *Augmentative and Alternative Communication, 7,* 204–214.

Cipani, E., & Spooner, F. (1994). *Curricular and instructional approaches for persons with severe disabilities.* Needham Heights, MA: Allyn & Bacon.

Crimmins, D.B., & Berotti, D. (1996). Supporting increased self-determination for individuals with challenging behaviors. In D.H. Lehr & F. Brown (Eds.), *People with disabilities who challenge the system* (pp. 379–402). Baltimore: Paul H. Brookes Publishing Co.

Devault, G., Turnbull, A., & Horner, R. (1994). *Why does Samantha act like that? A positive behavior support story of one family's success.* Lawrence, KS: Beach Center on Families and Disability.

Doll, B., Sands, D.J., Wehmeyer, M.L., & Palmer, S. (1996). Promoting the development and acquisition of self-determined behavior. In D.J. Sands & M.L. Wehmeyer (Eds.), *Self-determination across the life span: Independence and choice for people with disabilities* (pp. 65–90). Baltimore: Paul H. Brookes Publishing Co.

Durand, V.M. (1990). *Severe behavior problems: A functional communication training approach.* New York: Guilford Press.

Dyer, K., Dunlap, G., & Winterling, V. (1990). Effects of choice-making on the serious problem behaviors of students with severe handicaps. *Journal of Applied Behavior Analysis, 23,* 515–524.

Field, S., & Hoffman, A. (1996). Promoting self-determination in school reform, individualized planning, and curriculum efforts. In D.J. Sands & M.L. Wehmeyer (Eds.), *Self-determination across the life span: Independence and choice for people with disabilities* (pp. 197–213). Baltimore: Paul H. Brookes Publishing Co.

Glatthorn, A.A. (1992). *Teachers as agents of change: A new look at school improvement.* Washington, DC: National Education Association.

Gothelf, C.R., & Brown, F. (1996). Instructional support for self-determination in individuals with profound disabilities who are deaf-blind. In D.H. Lehr & F. Brown (Eds.), *People with disabilities who challenge the system* (pp. 355–377). Baltimore: Paul H. Brookes Publishing Co.

Gothelf, C.R., Crimmins, D.B., Mercer, C.A., & Finocchiaro, P.A. (1994). Teaching choice-making skills to students who are deaf-blind. *Teaching Exceptional Children, 26,* 13–15.

Gothelf, C.R., & Mercer, C.A. (1996). Preventing behavior problems: A problem-solving approach to restructuring classrooms. *TASH Newsletter, 22*(7), 22–23.

Halle, J. (1987). Teaching language in the natural environment: An analysis of spontaneity. *Journal of The Association for Persons with Severe Handicaps, 12,* 28–37.

Hanline, M.F., & Fox, L. (1993). Learning within the context of play: Providing typical early childhood experiences for children with severe disabilities. *Journal of The Association for Persons with Severe Handicaps, 18,* 121–129.

Haring, T.G., & Breen, C. (1989). Units of analysis of social interaction outcomes in supported education. *Journal of The Association for Persons with Severe Handicaps, 14,* 255–262.

Heber, R.F. (1959). A manual on terminology and classification in mental retardation. *American Journal of Mental Deficiency Monograph Supplement, 64*(2).

Heward, W.L., & Orlansky, M.D. (1992). *Exceptional children: An introductory survey of special education.* New York: Merrill Education.

Johnson, J.M., Baumgart, D., Helmstetter, E., & Curry, C.A. (1996). *Augmenting basic communication in natural contexts.* Baltimore: Paul H. Brookes Publishing Co.

Koegel, L.K., Koegel, R.L., & Dunlap, G. (Eds.). (1996). *Positive behavioral support: Including people with difficult behavior in the community.* Baltimore: Paul H. Brookes Publishing Co.

Kohn, A. (1993). *Punished by rewards: The trouble with gold stars, incentive plans, A's, praise and other bribes.* Boston: Houghton Mifflin.

Luckasson, R., Coulter, D.L., Polloway, E.A., Reiss, S., Schalock, R.L., Snell, M.E., Spitalnik, D.M., & Stark, J.A. (1992). *Mental retardation: Definition, classification, and systems of supports* (9th ed.). Washington, DC: American Association on Mental Retardation.

Lucyshyn, J.M., Horner, R.H., & Ben, K.R. (1996). Positive behavioral support with families. *TASH Newsletter, 22*(7), 31–33.

Maccoby, E.E. (1984). Middle childhood in the context of the family. In W.A. Collins (Ed.), *Development during middle childhood: The years from six to twelve* (pp. 184–239). Washington, DC: National Academy Press.

Meyer, L.H., & Evans, I.M. (1989). *Nonaversive intervention for behavior problems: A manual for home and community.* Baltimore: Paul H. Brookes Publishing Co.

Meyer, L.H., & Evans, I.M. (1993). Meaningful outcomes in behavioral intervention: Evaluating positive approaches to the remediation of challenging behaviors. In J. Reichle & D.P. Wacker (Eds.), *Communication and language intervention series: Vol. 3. Communicative alternatives to challenging behavior: Integrating functional assessment and intervention strategies* (pp. 407–428). Baltimore: Paul H. Brookes Publishing Co.

Meyer, L.H., & Janney, R. (1989). User-friendly measures of meaningful outcomes: Evaluating behavioral interventions. *Journal of The Association for Persons with Severe Handicaps, 14,* 263–270.

Meyer, L.H., Peck, C.A., & Brown, L. (Eds.). (1991). *Critical issues in the lives of people with severe disabilities.* Baltimore: Paul H. Brookes Publishing Co.

Mithaug, D.E. (1996). The optimal prospects principal: A theoretical basis for rethinking instructional practices for self-determination. In D.J. Sands & M.L. Wehmeyer (Eds.), *Self-determination across the life span: Independence and choice for people with disabilities* (pp. 147–165). Baltimore: Paul H. Brookes Publishing Co.

Mount, B. (1988). *Interactive planning: New tools for collaborative planning in complex environments.* New York: Graphic Futures.

Munk, D.D., & Repp, A.C. (1994). The relationship between instructional variables and problem behavior: A review. *Exceptional Children, 60,* 390–401.

Neel, R.S., & Billingsley, F.F. (1989). *IMPACT: A functional curriculum handbook for students with moderate to severe disabilities.* Baltimore: Paul H. Brookes Publishing Co.

Reichle, J. (1991). Describing initial communicative intents. In J. Reichle, J. York, & J. Sigafoos, *Implementing augmentative and alternative communication: Strategies for learners with severe disabilities* (pp. 71–88). Baltimore: Paul H. Brookes Publishing Co.

Reichle, J., & Wacker, D.P. (Eds.). (1993). *Communication and language intervention series: Vol. 3. Communicative alternatives to challenging behavior: Integrating functional assessment and intervention strategies.* Baltimore: Paul H. Brookes Publishing Co.

Rowland, C. (1990). Communication in the classroom for children with dual sensory impairments: Studies of teacher and child behavior. *Augmentative and Alternative Communication, 6,* 262–274.

Rowland, C., & Schweigert, P. (1993). Analyzing the communication environment to increase functional communication. *Journal of The Association for Persons with Severe Handicaps, 18,* 161–177.

Sage, D.D., & Burrello, L.C. (1994). *Leadership in educational reform: An administrator's guide to changes in special education.* Baltimore: Paul H. Brookes Publishing Co.

Sailor, W., Gee, K., & Karasoff, P. (1993). Full inclusion and school restructuring. In M.E. Snell (Ed.), *Instruction of students with severe disabilities* (4th ed., pp. 1–30). New York: Merrill Education.

Sands, D.J., & Wehmeyer, M.L. (1996). Future directions in self-determination: Articulating values and policies, reorganizing organizational structures, and implementing professional practices. In D.J. Sands & M.L. Wehmeyer (Eds.), *Self-determination across the life span: Independence and choice for people with disabilities* (pp. 331–334). Baltimore: Paul H. Brookes Publishing Co.

Schön, D.A. (1983). *The reflective practitioner: How professionals think in action.* New York: Basic Books.

Schloss, P.J., Alper, S., & Jayne, D. (1993). Self-determination for persons with disabilities: Choice, risk, and dignity. *Exceptional Children, 60,* 215–225.

Shumway, D.J., & Nerney, T. (1996). Pursuing self-determination. *Exceptional Parent, 26,* 22–27.

Siegel-Causey, E., & Downing, J. (1987). Nonsymbolic communication development: Theoretical concepts and educational strategies. In L. Goetz, D. Guess, & K. Stremel-Campbell (Eds.), *Innovative program design for individuals with dual sensory impairments* (pp. 15–48). Baltimore: Paul H. Brookes Publishing Co.

Siegel-Causey, E., & Ernst, B. (1989). Theoretical orientation and research in nonsymbolic development. In E. Siegel-Causey & D. Guess (Eds.), *Enhancing nonsymbolic communication interactions among learners with severe disabilities* (pp. 15–51). Baltimore: Paul H. Brookes Publishing Co.

Skinner, B.F. (1957). *Verbal behavior.* New York: Appleton-Century-Crofts.

Skrtic, T.M. (1991). *Behind special education: A critical analysis of professional culture and school organization.* Denver: Love Publishing Co.

Snell, M.E., & Brown, F. (1993). Instructional planning and implementation. In M.E. Snell (Ed.), *Instruction of students with severe disabilities* (4th ed., pp. 99–151). New York: Merrill Education.

Van de Ven, A.H. (1980). Problem solving, planning and innovation: Part II. Speculations for theory and practice. *Human Relations, 33,* 757–779.

Wehmeyer, M.L. (1992). Self-determination and the education of students with mental retardation. *Education and Training in Mental Retardation, 27,* 302–314.

Wehmeyer, M.L. (1996). Self-determination as an educational outcome: Why is it important to children, youth, and adults with disabilities? In D.J. Sands & M.L. Wehmeyer (Eds.), *Self-determination across the life span: Independence and choice for people with disabilities* (pp. 17–36). Baltimore: Paul H. Brookes Publishing Co.

Williams, R. (1991). Choices, communication, and control: A call for expanding them in the lives of people with severe disabilities. In L.H. Meyer, C.A. Peck, & L. Brown (Eds.), *Critical issues in the lives of people with severe disabilities* (pp. 543–544). Baltimore: Paul H. Brookes Publishing Co.

The View from
the Student's Side of the Table

Cecelia Ann Pauley

I love Trinity College. I make all my own decisions. I also made the decision to come here. I feel great when I can decide what happens to me. It was not always that way.

When I was in elementary school, they did not invite me to my individualized education program (IEP) meetings. They discussed my program for the next year with my parents and then told me what to do. I did not like it. I felt like I was not important. I also had no interest in school. I did not learn much.

Unlike most students with Down syndrome in the United States, when Cecelia Ann Pauley was a senior at Winston Churchill High School in Potomac, Maryland, she was fully included in general education classrooms. Her numerous school activities included serving as a cheerleader for the varsity football team, singing in the chorus, and being a member of the Spanish Club. Because she wants to communicate her experiences, and because of her firsthand knowledge of the importance of involving students with disabilities in their education programs, Ms. Pauley has worked closely with her father to prepare and deliver speeches across the country on the topic of inclusion and education of students with disabilities. This chapter provides Ms. Pauley's viewpoint on the importance of student involvement.

My IQ score dropped by 14 points. I did not know that I had any say in my future. I felt sad.

In middle school, I attended IEP meetings for the first time. Everyone talked about me, but no one let me say anything. Sometimes I tried to say something, but no one listened. People talked and talked, and I got bored. The meetings were boring, and I hated them. When my teachers said nice things about me, I felt good. But they used a lot of words I did not know, and I wanted the meetings to end. Sometimes I put my head on the desk and went to sleep. Then they would decide what I would do the next year. But they never asked me what I wanted to do. In the eighth grade, they asked me if I wanted to go to Churchill High School with my classmates. I said I did. The county did not want to let me go to Churchill, so we had to fight to get them to change their decision. I am glad they did. This was the first time I had a say in what was going to happen to me in school.

In the seventh grade, my mom and dad asked me the questions on the Making Action Plans (MAPs) survey (Forest & Pearpoint, 1992; Vandercook, York, & Forest, 1989). They asked me at home. They had talked to me before about what I wanted, but I did not know what choices I had. This was the first time I felt like I had a choice in what I wanted to do. These were my answers to the questions:

1. *Who is Cecelia?* "I am a good person."
2. *What are Cecelia's strengths?* "I like to have fun. I like to sing and dance and act in plays. I like people."
3. *What are Cecelia's needs?* "I need to listen to my teachers more. I need to study more."
4. *What is Cecelia's vision for herself?* "I want to have a job. I want to get married. I want to have kids. I want to have a house. I want to be able to travel. I want to visit my sister Cathy."
5. *What is Cecelia's nightmare for herself?* "If all of my family went away."

I felt happy when my dad asked me these questions. I wanted people to know how I felt. But I did not know anyone except my family cared. Sometimes I felt good about being me. Sometimes I did not. I felt upset that I could not tell people how I felt. This was the first time that I felt like what I wanted mattered. It changed my whole life.

My dad talked to me about inclusion. I did not know what *inclusion* meant. He told me that I could go to school with my friends near my house and be in class with them. I thought that was neat. I wanted to be with my friends and go to school with them. My dad then had the teachers at Cabin John Middle School hold a special IEP meeting. He told them I wanted to be included in general classes in the eighth grade. I was mainstreamed for the first time in English, science, and math. I liked that. I think my friends liked having me in their class, too.

In high school, I was not invited to my 60-day IEP review meeting the first year. The teachers made all the decisions without me. I began to attend IEP meetings in the tenth grade, but the teachers did not ask me what I wanted. My dad asked me at home, and then he and my mom spoke for me in the meetings. At the end of the tenth grade, my guidance counselor, Mrs. Suter, asked me what courses I wanted to take the next year. I picked my classes. Some of the classes got changed in the IEP meeting, but they asked me first. I liked that. At the end of the eleventh grade, Mrs. Suter asked me what classes I wanted to take in the twelfth grade. I picked my classes. I got to take all of them that time. I felt great.

I also made my own choices about what I would do after school. I was involved in a lot of different things, and, in my junior and senior years in high school, I had to choose between several different activities. For example, I was in Girl Scouts. I also was in the tennis clinic at Potomac Community Resources. They both met on the same night, so I had to choose between them. I chose the tennis clinic. I had wanted to be in the school musical revue. The rehearsals conflicted with my rehearsals for the plays at the Bethesda Academy of the Performing Arts (BAPA). I had to choose which show I would be in. I chose the BAPA play because we got to write our own plays and then act in them.

In my senior year, I made a lot of decisions myself. I wanted to go with the chorus on an overnight bus trip to Orlando, Florida, to sing in a national competition. To go, I had to save my money. I decided not to go to some movies to save enough money to pay for the trip. On this trip, I decided I wanted to visit Disney World and Universal Studios with four of my friends. I saved my money to pay for the trip. My music teacher asked me to try out for the chorus of the rock-and-roll musical revue, "Blast from the Past," at school. I wanted to be in it, but I had to work during rehearsal times. My teacher agreed to rehearse the numbers I would be in on the days I could be at rehearsals. It was fun being in "Blast." I also chose to act in BAPA plays. The times did not conflict during my senior year, and I could be in both. That was a lot of fun.

At church, I decided I wanted to sing in the teen choir and be an altar server. When I was 18, I asked if they would let me be a eucharistic minister, and they did. I got to give communion to my mom and dad and all my friends. That was neat.

I also had a job. I applied at many places. My job coach asked me what kind of job I wanted, and I told her that I wanted to work in a nursing home, hospital, or restaurant. I went for a job interview at one nursing home far away from my house, but they hired someone else. Then I went for an interview at Manor Care, a nursing home near my house. They could not hire me, but they agreed to let me work as a volunteer on two afternoons per week. I played games with the people who lived there and also talked with them. I also helped set the table for dinner. I had a good time there.

I also interviewed for a job at Flaps Restaurant. Bob and Grace Rood, the owners, hired me. At first, I worked one afternoon per week preparing food for dinner. I peeled carrots, potatoes, onions, and so forth. I did not like peeling and slicing onions, because they brought tears to my eyes. After I had worked at Flaps for a while, Bob and Grace asked me if I would like to work two afternoons per week. I told them I would love to. They liked me, and I liked working with them.

During my junior year, I visited several colleges. All of my friends visited colleges that year, too. I visited Trinity College in Burlington, Vermont. I liked it. I decided I wanted to go there. Trinity has a neat program called Enhance for kids like me. We go to three classes with everyone else, have a part-time job, and have two life skills classes each semester. I think it is a great opportunity for me.

During my senior year, I started to get scared to leave home. My dad was working with our community college, Montgomery College, to start a program there. This program would be nearer to home than Trinity, so I decided that I wanted to go to Montgomery College. I was accepted into the Enhance program at Trinity. But I was not sure I wanted to attend. My dad told me that I could make my own decision about what I wanted to do after graduation. I could attend Trinity. I could attend Montgomery College. I could get a job and not go to school at all. I felt great that I could make that decision. I decided to go to Montgomery College.

Before I told Trinity that I did not want to go there, I visited the school once more. I met my suitemate Lisa Badore. She was neat. I told her I was going to Montgomery College. Then I saw my dorm room. It was nice. I walked through the dorm and looked at every room. There were 30 beds in my dorm. If I went to Trinity College, I would have 30 friends. I decided to go to Trinity. I made a smart decision.

What subjects am I taking? I met with my friend, Linda Murray, Director of the Enhance program. She asked me what subjects I wanted to take. I had to take two life skills courses and the freshman seminar. The other two courses I could pick. I looked at the list of courses and picked music and acting. I did not get to take them, though. Instead, I am taking a computer course and an English course. I will take music and acting later. The two life skills courses are 1) Jobs: Finding Them and Keeping Them and 2) Adult Problem Solving. My favorite class is my computer class. I can log on to the computer and send e-mail to my family and friends. They all send e-mail to me, too.

I love Trinity. I have a lot of friends. I like my teachers. Everyone likes me. I am learning a lot. I have a telephone in my room, and I cali home whenever I want. I usually call home on weekends. Sometimes I call early in the morning or late at night. I decide when I want to call home.

I also wanted to have a job, so I asked the manager of the cafeteria if she would hire me. She asked me to fill out an application, and I did. She called my references and then hired me. I work in the kitchen on Saturdays preparing food for dinner. I sweep and mop the floor, set out the salt and pepper shakers for dinner, clean the shelves, store food, and break down storage boxes. As the people in the cafeteria get to know me better, I am sure that they will let me do more things. I like working in food service.

Recently, I had an interview with a job counselor from Transition II. They have an office on campus. They are going to help me find more jobs so that I will have a lot of different job experiences. They also will help train me so that I can do my jobs well. One place I would like to work is in an office. That is why I want to work with computers. If I can use the computer, it will be easier to find a job in an office. I would also like to work in a video store, toy store, or hospital.

So that I could sing, I joined the chapel choir. I sing at mass every Sunday night. I also am a eucharistic minister. So that I could act, I began going to play practice one night per week. I love to act, and this gives me a chance to have some fun. I will be the judge in a play in November. I also want to exercise. Last week I started doing aerobics with my friends. I pulled a muscle in my back. I went to see the doctor, and he gave me some medicine.

On September 25, 1996, the National Council for Communicative Disorders gave me an Exceptional Youth Award at the French Embassy in Washington, D.C. That was neat. Ten of us were honored. William Shatner, who played Captain Kirk in *Star Trek* and has tinnitus, was given an award by U.S. Senator John Glenn. Scatman John, a jazz singer and pianist who stutters, also was honored. I got to dance with Scatman John at the reception after the awards ceremony. I also had my picture taken with him and with Senator Glenn. It was one of the happiest nights of my life.

After I returned to Trinity, the student Senate asked me to speak at one of their meetings to tell them about the award. I did. I liked being at the Senate meeting, so I asked if I could be one of the members. They agreed, and I now represent my dorm and the Enhance program in the student Senate.

The Senate meets every 2 weeks to handle student complaints, consider student suggestions, set student policy, and approve applications for new clubs. One of the suggestions that we approved was to cover the murals in the cafeteria with bulletin boards so that we can display student artwork on them.

One of the biggest decisions I make is what to do each day and when to do it. I keep a calendar, and I write in it when I am going to clean my room, do my laundry, study with my friends, watch television, go to meetings, work, do aerobics, walk, help teachers, go shopping, go to a restaurant, and go to the fitness center. Mary Beth Doyle, my freshman seminar mentor, helps me with this; but I decide when I am going to do all these things. My favorite restaurants are a Chinese restaurant, Pizza Hut, and Ben and Jerry's ice cream store.

Every day I make my own decisions. I decide when I am going to get up, when I am going to eat, when I do my laundry, when I get a haircut, when I go shopping, whether to eat in the cafeteria or cook in my room, and what to buy when I go shopping. I love it.

I like all my friends here and my activities, but Trinity is far from my home. I miss my mom and dad, my brother and sisters, and my nephews and nieces very much. I think about them a lot. My friends go out shopping with me and help me keep busy so I will not miss my family too much. But I still miss them a lot.

Weekends are especially lonely, so I call my mom and dad every Saturday and Sunday. Some weekends I go home with my suitemate, Lisa. I like going to her house. She has a big black-and-white cat named George. I like to play with him.

In the spring, Trinity has an alternative spring break week. Instead of going to Florida on spring break, the students spend the week working with the poor. This year we can go to Washington, D.C., or to West Virginia. Last night we had a meeting to decide where we wanted to go. I listened to what we were going to do in both places. I decided that I would go to West Virginia. In West Virginia, we are going to help people repair their houses. I want to learn how to repair houses and build them. That is why I picked West Virginia.

We have dorm meetings every week. We talk about different things. I participate in the discussions with everyone else. I think that they all like to hear my opinions.

I am learning a lot here. I also am teaching people a lot. Every day people relax more with me. They see that I can do a lot of things they did not know I could do. The other day I saw a mom and a dad with their baby. I like babies, so I went over and touched the baby on the arm. I also rocked the carrier. They were not comfortable when I did that. I started to talk to them. I told them I like babies. I told them about my nephews and nieces and how I play with them. I told them my sister just had a new baby, too. We talked for a long time. Pretty soon they relaxed.

Every day I get to make more decisions. I love it. After I graduate from Trinity, I will have to decide whether I want to live in Vermont, return to Maryland, or live somewhere else. I also will have to decide what job I want and whether I want to get married. I do not know what my decisions will be, but because I make decisions now I know I will be able to make good decisions later on. All I want is a chance to make decisions about my future. Give me a chance, and I will learn.

REFERENCES

Forest, M., & Pearpoint, J. (1992). MAPS: Action planning. In J. Pearpoint, M. Forest, & J. Snow, *The inclusion papers: Strategies to make inclusion work* (pp. 52–56). Toronto: Inclusion Press.

Vandercook, T., York , J., & Forest, M. (1989). MAPS: A strategy for building the vision. *Journal of The Association for Persons with Severe Handicaps, 14*(3), 205–215.

II

PROMOTING STUDENT INVOLVEMENT IN THE EDUCATION-PLANNING AND DECISION-MAKING PROCESS

7

Self-Advocacy Strategy Instruction

Enhancing Student Motivation, Self-Determination, and Responsibility in the Learning Process

Anthony K. Van Reusen

Many general, remedial, and special education teachers have increasingly become aware of the need to directly address the motivation and personal responsibility of students for learning and/or improving their academic, social, and career-related skills. Consequently, some teachers have begun to use motivation strategies. Motivation strategies are techniques and procedures that involve students in key aspects of the teaching–learning process, thereby increasing the students' intrinsic commitment to learn. These strategies focus on helping students identify their own learning strengths. They also enable students to learn how to identify and prioritize their needs, choose and monitor

---

The instructor's manual for teaching *The Self-Advocacy Strategy for Education and Transistion Planning* can be obtained from Edge Enterprises, Inc., Post Office Box 1304, Lawrence, Kansas 66045; (913) 749-1473.

their goals, and successfully work toward the attainment of goals. Thus, the term *motivation strategies* refers to specific processes that students can acquire and use to increase their interest in and efforts toward learning while gaining greater control over their own lives (Van Reusen, Bos, Schumaker, & Deshler, 1987, 1994).

Motivation strategies are important because they can be used to increase students' involvement in key decision-making and planning processes related to instruction and performance. These strategies enable students to decide what education and/or transition goals are important to them and can be used by teachers and others to help students understand and consider how their individual strengths, needs, and limitations affect their ability to successfully complete tasks. They also enable students to set goals and regulate their progress toward achieving their goals. Motivation strategies can provide students with a sense of direction, control, and ownership over the learning process, both in and out of school.

One example of a motivation strategy is *The Self-Advocacy Strategy for Education and Transition Planning,* also known as I PLAN (Van Reusen et al., 1994), which targets "an individual's ability to effectively communicate, convey, negotiate, or assert one's interests, desires, needs, and rights" (p. 1). The strategy assumes the importance of students' abilities to make informed decisions and take responsibility for those decisions. In addition, the idea of teaching students how to make effective learning and development decisions and use self-advocacy skills is based on research that has shown that students who have positive self-perceptions and perceived choice and control over their learning experiences are more willing and more motivated to work successfully with the adults in their environment than students who do not (Brown, 1988; Perlmuter & Monty, 1977, 1979; Schunk, 1982, 1985, 1989; see also Chapter 3).

Furthermore, by teaching students how to make effective decisions and by providing them with opportunities to make important learning and development decisions, they can be empowered to become active participants in directing their own futures and advocating for their own interests. However, *empowering students* does not mean providing them with complete freedom to do whatever they want whenever they please. Instead, it means teaching students how to make informed learning and development decisions and choices. It also means teaching students how to take responsibility for their decisions, choices, or actions and how to effectively advocate for themselves. Such instruction is directed toward increasing students' awareness and understanding that, regardless of the learning context or situation, ultimately they control what, how, how well, and why they learn. Before proceeding with an overview and description of *The Self-Advocacy Strategy for Education and Transition Planning,* a brief review of current research and information on student motivation patterns, school responses, and the critical links among intrinsic motivation, self-determination, and learning is appropriate.

STUDENT MOTIVATION PATTERNS

Research on the motivation characteristics of today's diverse school-age population indicates that students with and without learning, behavior, and developmental disabilities exhibit intra-individual patterns of motivation, attribution, and cognition for learning (Borkowski, Carr, Rellinger, & Pressley, 1990; Borkowski, Estrada, Milstead, & Hale, 1989; Maehr & Midgley, 1991; Pintrich, Anderman, & Klobucar, 1994). Studies examining children and youth with severe learning disabilities and students with behavior disorders have shown that some of these students, particularly those experiencing ongoing academic failure, often develop negative beliefs and behaviors in varying degrees that interfere with optimal learning (Adelman, 1978; Adelman & Taylor, 1983b; Chapman, 1988; Deshler, Schumaker, & Lenz, 1984).

In examining students' locus of control (i.e., whether one perceives control over life to be internally or externally mediated), Pascarella, Pflaum, Bryan, and Pearl (1983) found that students identified as having an internal locus of control demonstrated greater performance in less structured conditions than in more structured conditions, whereas students identified as exhibiting an external locus of control demonstrated greater progress in more structured conditions. In a review of research studies comparing the attributions of adolescents with and without learning disabilities, Huntington and Bender (1993) indicated that more adolescents with learning disabilities than their peers without learning disabilities tend to demonstrate an external locus of control orientation. In redirecting learning behavior, Edwards and O'Toole (1985) demonstrated the effectiveness of self-control instruction for students with behavior disabilities. Research has also demonstrated that some students with learning disabilities have lower self-concepts than their peers without disabilities, with greater decrements for academic self-concept than for general self-worth (for a review, see Chapman, 1988). In addition, students with mental retardation have also been found to exhibit differential patterns of motivation, field dependence/independence, and attributions for learning (Polloway & Epstein, 1985; Polloway & Smith, 1983; Reschly, 1987). These intra-individual patterns are believed to differentially influence students' behavior and academic performance in various instructional contexts, both in and out of school. Although teachers and other professionals often acknowledge student motivation and responsibility for learning, these behaviors are infrequently addressed in many educational settings.

Even when students possess the cognitive, linguistic, social, and academic skills necessary to learn new skills, acquire information, or complete tasks, some students exhibit a pattern of behavior referred to as *learned helplessness* (Seligman, 1975). This behavior is characterized by low expectation of success and an insufficient amount of time and effort expended toward the completion of tasks or assignments. It is also characterized by the beliefs that failures are caused by skill impairments or lack of ability and that successes are due to external events beyond the student's control (Chapman, 1988; Pascarella et al., 1983; Pintrich et al., 1994). For example, some students may believe that their poor school performance is caused by the amount and complexity of assigned tasks or the quality of instruction that teachers provide rather than by internal, controllable factors such as the use of effective learning skills and strategies, time management skills, and the ability to monitor and regulate one's efforts and progress. As a result, some students are believed to demonstrate apathy toward learning new skills or trying new tasks, and some fail to set goals for themselves. Others may begin but set unrealistic goals for themselves and quit when their expectations are not met. Still other students, although appearing to spend time on tasks, may engage in mindless or unproductive learning by participating passively in the learning process (Bryan, 1986; Licht & Kistner, 1985; Torgesen, 1982). Some may even use verbal and nonverbal defiance, aggression, or antisocial behaviors and actions to avoid tasks. Indeed, there are students who simply choose not to participate in the learning process even when the tasks or assignments are developmentally appropriate and relevant. Students with chronic or pervasive learning and motivation problems are often placed in remedial, alternative, and special education programs in elementary and secondary schools and later in vocational and rehabilitation counseling programs.

The dilemma for many of these students is their dependency on teachers, parents, peers, and others for direction, decision making, goal setting, problem solving, feedback, and reinforcement as they move through various school settings and into adulthood. To help those students acquire the skills and behaviors needed to effectively learn or work independently as well as interdependently with others, less structured situations are suggested. However, such contexts are usually the very situations in which these students experience difficulty. Moreover, when teachers, parents, and others provide highly structured situations in which all goals and decisions are made for the students, they may be perpetuating students' dependency. In short, many of these students become dependent on teachers and parents, instructional conditions, materials, or accommodations to demonstrate progress that can undermine their development and use of self-directed behavior and independent learning or performance.

Unfortunately, such problematic motivation characteristics (e.g., negative beliefs, learned helplessness, lack of interest or effort, passive learning, learning dependency, avoidance behaviors) about learning and school can continue into adulthood with serious consequences. For example, in far too many instances, students with learning disabilities and behavior problems quit or graduate from high school without realistic goals or plans for the future such as additional training or schooling. Many are unprepared or underprepared for the responsibilities of adult life, including personal and professional relationships, employment, and full participation in their communities. To the contrary, capable learners perceive their successes and failures in and out of school as being the result of controllable factors such as the degree to which they set and work toward goals. These students are resourceful, persistent, and committed to practice and mastery of the learning process. Capable learners are volitional in that they resist distractions as well as direct and regulate their thinking and behavior. Furthermore, these students arrange their physical and social contexts to facilitate successful performance. They are also found to invest the time, effort, and energy necessary to complete tasks, and they monitor and evaluate their progress toward the attainment of goals (Zimmerman, 1994; Zimmerman, Bandura, & Martinez-Pons, 1992).

School Responses to Student Motivation Problems

When confronted with student motivation problems, many school programs have directed their efforts toward changing or manipulating factors within the learning context, outside of student control (i.e., external or extrinsic manipulation). For example, many teachers and researchers use and recommend the use of behavior management interventions that are based on principles of operant conditioning. These interventions focus on the use of positive (external) reinforcement systems (Deutsch-Smith & Pedrotty-Rivera, 1995; Repp, Felce, & Barton, 1991; Shores, Gunter, Denny, & Jack, 1993), and they usually involve reward systems (i.e., token economies, point systems, verbal praise) that are used to increase the amount of time spent on tasks and enhance assignment completion, response rates, and appropriate behavior. The tokens or points are then exchanged by students for privileges at school or at home. These systems are also used to decrease or eliminate inappropriate behaviors. For example, teachers and others may use a response cost procedure in which a specified amount of a reinforcer is removed or applied following a particular behavior. Through these systems, students earn tokens or points for exhibiting desired behaviors and completing assignments and tasks, and they can lose their tokens or points for failing to complete assignments or for disruptive behavior.

Limitations of External Controls

It is important to recognize that though behavior management interventions can be very effective and necessary for eliciting desired behaviors from some students, they also have several limitations. First, a heavy reliance on rewards may increase student dependence on external reinforcement (Lepper, 1988; Lepper & Greene, 1978; Lepper, Greene, & Nisbett, 1973; Lepper & Hodell, 1989). In essence, some students may be willing to put forth time and effort or to complete tasks only when rewards are available. Second, some research indicates that external reinforcement systems often cannot be faded without simultaneously decreasing student performance (Kazdin, 1982; O'Leary & Drabman, 1971). Third, for some students with developmental delays or severe language and learning problems, the use of external positive reinforcement (e.g., rewards, verbal praise) in combination with interactive modeling strategies may produce confusion. That is, some students may be uncertain about what behavior is being reinforced, or the reinforcer (including verbal praise) may serve as a distraction (Biederman, Davey, Ryder, & Franchi, 1994). Fourth, the use of external controls may actually interfere with the students' intrinsic motivation for acquiring skills and knowledge, a circumstance that can undermine the development and maintenance of the ability to independently work, learn, or complete tasks.

By primarily emphasizing external control mechanisms, many school programs and teachers overlook intra-individual patterns of student motivation and the critical role of intrinsic motivation and self-determination in developing or enhancing learner independence. In addition, many programs do not differentiate instructional or behavioral interventions based on the students' motivation patterns or belief systems. These programs often fail to help students establish or alter their belief systems about the value of learning and school. Many programs do not include students in the determination of their learning needs and responsibilities or do not involve them in the process of developing goals for improving performance both in and out of school.

INTRINSIC MOTIVATION, SELF-DETERMINATION, AND LEARNING

Theorists and researchers involved in the study of motivation (e.g., Boggiano et al., 1992; Cameron & Pierce, 1994; Deci & Ryan, 1985; Mook, 1987) have described intrinsic motivation as an important energizer of human behavior that is believed to be based on the individual's need for competence and self-determination (i.e., internal control). In other words, individuals are described as intrinsically motivated when they complete activities or exhibit behavior because of an inner desire to succeed or to act appropriately (i.e., competence) and act out of choice based on perception of need (i.e., self-determination). More important, intrinsic motivation and self-determination are believed to have a critical role in the human ability to understand and regulate one's own behavior and actions (Deci & Ryan, 1985; Spaulding, 1992; Weiner, 1980). Thus, when students perceive themselves as competent and self-determining in their learning attempts, they are more likely to commit themselves and to direct their efforts toward the attainment of learning goals or the successful completion of tasks. In many schools and classrooms, students may be viewed as intrinsically motivated when they are minimally compliant and cooperative in working on tasks, completing assignments, or learning new skills. Those who are frequently noncompliant or who fail to direct their efforts and effectiveness toward meeting classroom expectations are often described as unmotivated or inactive learners (Adelman & Taylor, 1983a, 1983b; Torgesen, 1982).

In emphasizing self-determination as an important outcome for children and youth with disabilities, Wehmeyer (1996) defined *self-determination* as the attitudes and abilities necessary to act as the primary causal agent in one's life and to make choices and decisions regarding one's quality of life, free from external influences or interference. Furthermore, Wehmeyer (1992, 1995, 1996) and Wehmeyer and Schwartz (1997) contended that self-determination is predicated on the individual's acquisition and use of specific skills, behaviors, and attitudes that are learned across the life span and associated primarily with reaching adulthood and fulfilling adult roles.

More specifically, Wehmeyer (1996); Wehmeyer, Kelchner, and Richards (1996); and Wehmeyer and Schwartz (1997) posited that for the emergence of self-determination to occur, students need to acquire or develop a compilation of skills, behaviors, attitudes, and beliefs. Wehmeyer (1996) and Wehmeyer et al. (1996) referred to this compilation as the *components or essential elements of self-determination*. This compilation involves the degree to which individuals are metacognitively, motivationally, and behaviorally autonomous in directing, monitoring, and regulating their thoughts, actions, or behaviors. It also includes but is not limited to engaging in actions or activities based on one's self-knowledge or awareness of strengths, limitations, interests, preferences, or abilities. It includes the ability to solve problems, set and attain goals, exhibit an internal locus of control, demonstrate positive attributions of efficacy and outcome expectancy, and reward oneself when goals are attained or tasks successfully completed. This compilation also encompasses the ability to identify one's current and future needs, gain access to and use information and resources, plan and complete tasks, expend personal time and effort, and take responsibility for one's actions or behaviors. It involves acting on one's beliefs and using verbal and nonverbal skills necessary for effective communication, including knowing how and when to ask questions, compare ideas, be assertive or persistent, negotiate, and/or make informed decisions and choices. These interrelated skills, behaviors, and attitudes are all sufficiently complex, and their acquisition or development can be difficult for many students. In short, concerns about student motivation, involvement, and responsibility in the teaching–learning process along with the postschool outcomes of students with disabilities, particularly those with learning disabilities and behavior problems, have elevated the critical link of intrinsic motivation and self-determination in the effectiveness of intervention programs for students receiving general, special, or remedial education (Bos & Van Reusen, 1991; Carter-Ludi & Martin, 1995; Ellis, Deshler, Lenz, Schumaker, & Clark, 1991; Field, 1996; Hoffman & Field, 1995; Martin & Huber Marshall, 1995).

Implications for Enhancing Students' Intrinsic Motivation and Self-Determination

When applied to the motivational characteristics of students with disabilities and others at risk for failure in school, the constructs of intrinsic motivation and self-determination have two major implications. First, if education and/or transition programs for this population are to be effective, these students need to be taught how to reflect, explore, and act on their beliefs about the causes of their success or failure, both in and out of school. Second, efforts to address the intrinsic motivation and self-determination of these students require teachers, parents, and others to recognize the need for students to be involved in determining and advocating for their learning and development needs, outcomes, and experiences. Indeed, these students need ongoing opportunities to actively and directly participate in planning, carrying out, and monitoring their individualized education programs (IEPs) and/or individualized transition plans (ITPs) (see Chapter 3). Thus, efforts to enhance the intrinsic motivation and self-determination of students may need to be directed in a twofold approach. This approach includes teaching students how to make decisions about their learning and development needs and providing them with opportunities to make decisions or choices.

Creating Opportunities for Student Decision Making and Success

As noted in Chapter 3, it must be emphasized that teaching students how to make effective decisions and choices is of little value unless schools, teachers, parents, and others provide real opportunities and experiences for students with disabilities and others with learning and performance problems to engage in active and responsible decision making. Specifically, students need to have a major voice in making decisions and choices regarding their IEPs and ITPs. More specifically, they need to be actively involved in making decisions and choices before, during, and after instruction. Concurrently, students need opportunities in which they are given responsibility for their decisions and choices. In this way, the instruction process is guided and driven by students' goals, not by teachers' goals.

Teachers, other education professionals, and parents who want to enhance students' intrinsic motivation, self-determination, and responsibility for learning and development must be willing to create and maintain environments that promote and provide students with opportunities for success. Providing opportunities or situations in which students with disabilities and others can make decisions and choices but have little chance of attaining success is unproductive. Similarly, it is important to recognize that differences exist in students' individual perceptions of education and transition needs, goals, skills, beliefs, and motivations. These differences need to be identified and accommodated.

One way to accommodate or to address such differences is to examine available instruction programs or services to make sure that a variety of materials, content, and options for learning and development opportunities are offered. Nonetheless, if students have the capacity and are given opportunities to make decisions and choices but are not permitted to pursue those decisions or choices, then their interest and effort in working toward their goals will be undermined. Keeping this twofold approach in mind helps to maintain students' perceptions of choice, control, commitment, and effort to learn and achieve in school and in life. The Self-Advocacy Strategy described and presented in the remaining sections provides teachers, parents, and students with a framework for teaching students the skills and behaviors needed to make plans and carry out those plans. These skills help students to make successful transitions within and between education settings and to the work force, adult life, and their communities.

THE SELF-ADVOCACY STRATEGY FOR EDUCATION AND TRANSITION PLANNING

The Self-Advocacy Strategy for Education and Transition Planning was designed to increase student participation, decision making, and communication during IEP/ITP conferences (see Van Reusen & Bos, 1990, 1994; Van Reusen et al., 1987; Van Reusen, Deshler, & Schumaker, 1989). This research-based strategy was revamped, improved, and updated to more effectively address the complex education and/or transition concerns of students with disabilities and others who exhibit learning and performance problems. The updated version was created to better assist students, parents, teachers, and others who are involved in planning and carrying out the requirements of IEPs and ITPs. This strategy also incorporates developments in strategic instruction, motivation, self-determination, and self-advocacy research. Many of the changes found in The Self-Advocacy Strategy stem from invaluable feedback and suggestions provided by the students, parents, teachers, researchers, and other professionals who used the original strategy.

Purpose of The Self-Advocacy Strategy

The purpose of The Self-Advocacy Strategy is fivefold. First, as a motivation strategy, it is designed to enable students to systematically gain a sense of control and influence over their own learning and development. Second, the strategy emphasizes the role and importance of intrinsic motivation and self-determination by focusing students' attention on their learning and transition skill strengths. Third, mastery of the strategy prepares students to take an active role in making decisions related to their learning and development experiences. Fourth, the strategy provides students with a way of getting organized before any type of conference or meeting. Finally, the steps of the strategy remind students about behaviors and techniques needed for effectively communicating and advocating their education and/or transition needs and goals.

Focus of Instruction

Instruction in The Self-Advocacy Strategy is specifically designed to increase students' investment in their own learning, their intrinsic motivation, and their commitment to learn. Furthermore, although students can use this strategy to prepare for and participate in any type of conference or meeting, the focus of instruction is on the importance of students' becoming active and responsible participants in determining their lives by advocating for and negotiating their own futures. Through Self-Advocacy Strategy instruction, students and others learn how to determine their education and/or transition strengths, areas in which they can improve or learn, and choices for learning or needed accommodations. In addition, they learn how to set goals for learning and preparing themselves for the transition from school to adult life. With regard to transition, students learn how to identify their current needs in areas such as independent living skills, career and employment skills, financial and consumer skills, social and family living skills, citizenship and legal skills, health and wellness skills, community resource skills, and leisure and recreational skills. Moreover, they learn how to communicate this information in a productive manner during conferences or meetings and take an active role in making decisions. Thus, the instruction provides students, parents, and others with a strategic system or framework for making plans and carrying out those plans related to successful educational experiences and transitions from school to adult life, community settings, and the work force.

The strategy comprises five steps called the I PLAN steps and five communication behaviors called the SHARE behaviors. These steps and communication behaviors form the strategic system previously mentioned. The acronym I PLAN is used to help students remember the five steps involved in the strategy (Table 1). Each letter in I PLAN cues students to use each step of the strategy. Students also learn how to use the SHARE behaviors, which are basic techniques for effective communication (Table 2).

The Self-Advocacy Strategy is also centered on specific instruction procedures, materials, and activities for preparing students to actively participate in two types of conferences: education-planning conferences and transition-

Table 1.   The steps of The Self-Advocacy Strategy

Step 1	Inventory your
	Strengths
	Areas to improve or learn
	Goals
	Choices for learning or accommodations
Step 2	Provide your inventory information
Step 3	Listen and respond
Step 4	Ask questions
Step 5	Name your goals

From Van Reusen, A.K., Bos, C.S., Schumaker, J.B., & Deshler, D.D. (1994). *The Self-Advocacy Strategy for Education and Transition Planning* (p. 130). Lawrence, KS: Edge Enterprises; reprinted by permission.

Table 2.   SHARE behaviors from The Self-Advocacy Strategy

S	Sit up straight
H	Have a pleasant tone of voice
A	Activate your thinking
	Tell yourself to pay attention
	Tell yourself to participate
	Tell yourself to compare ideas
R	Relax
E	Engage in eye communication

From Van Reusen, A.K., Bos, C.S., Schumaker, J.B., & Deshler, D.D. (1994). *The Self-Advocacy Strategy for Education and Transition Planning* (p. 129). Lawrence, KS: Edge Enterprises; reprinted by permission.

planning conferences. In some states and school districts, these conferences are conducted independently of each other. In other states and school districts, education- and transition-planning conferences or meetings take place simultaneously. In deciding which type of conference to conduct, those wanting to teach this strategy should think about their students and whether they need to focus primarily on education planning, transition planning, or both. For elementary school–age students, education-planning conferences may be the best choice. For adolescents and adults, including those who have already left school, transition-planning conferences are more appropriate. For middle school, junior high, or high school students, both education- and transition-planning conferences may be appropriate. In any case, it is important to remember that all students who are determined to be eligible for special education services are required by federal regulations to have an IEP that is developed in a planning conference before they are placed in a special education program and before they receive any special education services. In addition, students receiving special education services are required to have transition goals addressed in their IEPs by the time they are 14 years old.

Because of the major differences between the two types of conferences and the different needs of students, three different inventories were developed for use in teaching the "I" step of the strategy. These inventories are an education inventory with education skill lists, a modified education inventory called My Personal Inventory (for younger students in Grades 2–5), and a transition inventory (for students in middle, secondary, and postsecondary schools) with transition skill lists. Depending on the unique individual needs and ages of students, either one of the inventories is selected or parts of the inventories are selected and combined into an inventory that is then completed by students individually during the third stage of the instructional sequence (see the next section) but prior to their participation in a meeting or conference. The teacher or other students provide assistance to students who have difficulty in providing written responses. Regardless of the inventory used, this step of the strategy provides students with a decision-making process for determining and listing their perceived education and/or transition strengths, areas for improvement or learning goals, needed accommodations, and choices for learning. Students then use this information as they learn to become active participants in advocating for and negotiating their own futures across various settings and contexts.

The Self-Advocacy Strategy was written to reflect the knowledge and technology involved in providing effective strategic instruction to increase acquisition and generalization. Therefore, teachers, parents, and others will find the strategy to be organized around the instructional stage model (see the next section), with each stage using lesson organizers to promote student learning, goal attainment, and use of the strategy.

THE INSTRUCTION SEQUENCE

The Self-Advocacy Strategy is taught by using a modified version of the acquisition and generalization stages that were developed and expanded as part of the Strategic Intervention Model (SIM) (Ellis et al., 1991). Students with disabilities and others with learning and behavior problems who participated in field test studies of the strategy demonstrated mastery when the instructional stages, as presented in Figure 1, were implemented. The description in the next section summarizes the instruction stages and sequences used to teach the strategy.

Instruction Stages

Stage 1: Orient and Obtain Commitment to Learn   During this stage, students are introduced to the concept of education and transition planning, the purpose of The Self-Advocacy Strategy, and how learning this strategy can give them more power and control over their own learning and development, both in and out of school. Students are also asked to make a commitment to learn the strategy, and the instructor makes a commitment to teach the strategy to the students. In working with older students, experience has shown that student effort and involvement in the instruction process is greater when students make a verbal or written commitment and the instructor or teacher makes a similar commitment.

Stage 2: Describe   This stage is designed to provide students with a picture that details the nature of skills to be taught and the advantages of using those skills. First, students are provided with definitions of IEP and/or ITP conferences. Next, the types of meetings or conferences in which students are likely to participate and the characteristics of those meetings are described. Then students are shown how they can personally benefit from applying The Self-Advocacy Strategy in the meetings or conferences they attend as well as in day-to-day situations. During this stage, an interactive format is used. Students are presented with situations and settings in which using the strategy made

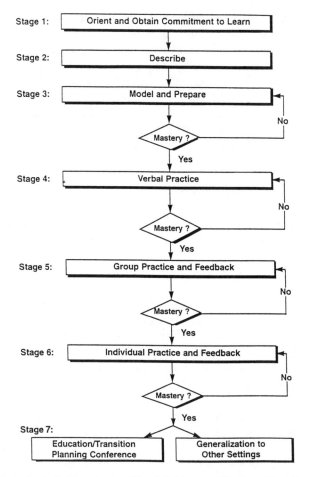

Figure 1.   Instruction stages of The Self-Advocacy Strategy. (From Van Reusen, A.K., Bos, C.S., Schumaker, J.B., & Deshler, D.D. [1994]. *The Self-Advocacy Strategy for Education and Transition Planning* [p. 129]. Lawrence, KS: Edge Enterprises; reprinted by permission.)

a difference for other students. Discussion with the students about the kinds of results and advantages that can be attained by learning and using the strategy has been found to enhance student commitment, interest, and strategy use.

Stage 3: Model and Prepare   Students learn a skill better if they can see and hear others perform it first rather than just receiving a description of what to do. In other words, they learn the skills by imitating good models. Therefore, the I PLAN steps of the strategy are demonstrated in this stage. The instructor or teacher needs to use a "think aloud" teaching format or routine for students to hear someone verbalize the necessary cognitive processes and see the overt behaviors used to perform the strategy. The "I," or "inventory," step of I PLAN requires the longest time to model because in it students complete their education or transition inventory. Owing to the time requirements (three 40- to 50-minute lessons), instruction during this stage is designed so that first each part of the inventory step is modeled and then the students complete that part. When the demonstration of the inventory step is concluded, the students have a completed inventory that they bring to their IEP and/or ITP conferences. After the inventory is completed, the remaining steps of the strategy, which focus on learning how and when to communicate during a conference or meeting, are demonstrated. In this manner, all of the I PLAN steps, the cognitive processes, and the overt behaviors involved in performing the strategy steps are presented clearly and explicitly.

As stated previously, the model-and-prepare stage requires the most time to complete because the students complete an inventory as part of this instructional stage. In view of the fact that differences exist in the scope and purpose of IEP and ITP conferences, The Self-Advocacy Strategy contains two different model-and-prepare stages. If a decision is made to combine the two conferences into the same conference, components of the IEP inventory and the ITP inventory can be selected to reflect the unique needs of a student. For example, the social skills planning section of the education inventory might be omitted because the ITP inventory contains a social and family living section. Components of the ITP inventory may be selected because they may be more appropriate for some students. For instance, a student's ITP inventory may reflect his or her needs to focus on independent living skills, whereas another student's ITP inventory may focus primarily on financial and consumer skills or community involvement skills.

Stage 4: Verbal Practice   Prior to actual use of the strategy, students should be able to accurately name the strategy steps and communication behaviors in detail, including where, when, and how they can use the strategy. Specifically, this instructional stage is used to ensure that students know what to do and how to act during each step of the strategy. Through an interactive questioning process, students are first asked about each of the I PLAN steps and where, when, and why they need to use each step. Next, they are asked to verbally rehearse the I PLAN steps and SHARE behaviors. This instructional activity helps facilitate students' independent use of the strategy in the future. The verbal practice activities (i.e., elaboration and rehearsal) provided in this stage can be quickly and effectively carried out with groups of students through rapid-fire exercises in which the instructor points to students in succession and each student names or explains a strategy step or answers a specific question about the strategy. Once students demonstrate their knowledge about the strategy steps and each step's purpose, they can practice individually or in small groups. Students practice in this manner until they can name and explain the steps and associated behaviors without help. Each student's knowledge is evaluated individually and recorded on a checklist.

Stage 5: Group Practice and Feedback   After students demonstrate both understanding and mastery of the steps, behaviors, and concepts of the strategy, they participate as a group in a simulated conference. In this stage, the instructor first reviews what takes place during a particular type of meeting or conference, including who might participate and what the student's responsibilities involve. Next, the instructor conducts a simulated conference or meeting by directing questions and statements to individual students in the group and requiring a response from the student being questioned. After each response, the instructor and the other students provide corrective feedback on how each student effectively used the strategy (e.g., whether the student looked at the conference participants while talking, used a pleasant tone of voice, responded in complete statements, or referred to his or her inventory). During this step, a group practice score sheet is used to score each student's performance. Simulated practice activities continue until the students consistently use the strategy effectively.

The use of corrective feedback during this stage is perhaps the most important element of the instruction process. Research has shown that students make the greatest gains when they receive specific, well-timed feedback. Students with learning disabilities often continue to perform or practice incorrect responses, thus delaying mastery without such feedback. To facilitate the corrective feedback process, audiotaping or videotaping simulated conference activities and having students listen to or watch some of the responses and comments can be very helpful. Similarly, the audio- or videotaping of the simulated conference is also useful in the next stage of instruction.

Stage 6: Individual Practice and Feedback   In this stage, the instructor or teacher meets with students individually to allow for individual practice, corrective feedback, and mastery. First, the student's participation in the simulated conference (conducted in Stage 5) is reviewed. The student is asked to self-evaluate his or her performance during the simulated conference, and then the instructor provides corrective feedback regarding the student's use of the strategy steps and the communication behaviors. Next, the strategy steps and communication behaviors are reviewed once again. Then another simulated conference or meeting is conducted with the student in a one-to-one format. Corrective feedback and additional practice for the student are provided as needed. As in the previous stage, audio- or videotaping individual simulated conferences facilitates the provision of corrective feedback. This type of individual practice and corrective feedback continues until the student demonstrates mastery, which typically requires 10–15 minutes. Finally, the student is given an opportunity to ask questions about the specific type of conference or meeting in which he or she will participate, and then the instructor provides a quick last review.

Because this stage is designed to promote acquisition durability of the strategy, the instructor or teacher needs to reduce the amount of prompts and cues provided in earlier stages. Using this fading technique, each student becomes more responsible for taking the initiative and becomes more actively involved in using the strategy. Individual corrective feedback during this stage of the instruction sequence is just as critical as during the earlier stages. However, instead of the instructor or teacher assuming the major responsibility for the corrective feedback process in this stage, the student becomes responsible for reflection, self-regulation, and self-evaluation. This is accomplished by asking the student questions about his or her use of the strategy steps and communication behaviors, thereby enabling the student to reflect on and analyze his or her effectiveness in applying the strategy.

Stage 7: Generalization to Other Settings   Mastering The Self-Advocacy Strategy serves little purpose unless it is used at intended times and in intended settings. In other words, the critical measure or "acid test" of effective instruction is the degree to which students can apply the strategy in the real world and maintain as well as adapt its use over time. This concept is known as *generalization*. Therefore, in this stage, students are ready to use the strategy independently during actual conferences or meetings, and they are given assistance in adapting the strategy to a variety of meetings or conferences (i.e., job interviews, performance evaluations, negotiating with parents, club or team meetings). Three distinct generalization phases are addressed in this stage. The first phase, Preparing for and Conducting a Planning Conference, provides students with individual opportunities to directly apply their acquired self-advocacy skills in an IEP or ITP conference. The second phase, Preparing for Other Uses of the Strategy, makes students aware of other formal and informal situations or circumstances in which they can apply the strategy, as well as ways in which they may need to adjust the strategy. The third and final phase, Preparing for Subsequent Conferences, is used with students to review the purpose of particular conferences or meetings and the importance of their participation. Again, students are provided with a review of the strategy and an opportunity to update their IEP and/or ITP inventories. This generalization stage is also used to ensure that the students have maintained their understanding and use of the strategy before participating in any subsequent meetings or conferences in which they need to advocate for themselves.

Related Concepts and Skills Embedded in the Strategy

Students acquire numerous related concepts and skills embedded in the strategy. These related concepts and skills are believed to be important to the construct of *self-regulation*, in which students monitor their own thinking, behavior, or actions through language mediation while learning. Subsequently, students are expected to take active roles in learning the strategy by first describing overtly the steps and behaviors of the strategy during the instruction process. Once they have demonstrated mastery, the focus of instruction also addresses the need for students to adapt the strategy to various situations by covertly using corrections or fix-up strategies and techniques when problems are encountered. Through this process, a deliberate progression of instruction from teacher- to student-mediated instruction during Stages 4–7 of the instruction sequence emphasizes the importance of self-regulated behavior on the part of students. Other related concepts and skills embedded in the strategy include

- Nonverbal and verbal behaviors necessary for good communication
- Benefits of self-talk
- Active versus passive listening
- Self-knowledge and self-awareness skills
- Social and practical skills
- Informed decision making
- Planning
- Conversation skills
- Information gathering
- Acceptance of criticism and feedback
- Questioning
- Negotiation and problem solving
- Acceptance of responsibility

Opportunities for Student Self-Advocacy in and out of School

Students have a variety of formal and informal opportunities to advocate for themselves in responding to an intricate network of learning, performance, and social demands or expectations. For example, formal planning conferences occur routinely in special, remedial, and general education programs. These conferences provide excellent opportunities for students to engage in self-advocacy and make decisions and choices regarding their learning and development needs and experiences. They include the IEP planning conference, the ITP planning conference, and the individualized vocational education program (IVEP) planning conference, to name a few. Unfortunately, some research has demonstrated that the majority of these conferences are mechanical and compliant at best and that students are rarely given the opportunity to participate in them, let alone be included in the decision-making process related to instruction, intervention, or placement decisions (Smith, 1990a, 1990b). Once students have learned The Self-Advocacy Strategy sufficiently, they can use it to prepare for and participate in an array of conferences, perhaps making the conferences more beneficial for everyone involved.

Similarly, students often meet with school counselors on a more informal basis to plan class schedules or to prepare for their futures. These informal conferences may include discussions about college or other postsecondary training. In these situations, students are routinely asked to make decisions about, as well as to plan for, their current and future needs and goals. Likewise, teachers and administrators across the grade levels often request informal conferences with parents or guardians at which students are asked to be in attendance. In these situations, students' abilities to rationally communicate and advocate a course of action may be the difference between their willingness to change or modify their behavior and efforts and their continuing to have difficulties and problems in school.

Inside the classroom, students are routinely confronted with situations that often require them to advocate a course of action. These situations include daily informal interactions with their peers, working with other students on assignments, asking questions, providing information, comparing information and ideas, or setting goals. Similarly, outside the classroom and particularly in unstructured situations, students have many more opportunities to interact with each other and make decisions or choices. These situations and opportunities include transition or breaktimes between classes, lunchtime in the cafeteria, recess, and after-school activities. In all of these situations, students may find themselves in circumstances in which they must self-advocate. More specifically, most of these circumstances and situations require students to use some if not all of the I PLAN steps and the SHARE communication behaviors.

In the same way, students frequently find themselves in situations outside of school where they need sound self-advocacy skills. Some of these situations include meeting informally with their parents or guardians to resolve a problem or to negotiate permission. Another common situation involves choosing a place to go to or an activity to do with friends that will not result in negative consequences. Perhaps more important are those situations where the ability to self-advocate may be critical for one's success, including knowing how to prepare for and participate in a job interview or performance evaluation. In the community, people often find themselves as consumers having to advocate a course of action, such as getting a refund or cash credit for or exchanging an item previously purchased that needs to be returned for some reason.

Sometimes, as a result of poor decision making or choice of actions, students find themselves in trouble with the law and become adjudicated and thus need to meet with judges, court-appointed social workers, probation officers, or youth evaluators. In these situations, their ability to advocate a course of action may result in their not being incarcerated. In summary, students are confronted with numerous situations and circumstances in which the ability to successfully self-advocate and be active participants in the decision-making process directly affects their education and other life experiences.

CONCLUSIONS

The Self-Advocacy Strategy for Education and Transition Planning is an effective tool that can be used to involve students, both young and old, in planning their IEPs and/or ITPs, with the ultimate goal being increasing their intrinsic motivation, self-determination, and responsibility in the learning process, both in and out of school. This strategy focuses on helping students to determine and verify their beliefs about their education and transition strengths, make informed learning and development decisions, and advocate for themselves. The strategy is used to teach students to identify and prioritize needs; to set and attain goals; and to increase their interest in, effort toward, and commitment to learning and performing. In providing students with opportunities to learn and use decision-making and self-advocacy skills, teachers, parents, and other professionals can better prepare students with disabilities, as well as those with learning and performance problems, to become full participants in their communities and in society.

REFERENCES

Adelman, H.S. (1978). The concept of intrinsic motivation: Implications for practice and research with the learning disabled. *Learning Disability Quarterly, 1,* 43–54.

Adelman, H.S., & Taylor, L.S. (1983a). Classifying students by inferred motivation to learn. *Learning Disability Quarterly, 6,* 201–206.

Adelman, H.S., & Taylor, L.S. (1983b). Enhancing motivation for overcoming learning and behavior problems. *Journal of Learning Disabilities, 16,* 384–392.

Biederman, G.B., Davey, V.A., Ryder, C., & Franchi, D. (1994). The negative effects of positive reinforcement in teaching children with developmental delay. *Exceptional Children, 60,* 458–465.

Boggiano, A.K., Shields, A., Barrett, M., Kellam, T., Thompson, E., Simons, J., & Katz, P. (1992). Helplessness deficits in students: The role of motivational orientation. *Motivation and Emotion, 16,* 271–296.

Borkowski, J., Carr, M., Rellinger, E., & Pressley, M. (1990). Self-regulated cognition: Interdependence of metacognition, attributions, and self-esteem. In B.F. Jones & L. Idol (Eds.), *Dimensions of thinking and cognitive instruction* (pp. 53–92). Hillsdale, NJ: Lawrence Erlbaum Associates.

Borkowski, J., Estrada, M., Milstead, M., & Hale, C. (1989). General problem solving skills: Relations between metacognition and strategic processing. *Learning Disability Quarterly, 12,* 57–70.

Bos, C.S., & Van Reusen, A.K. (1991). Academic interventions with learning disabled students: A cognitive/metacognitive approach. In J.E. Obrzut & G.W. Hynd (Eds.), *Neuropsychological foundations of learning disabilities* (pp. 659–683). San Diego: Academic Press.

Brown, A. (1988). Motivation to learn and understand: On taking charge of one's own learning. *Cognition and Instruction, 5,* 311–321.

Bryan, T. (1986). Personality and situational factors in learning disabilities. In G. Parlidis & D. Fisher (Eds.), *Dyslexia: Its neuropsychology and treatment* (pp. 215–230). New York: John Wiley & Sons.

Cameron, J., & Pierce, W.D. (1994). Reinforcement, reward, and intrinsic motivation: A meta-analysis. *Review of Educational Research, 64,* 363–423.

Carter-Ludi, D., & Martin, L. (1995). The road to personal freedom: Self-determination. *Intervention in School and Clinic, 30,* 164–169.

Chapman, J.W. (1988). Learning disabled children's self-concepts. *Review of Educational Research, 58,* 347–371.

Deci, E.L., & Ryan, R.M. (1985). *Intrinsic motivation and self-determination in human behavior.* New York: Plenum Press.

Deshler, D.D., Schumaker, J.B., & Lenz, B.K. (1984). Academic and cognitive interventions for LD adolescents: Part I. *Journal of Learning Disabilities, 17,* 108–117.

Deutsch-Smith, D., & Pedrotty-Rivera, D. (1995). Discipline in special education and general education settings. *Focus on Exceptional Children, 27*(5), 1–14.

Edwards, L.L., & O'Toole, B. (1985). Application of the self-control curriculum with behavior disordered students. *Focus on Exceptional Children, 17*(8), 1–8.

Ellis, E.S., Deshler, D.D., Lenz, B.K., Schumaker, J.B., & Clark, F.L. (1991). An instructional model for teaching learning strategies. *Focus on Exceptional Children, 23*(6), 1–23.

Field, S. (1996). Self-determination instructional strategies for youth with learning disabilities. *Journal of Learning Disabilities, 29,* 40–52.

Hoffman, A., & Field, S. (1995). Promoting self-determination through effective curriculum development. *Intervention in School and Clinic, 30,* 134–141.

Huntington, D.D., & Bender, W.N. (1993). Adolescents with learning disabilities at risk? Emotional well-being, depression, suicide. *Journal of Learning Disabilities, 26,* 159–166.

Kazdin, A.E. (1982). The token economy: A decade later. *Journal of Applied Behavior Analysis, 15,* 431–445.

Lepper, M.R. (1988). Motivational considerations in the study of instruction. *Cognition and Instruction, 5,* 289–310.

Lepper, M.R., & Greene, D. (Eds.). (1978). *The hidden costs of rewards: New perspectives of the psychology of human motivation.* Hillsdale, NJ: Lawrence Erlbaum Associates.

Lepper, M.R., Greene, D., & Nisbett, R.E. (1973). Undermining children's intrinsic interest with extrinsic reward: A test of the overjustification hypothesis. *Journal of Personality and Social Psychology, 29,* 129–137.

Lepper, M.R., & Hodell, M. (1989). Intrinsic motivation in the classroom. In C. Ames & R. Ames (Eds.), *Research on motivation in education* (Vol. 3, pp. 73–105). New York: Academic Press.

Licht, B.G., & Kistner, J.A. (1985). Motivational problems of learning disabled children: Individual differences and their implications for treatment. In J.K. Torgesen & B.Y.L. Wong (Eds.), *Psychological and educational perspectives on learning disabilities* (pp. 225–255). Orlando, FL: Academic Press.

Maehr, M.L., & Midgley, C. (1991). Enhancing student motivation: A school-wide approach. *Educational Psychologist, 26,* 399–427.

Martin, J.E., & Huber Marshall, L. (1995). ChoiceMaker: A comprehensive self-determination transition program. *Intervention in School and Clinic, 30,* 147–156.

Mook, D.G. (1987). *Motivation: The organization of action.* New York: W.W. Norton.

O'Leary, K.D., & Drabman, R. (1971). Token reinforcement programs in the classroom: A review. *Psychological Bulletin, 75,* 379–389.

Pascarella, E., Pflaum, S., Bryan, T., & Pearl, R. (1983). Interaction of internal attributions for effort and teacher response mode in reading instruction: A replication note. *American Educational Research Journal, 5,* 173–176.

Perlmuter, L.C., & Monty, R.A. (1977). The importance of perceived control: Fact or fantasy? *American Scientist, 65,* 759–765.

Perlmuter, L.C., & Monty, R.A. (Eds.). (1979). *Choice and perceived control.* Hillsdale, NJ: Lawrence Erlbaum Associates.

Pintrich, P.R., Anderman, E.M., & Klobucar, C. (1994). Intraindividual differences in motivation and cognition in students with and without learning disabilities. *Journal of Learning Disabilities, 27,* 360–370.

Polloway, E.A., & Epstein, M.H. (1985). Current issues in mild mental retardation: A survey of the field. *Education and Training of the Mentally Retarded, 20,* 171–174.

Polloway, E.A., & Smith, J.D. (1983). Changes in mild mental retardation: Populations, programs, and perspectives. *Exceptional Children, 50,* 149–159.

Repp, A.C., Felce, D., & Barton, L.E. (1991). The effects of initial intervention size on the efficacy of DRO schedules of reinforcement. *Exceptional Children, 57,* 417–425.

Reschly, D. (1987). Learning characteristics of mildly handicapped students: Implications for classification, placement, and programming. In M.C. Wang, M.C. Reynolds, & H.J. Walberg (Eds.), *Handbook of special education: Vol. 1. Research and practice: Learner characteristics and adaptive education* (pp. 253–271). New York: Pergamon Press.

Schunk, D. (1982). Effects of effort and attributional feedback on children's perceived self-efficacy and achievement. *Journal of Educational Psychology, 74,* 548–556.

Schunk, D. (1985). Participation in goal setting: Effects on self-efficacy and skills of learning disabled children. *Journal of Special Education, 19,* 307–317.

Schunk, D. (1989). Self-efficacy and cognitive skill learning. In C. Ames & R. Ames (Eds.), *Research on motivation in education: Vol. 3. Goals and cognitions* (pp. 13–44). San Diego: Academic Press.

Seligman, M.E.P. (1975). *Helplessness: On depression, development and death.* San Francisco: W.H. Freeman.

Shores, R.E., Gunter, P.L., Denny, K.R., & Jack, S.L. (1993). Classroom influences on aggressive and disruptive behaviors of students with emotional and behavioral disorders. *Focus on Exceptional Children, 26*(2), 1–10.

Smith, S.W. (1990a). Comparison of individualized education programs (IEPs) of students with behavior disorders and learning disabilities. *Journal of Special Education, 24*(I), 85–100.

Smith, S.W. (1990b). Individualized education programs (IEPs) in special education: From intent to acquiescence. *Exceptional Children, 57,* 6–14.

Spaulding, C.L. (1992). *Motivation in the classroom.* New York: McGraw-Hill.

Torgesen, J.K. (1982). The learning disabled child as an inactive learner: Educational implications. *Topics in Learning and Learning Disabilities, 2,* 45–52.

Van Reusen, A.K., & Bos, C.S. (1990). I PLAN: Helping students communicate in planning conferences. *Teaching Exceptional Children, 22*(IV), 30–32.

Van Reusen, A.K., & Bos, C.S. (1994). Facilitating student participation in individualized education programs through motivation strategy instruction. *Exceptional Children, 60,* 466–475.

Van Reusen, A.K., Bos, C.S., Schumaker, J.B., & Deshler, D.D. (1987). *The Education Planning Strategy.* Lawrence, KS: Edge Enterprises.

Van Reusen, A.K., Bos, C.S., Schumaker, J.B., & Deshler, D.D. (1994). *The Self-Advocacy Strategy for Education and Transition Planning.* Lawrence, KS: Edge Enterprises.

Van Reusen, A.K., Deshler, D.D., & Schumaker, J.B. (1989). Effects of a student participation strategy in facilitating the involvement of adolescents with learning disabilities in the individualized educational program planning process. *Learning Disabilities: A Multidisciplinary Journal, 1,* 23–34.

Wehmeyer, M.L. (1992). Self-determination and the education of students with mental retardation. *Education and Training in Mental Retardation, 27,* 302–314.

Wehmeyer, M.L. (1995). A career education approach: Self-determination for youth with mild cognitive disabilities. *Intervention in School and Clinic, 30,* 157–163.

Wehmeyer, M.L. (1996). Self-determination as an educational outcome: Why is it important to children? In D.J. Sands & M.L. Wehmeyer (Eds.), *Self-determination across the life span: Independence and choice for people with disabilities* (pp. 17–36). Baltimore: Paul H. Brookes Publishing Co.

Wehmeyer, M.L., Kelchner, K., & Richards, S. (1996). Essential characteristics of self-determined behaviors of adults with mental retardation and developmental disabilities. *American Journal on Mental Retardation, 100,* 632–642.

Wehmeyer, M.L., & Schwartz, M. (1997). Self-determination and positive adult outcomes: A follow-up study of youth with mental retardation or learning disabilities. *Exceptional Children, 63,* 245–255.

Weiner, B. (1980). *Human motivation.* New York: Holt, Rinehart & Winston.

Zimmerman, B.J. (1994). Dimensions of academic self-regulation: A conceptual framework for education. In D.H. Schunk & B.J. Zimmerman (Eds.), *Self-regulation of learning and performance, issues and educational applications* (pp. 3–21). Hillsdale, NJ: Lawrence Erlbaum Associates.

Zimmerman, B.J., Bandura, A., & Martinez-Pons, M. (1992). Self-motivation for academic attainment: The role of self-efficacy beliefs and personal goal-setting. *American Educational Research Journal, 29,* 663–676.

Whose Future Is it Anyway?

A Student-Directed
Transition-Planning Program

Michael L. Wehmeyer

There are a growing number of programmatic efforts to involve students in their transition programs, many of which are presented in this text. These programs usually are one of two types—student-directed transition-planning programs or self-advocacy programs—although most efforts incorporate components of both types. *Student-directed transition-planning programs* typically emphasize student direction of the education-planning process, are often written expressly for students to implement, and typically use the individualized education program (IEP) or individualized transition plan (ITP) meeting as the fulcrum for activities. *Self-advocacy programs* tend to emphasize the development of skills related to leadership, assertive communication, individual rights and responsibilities, and advocacy ef-

The *Whose Future Is it Anyway? A Student-Directed Transition-Planning Program* curriculum is published by and available from The Arc National Headquarters, 500 East Border Street, Suite 300, Arlington, Texas 76010; (800) 433-5255.

forts; are less likely to use the IEP meeting itself as a central focus; and are generally implemented by someone other than the student, such as the classroom teacher.

There are limitations to relying on the educational and transition-planning process, specifically on the annual meeting, as a means to promote student involvement or self-determination (see Chapters 1 and 2 for further discussion of this topic). However, there is also a good reason to actively pursue increased student involvement in planning meetings: Quite simply, the IEP and ITP meetings provide an opportunity for students to show that they have the capacity and motivation to assume responsibility for their learning and a vision for their future and a plan (e.g., goals, objectives) to make that vision a reality and that, indeed, they deserve the opportunity to do so. The IEP and ITP meetings provide an opportunity for the student to see him- or herself as having control over his or her life and for significant others to see the student as capable and competent.

This potential for providing students with greater control over their learning stands in stark contrast to how students typically perceive such meetings. Our experience has been that many students view education-planning meetings as a time when adults talk about what students cannot do, what students have not accomplished, and what these adults believe needs to happen to correct these problems. Instead of being an opportunity for the student to experience control, such meetings too often offer students further proof that they have no control.

Efforts to enable students to participate in their education-planning meetings can have multiple benefits. First, such efforts provide students with self-advocacy and self-determination skills that will benefit them throughout their lives. Second, just the effort to involve students, in and of itself, sends a message to students that they are valued and capable. Third, such efforts may influence the process itself, as well as other participants in the process, and make it more equitable and beneficial for students.

This chapter describes one such effort, called *Whose Future Is it Anyway? A Student-Directed Transition-Planning Program* (Wehmeyer & Kelchner, 1997), that was developed and field tested for use with adolescents who have cognitive disabilities. (The *Whose Future Is it Anyway? A Student-Directed Transition-Planning Program* curriculum is published by and available from The Arc National Headquarters, 500 East Border Street, Suite 300, Arlington, Texas 76010; 1-800-433-5255.) *Whose Future Is it Anyway?* is designed to enable learners, primarily students with mental retardation and learning disabilities, to assume a more meaningful role in their transition-planning process. The following section describes the materials and the instructional process. Subsequent sections report the results of the yearlong field test of the materials with students who have cognitive disabilities.

CURRICULUM DEVELOPMENT

Since 1990, The Arc of the United States: A National Organization on Mental Retardation has conducted research in and developed curricular and assessment materials to promote self-determination (see Chapter 1). Among the findings from the research and assessments was that females with cognitive disabilities were more likely than their male peers to hold perceptions of control that were maladaptive to becoming more self-determined (Wehmeyer, 1994).

There are well-documented findings that young women with disabilities graduate from secondary education programs to less positive adult outcomes. Research indicates that males with disabilities are more likely than females to be employed, to work full time, and to remain so. When employed, females with disabilities are more likely to be employed in unskilled jobs than males in spite of a lack of differences between sexes in IQ scores, achievement, and basic job skills. Hasazi, Gordon, and Roe (1985) found that males with disabilities leaving school were 30% more likely than females to be employed. Hasazi, Johnson, Hasazi, Gordon, and Hull (1989) found that female students without disabilities were twice as likely to be employed as were female students with disabilities 1 year after high school and three times more likely than females 2 years postgraduation. They found that males were consistently more likely to be employed than females, both for students with and without disabilities, but that the degree of gender difference was greater for students with disabilities.

Sitlington and Frank (1993) found that females with mental retardation or learning disabilities were less likely than males to find competitive employment after high school and earned significantly less per hour when employed. Scuccimarra and Speece (1991) determined that, among students with mild disabilities 2 years out of high school, females had a significantly higher rate of unemployment (48%) than males (9%), females were more likely to work in unskilled occupations, and more males (25%) than females (9%) earned $5 or more per hour.

Given that increased self-determination has been linked to more positive adult outcomes for students with cognitive disabilities (Wehmeyer & Schwartz, 1997) and an enhanced quality of life for adults with mental retardation (Wehmeyer & Schwartz, in press), I and my colleagues were interested in designing an intervention that would enable young women to become more self-determined and take greater control over their education and their lives. Pioneering efforts by Martin and colleagues (Martin & Huber Marshall, 1995; Martin, Huber Marshall, & Maxson, 1993) to teach self-determination skills through the IEP process had illustrated the potential benefits of working with students to assume greater control in their planning processes. Given the federal mandates for student involvement in transition planning (see Chapter 1) and the general importance of involving students in such planning, I and my colleagues believed that one way to change students' perceptions about control in their lives, particularly those of females with cognitive disabilities, was to enable them to take meaningful roles in their ITP processes.

Whose Future Is it Anyway? was written to achieve this end. The development of the curriculum was guided by several overarching principles. First, I and my colleagues wanted the materials to be student directed. Most educational materials are written for teachers as the end users, and, as such, instruction proceeds from the teacher to the student. *Whose Future Is it Anyway?* was developed with the student in mind as the end user. The intent was to keep the student in control of his or her learning experience as much as possible.

Second, although student acquisition of specific self-determination and self-advocacy skills was one envisioned outcome, the primary outcome of the curriculum was to provide students with the information that they needed to take more control over their meetings. There is a reciprocity between taking control and perceiving oneself as being in control. That is, the way that individuals often develop adaptive perceptions of control in their lives and come to believe that they can exert influence on desired outcomes is to "jump into the deep end" and experience control. It was hoped that through this process students would learn a few fundamental self-determination and self-advocacy skills and become further motivated to learn more such skills.

Third, although the teacher's role in the curriculum is different from typical teacher-directed instructional programs, we believed that the teacher was the key to success for the student. Many students with disabilities lack the experiences, skills, or confidence to work through a curriculum independently. If students were to learn about the curriculum, work through the curriculum, and eventually take a greater role in their educational program, it would be because their teacher provided the information, support, advocacy, and instruction needed to succeed. Based on these basic principles and with funding from the U.S. Department of Education's Women's Educational Equity Act program, we developed and field tested the *Whose Future Is it Anyway?* curriculum. The curriculum is described in the section that follows.

CURRICULUM OVERVIEW

Whose Future Is it Anyway? consists of 36 sessions that introduce students to the concepts of transition and transition planning and enable students to self-direct instruction related to 1) being aware of oneself and one's disability; 2) making decisions about transition-related outcomes; 3) identifying and securing community resources to support transition services; 4) writing and evaluating transition goals and objectives; 5) communicating effectively in small groups; and 6) developing skills to become an effective team member, leader, or self-advocate.

Role of the Student

The level of support needed by students to complete activities varies a great deal. Some students who experience difficulty reading or writing may need almost one-to-one support to progress through the materials, whereas other students can complete the process independently. However, it is not the degree to which students are independent in the accomplishment of activities that represents the essence of student-directed learning, but rather the degree to which students have and believe they have control over the process. The materials make every effort to ensure that students retain this control while receiving the support they need to succeed.

Role of the Teacher

As mentioned previously, the teacher's role in implementing *Whose Future Is it Anyway?* is different from more traditional teacher-directed instructional strategies or materials. In fact, the teacher's role in *Whose Future Is it Anyway?* combines a number of roles: facilitator, teacher, and advocate. The growing use of person-centered planning procedures has acclimated many teachers to the role of facilitator. A facilitator's responsibility is to do whatever it takes to enable the student to succeed. Although for the sake of simplicity the term *coach* is used throughout the process, there are important differences between traditional coaching roles and facilitation. These differences revolve around the authority vested in the coach. Technically, a person could facilitate a discussion or a process without having broad knowledge about the given topic. This is just the opposite for coaches, who are supposed to possess a great deal of knowledge about the topic. A facilitator needs to provide support without seeming to be the authoritarian figure who has all the answers. Students' self-understanding will emerge only in a nonjudgmental atmosphere in which their efforts are valued and supported.

The second role, that of teacher, seems counterintuitive to that of facilitator. A *teacher*, by definition, is someone who has expertise in an area and whose job it is to use that expertise to change students. However, *Whose Future Is it Anyway?* emphasizes to students that all people depend on others to a certain extent and that teachers are a valuable resource for information about education and the educational planning process. The student will need to tap into that expertise and information if he or she is to succeed. The key is that it is the student who requests or seeks the information. In addition, *Whose Future Is it Anyway?* is a learning tool. Just because a teacher is not lecturing or using more traditional teaching models does not mean that he or she is not teaching the student.

The third role is that of an advocate. In this sense, it is not intended to mean advocacy on behalf of the student against any particular event or entity. Instead, the teacher's role is to communicate to the student that he or she can succeed, that he or she will be provided support throughout the process, and that the shared goal is a successful transition. This may mean that teachers do have to advocate on behalf of the student, particularly in situations in which the planning process does not allow student involvement. However, the important aspect of this role is that teachers must work collaboratively with students to achieve a shared goal.

Best Use of the Curriculum

Ideally, students should be able to acquire the *Whose Future Is it Anyway?* student materials and begin to work through them individually. In reality, the time demands on teachers, the reading and writing abilities of students with cognitive and developmental disabilities, and the structure of most classrooms make this difficult. Given these realities, the materials have been field tested for group use as well as for individual use. Group use implies that students work in groups to read through the lesson and get an understanding of the task or tasks at hand; it does not imply that the students respond in groups. There are some lessons where group responses may be possible as long as all students are involved. In other lessons, the responses must be individually determined.

Because most planning meetings are held annually, the materials are written so that a student can begin to work on *Whose Future Is it Anyway?* immediately after his or her planning meeting and, by devoting 1 or 2 hours per week to the process, can complete all activities before the following year's planning meeting. It is best to schedule instruction so that students can quickly apply the skills that they have acquired at the planning meeting. If the materials are used in a "unit" format in which the student devotes more time to the process, this instruction should occur just before the planning meeting.

One of the advocacy tasks that teachers must assume is to make sure that the process does not contribute to students' sense of helplessness. If students work through the materials, they must have the opportunity to meaningfully participate in their planning meetings. Teachers may need to work with other team members, including administrators, diagnosticians, transition specialists, and other professionals to guarantee that they understand and support the goals that the student is working to achieve.

Depending on how early instructional emphasis in transition begins, *Whose Future Is it Anyway?* can be used with students ages 14–21. It is likely that students will benefit most from early and repeated use of the materials. This does not mean that students repeat the process each year. The materials can serve as a structure by which students are involved in educational planning each year. Students do not necessarily need to repeat all the activities but can use the completed materials as an ongoing resource. It may not hurt, however, to repeat the process once if it is used with students younger than 18 years of age.

Students with cognitive disabilities receive their education in a wide array of instruction environments, from general education classrooms to separate campus, self-contained classrooms. Although I believe that self-determination is linked to the movement toward inclusive educational experiences (Sands & Wehmeyer, 1996) and that students with mental retardation should receive their education in the same settings as their peers without disabilities (The Arc, 1992), I did not want to make the materials placement specific. Because it is designed to be student directed, *Whose Future Is it Anyway?* can be used in virtually any education environment.

Curriculum Outcomes

Student outcomes vary a great deal. Some students complete the process and go on to take an active role in their educational planning. Other students participate in the process but may not "lead" their planning meetings. The intended outcome is for students to increase their participation in the education-planning and decision-making processes. This outcome varies considerably among students. Field testing indicated that, if nothing else, students who participate in the program have a better understanding of transition planning.

WHOSE FUTURE IS IT ANYWAY?
A STUDENT-DIRECTED TRANSITION-PLANNING PROGRAM

As mentioned previously, *Whose Future Is it Anyway?* consists of 36 lessons in six instructional units or sections. Each unit is described in the following sections.

Section 1: Getting to Know You

Section 1 (called *Getting to Know You*) introduces the concepts of transition and education planning; provides information about transition requirements in the Individuals with Disabilities Education Act (IDEA) of 1990 (PL 101-476) and its amendments (Individuals with Disabilities Education Act Amendments of 1991 [PL 102-119] and Individuals with Disabilities Education Act Amendments of 1997 [PL 105-17]) and enables students to identify who has attended past planning meetings, who is required to be present at such meetings, and who they want involved in their planning processes. Using an exercise depicted in Figure 1, students identify people from five areas of their lives (friends, family, school, neighborhood, church/community) who might participate in planning activities. Later in the section, they are introduced to four primary transition outcome areas (employment, community living, postsecondary education, recreation and leisure). Activities throughout *Whose Future Is it Anyway?* focus on these transition outcome areas.

The remainder of the sessions in this section discuss the topics of disability and disability awareness. Students are encouraged to identify their unique

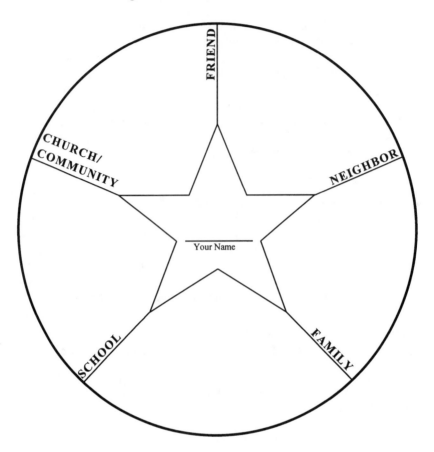

Figure 1.   Support circle sheet from Section 1 of *Whose Future Is it Anyway?*

characteristics, including their abilities and interests. Participants then identify unique learning needs related to their disabilities. This process begins with a discussion of stereotypes associated with disability and the possible negative impact of such stereotypes. Finally, students identify their unique learning needs resulting from their disabilities. They also identify the services and supports, called *MULES* (My Unique Learning and Educational Supports), that they can use to succeed in school.

Section 2: Making Decisions

The second section (called *Making Decisions*) introduces a decision-making process that students then apply to making decisions about the four transition outcome areas. This process involves the application of a simple problem-solving process represented by the acronym DO IT!, which stands for Define your problem, Outline your options, Identify the outcome of each option, Take action, and ! (get excited). Students learn the DO IT! process by working through each step to make a decision about a potential living arrangement and then applying the process to make decisions about the three other transition outcome areas. In the final session in this section, students learn to use the DO IT! process to give informed consent and apply this specifically to the ITP planning meeting.

Section 3: How to Get What You Need, Section 101

The third section (called *How to Get What You Need, Section 101*) enables students to locate community resources identified in previous planning meetings that are intended to provide supports in each of the transition outcome areas. Students identify such supports if available and then gather information about each community resource. They are encouraged to think about alternative community supports, including those available to all citizens (e.g., banks, real estate agents) and those specific to people with disabilities (e.g., vocational rehabilitation, supported employment). At the end of this section, students are asked to identify the MULES that they can use to become more independent as adults. Because this focuses on obtaining support in the community and not just at school, MULES is redefined as meaning My Unique Life Elevating Supports.

Section 4: Goals, Objectives, and the Future

Section 4 enables learners to apply a set of rules, called *WIGOUT* (Writing Instructional Goals and Objectives for Use in Transition) rules, to identify transition-related goals and objectives that are currently in their IEPs or on their ITP forms, evaluate these goals based on their own transition interests and abilities, and develop additional goals to take to their next planning meetings. These rules, depicted in Table 1, provide students with guidelines for

Table 1. WIGOUT (Writing Instructional Goals and Objectives for Use in Transition) rules

Rule number	Rule description
WIGOUT Rule 1	Goals and objectives for your school program should be written to reach outcomes you have helped to decide on and that are based on your unique interests and abilities.
WIGOUT Rule 2	You have to write goals that you can reach and that you have some control over achieving.
WIGOUT Rule 3	Goals and objectives have to be measurable. This means that you have to be able to tell how you are doing on them.
WIGOUT Rule 4	Goals and objectives should have a time to start and a time to end.
WIGOUT Rule 5	Goals and objectives should be written in terms of expected outcomes.

evaluating and developing educational goals. Students learn what goals and objectives are, how they should be written, and ways to track progress on goals and objectives. The intent is not to make students proficient in writing educational goals, but instead to provide an overview of what they can expect when they examine their goals.

Section 5: Communicatin'

The fifth section (called *Communicatin'*) introduces effective communication strategies for small-group situations, such as the ITP meeting. Students work through sessions that introduce different types of communication (e.g., verbal, body language) and how to interpret these communicative behaviors, what the differences are between aggressive and assertive communication, how to effectively negotiate and compromise, when to use persuasion, and what other skills will enable them to be more effective communicators during ITP meetings. Students are introduced to a set of rules that can make them better listeners as well. These rules, called *get reAL* (*get re*sults from *A*ctive *L*istening), encourage students to look at the speaker, to ask questions, and to take notes, as well as not to interrupt. Through this section, students generate a list of at least four issues that they want to discuss at their transition-planning meetings and determine the best ways to communicate these issues.

Section 6: Thank You, Honorable Chairperson

The final session enables students to learn types and purposes of meetings, steps to holding effective meetings, and roles of the meeting chairs and team members. Students are encouraged to work with school district personnel to take meaningful roles in planning for and participating in the meetings, including the possibilities of chairing their ITP meetings. Students review the previous sections and use that review process to create support sheets of things they can do in their meetings.

CURRICULUM EFFICACY

Wehmeyer and Lawrence (1995) reported findings of a study to evaluate the educational efficacy of the *Whose Future Is it Anyway?* curriculum. Field testing of the *Whose Future Is it Anyway?* materials was conducted in an urban school district with students who were identified as having cognitive disabilities, primarily learning disabilities or mental retardation. Instruction with the curriculum began early in the school year and continued through the spring of that school year, at which time all students' IEP planning meetings were scheduled. A special education teacher employed by The Arc was present during the entire field test and served as the primary facilitator for instructional activities. Students involved in the field test received instruction for approximately 1 hour per week for the duration of the school year.

The purpose of the field test was to evaluate the effects of the process on students' self-determination and perceptions about their abilities to participate in the planning process. To evaluate the first, teachers and students involved in the field test were interviewed. To evaluate the latter, students were asked to complete measures of student self-determination, perceptions of control, and self-efficacy for participation in IEP planning (see Wehmeyer & Lawrence, 1995, for details of instrumentation) both before and after they worked through the curriculum.

There were significant changes in scores on self-efficacy and outcome expectancy for education planning among students involved in the curriculum, indicating that students believed that they possessed more skills that were necessary to participate in their IEP planning meetings and believed that if they exhibited these skills, preferred outcomes related to their involvement in the meetings would occur. This trend was particularly strong for young women in the sample.

Anecdotal information from students suggested that they did enjoy, as well as benefit from, the process. When asked to identify their favorite part of the program, students identified 1) finding out about community resources, 2) learning about jobs, 3) learning about "myself" and testing, 4) learning about the law (specifically IDEA), 5) talking about their futures and what they wanted to do after graduation, and 6) learning to do things on their own. When asked to identify their least favorite aspect of the process, the students identified only the writing involved. When asked what they had learned about themselves, students responded that they had learned that they could be more independent by seeking support, could benefit from postsecondary education, and could set goals that would provide direction for their lives.

During our field testing, we encountered situations that illustrated how difficult it is to change the system and to begin to rebuild students' beliefs. Despite the best intentions and sincere efforts on the part of the project personnel and the school personnel to enable students to play more meaningful roles in the process, the process broke down on several occasions. For example, team members who were added at the last minute were unaware of students' involvement in the field test. Also, personnel who were involved in the instructional activities were transferred within or left the school district, and replacements who took over were unaware of students' activities. Finally, the time constraints involved in having meetings for all students too frequently curtailed the opportunities for students to participate and often gave the impression that the decisions were made before the meetings began. Teachers implementing the curriculum need to be aware that they undoubtedly will encounter barriers to successful student involvement.

CONCLUSIONS

In the end, however, our experiences proved that barriers to student involvement in transition planning are not insurmountable and that *Whose Future Is it Anyway?* can enable learners with cognitive disabilities to play a meaningful role in the transition-planning process. In addition to the gains in self-efficacy and outcome expectancy scores, students were able to participate in a meaningful manner. Students were often more animated and one student noticed that a school representative who should have attended the meeting was absent. Students who previously had remained quiet or withdrawn, expressed their opinions and ideas and advocated for preferred goals. Although all students did not make such dramatic gains, enough did so to provide optimism that efforts to promote student involvement through programs like *Whose Future Is it Anyway?* and other programs in this book can make a significant difference in the lives of students with disabilities.

REFERENCES

The Arc. (1992). *Position statement on education.* Arlington, TX: Author.

Hasazi, S.B., Gordon, L.R., & Roe, C.A. (1985). Factors associated with the employment status of handicapped youth exiting high school from 1979–1983. *Exceptional Children, 51,* 455–469.

Hasazi, S.B., Johnson, R.E., Hasazi, J.E., Gordon, L.R., & Hull, M. (1989). Employment of youth with and without handicaps following high school: Outcomes and correlates. *Journal of Special Education, 23,* 243–255.

Individuals with Disabilities Education Act (IDEA) of 1990, PL 101-476, 20 U.S.C. §§ 1400 *et seq.*

Individuals with Disabilities Education Act Amendments of 1991, PL 102-119, 20 U.S.C. §§ 1400 *et seq.*

Individuals with Disabilities Education Act Amendments of 1997, PL 105-17, 20 U.S.C. §§ 1400 *et seq.*

Martin, J.E., & Huber Marshall, L. (1995). ChoiceMaker: A comprehensive self-determination transition program. *Intervention in School and Clinic, 30,* 147–156.

Martin, J.E., Huber Marshall, L., & Maxson, L. (1993). Transition policy: Infusing self-determination and self-advocacy into transition programs. *Career Development for Exceptional Individuals, 16,* 53–61.

Sands, D.J., & Wehmeyer, M.L. (1996). Future directions in self-determination: Articulating values and policies, reorganizing organizational structures, and implementing professional practices. In D.J. Sands & M.L. Wehmeyer (Eds.), *Self-determination across the life span: Independence and choice for people with disabilities* (pp. 331–344). Baltimore: Paul H. Brookes Publishing Co.

Scuccimarra, D., & Speece, D.L. (1991). Employment outcomes and social integration of students with mild handicaps: The quality of life two years after high school. *Journal of Learning Disabilities, 25,* 213–219.

Sitlington, P.L., & Frank, A.R. (1993). Success as an adult: Does gender make a difference for graduates with mental disabilities? *Career Development of Exceptional Individuals, 16,* 171–182.

Wehmeyer, M.L. (1994). Perceptions of self-determination and psychological empowerment of adolescents with mental retardation. *Education and Training in Mental Retardation and Developmental Disabilities, 29,* 9–21.

Wehmeyer, M.L., & Kelchner, K. (1997). *Whose Future Is it Anyway? A student-directed transition-planning program.* Arlington, TX: The Arc National Headquarters.

Wehmeyer, M.L., & Lawrence, M. (1995). Whose future is it anyway? Promoting student involvement in transition planning. *Career Development for Exceptional Individuals, 18,* 69–83.

Wehmeyer, M.L., & Schwartz, M. (1997). Self-determination and positive adult outcomes: A follow-up study of youth with mental retardation or learning disabilities. *Exceptional Children, 63,* 245–255.

Wehmeyer, M.L., & Schwartz, M. (in press). The relationship between self-determination and quality of life for adults with mental retardation. *Education and Training in Mental Retardation and Developmental Disabilities.*

Next S.T.E.P.

Student Transition and Educational Planning

Andrew S. Halpern

Since the early 1990s, I and several of my colleagues in Oregon have been developing a curriculum that is focused on self-directed transition planning for adolescents and young adults with and without disabilities (Halpern et al., 1997). This curriculum is called *Next S.T.E.P.: Student Transition and Educational Planning*. Over the course of development, we have field-tested and evaluated the curriculum with about 300 teachers and more than 5,000 students and their families. Evaluation efforts have included weekly feedback from teachers; observations of classroom sessions; and multiple focus group sessions with teachers, students, and families. We have also collected some information about the initial impact of the curriculum on the students. As an outcome of this process, we have not only produced our curriculum but also developed some convictions about the desirable components of *any* curriculum that addresses self-directed transition planning.

The *Next S.T.E.P.* curriculum is available from PRO-ED, 8700 Shoal Creek Boulevard, Austin, Texas 78758-6897; (800) 397-7633.

PROPOSITIONS FOR SUCCESSFUL
ENGAGEMENT IN SELF-DIRECTED TRANSITION PLANNING

So, what are some of the elements required to help students to engage success-fully in self-directed transition planning? As I have given thought to this question in light of our own work and also the work of others, I have formulated 10 propositions that, for me anyway, point the way. I have structured this chapter around these propositions, which have been developed to address instructional design. All of these issues are addressed in the *Next S.T.E.P.* curriculum, but they may also be relevant for other curricula as well. I have therefore chosen to present very few details about our curriculum; instead, the focus of the discussion is on the general principles underlying it. Specifically, I will share these 10 propositions with you, along with some of my reasons for believing them to be true.

Proposition 1: Students Must Be *Taught* How to Do Transition Planning

For the most part, students do not learn to plan for their transition from school to adult life through incidental learning. Transition planning is not something that students acquire naturally, so it needs to be embedded in some form of in-struction or guidance (Gelatt, 1962; Halpern, 1994; Krumboltz & Hamel, 1977; Szymanski, 1994; Szymanski, Turner, & Hershenson, 1992). Students will learn how to *do* transition planning only by *doing* transition planning. Al-though the planning "process" is similar for most people, the "content" of each student's plan is individualized. This calls for an intricate mixture of teaching "general concepts" and providing students with "structured opportu-nities" for developing their own plans. When the focus of a lesson is on learn-ing about transition planning, a group-oriented lecture and discussion format often works best, accompanied by numerous group activities. As the lessons progress into how to develop a transition plan, each student begins to travel down his or her own unique path. At this stage in the curriculum, teachers must begin to individualize instruction. The balancing of group and individu-alized instruction is ultimately a teacher judgment, depending on the needs of the students and the availability of instructional aides for assisting the teacher.

The need to *teach* students how to engage in self-directed transition plan-ning presents a delicate dilemma. Even as adolescents are still learning how to assume increasing levels of responsibility for their own life decisions, teach-ers are exercising substantial control through the structure of the instructional process. Teachers usually tell students "what" to learn and often "how" to learn. However, as adolescents become increasingly skillful and responsible in doing self-directed transition planning, the teacher must let go and provide ever-decreasing amounts of support and guidance. Parents, of course, face a similar dilemma as their children begin to show interest in leaving home.

Proposition 2: Students Are Not "Naturally" Motivated to Do Transition Planning, Which Creates a Potential Barrier to Getting Them Involved in This Process

Many adolescents and young adults are *not* naturally inclined to engage in transition planning. To this age group, the "future" seems far away and much less interesting than what to do this afternoon or next week. At this stage in their lives, adolescents also tend to believe that they have much more control over short-range decisions than over long-range plans. "Why bother worrying about something," they ask, "because the future is far away and you probably can't do much about it anyway?" This is the real-life context that must be acknowledged as a starting point in the design of instruction for teaching adolescents and young adults how to do transition planning.

The first business of any transition-planning curriculum must focus on arousing student interest in the need for doing transition planning. Many students do not think much about what they want to do after high school and how such long-range goals might affect their current goals and activities. Most students are struggling to gain control over their own choices and decisions, and this struggle may potentially bring them into conflict with teachers and parents.

There are several ways in which a transition-planning curriculum can address this motivational component. During the early lessons of a transition-planning curriculum, students become motivated to participate only if they can begin to see the relevance of doing long-range planning in spite of their general disbelief in either the efficacy or enjoyableness of such activities. This means that the early lessons must somehow accomplish two purposes:

1. Sensitizing students to the relevance of transition planning in their own lives
2. Encouraging students to believe that they can actually do something useful if they engage in such planning

To accomplish these purposes, early lessons must be entertaining as well as instructive and must include numerous real-life examples of transition issues prevalent in student lives that might benefit from systematic planning. No planning strategies are required at this point in the curriculum. An emerging perception of personal need for such strategies provides the motivation for students to become engaged.

The next phase of a transition-planning curriculum should involve helping students to acquire or hone the skills they need to do transition planning effectively. From the perspective of motivation, two outcomes must occur during this phase of the curriculum to keep students engaged in the process:

1. They must begin to sense that they are actually gaining control over some important decisions in their lives.
2. They must begin to develop a concrete transition plan that reflects their own needs, interests, and abilities.

Gaining a perception of control at the beginning may be little more than suspending disbelief that adults are actually willing to sacrifice some of their control. The perception of gaining control solidifies when the student develops his or her own transition plan. This does not mean that parents and teachers must simply acquiesce to student demands. A self-directed plan places the student in the driver's seat, so to speak, but the car cannot function without fuel and the maintenance services, which must be provided by significant others. As discussed in Chapter 3, student decision making benefits from support provided by parents and teachers. Lessons that reinforce this interdependence are motivational for the student, who will thus be learning productive ways of interacting assertively and effectively with authority figures.

Engaging in the planning process and developing a concrete plan are necessary but not sufficient outcomes of an effective transition-planning curriculum. Actually accomplishing a plan requires an entirely different set of skills and provides unique and different opportunities for student reinforcement. During the part of the curriculum that addresses plan implementation, students must

1. Experience some success in achieving at least part of their transition plans
2. Learn that if part of a plan does not work, their response should be to modify the plan rather than to simply acknowledge and accept defeat

As students learn and practice these plan implementation skills, they begin to experience the most powerful motivation-enhancing feelings that a good transition-planning curriculum can deliver. Students learn how to make their plans succeed, and success is almost guaranteed because problems can usually be overcome by changing either one's tactics or one's expectations. Students find it motivational to learn that there are many shades of gray between getting exactly what one wants and feeling the despair of failure.

Proposition 3: Self-Evaluation Is an Essential Foundation for Engaging Successfully in Transition Planning

The basic principle behind Proposition 3 is that students must gain an understanding of who they are before they can explore meaningfully who they might become—that is, they must follow the advice of Socrates, "Know thyself," and Shakespeare, "To thine own self be true." Although Socrates and Shakespeare were probably not particularly interested in transition planning, they both understood that all people need the foundation of an accurate understanding of who they are before considering who they might become. Adolescents and young adults must be taught to think about their likes, dislikes, strengths, and weaknesses before setting personal goals that will guide them into the future.

Traditional assessment practices do not encourage this type of self-evaluation. Most educational assessments are performed as tests of student behavior. An expert, often a teacher, requires the student to demonstrate ability or proficiency under structured and controlled conditions. The outcomes of assessment are used to make decisions about the student, with someone other than the student being the decision maker. Will the student be admitted into a program? What grade will the student receive? What additional instruction does the student need in reading or math? Rarely are the results of such assessments placed under the student's control for interpretation and use.

Even though the traditional uses of assessment have almost entirely fallen into a diagnostic-prescriptive approach, there is no reason to confine the purposes of assessment in such a way, as discussed in Chapter 4. It is thinkable, and has been argued with passion (Vash, 1984), that the person being assessed can and should control both the type of assessments that are performed and the eventual use of the assessment outcomes. In a sense, Vash (1984) argued that the person being assessed should "hire" the assessment expert to serve as a personal consultant, leaving the ultimate decision making to the "employer" (e.g., the person who hired the consultant). Such an approach is totally empowering and places responsibility for the use of assessment information within the context of self-directed planning, where it belongs.

Although this way of viewing assessment is not typical in the disability education field, there are some emerging examples of self-evaluation approaches being used for the purpose of helping adolescents with disabilities to engage effectively in transition planning (Clark & Patton, 1997; Halpern et al., 1997; Wehmeyer, 1995b). Such approaches must be built into any curriculum that addresses transition planning as a foundation for engaging in such planning.

Lessons in this area should begin with the assumption that students have had little or no experience with an assessment approach purporting to place them in charge of interpreting and using the outcomes of assessment. It is more likely for students to be somewhat fearful of assessment practices, expecting that the traditional approaches will be used.

Given this likely set of expectations about assessment, the first instructional unit in self-directed assessment should probably help students understand and appreciate the difference between most traditional assessments they have experienced and the new approach they will be learning that focuses on self-evaluation. After students have been made to feel comfortable with the viability and utility of this approach to assessment, they must then learn how to actually conduct a useful self-evaluation. These lessons, at minimum, have two distinct purposes. They will teach students the following:

1. How to conduct a self-evaluation using one or more appropriate instruments that would be introduced and described through these lessons
2. How to interpret the outcomes of the self-evaluation by taking charge of the interpretation process

The final lessons addressing self-evaluation should focus on teaching students to use their assessment outcomes to help them identify appropriate transition goals and activities to include in their transition plans. The focus of these lessons is clearly on teaching students how to engage successfully in the process of self-evaluation.

But what about instrumentation? What raw data should students use to help them perform meaningful self-evaluations? There is no single correct answer to this question. All types of assessment information are potentially useful, including traditional psychometric tests, curriculum-based assessments, behavioral observations, and rating scales. The issue is not so much about what information is collected but rather how the information is used and who is ultimately responsible for making the interpretations.

We have chosen to use a rating instrument, the *Transition Skills Inventory*, in the *Next S.T.E.P.* curriculum (Halpern et al., 1997). This inventory evaluates student skills in the same areas that students are expected to consider as they develop their transition goals. Students evaluate themselves, as do their teachers and parents, using the same set of items. Differences of opinion are treated as an invitation to discuss possible reasons for viewing student performance differently rather than as a sign of unreliable assessment. In the end, students develop a sense of their strengths and weaknesses, and they use this information to help them develop their transition plans.

Proposition 4: Students Should Explore the Areas of Personal Life, Jobs, Education and Training, and Living on One's Own When They Do Transition Planning

The essence of transition planning asks adolescents to consider what they want to become when they leave school as young adults and what they need to do to begin moving themselves toward those future goals. Over the years, numerous descriptions and taxonomies have been proposed to conceptualize the adult adjustment of people with disabilities (Brown, Bayer, & MacFarlane, 1988; Chadsey-Rusch, Rusch, & O'Reilly, 1991; Edgerton, 1990; Goode, 1990; Halpern, 1993; Nirje, 1970; Parmenter, 1988; Schalock, 1990; Taylor & Bogdan, 1990). Most of these studies, however, were produced from the perspectives of theoreticians, researchers, policy makers, and service providers. As these professional adults have struggled with defining the good life and developed ever-increasing nuances in proposed taxonomies, the field has progressed in gaining clarification about the broad purposes and desired outcomes of transition planning.

However, adolescents with disabilities have rarely been engaged in this dialogue. Assuming that a transition-planning curriculum has been successful in simply getting their attention and securing their motivation to participate, students probably will not even have a working vocabulary for identifying transition goals during the early phases of such a curriculum. The establishment of such a working vocabulary must be one of the first purposes of a curriculum on transition planning.

When we cut through the various professional taxonomies to look for commonalities, we identified four areas that adolescents should consider as they begin to develop their transition goals:

1. Personal life
2. Jobs
3. Education and training
4. Living on one's own

These areas capture the essence of the professional taxonomies using language that is easy for the students to learn and appreciate as being relevant to their own emerging lives as young adults.

Personal Life   If anything can be regarded as a hook for beginning to think about transition goals, the quality of one's personal life is a prime candidate. We are all interested in such topics as learning how to get along better with other people and exploring new ways of using leisure time effectively. This content area serves as a good first topic in an adolescent's beginning vocabulary for transition planning.

Jobs   Like it or not, adolescents are bound to frequently hear the question, "What do you want to do when you grow up?" Many adolescents find part-time jobs while still in school, usually to earn money for immediate needs and desires rather than to explore career possibilities. In other words, we can almost count on adolescents being exposed, in one way or another, to the need for work and the dynamics of work. This is a good foundation to exploit in a transition-planning curriculum. We should encourage students to explore systematically some possible matches between their interests and skills and job opportunities that might draw upon these interests and skills.

Education and Training   Most adolescents can relate to the question of whether and how they will graduate from high school. The consequence of not attending to this question, at worst, is dropping out of school, an event that occurs far too frequently and often portends devastating consequences. For students who remain in school, an issue that often catches their attention is whether they need additional education or training to accomplish their vocational goals and what they need to do to secure such training. Students should be encouraged to explore the answers to such questions.

Living on One's Own   Most adolescents begin to fantasize while they are still in school about "getting a pad of their own." This is a normal manifestation of a growing urge to become independent. It is surprising, therefore, how little adolescents actually know about what it takes to gain such independence. Endless research (see, e.g., the review by Chadsey-Rusch et al., 1991) shows that many adolescents know little about such things as money management, finding and securing housing, preparing meals, home management, and gaining access to the community resources that one needs to function independently. Students should be encouraged to explore the discrepancy between their desire to become independent and their ability to do so.

An important lesson that should also be reinforced during this phase of the curriculum is that one does not need to be a Lone Ranger to live as an adult independently. The word *independent* is actually misleading. Few people, with or without the challenge of a disability, live in total isolation from other people. In the normal interplay of human interactions, we sometimes give help and nurturance to others, and we sometimes receive help and nurturance from others. The free flow of mutual support is a vital characteristic of a well-functioning community. We sometimes tend to forget that interdependence is the true goal of independent living. This is because human nature and American social mores tend to emphasize individual achievement and competition as being more fundamental than community prosperity and collaboration.

We do not want to teach our students that it is somehow "wimpy" to rely on other people while still being responsible for planning one's own life. Knowing when to ask for help and being able to use help effectively are important transition skills. The need for such skills occurs at every stage of the planning process. Students must learn that it is desirable to use help wisely and that this is not the manifestation of a character flaw. The curriculum must reinforce this concept repeatedly.

Proposition 5: Students Benefit from Assistance and Structure to Identify Transition Goals and Develop Individualized Transition Plans

A working vocabulary for transition goals, a developing motivation to participate in the transition-planning process, and a carefully executed self-evaluation are, of course, only useful preliminary steps along the road of transition planning. There are many possible concrete goals that one might choose to pursue within each of the four transition areas just described. To minimize potential confusion that might then become a stumbling block for students, a curriculum on transition planning should identify specific goal choices and very concrete activities for students to select as they develop their transition plans. This catalog of goal and activity possibilities becomes a foundation for actual student choices. If this catalog somehow does not tap a particular student's needs and interests, the structure provided within the catalog should be sufficient to help the student to generate a unique goal and/or activity that is personally relevant.

At this point in the curriculum, students are highly involved in developing their own transition plans. Instruction begins to take on the form of individualized coaching and tutoring rather than group instruction. The intended outcome is for each student to create a unique plan that accommodates individual needs, preferences, and abilities.

If you accept my argument that transition planning should address four main areas of concern—personal life, jobs, education and training, and living on one's own—then it follows that transition plans should also include something in each of these areas. Following our belief that students should be able to choose from a catalog of possibilities, we have identified 12 goal possibilities in our own curriculum (Halpern et al., 1997) from which students may make their selections. Table 1 displays these goal choices.

Goal statements alone, of course, are not sufficient to provide students with structure and guidance for implementing their transition plans. A fully developed plan must also contain a description of activities that students will pursue to attain their goals, proposed time lines for accomplishing activities, identification of resources on which students can draw for help, and concrete indicators to determine whether goals have been achieved. To provide the reader with a sense of this flow of information within a plan, Table 2 displays some of the activities that we have developed in the *Next S.T.E.P.* curriculum (Halpern et al., 1997) for a few of the goals.

Table 1. Goal possibilities in the *Next S.T.E.P.* curriculum

Personal Life
    I will explore new ways to use my leisure time.
    I will learn new ways for getting along better with others.
    I will explore effective ways to improve my physical, mental, or spiritual health.

Jobs
    I will begin to explore jobs that match my interests and what I do well.
    I will sample jobs in my school or community that match my interests and goals.
    I will obtain a paid job in my interest area.

Education and Training
    I will make a plan for completing high school.
    I will make a plan for getting vocational training.
    I will make a plan for getting a college degree.

Living on One's Own
    I will learn the skills I need to live on my own.
    I will learn how to use community resources to help me be independent.
    I will learn how to be a good citizen and stay out of trouble.

Table 2.   Activities from the *Next S.T.E.P.* curriculum

I will learn new ways for getting along with others.
  I will listen more carefully to what other people are saying.
  I will disagree with someone in a way that helps to resolve the problem.
  I will make new friends.
  I will accept criticism without getting angry.
  I will ask for advice and use the advice.

I will find out more about several jobs that interest me.
  I will go to the library and read some books or articles about these jobs.
  I will use a computerized Career Information Service to locate information about these jobs.
  I will talk to people who are already working in these areas.
  I will visit the state employment agency to find out more about these jobs.
  I will do volunteer work that will help me learn more about these jobs.

I will make a plan for completing high school.
  I will learn what the requirements are for graduating from my high school.
  I will learn about the advantages and disadvantages of getting a GED.
  I will learn about the alternative high school completion programs that are available in my community.
  I will visit an alternative high school program in my community.
  I will list the advantages and disadvantages of the different possibilities that I have discovered.

A fully developed transition plan would include more information than is displayed in Tables 1 and 2. This additional information would complete the documentation of logistics for implementing the plan and evaluating whether it has been completed successfully. Types of additional information include 1) time lines for completing activities, 2) resources that the student may need to help him or her to complete an activity successfully, 3) check-in dates for monitoring progress, and 4) a clear indication of evaluation criteria that one might examine to determine whether the transition goal has been accomplished. The lessons during this phase of the curriculum teach students how to use this planning structure to facilitate their own transition-planning process.

The development of a good plan, however, does not automatically translate into the acquisition of many important skills that the student needs to actually implement the plan. By successfully completing a transition-planning curriculum, the student

* Becomes motivated to do transition planning
* Learns and exercises planning skills
* Develops a personally relevant transition plan
* Self-monitors implementation of his or her own plan

The actual implementation of the transition plan, however, requires that the student engage in a variety of activities above and beyond those that structure the development of a plan.

Perhaps an example will help to illustrate this distinction. Table 2 identifies a personal life planning goal that involves learning how to get along better with other people. Some possible activities to facilitate the achievement of this goal include 1) listening more carefully, 2) engaging in constructive dialogue when there is a disagreement, 3) learning how to make new friends, 4) accepting criticism without getting angry, and 5) learning how to ask for advice and help from others. Many other activities are possible in pursuit of this goal, and the curriculum encourages students to think of other possibilities that are personally relevant.

A transition-planning curriculum helps students to identify and select such activities to include in their plans; however, it does not teach students the actual skills that are embedded in selected activities. The acquisition of such skills requires additional instruction supported by other curriculum materials.

Because of this distinction between teaching students to plan and teaching students how to accomplish their plans, a transition-planning curriculum cannot be successful unless it is supported by other curricula dealing with implementation skills. In the development of the *Next S.T.E.P.* transition-planning curriculum (Halpern et al., 1997), we have found that the lessons in this curriculum work best when taught twice per week and augmented with additional instruction in related areas. I return to this logistical consideration later in the chapter.

Proposition 6: To the Maximum Extent Possible, Students Should Develop and Direct Their Own Transition-Planning Meetings

The culminating event in the process of developing a transition plan should be a student-directed transition-planning meeting, connected to the student's individualized education program (IEP) meeting if appropriate. The student and his or her teacher and parents typically attend this meeting, although others may also be invited, including friends of the student or people in the community who might be able to help the student to reach his or her goals. During this meeting, the student presents his or her tentative transition plan and receives helpful feedback from the others who are present. Program developers have found this event to be a powerful part of the total transition-planning process (Halpern, 1994; Martin, Marshall, & Maxson, 1993; Wehmeyer, 1995a). Students become empowered to make choices. Teachers and parents are often amazed by the skill and maturity students show as they take charge in a socially desirable manner. Everyone present becomes highly involved in addressing transition issues and concerns that in the past may have been swept under the rug.

The history of student involvement in the IEP process is not a good model for what I am suggesting (Benz, Johnson, Mikkelsen, & Lindstrom, 1995; Gerry & McWhorter, 1991; Mount & Zwernik, 1988; Nisbet, Covert, & Schuh, 1992; Stowitschek & Kelso, 1989). More often than not, the IEP meeting has been largely controlled by teachers, with little engagement or involvement of parents or students. With this type of experiential history, the new legal presence of transition-planning requirements within the IEPs of adolescents is hardly a guarantee that students will suddenly become meaningfully involved in the process.

In essence, we are faced with discrepancies in both the motivation and the skills of students. Students are likely to have little desire to participate actively in a transition-planning meeting, and they have few skills that would help them to do so successfully. A transition-planning curriculum must respond to both of these discrepancies by teaching students how to play an assertive role in their transition-planning meetings and by encouraging students to make such an attempt in spite of the fact that their previous involvement in such meetings has probably not been satisfying.

Assuming that students can be motivated to participate assertively, they need to learn and practice a variety of skills including

- Selecting and inviting the participants
- Introducing the participants
- Presenting their plans
- Encouraging and processing feedback from other participants
- Responding positively to suggestions from other participants
- Closing the meeting and arranging for follow-up activities

Lessons within a transition-planning curriculum must address these skills. Furthermore, the lessons must be sensitive to varying levels of involvement and assertiveness that different students may be prepared to learn and practice at any given time. Taking charge of a planning meeting is not an "all-or-nothing" dichotomy. It may take years for students to reach their full potential for self-direction.

Proposition 7: Students Must Learn How to Actually Implement Their Transition Plans

Planning is not a static event. No one is able to foresee the future with total accuracy, and the activities one chooses to implement a transition plan are likely to encounter varying degrees of success. The ultimate success of a plan, therefore, requires the following:

1. Follow-through on commitments
2. Self-monitoring of accomplishments
3. Adjustments to the plan when things do not work entirely as planned

To encourage students to engage effectively in this implementation phase of the transition-planning process, an effective curriculum on transition planning must develop some self-monitoring tools and procedures for students to use and for teachers to guide.

The lesson structure at this point in the curriculum has two distinct purposes: 1) coaching students with the implementation of their own transition plans and 2) providing students with opportunities to share their implementation experiences with one another for the purposes of mutual reinforcement and brainstorming ways for overcoming obstacles. The foundation for these two distinct lesson strands is identical. Students must develop a weekly strategy for attacking their goals and activities. In essence, they must break their efforts into a series of small steps, each of which is

- Clearly related to a specific goal that the student has adopted
- Completable within a short period of time (preferably 1 week)
- Provable and documentable

The lessons involve teaching students how to identify these small steps, proceed with their implementation, and overcome any barriers that they may encounter in the process either by extended practice or by altering the nature of the difficult steps.

Proposition 8: Whenever Possible, Parents Should Participate in a Curriculum that Focuses on Self-Directed Transition Planning

Parental involvement is almost essential in any curriculum that purports to address transition planning. At one level of thinking, the need for such involvement seems obvious. Parents typically exercise a profound influence over their children, for better or for worse, and want their children to succeed in life. Parents also typically struggle with issues of control over their children's lives. Do parents let their sons or daughters learn from living, or do they try to prevent them from making obvious mistakes? Adolescents, however, struggle with their growing need for independence. They want to take charge of their own lives, yet they are usually not quite certain how to do so effectively.

These strong undercurrents surrounding the issue of control are a powerful context within which transition-planning curricula must operate. Some parent–student combinations work well, whereas others do not. Most troublesome, of course, are those situations in which the student is totally and unreasonably rebellious or in which the parent is dysfunctional or abusive.

In spite of these variations, the best context for transition planning involves cooperation and collaboration between the parent and the student. Certainly there are some exceptions, and teacher judgment is required to identify these exceptions. In such situations in which a parent is not available or suitable, it may be possible to find a parent surrogate such as a friend or relative who is willing and able to play the parental role.

There are four possible ways that parents or surrogates can become involved in transition-planning efforts. They can

1. Become aware of what the student is doing and be generally supportive at home
2. Become actively involved in certain lessons in which parent participation is especially important
3. Participate as a strong collaborator in the student's planning meeting
4. Support the student in the implementation of his or her transition plan

A good curriculum for transition planning should include methods for helping parents or surrogates to become involved in each of these ways.

Proposition 9: A Curriculum Embedded within an Existing Instructional Program Is the Best Way to Provide Instruction in Self-Directed Transition Planning

Teachers do not want to have to engage in transition-planning efforts as an after-school activity. They already have plenty of committee work and other extracurricular activities on their agendas. If teachers are going to become seriously involved in teaching self-directed transition planning, they need to do so in a way that is part of their formal workload and that provides them with teaching credit for their efforts. Similarly, students, for the most part, do not want to do transition planning as an extracurricular activity. If they are really going to engage in such planning efforts seriously and intensively, they want to do it in a way that provides them with course credit as well. This may sound like a small point, but the typical career education activities found in schools are often provided only within counseling centers and are simply not available as part of an instructional program.

Assume that your school district is enlightened and offers transition planning as part of an instructional program. We have found through our field studies that a transition-planning curriculum usually cannot be offered as a full-time class that meets five times per week. The homework between lessons often requires a fair amount of time to complete, especially if parental involvement is to occur meaningfully. Simply finding a time when parents and students can get together is sometimes a major achievement; therefore, a schedule of two or three classes per week seems to be ideal.

What is the teacher going to do with the rest of the time during those off days when he or she is not teaching transition planning? We found that teachers resolved this problem in many different ways, embedding their transition-planning instruction in classes with approximately 40 different titles. The classes that seemed to work best were those in which the content was relevant to transition planning. For example, if the teacher is teaching transition planning some days, it might be beneficial to teach some life skills, vocational skills, independent living skills, or personal care skills during the other days so that students can see the relationship between planning how to do these things and actually learning how to do them. However, instruction does not have to be delivered this way. We found that sometimes transition planning can be taught with seemingly off-task subjects such as remedial reading or mathematics. Nonetheless, the classes that put transition planning in a context that is clearly relevant to other related material have seemed to work best. For these reasons, we recommend that a transition-planning curriculum be incorporated into other relevant classes, thereby spreading out lessons to facilitate homework but still keeping them embedded within a course for which both teachers and students can receive credit.

Proposition 10: Transition Planning Is a Problem-Solving Process That Students Will Need to Use Throughout Their Lives

Regardless of the goals students choose to work on at any given point in time, they are likely to change their minds as they grow older and have new experiences. It is more important to learn a transition-planning process than to select perfectly appropriate goals. This is almost self-evident. Any time transition planning is taught, students have to be helped to develop an actual plan. They have to pick some goals on which to work, and they have to make some progress toward achieving those goals. However, there is no way that a 14-, 17-, or 21-year-old is going to be able to accurately project the kinds of things that he or she wants to do or to become 2 years, 5 years, or 10 years down the road. None of us could probably do that when we were that age, or even now! Goals are going to change and thus are going to need to be adjusted. This means that the ultimate goal of any instruction provided in this area is teaching students the process of transition planning. Students will need to use the skills that they learn again and again, especially when future needs arise and an instructor will not be around to look over their shoulders.

When students move into the self-monitoring phase of a transition-planning curriculum, they find that transition goals and activities frequently require modification for a variety of reasons. As students become proficient in making such modifications, they also become increasingly empowered to engage in transition planning with decreasing levels of support from their parents and teachers. To the extent that this occurs, the ultimate intent of the curriculum will have been accomplished. Students will have learned an approach to problem solving, in the context of making transitions, that will serve them well for the rest of their lives.

IMPACT EVIDENCE

Teaching an entire approach to problem solving is a lofty goal for any curriculum or set of curricula to achieve. It would be reasonable to ask whether there is any empirical evidence that students can actually learn how to engage successfully in self-directed transition planning. As of 1998, there was no line of research that examined this issue systematically, thoroughly, and empirically. However, there is some evaluation information from our own field studies that I will share with you.

As part of the field study process, teachers and students were asked to give their opinions on the impact of *Next S.T.E.P.* once they had finished using it, focusing in particular on their perceptions of student self-direction within the transition-planning process. Teachers were asked to provide ratings of student engagement and involvement throughout the curriculum. In addition, both teachers and students were asked to provide ratings of student self-direction in their planning meetings, satisfaction with the resulting transition plan, and student growth in problem-solving behavior that extended beyond the tasks required by the curriculum and yet appeared to be an outcome of participating in the curriculum.

The information obtained is encouraging. With respect to engagement, teachers reported that less than 5% of the total sample was disengaged throughout the curriculum. More than 50% were rated as "highly engaged." The subsample of students without disabilities received the highest percentage, 57%, of "highly engaged" ratings. This is particularly interesting since most of the students without disabilities experienced the curriculum in inclusive settings, working together with students who were disabled. There are not many reported examples of successful inclusive instruction in high school settings, and it appears that transition planning may provide a good opportunity for such instruction.

When reflecting on their transition-planning meetings, 53% of the students and 60% of the teachers described these meetings as being "primarily" student led. Only 14% of the students and 7% of the teachers viewed these meetings as being led by teachers. In other words, approximately 90% of the students, from both student and teacher perspectives, took *some* level of responsibility for directing their own meetings. This is an amazing finding, when juxtaposed with the widely reported negligible involvement of students in their own IEP meetings.

One outcome of participation in a transition-planning curriculum should be student production of a concrete transition plan. A question worth asking is whether a high level of student involvement in this effort would result in satisfaction with the final product. We were quite pleased by the findings that were reported. Only 2% of the students and 6% of the teachers were dissatisfied with the transition plans produced by the students. Approximately 60% of both groups were "very satisfied" with the plans that emerged. This was true for students both with and without disabilities.

The final question pertained to the "sustainability" of the problem-solving strategy that students learned as a consequence of participating in the *Next S.T.E.P.* curriculum. Would such skills generalize into other aspects of the students' lives where problem solving was needed? When addressing this question, nearly two thirds of both students and teachers reported that completion of the curriculum resulted in an increase in student motivation, skill, and confidence about taking charge of their important life decisions. Less than 1% reported a decrease in these areas.

Although these findings are promising, much more will have to be done in the way of research and evaluation before we can be confident about the impact of instruction on self-directed transition planning. We do, however, appear to have reason to be optimistic.

CONCLUSIONS

Before closing, I would like to remind readers of the major assumption that underlies the need for a curriculum in the area of self-directed transition planning. Adolescents and young adults desperately want to take charge of their own lives effectively, yet they do not always know how to do so effectively; furthermore, they are not always supported by parents or teachers in this endeavor. This tension between emerging adults and their authority figures was eloquently described by an adolescent, Katherine Zondlo, in the June 10, 1996, edition of *Newsweek*. Zondlo focused on disrespect as a source of this tension, as illustrated by adults referring to adolescent attitudes and behavior as being "just a phase." She wrote,

> "It's just a phase" is a belittling and harmful remark, but one that adolescents hear almost every day to dismiss behavior that adults simply don't want to understand. . . . When I got my nose pierced in November, for instance, my parents' first remark was *"When* you decide to take that thing out, will the hole close up?" It didn't occur to them that I might not ever take it out. When I chose to become a vegetarian, I heard, "You'll give this up as soon as you get hungry for a pepperoni pizza." . . . I'm saddened by adults who say "it's just a phase" when I speak of my hopes and dreams. . . . The adults I am drawn to are those who have not completely forgotten their adolescence and its open-mindedness. They believe in me and my abilities, and encourage me to attain my goals. (p. 14)

This is not to say, of course, that all conflicts between adolescents and adults are the result of adult insensitivity. This is, however, one area over which we should have some control. We need to teach adolescents how to take charge of their own lives, under appropriate guidance and supervision, and then let them know that we really mean it.

REFERENCES

Benz, M., Johnson, D., Mikkelsen, K., & Lindstrom, L. (1995). Improving collaboration between schools and vocational rehabilitation: Stakeholder identified barriers and strategies. *Career Development for Exceptional Individuals, 18,* 133–144.

Brown, R., Bayer, M., & MacFarlane, C. (1988). Quality of life amongst handicapped adults. In R. Brown (Ed.), *Quality of life for handicapped people* (pp. 111–140). London: Croom Helm.

Chadsey-Rusch, J., Rusch, F.R., & O'Reilly, M. (1991). Transition from school to integrated communities. *Remedial and Special Education, 12,* 23–33.

Clark, G., & Patton, J. (1997). *Transition planning inventory.* Austin, TX: PRO-ED.

Edgerton, R. (1990). Quality of life from a longitudinal perspective. In R. Schalock & M. Begab (Eds.), *Quality of life: Perspectives and issues* (pp. 149–160). Washington, DC: American Association on Mental Retardation.

Gelatt, H.B. (1962). Decision-making: A conceptual frame of reference for counseling. *Journal of Counseling Psychology, 9,* 240–245.

Gerry, M.H., & McWhorter, C.M. (1991). A comprehensive analysis of federal statutes and programs for persons with severe disabilities. In L.H. Meyer, C.A. Peck, & L. Brown (Eds.), *Critical issues in the lives of people with severe disabilities* (pp. 495–525). Baltimore: Paul H. Brookes Publishing Co.

Goode, D. (1990). Thinking about and discussing quality of life. In R. Schalock & M. Begab (Eds.), *Quality of life: Perspectives and issues* (pp. 41–57). Washington, DC: American Association on Mental Retardation.

Halpern, A. (1993). Quality of life as a conceptual framework for evaluating transition outcomes. *Exceptional Children, 59,* 486–498.

Halpern, A. (1994). The transition of youth with disabilities to adult life: A position statement of the Division on Career Development and Transition, Council for Exceptional Children. *Career Development for Exceptional Individuals, 17,* 115–124.

Halpern, A., Herr, C., Wolf, N., Doren, B., Johnson, M., & Lawson, J. (1997). *The Next S.T.E.P. (Student Transition and Educational Planning) Curriculum.* Austin, TX: PRO-ED.

Krumboltz, J.D., & Hamel, D.A. (1977). *Guide to career decision-making skills.* New York: College Entrance Examination Board.

Martin, J.E., Huber Marshall, L., & Maxson, L. (1993). Transition policy: Infusing self-determination and self-advocacy into transition programs. *Career Development for Exceptional Individuals, 16,* 53–61.

Mount, B., & Zwernik, K. (1988). *It's never too early, it's never too late: A booklet about Personal Futures Planning.* Minneapolis, MN: Metropolitan Council.

Nirje, B. (1970). The normalization principle: Implications and comments. *Journal of Mental Subnormality, 16,* 62–70.

Nisbet, J., Covert, S., & Schuh, M. (1992). Family involvement in the transition from school to adult life. In F.R. Rusch, L. DeStefano, J. Chadsey-Rusch, L. Phelps, & E. Szymanski (Eds.), *Transition from school to adult life: Models, linkages, and policy* (pp. 407–424). Sycamore, IL: Sycamore Publishing Co.

Parmenter, T. (1988). An analysis of the dimensions of quality of life for people with physical disabilities. In R.I. Brown (Ed.), *Quality of life for handicapped people: A series in rehabilitation education* (pp. 7–36). London: Croom Helm.

Schalock, R. (1990). Attempts to conceptualize and measure quality of life. In R. Schalock & M. Begab (Eds.), *Quality of life: Perspectives and issues* (pp. 141–148). Washington, DC: American Association on Mental Retardation.

Stowitschek, J., & Kelso, C. (1989). Are we in danger of making the same mistakes with ITP's as were made with IEP's? *Career Development for Exceptional Individuals, 12,* 28–32.

Szymanski, E. (1994). Transition: Life-span and life-space considerations for empowerment. *Exceptional Children, 60,* 402–410.

Szymanski, E., Turner, K., & Hershenson, D. (1992). Career development and work adjustment of persons with disabilities: Perspectives and implications for transition. In F.R. Rusch, L. DeStefano, J. Chadsey-Rusch, L. Phelps, & E. Szymanski (Eds.), *Transition from school to adult life* (pp. 391–406). Sycamore, IL: Sycamore Publishing Co.

Taylor, S., & Bogdan, R. (1990). Quality of life and the individual's perspective. In R. Schalock & M. Begab (Eds.), *Quality of life: Perspectives and issues* (pp. 27–40). Washington, DC: American Association on Mental Retardation.

Vash, C. (1984). Evaluation from the client's point of view. In A. Halpern & M.J. Fuhrer (Eds.), *Functional assessment in rehabilitation* (pp. 253–268). Baltimore: Paul H. Brookes Publishing Co.

Wehmeyer, M. (1995a). A career education approach: Self-determination for youth with mild cognitive disabilities. *Intervention in School and Clinic, 30,* 157–163.

Wehmeyer, M. (1995b). *The Arc's Self-Determination Scale.* Arlington, TX: The Arc National Headquarters.

Zondlo, K. (1996, June 10). As I see it. *Newsweek,* 14.

10

TAKE CHARGE for the Future

A Student-Directed
Approach to Transition Planning

Laurie E. Powers, Alison Turner, Dean H. Westwood,
Constance Loesch, Anne Brown, and Charity Rowland

Adolescents and young adults with disabilities experience significant barriers
to employment, postsecondary training, and independent living following
high school (Blackorby & Wagner, 1996; Valdes, Williamson, & Wagner, 1990).
Adolescents with disabilities also drop out of high school at a higher rate than
adolescents without disabilities (Valdes et al., 1990). Case studies (Lichten-

This chapter was funded in part by Grant H158U50001 awarded by the U.S. Department of Education, Office of Special Education and Rehabilitative Services
(OSERS). The opinions expressed herein are exclusively those of the authors, and no
official endorsement by OSERS should be inferred.

Certain portions of this chapter are based on material previously published in
Powers, L.E., Sowers, J.-A., Turner, A., Nesbitt, M., Knowles, E., & Ellison, R. (1996).
TAKE CHARGE: A model for promoting self-determination among adolescents with
challenges. In L.E. Powers, G.H.S. Singer, & J.-A. Sowers (Eds.), *On the road to autonomy: Promoting self-competence in children and youth with disabilities*
(pp. 291–322). Baltimore: Paul H. Brookes Publishing Co.

stein, 1993; Lichtenstein & Michaelides, 1993; Zetlin & Hosseini, 1989) suggested that, following high school, many young adults with disabilities find themselves confused about the future, socially isolated, and unable to get jobs and establish independent residences. Prior to leaving school, youth are often disengaged from their high school experiences and transition-planning activities, and they receive little assistance in formulating and implementing individualized goals for independent living, employment, and college.

Consensus regarding the value of transition support for youth with disabilities, based on students' interests and preferences, is reflected in the inclusion of a transition mandate in the Individuals with Disabilities Education Act (IDEA) of 1990 (PL 101-476). The Individuals with Disabilities Education Act Amendments of 1997 (PL 105-17) extended this mandate to students ages 14 and older. The transition provisions of IDEA provide an impetus for promoting the involvement of students with disabilities in the development, implementation, and oversight of their transition plans. Likewise, increasing emphasis on the importance of transition planning for youth in general education programs is evident in school-to-work, school reform, and outcomes-based education initiatives that are under way.

Researchers, educators, service providers in the community, self-advocates, and families generally agree that the promotion of student involvement in transition planning must be considered a priority if the quality and responsiveness of transition supports are to be improved. Although significant attention has been devoted to identifying methods of promoting parent and professional participation in education and transition planning, comparatively little focus has been placed on directly preparing students to assume responsibility for their own planning. In many instances, students are not present at education- or transition-planning meetings, and most students who do attend their meetings passively accede to the wishes of the adult participants. As a result, students miss important opportunities to learn and apply transition-planning skills, have minimal input into the development of their own transition goals, and assume little responsibility for the implementation of their own goals. As a result, the burden of goal achievement often rests on professional staff and families who, although committed to supporting the student, may have expectations that are different from the student as well as many competing responsibilities. If youth are to learn how to become the key change agents in their adult lives, emphasis must be shifted from transition planning *for* youth to transition planning *with* youth.

This chapter describes a comprehensive model, *TAKE CHARGE for the Future*, that is designed to promote the transition planning of youth ages 15–17 with and without disabilities. The model has been implemented by school districts and community organizations collaboratively. *TAKE CHARGE for the Future* has as its centerpiece student-directed participation in personally relevant transition-planning and preparation activities in school, community, and home settings. Students learn that they are responsible for promoting their own successful transitions; are exposed to specific strategies to help them identify, communicate, and achieve their transition goals; and are provided with the information and support necessary to ensure their success in achieving their transition goals. Students have access to self-help materials, coaching, and support to enable them to assume primary responsibility for identifying their transition goals, conducting their transition-planning meetings, formulating systematic plans for goal attainment, and performing activities to achieve their goals. Information and support are concurrently provided to school staff and families to expand their respective capacities to assist youth. Peer support and mentorship opportunities are organized to bolster students' transition knowledge, confidence, and support networks. Students participate in the design and implementation of the model at all levels, including materials development, the structuring of peer support activities, and dissemination. This chapter provides an overview of the conceptual and empirical foundations of *TAKE CHARGE for the Future,* describes its major intervention components, and discusses its implications for the design and delivery of transition supports.

> "Before TAKE CHARGE for the Future, I never thought I'd apply to college, and I've done that. I didn't used to think much about my future. Boy, has that changed. It feels good."
>
> *Josh*

CONCEPTUAL FOUNDATIONS

The *TAKE CHARGE for the Future* model is informed by knowledge related to the involvement of parents, community agencies, and school staff in education planning and to the facilitation of student self-determination.

Promoting Involvement of Families, School Staff, and Community Organizations in Education Planning

There is widespread agreement that family involvement in education planning is best promoted by emphasizing parent–staff collaboration (Bailey, 1987), providing logistical accommodations (Walker & Singer, 1993), facilitating parents' decision making and empowerment (Dunst & Trivette, 1989; Zeitlin & Williamson, 1988), providing culturally responsive support (Turnbull & Turnbull, 1996), and assisting families to activate natural supports (Nisbet, 1992).

Likewise, the literature suggests that several strategies can promote the involvement of teachers, related-services staff, and community members in effective transition planning. These strategies include clear role definition; team collaboration; systematic goal identification, problem solving, and decision making; collaborative consultation; and positive communication (Cooley, 1991; Giangrego, Cloninger, & Iverson, 1998; Powers & Sowers, 1994; Sileo, Rude, & Luchner, 1988). As applied to the goal of promoting student involvement in transition planning, this information suggests that, within the context of family culture and values, models should provide opportunities for

- Students' identification and selection of transition goals
- Students' decision making regarding choice of services
- Students' mobilization of natural and professional supports
- Students' skill development in transition plan development and collaboration
- Students' assumption of responsibilities and equal status in planning
- Ongoing encouragement, coaching, and support for students
- Structuring of transition-planning meetings around the comfort of the students
- Training and support to assist professionals in supporting student involvement through positive communication, collaborative inclusion, and providing necessary help

Facilitation of Self-Determination

Self-determination refers to personal attitudes and abilities that facilitate an individual's desire for and pursuit of goals. The expression of self-determination is reflected in personal attitudes of empowerment and self-directed action to achieve personally valued goals (Powers, Wilson, et al., 1996). Twenty-six model demonstration projects and several research projects have been funded specifically to investigate the nature, promotion, and assessment of self-determination (see U.S. Department of Education, 1992, for an overview of some of these projects). These activities have culminated in the identification of validated factors essential to the promotion of self-determination among youth with disabilities, including self-determination skills development, mentoring and modeling, community-based experiential learning, futures planning, and involvement in transition planning (Ward & Kohler, 1996).

Several conceptual models, some of which are described in this book, have been developed to explain the emergence of self-determination (see Chapters 1 and 2). From the professional's perspective, self-determination can be conceptualized as an outcome of mastery motivation and self-efficacy expectations.

Mastery Motivation   Mastery motivation is characterized by perceived competence, self-esteem, maintenance of an internal locus of control, and internalization of goals and rewards (Harter, 1981). It is achieved through repeated attempts and reinforcement of success. Students who possess mastery motivation exhibit a demonstrated willingness to expend effort in domains that are historically associated with success. Parents and professionals who encourage mastery motivation do not require too little of the child and thereby reinforce passivity or demand too much and thereby set the stage for failure (Lindemann, 1981). As children mature, they are encouraged to set their own goals, take acceptable risks, and self-advocate (Powers, Singer, & Todis, 1996).

Self-Efficacy Expectations   According to Bandura (1977, 1986), behavior depends on both outcomes expectations and personal efficacy expectations. *Outcomes expectations* refers to beliefs about whether a particular behavior will lead to a particular consequence. *Personal efficacy expectations* refers to a person's belief about his or her capability to perform a desired behavior in a specific context. Such expectations do not reflect a person's skills but rather one's judgment of what one can do with whatever skills one possesses. Youth with high levels of self-efficacy are more likely to make choices, attempt new behaviors, and persevere through difficult tasks than youth with low self-efficacy (Bandura, 1977). A growing body of evidence indicates that self-efficacy beliefs are an important predictor of academic success (Graham & Harris, 1989), motivation (Schunk, 1989), and functional well-being (Dolce, 1987). Self-efficacy appraisals are affected by performance accomplishments and mastery experiences; vicarious learning from role models; social persuasion provided by family, peers, and educators; and physiological feedback mediated by the use of self-regulation strategies.

Key to the promotion of self-efficacy appraisals is maximizing self-attribution of competence. Although external reinforcement of achievement clearly bolsters the confidence of youth, adolescents' personally attributing achievement to their own decisions and actions is essential. To promote their self-attribution of competence, youth must have opportunities to obtain and use information, skills, and support. Ideally, such opportunities should facilitate self-help among youth, provide those skills and supports necessary to give youth a reasonable chance for success, and highlight self-attribution of accomplishment of youth.

Implications for Student Involvement in Transition Planning   The conceptual information described in the preceding section suggests that an effective model for promoting youth involvement in transition planning must have as its centerpiece implicit and explicit support of youth as effective change agents in their own lives who are capable of exercising personal control and making their own decisions. Interventions designed to assist youth must provide for their primary implementation of strategies, with other participants acting as facilitators and support providers.

The empowerment of youth is also clearly a socioecological process that is interdependent with the support capacities of those who are important in the lives of youth. Parents and educators who themselves have high levels of self-determination are typically more effective in supporting the self-determination of youth than are those with low levels of self-determination. If youth are to be empowered to become active in their transition planning, their families and educators must also be assisted in developing and expressing their capabilities to support youth. Thus, the same resources that youth require to express self-determination in transition planning are needed by families and educators: opportunities to obtain and use information, skills to encourage and help youth, and support resources that enable families and educators to use their capacities to assist youth. *Our experiences in working with teenagers suggest that when educators and families are provided with information, strategies, and validation of their support capabilities, educators and families become increasingly interested and proficient in assisting youth to become active in transition planning.*

EMPIRICAL SUPPORT FOR *TAKE CHARGE FOR THE FUTURE*

Empirical validation of the efficacy of the *TAKE CHARGE for the Future* model is provided by three sources:

1. Findings (Powers, Turner, Matuszewski, & Wilson, 1996) that support the efficacy of *TAKE CHARGE*, the original self-determination model that provides the basis for *TAKE CHARGE for the Future*
2. Findings from a qualitative study (Powers, Turner, Phillips, & Matuszewski, 1996) of critical factors support student involvement in transition planning
3. Preliminary findings (Powers, Turner, & Matuszewski, 1997) from the field test of *TAKE CHARGE for the Future* validate its effectiveness

Validation of *TAKE CHARGE for the Future*

The *TAKE CHARGE for the Future* model is adapted from the original *TAKE CHARGE* approach, which focuses on promoting the self-determination of middle school and high school youth with and without disabilities (Powers, Sowers, et al., 1996). *TAKE CHARGE* is an integrated self-determination promotion approach that includes student coaching, mentorship, peer support, and parent support. Findings from a controlled field test of *TAKE CHARGE* substantiate its impact on promoting students' empowerment, students' identification and pursuit of goals, and healthy psychosocial adjustment of students (Powers, Turner, Phillips, & Matuszewski, 1996). Qualitative findings also support the efficacy of *TAKE CHARGE* for promoting students' confidence and independent functioning and parents' and staff's perceptions of students' capabilities (Powers, Sowers, et al., 1996). Additional program evaluation findings based on a study of approximately 200 youth suggested that *TAKE CHARGE* can be successfully delivered in inclusive classroom environments.

"My son learned so much about setting goals and working to reach them. . . . I have learned that my son can problem-solve if something happens. . . . Now that I know this I am very excited to see him doing things."

Helen

Qualitative Study of Student Involvement in Transition Planning

The design of *TAKE CHARGE for the Future* is also based on the findings of a qualitative interview study designed to identify specific factors that promote student participation in transition planning (Powers, Turner, Matuszewski, & Wilson, 1996). The study was conducted with a purposive sample of 12 students ages 16–18 who did not actively participate in transition planning, their parents, and school staff ($N = 36$). Each interview was audiotaped, transcribed verbatim, coded, and analyzed. Some of the key findings are summarized in the following sections.

Student Themes Students reported that they were interested in being more involved in their planning. To be active in the process, however, youth wanted the other participants to listen to and demonstrate respect for their ideas and input. Several youth specifically reported that their transition-planning meetings were heavily focused on employment, and, although they realized that work is important, these youth wished that other interests such as independent living would be regarded. Youth also wanted clearer explanations of how the transition-planning process works, with less use of jargon. They requested accommodations such as assistance in preparing for their meetings and with note taking during their meetings. Several youth reported difficulty in speaking up at meetings and requested help in becoming more assertive. The final theme that emerged from youth related to the importance of support from others. Youth generally agreed that the encouragement and help they receive from their families is most important. Several youth also indicated that they would like to meet successful adults who faced similar challenges during high school.

Family Themes Parents typically indicated that they were concerned that their sons' and daughters' input would not be respected and that their children lacked the ability to self-advocate. Most parents reported that they would support their children's involvement if their sons and daughters were provided with help to successfully advocate for their needs. Many parents indicated that they were unsure of ways to support their children's successful participation. Like the students, parents also reported experiencing confusion about the transition-planning process and their roles. Parents wanted to feel respected by staff and have meetings focus on creative problem solving rather than on pro forma approval of a preprepared plan. Finally, parents indicated that they believed that school staff had unrealistic expectations of the support families could provide, given that most parents work and have numerous additional financial, personal, and family obligations. They emphasized the importance of working with families to identify feasible approaches for families to assist youth.

Staff Themes   School staff generally agreed that transition planning should be provided in a focused way for all students and that youth should be more involved in the planning process. Staff reported, however, that students need skills, structure, and allies in order to participate successfully and that educators have difficulty finding the time to help youth individually. Staff also indicated that interagency coordination is important to the success of transition-planning efforts, with the organization of small teams specifically devoted to assisting a particular student being the most effective approach. Staff indicated that they require increased administrative support for their devotion of time to assist youth with transition planning.

Field Test of TAKE CHARGE for the Future

Based on the qualitative findings (Powers, Turner, Matuszewski, & Wilson, 1996), the *TAKE CHARGE* self-determination model was modified to address the specific issues identified by students, staff, and parents. The adapted model, *TAKE CHARGE for the Future*, includes coaching for youth in the application of transition-planning skills, peer support and mentoring, information and support for families to increase their capabilities to assist youth, and staff training and technical assistance in strategies to more effectively support youth and their parents.

The *TAKE CHARGE for the Future* model is being field tested by school districts, independent living centers, and parents' organizations in New Hampshire, North Carolina, Oregon, Texas, and Wisconsin. Students' self-reports, parents' reports, and behavioral observation data are being systematically collected for all youth participating in field test studies (Powers et al., 1997). Analysis of the first wave of controlled field test evaluation data (Powers et al., 1997) provides strong evidence to suggest that participation in *TAKE CHARGE for the Future* enhances student identification and achievement of transition goals, levels of participation in transition-planning meetings, and perceptions of personal empowerment to influence transition services and supports. Educators who have implemented *TAKE CHARGE for the Future* report that students using it are more active in their transition planning. Most important, these educators report enhanced commitment and confidence in their own abilities to involve students in transition planning.

Approximately 200 youth with and without disabilities are also participating in replication activities. The model provides for many different replication options, and technical assistance efforts are focused on assisting school districts and communities to select and implement those options that they believe have the highest probability of success in their communities. Through this process, we are learning both that no one model fits all needs and that flexible approaches tailored to effectively address most local conditions can be used. The following section provides an overview of the major components of *TAKE CHARGE for the Future* and describes some of the component variations that can be implemented successfully to assist youth with transition planning.

"*TAKE CHARGE for the Future* has coached, not forced me to set goals and follow through on them. . . . I am no longer feeling the need to hurt others for personal gain. I have turned the ruthlessness into positive ambition."

Zachary

TAKE CHARGE FOR THE FUTURE MODEL COMPONENTS

The *TAKE CHARGE for the Future* model is an integrated, socioecologically based approach that includes coaching youth in the application of transition-planning involvement skills, support from mentors and peers, support from parents, and training and technical assistance for staff.

Component 1: Coaching for Youth

The *TAKE CHARGE for the Future* model uses in situ coaching to assist youth to learn transition-planning skills. All skills are learned in the context of youth applying the skills in identifying and working to achieve their transition goals. As shown in Table 1, coaching can be delivered individually, in a classroom, or in an intensive conference or workshop. Classroom-based coaching can be incorporated in an existing course. For example, *TAKE CHARGE for the Future* was incorporated in an English course for one period per week. The content of the English course was further modified to include writing essays and reading novels related to directing one's future. Coaching can also be delivered as a modular course conducted with a complementary course such as study skills, physical education, or health education. In this situation, students who are taking a complementary course are also invited to enroll in *TAKE CHARGE for the Future*; however, the content of the other course is unmodified. Finally, the curriculum can be offered as a stand-alone class elective; in this case, it is included in the course guide, and enrollment is open to all students.

Table 1.   Coaching variations

Individual coaching
Classroom-based coaching
Integrated with an existing course
Modular course or with a complementary course
Stand-alone elective
Intensive conference or workshop

Coaches may be educators, related-services personnel, guidance counselors, instructional assistants, school nurses, staff or volunteers from community agencies, or any other individuals who are willing to commit to regular meetings with youth. Coaching is typically delivered either for two 45-minute periods per week for one semester or for one class period per week for the entire school year.

Coaching Principles   Several principles of effective coaching have been articulated:

- *Work through youth, not around them*: Communicate respect to youth by providing them with the information and feedback that they need to make informed choices, soliciting their ideas, and obtaining their approval and input before intervening with their parents or with other significant people in their lives.
- *Respect individual differences in learning and maturity*: Some students may require fairly directive coaching, whereas others may need the coach to merely check in, provide intermittent support, and praise their progress.
- *Help youth learn how to direct the support that others provide*: Coach students to identify occasions when they may need the coach's or others' help, to request help, and to oversee the help that the coach or others provide.
- *Keep communication open and positive*: The coach must avoid being judgmental or reactive when a student chooses a goal or a strategy with which the coach is uncomfortable. For example, one student shared that his dream was to be a pimp. Rather than responding with distaste or rejection, the student's coach said that she was not comfortable helping him to work toward that specific goal but that she wanted to understand what it was about being a pimp that he found attractive. The coach was then able to help the student identify other, socially acceptable goals related to his interests.
- *Interpret lack of follow-through as a need for support*: Assume that poor follow-through is a sign either that the activity is too complex or intimidating for the student or that the student requires additional support or resources to accomplish it. Explore with the student what is getting in the way and try to define a more effective approach.

Progression through the *TAKE CHARGE for the Future* curriculum is student directed. Adolescents are told that they are responsible for taking charge of their lives, and they are challenged to take the lead. Coaches provide instruction to assist youth to learn particular strategies; however, their major roles are to facilitate cooperative learning among youth, to provide support for individual goal achievement, and to model effective strategies. They assist youth to review their self-help materials, acknowledge their progress, occasionally challenge youth to take action, and facilitate positive relationship building between students and those who can assist them.

Assisting youth to cultivate allies is a critical activity, particularly for youth who have had a troubled past. Students with histories of disruptive behavior often have developed reputations that make staff reluctant to trust them or to provide them with opportunities. To assist these youth, it is critical that the coach run interference by providing staff with information about the student's goals and motivation, emphasizing the importance of the staff's support for the student, and offering to provide assistance if problems arise.

TAKE CHARGE for the Future *Skills*   *TAKE CHARGE for the Future* introduces youth to the application of three major categories of skills: achievement, partnership, and self-regulation. Skills are presented in a self-help guide that leads youth through the process. Skills are presented as generic strategies for transition planning and goal achievement, with each strategy being presented as a small number of systematic steps. The major strategies in *TAKE CHARGE for the Future* are presented in Table 2. Youth are also provided with companion informational materials in adolescent-friendly formats. Companion materials provide basic information and tips about making and keeping friends, getting into college, getting a job, and living on one's own. (A detailed review of many of these fundamental self-determination skills is found in Powers, Sowers, et al., 1996.) *TAKE CHARGE for the Future* assists youth to apply these skills to the achievement of their transition goals.

Table 2.   Generic skills developed in *TAKE CHARGE for the Future*

Achievement	Partnership	Self-regulation
Dream	Schmooze	Think positively
Set goals	Be assertive	Manage other people's discouragement
Organize your planning meeting	Negotiate	Focus on your accomplishments
Problem solve		Hang tough
Prepare	Manage help	Track and reward your progress
Keep it going!		

Adapted from Powers, Sowers, et al. (1996).

Students learn additional strategies specifically related to organizing and conducting their transition-planning meetings.

In association with learning strategies to communicate their dreams and goals and to develop allies, youth identify people whom they would like to participate in their transition-planning meetings. They also have the option of identifying an *organizer*, meaning a person from whom they would like assistance in organizing their meetings. Students typically do choose to use an organizer, who may be a teacher, athletic coach, program manager, guidance counselor, or anyone else who the student selects. Students are free to choose their *TAKE CHARGE* coach as their organizer; however, they are encouraged to use the opportunity to develop a relationship with an additional person. Occasionally, youth elect to organize their own meetings; in that case, they receive back-up support from their *TAKE CHARGE* coaches.

As shown in Figure 1, youth identify priority activities associated with the achievement of each of their goals. They identify the subactivities that

---

Sample Transition Plan Worksheet

Name: _Florence_   Date: _3-19_
Goal: _Get an after-school job_

Priority activities	What I need to do	What others will do	Deadline/ Check-in arrangements
1. Find out what kinds of jobs are available.	Talk to Mr. Sampson about job hunting.	**Mr. Sampson will call job bank.**	**Stop by next Thursday, fifth period.**
2. Make phone calls to see whether those places are hiring.	**Call employment office, check paper and postings at school.** Look up numbers and make calls.		
3. Practice the job interview.	Find someone to practice with.	**Mr. Hopewell will meet me tomorrow.**	**Stop by after school.**
4. Fill out applications.	Get someone's name when I apply, so I know whom to call. Set a time to call.	**Ask Ms. Smith to go over the application after I'm done.**	**Ask Ms. Smith tomorrow after first period.**

Figure 1.   Sample Transition Plan Worksheet.

they need to perform and develop ideas regarding what others can do to help them. Youth share this information during their planning meetings and solicit ideas and feedback from their participants. In most cases, students modify or specify additional details of their plans (shown in bold in Figure 1). They also establish and confirm deadlines for the completion of each activity.

Students are not expected to assume responsibility for implementing all of the tasks involved in organizing and carrying out their transition-planning meetings. Rather, they are encouraged to be the decision makers and to assume responsibility either for doing tasks themselves or for directing and supporting the people who assist them. The students' doing it themselves and effectively managing assistance from others are equally weighted with respect to their demonstrating independence. This approach is appropriate to the developmental capacities of youth and provides youth with opportunities to learn how to effectively foster interdependence. As shown in Figure 2, youth decide which parts of the meeting agenda they will lead and which parts they will delegate to others. However, they are responsible for deciding what they want to be communicated with regard to all parts of the agenda.

Participating in education- or transition-planning meetings is a novel experience for most general education students. Many students are particularly reluctant to invite their parents to these meetings. It is important that youth are encouraged to invite those people whom they most want to involve in their planning. Our experience suggests that the family members of general education youth are often interested in attending and that they are important contributors. As such, we encourage youth to invite their families; however, it is not required.

Traditionally, transition-planning meetings are focused on individual students. However, a small group of youth working together can organize and conduct a transition-planning meeting, invite their respective guests, and share the meeting time. This strategy seems to work well for students who are new to transition planning; benefit from peer support; and do not have complex, time-consuming issues to discuss. Group meetings appear to be most successful when they are conducted after school rather than during class time.

Component 2: Mentoring and Peer Support

Youth who participate in *TAKE CHARGE for the Future* are introduced to successful adults or older, more experienced teenagers with common interests who faced similar challenges when they were in high school. Youth are concurrently provided with opportunities to share information and experiences and to support each other in navigating their transition goals and challenges. Unlike many mentoring programs that focus on matching youth with successful adults, the primary goal of mentorship in *TAKE CHARGE for the Future* is to introduce youth to adults and other youth with whom they share common experiences. Mentors who are selected for *TAKE CHARGE for the Future*

Sample Transition-Planning Meeting Agenda and Notes		
Agenda items	Who will do the item	Key points I want to get across
1. Welcome everyone.	Me	Thank everybody for coming.
2. Explain the meeting's purpose.	Me	This meeting is about me trying to get ready for the future.
3. Ask everyone to introduce themselves.	Me	
4. Review what you have done.	Mr. Johnson	Tell them how I have thought about my life and my goals and that I have some things that I want to do. I have some goals that I want to go over, and then I would like to get their feedback.
5. Talk about your dream.	Me	I want to get a job to earn some money and maybe go to college. I am not sure when I want to move out. I might stay at home and help out for a while.
6. Talk about goals and activities.	Me	Pass out my plan sheet. I want to find an after-school job. I need ideas about who is hiring. Mr. Sampson, could you help? Could someone help me to practice interviewing and to fill out the applications?
7. Ask for feedback.	Me	
8. Summarize everything that has been decided.	Mr. Johnson	Go over what they are going to do and what my first steps are.
9. Thank everyone for participating.	Me	Remember to shake everyone's hand.

Figure 2. Sample transition-planning meeting agenda and notes.

have achieved success after graduating from school; however, their major qualification is having successfully dealt with challenges with which their protégés can relate (e.g., learning or behavior problems while in high school, substance abuse or gang involvement, social isolation in association with being a talented and gifted student or a special education student, experience as a teenage parent, having a physical disability).

The key elements of mentorship in *TAKE CHARGE for the Future* are mentoring activities between youth and more experienced adults or peers and peer support among youth at the same developmental level. Initially, peer support experiences were provided as a means of bringing youth and mentors together for group discussions; however, mentoring and peer support experiences are inextricably linked and have reciprocal impacts. For example, after meeting monthly with their mentors, a group of students requested additional peer meetings after school. At one of these meetings, a group of youth expressed concern that one of the students had not attended school for 2 weeks and had become reinvolved with a gang. Eight students and the Mentor Coordinator went to the missing student's neighborhood, located him, and asked him to return to school. The student returned and successfully completed the school year.

Mentoring programs can be organized by schools or by community organizations such as the Young Men's Christian Association (YMCA), Boys and Girls Clubs, and independent living centers. The major forms of mentorship are listed in Table 3.

Individual Activities with a Matched Adult or Older Peer   A student or protégé can be formally matched with an adult or an older peer of the same gender with whom the student shares similar interests and high school experiences. Protégés and their mentors are encouraged to participate in activities at least monthly. Although mentors and protégés are free to perform any activities that they choose, they are encouraged to select activities that will provide opportunities for youth to learn about living successfully as an adult. Mentors are assisted to anticipate opportunities to provide relevant information, address particular issues, or model strategies within the context of upcoming activities.

Workshops   Protégés are invited to participate in workshops that provide information and support related to adult life options, resources, and coping strategies. Workshops also provide youth with ongoing opportunities to share successful strategies and to validate their personal challenges and accomplishments. Workshops are conducted with youth and their matched mentors or with a group of youth and a group of mentors who, although not matched with one another, share interests and experiences at a group level. Workshops can be conducted during class, after school, in the evening, or on Saturdays. They can be conducted at school, at local colleges, or at other community sites.

Table 3.   Forms of mentoring activities

Individual activities with matched adults or older peers
Workshops for youth and their mentors
Individual activities with nonmatched adults or older peers introduced to students in workshops
Supplemental group outings

Workshop topics are selected by youth, and the meetings are cofacilitated by staff, youth, and mentors. A list of the most commonly selected workshop topics is presented in Table 4. Youth workshops are often conducted in partnership with parent workshops. In this instance, a workshop schedule is developed that reflects similar workshop topics that have been selected by youth and their parents. Each workshop begins with a whole-group discussion or with a presentation by a guest speaker. Next, the parents and the youth and mentors divide into two groups to discuss their particular interests. The workshop concludes with the whole group sharing their ideas and plans that have been stimulated by the workshop.

Individual Activities with Nonmatched Adults or with Older Peers with Whom They Have Been Connected Through Workshops   In association with their participation in workshops, mentors and youth naturally develop relationships with each other. These relationships can be expanded by encouraging youth and mentors to participate in individual activities. Although each mentor is requested to participate in monthly activities with at least one youth, he or she typically performs activities with different youth and youth typically have the opportunity to engage in activities with more than one mentor. This form of nonmatched individual mentorship enables youth to have experiences with different mentors. In many cases, youth select mentors based on shared interests and personal compatibility rather than on disability or other characteristics.

Supplemental Group Outings   Group activities conducted as a complement to workshops create additional opportunities for developing relationships among youth and mentors. Youth and mentors may choose to attend sporting events or concerts, participate in recreational activities, or visit community programs. The activities are selected and collaboratively planned by the students, their mentors, and staff utilizing the planning strategies that students are learning.

As shown in Table 5, these forms of mentorship can be creatively combined to address students' interests and needs within the parameters of local resources. Ideally, youth and mentors have opportunities to participate in some types of individual and group activities across multiple settings. If re-

Table 4.   Commonly selected mentoring workshop topics

Surviving high school
Money management
Getting a job
Living on one's own
Going to college
Dealing with gang pressure
Drug and alcohol issues

Table 5.   Mentorship variations

Variation	Form	Features
Enhanced	Individual activities (matched or unmatched) Workshops Group outings	Combines one-to-one relationship with peer support opportunities across multiple settings
Midsize	One-to-one matched *or* workshops plus group outings	Individual support *or* group support across multiple settings
Economy	Workshops among youth and mentors	Group support in one setting

sources are limited, however, conducting workshops or individual community activities is still very beneficial. If workshops are conducted, it is usually possible to support some unmatched follow-up activities between specific youth and mentors in the community. It is also fun and typically feasible for youth and mentors to plan one supplemental activity for the entire group.

Foundations for Mentorship: Recruitment, Training, and Ongoing Support   Although intuitively an appealing concept, mentorship is not automatically successful. It requires careful planning, support, and oversight. The design of a strong mentorship program begins with the careful ongoing recruitment of mentors. Recruitment of mentors requires building relationships with multiple referral sources, broad school and community education, and the formation of a network of mentors who can assist in recruiting future mentors. Mentors are recruited through local colleges, independent living programs, support groups, and other community organizations. Older students and former graduates of high schools that are participating in *TAKE CHARGE for the Future* activities are often good sources of mentor recruitment.

It is essential that mentors participate in a training program, during the course of which the purpose of mentoring and the mentor's roles and responsibilities are explained; procedures for selecting, organizing, and implementing workshops and activities with youth are detailed; and common challenges for mentors and youth are discussed and problem solved. Mentors benefit from learning specific strategies for initiating conversations with youth and parents during workshops, planning community activities, and responding to awkward or difficult questions (e.g., "Have you ever taken drugs?"). Mentor training is typically conducted during a 7-hour workshop that also provides participants with an opportunity to meet former mentors.

Regardless of their level of motivation, many busy mentors and youth do not attend workshops or participate in individual activities unless they are provided with ongoing support. Support for youth includes assistance in arranging transportation, obtaining parents' permission, and contacting a mentor to

plan an activity. Support for mentors includes workshop and activity re-
minders, transportation, check-ins following workshops and community activities, and coaching and discussion regarding awkward or difficult issues
broached by youth (e.g., sexuality). Support must also be available for parents
to inform them of their sons' or daughters' activities with mentors, to solicit
parents' input, and to assure them of the mentor's capabilities and the oversight role of the program staff.

Component 3: Parent Support

Clearly, parents and other family members play vital roles in transition planning for youth (Morningstar, Turnbull, & Turnbull, 1995). Family members
require information and support in order to optimally support teenagers. Parent support can be provided to parents, grandparents, aunts and uncles, older
siblings, permanent foster parents, or anyone who has a long-term supportive
relationship with a teenager. The purpose of parent support is to validate parent strengths, efforts, accomplishments, and values; help parents to identify
and shape their children's growth; assist parents in identifying strategies to
support their children's transition-planning efforts; provide opportunities for
parents to share their experiences and ideas with other parents who have had
similar experiences; foster parent, student, school, and community partnerships; and encourage parents to think about their own futures and what they
want for and from their children. It is essential that parents have access to
student-focused support as well as individualized family-centered support.
Parent support can be provided by coaches; parent support resources based in
schools or in school districts (e.g., parent liaisons, volunteer parents, parent–
teacher associations), parent support resources based in the community (e.g.,
family resource centers, parent-training programs, parent-to-parent groups,
parent outreach organizations), and mentors.

   TAKE CHARGE for the Future provides five primary methods of parent
support:

1. An orientation to the program
2. A guide written by parents that provides information about strategies that
   other parents may find useful in promoting the transition planning of their
   children
3. Regular updates from the *TAKE CHARGE* coach regarding the child's
   progress
4. Workshops or gatherings with other participating parents focused on information exchange, problem solving, and peer support
5. Individualized support to address the parents' questions and needs

   Parent Orientation   Parents of youth who participate in *TAKE
CHARGE for the Future* are provided with an orientation that includes infor-

mation about the program and invites parents to participate in parent support activities. A basic orientation can be provided in a letter. However, the most ideal orientation method is the sponsorship of an orientation meeting for parents conducted after school or in the evening. Such a meeting provides parents with opportunities to ask questions, meet other parents, and discuss whether they would like to participate in additional parent gatherings. Our experience suggests that a significant percentage of parents elect to attend orientation meetings.

The Parent Guide   Parents are provided with a guide containing general information about typical development of adolescents with and without disabilities, strategies that students are learning through *TAKE CHARGE for the Future*, and tips that parents can use to facilitate their children's involvement in transition planning. Parents are also provided with a glossary of commonly used secondary education and transition terms as well as bulletins, publications, and resource information related to their needs and interests.

Coaching Updates for Parents   It is essential that coaches contact parents on a regular basis. Parent updates can be provided through telephone calls, home–school notes, and during other encounters such as open houses. We recommend that updates be provided monthly and be structured to

- Overview the students' activities in *TAKE CHARGE for the Future*
- Seek the parents' report and input on their child's progress
- Brainstorm and problem solve strategies to address barriers to transition success
- Emphasize parents' and students' strengths
- Communicate respect and concern for the students and their families

Parent Gatherings   Parents or other family members are invited to participate in a series of two to five gatherings or workshops that may be conducted concurrently with the youth workshops. The focus of each meeting includes sharing of ideas and experiences, problem solving, validation of the efforts and accomplishments of participants, and discussion of specific topics that parents choose. A list of commonly selected meeting topics is presented in Table 6. Parent gatherings may be organized by a coach; however, typically, this is a form of parent support that is organized in partnership with parent programs at school or in the community.

Individualized Student- or Family-Centered Support   Individualized student- or family-centered support is provided by staff from schools or local community organizations participating in the intervention. Individualized support can be provided during the course of orientation activities, coaching updates, and parent gatherings. Individualized parent support often involves providing information, helping parents gain access to resources, and providing emotional support during difficult times. Although many school staff initially perceive that they do not have the resources to pro-

Table 6.   Parent workshop topics

Thinking about the future: Both the parents' and the child's
Working with the school system
College resources
Job resources
Gangs and drugs
Community resources

vide individualized support to families, simple strategies such as making a community resource guide available in the classroom for families who might want to drop by and sending home a note of interest or concern can be effective ways to reach many families. The capacities of school staff to provide individualized support can also be enhanced through establishing agreements with community organizations that can be available to families.

Component 4: Training and Technical Assistance for Staff

Many school staff report that they have difficulty in involving youth in transition planning. Obstacles that staff typically face include their lack of knowledge of systematic strategies to promote student involvement, limited administrative support for their devotion of time to this activity, and the absence of a schoolwide vision for transition planning. To build staff capacities, *TAKE CHARGE for the Future* incorporates a program of in-service training and technical assistance for educators, transition staff, and administrators.

In-Service Training   Staff involved in transition planning for youth are invited to participate in four 1-hour collaborative meetings. Training is conducted by the local *TAKE CHARGE for the Future* team and is scheduled at a time that is convenient for the participants. The meetings have four purposes: 1) to provide staff members with information about the model, 2) to assist staff in developing a vision for student participation in transition planning, 3) to discuss specific strategies to promote student involvement in transition planning, and 4) to promote teamwork. Staff select specific topics for the collaboration meetings. Table 7 lists commonly selected meeting topics. Much of the discussion is case based, using the experiences of students and staff taking part in *TAKE CHARGE for the Future* to illustrate key issues and strategies. Training is also provided to staff who students have selected as organizers for their planning meetings. Youth and parents may also participate in training activities, sharing their perspectives on the strategies that they find helpful and the ones that they believe are counterproductive.

Technical Assistance   Staff members, particularly those who agree to assist students in organizing transition-planning meetings, are provided with coaching to promote their application of strategies to promote stu-

Table 7.   Collaboration staff meeting topics

Developing a team vision for students' involvement
Organizer training
Strategies to collaboratively plan transition meetings
    with students
Encouraging students' participation in planning
    meetings
Assisting youth to achieve their transition goals
Working with parents

dent involvement. Technical assistance is provided in association with key events during the planning process and is adapted to accommodate the evolving needs of school staff. For example, a check-in is performed with key staff members prior to and following transition-planning meetings to promote staff members' readiness for the meeting and to debrief them afterward. Technical assistance may take the form of in situ observation and coaching, participation in planning meetings, or provision of resource information.

CONCLUSIONS

TAKE CHARGE for the Future offers a flexible approach to transition-planning activities that can be executed in various configurations as a function of students' needs and local conditions. The model facilitates mutual support and empowerment among youth, parents, staff, and mentors. Most important, it promotes the development of collaborative partnerships between schools and community organizations that have the potential to increase the range and intensity of support that is available to youth and their families.

TAKE CHARGE for the Future provides a model that challenges educators, students, and parents to exceed their traditional levels of involvement, responsibility, and partnership. It is not recommended for adoption by staff who desire a fixed, classroom-based curriculum, because its implementation requires creativity and teamwork that extends beyond the classroom. The model has several implications for the definition of and approach to transition planning, which are discussed in the list that follows:

1. *Transition planning must be defined and implemented as a series of achievement-oriented activities.* Although many educators value the importance of the transition-planning process, the accomplishment of transition activities such as getting a summer job or a driver's license appears to be most important to youth and their families. For this reason, learning planning skills within the context of achieving transition goals is essential.

2. *Transition planning must be creatively structured and implemented to address students' preferences.* Standard strategies for conducting transition planning, such as meetings with individual students, the use of professional-centered forms, and an emphasis on formal assessment of students' capabilities, must be replaced by flexible meeting or plan-sharing options, student-friendly documentation, and students' self-assessments.

3. *To effectively plan, students must be informed decision makers.* Although some progress has been made in communicating transition-planning information to parents, little information about transition options that is packaged for and directed toward youth audiences is available. Demystifying transition and providing students with accessible information about transition resources and methods that they can use to accomplish their goals are essential.

4. *Teamwork and collaboration are the vehicles for supporting youth and their families.* Transition planning is by definition an interdependent, team-focused activity. Our experience suggests that one of the major obstacles to implementing *TAKE CHARGE for the Future* and many other transition-planning approaches is the lack of opportunities to foster a shared vision and teamwork among general educators, special educators, guidance staff, and administrators. The development and support of interdepartmental transition work groups is essential to responding to students' needs.

5. *Transition planning transcends schools' walls.* The world is becoming increasingly complex and interrelated; expecting school staff to assume full responsibility for supporting the transition efforts of youth is no longer reasonable. Schools are responsible for actively cultivating relationships with community organizations that can assist youth and families, and community organizations are responsible for identifying creative ways to respond to opportunities to partner with school staff.

6. *Ultimately, the potential of all youth to learn, develop, and chart their futures must be respected.* The momentum that youth create through the successful direction of their transition-planning activities is evidence that if youth are trusted, provided with opportunities, and offered support, they are capable of becoming powerful change agents in their own lives and in the lives of others.

REFERENCES

Bailey, D.B., Jr. (1987). Collaborative goal-setting with families: Resolving differences in values and priorities for services. *Topics in Early Childhood Special Education, 7*(2), 59–71.

Bandura, A. (1977). Self-efficacy: Toward a unifying theory of behavior change. *Psychological Review, 84,* 191–215.

Bandura, A. (1986). *Social foundation of thought and action: A social cognitive theory.* Englewood Cliffs, NJ: Prentice-Hall.

Blackorby, J., & Wagner, M. (1996). Longitudinal postschool outcomes of youth with disabilities: Findings from the National Longitudinal Transition Study. *Exceptional Children, 62*(5), 399–413.

Cooley, E.A. (1991). *Investigating the effects of training and interdisciplinary teams in communication and decision-making skills.* Unpublished doctoral dissertation, University of Oregon, Eugene.

Dolce, J.J. (1987). Self-efficacy and disability beliefs in behavioral treatment of pain. *Behavior Research and Therapy, 25*(4), 289–299.

Dunst, C.J., & Trivette, C.M. (1989). An enablement and empowerment perspective of case management. *Topics in Early Childhood Education, 8*(4), 87–102.

Giangreco, M.F., Cloninger, C.J., & Iverson, V.S. (1998). *Choosing outcomes and accommodations for children (COACH): A guide to planning inclusive education* (2nd ed.). Baltimore: Paul H. Brookes Publishing Co.

Graham, S., & Harris, K.R. (1989). Component analysis of cognitive strategy instruction: Effects on learning disabled students compositions and self-efficacy. *Journal of Educational Psychology, 81*(3), 353–361.

Harter, S. (1981). A model of mastery motivation in children: Individual differences and developmental change. In W.A. Collins (Ed.), *The Minnesota symposium on child psychology* (Vol. 14, pp. 215–255). Hillsdale, NJ: Lawrence Erlbaum Associates.

Individuals with Disabilities Education Act (IDEA) of 1990, PL 101-476, 20 U.S.C. §§ 1400 *et seq.*

Individuals with Disabilities Education Act Amendments of 1997, PL 105-17, 20 U.S.C. §§ 1400 *et seq.*

Lichtenstein, J. (1993). Help for troubled marriages. In G.H.S. Singer & L.E. Powers (Eds.), *Families, disability, and empowerment: Active coping skills and strategies for family interventions* (pp. 259–277). Baltimore: Paul H. Brookes Publishing Co.

Lichtenstein, S., & Michaelides, N. (1993). Transition from school to young adulthood: Four case studies of young adults labeled mentally retarded. *Career Development for Exceptional Individuals, 16*(2), 183–196.

Morningstar, M.E., Turnbull, A.P., & Turnbull, H.R. (1995). What do students with disabilities tell us about the importance of family involvement in the transition from school to adult life? *Exceptional Children, 62*(3), 249–260.

Nisbet, J. (Ed.). (1992). *Natural supports in school, at work, and in the community for people with severe disabilities.* Baltimore: Paul H. Brookes Publishing Co.

Powers, L.E., Singer, G.H.S., & Todis, B. (1996). Reflections on competence: Perspectives of successful adults. In L.E. Powers, G.H.S. Singer, & J.-A. Sowers (Eds.), *On the road to autonomy: Promoting self-competence in children and youth with disabilities* (pp. 69–92). Baltimore: Paul H. Brookes Publishing Co.

Powers, L.E., & Sowers, J.-A. (1994). Transition to adult living: Promoting natural supports and self-determination. In S. Calculator & C. Jorgensen (Eds.), *Including students with severe disabilities in schools: Fostering communication, interaction, and participation* (pp. 215–248). San Diego, CA: Singular Publishing Group.

Powers, L.E., Sowers, J.-A., Turner, A., Nesbitt, M., Knowles, E., & Ellison, R. (1996). *TAKE CHARGE*: A model for promoting self-determination among adolescents with challenges. In L.E. Powers, G.H.S. Singer, & J.-A. Sowers (Eds.), *On the road to autonomy: Promoting self-competence in children and youth with disabilities* (pp. 291–322). Baltimore: Paul H. Brookes Publishing Co.

Powers, L.E., Turner, A., & Matuszewski, J. (1997). *Field-test of TAKE CHARGE for the Future: A student-directed transition-planning model.* Portland: Oregon Health Sciences University, Center on Self-Determination.

Powers, L.E., Turner, A., Matuszewski, J., & Wilson, R. (1996). *Qualitative perspectives of transition to adulthood among adolescents in special education.* Portland: Oregon Health Sciences University, Center on Self-Determination.

Powers, L.E., Turner, A., Phillips, A., & Matuszewski, J. (1996). *A controlled field-test of the efficacy of a multi-component model for promoting adolescent self-determination.* Portland: Oregon Health Sciences University, Center on Self-Determination.

Powers, L.E., Wilson, R., Matuszewski, J., Phillips, A., Rein, C., Schumacher, D., & Gensert, J. (1996). Facilitating adolescent self-determination: What does it take? In D.J. Sands & M.L. Wehmeyer (Eds.), *Self-determination across the life span: Independence and choice for people with disabilities* (pp. 257–284). Baltimore: Paul H. Brookes Publishing Co.

Schunk, D.H. (1989). Self-efficacy and cognitive achievement: Implications for students with learning problems. *Journal of Learning Disabilities, 22*(1), 14–22.

Sileo, T.W., Rude, H.A., & Luchner, J.L. (1988, December). Collaborative consultation: A model for transition planning for handicapped youth. *Education and Training in Mental Retardation, 23*(4), 333–339.

Turnbull, A.P., & Turnbull, H.R., III. (1996). Self-determination within a culturally responsive family systems perspective: Balancing the family mobile. In L.E. Powers, G.H.S. Singer, & J.-A. Sowers (Eds.), *On the road to autonomy: Promoting self-competence in children and youth with disabilities* (pp. 195–220). Baltimore: Paul H. Brookes Publishing Co.

U.S. Department of Education. (1992, Fall). *OSERS News in Print, 5*(2).

Valdes, K.A., Williamson, C.L., & Wagner, M.M. (1990). *National Longitudinal Transition Study of Special Education Students, 10*(7).

Walker, B., & Singer, G.H.S. (1993). Improving collaborative communication between professionals and parents. In G.H.S. Singer & L.E. Powers (Eds.), *Families, disability, and empowerment: Active coping skills and strategies for family interventions* (pp. 285–315). Baltimore: Paul H. Brookes Publishing Co.

Ward, M.J., & Kohler, P.D. (1996). Teaching self-determination: Content and process. In L.E. Powers, G.H.S. Singer, & J.-A. Sowers (Eds.), *On the road to autonomy: Promoting self-competence in children and youth with disabilities* (pp. 275–290). Baltimore: Paul H. Brookes Publishing Co.

Zeitlin, S., & Williamson, G.G. (1988). Developing family resources for adaptive coping. *Journal of the Division for Early Childhood, 12,* 137–146.

Zetlin, A.G., & Hosseini, A. (1989). Six postschool case studies of mildly learning handicapped young adults. *Exceptional Children, 55*(5), 405–411.

11

ChoiceMaker

Choosing, Planning, and Taking Action

James E. Martin and Laura Huber Marshall

Choices. . . . Life is full of choices. Self-determined people know how to choose. They know what they want and how to get it. From an awareness of personal needs, self-determined individuals choose goals. These goals are doggedly pursued until they are attained or adjusted. The goal attainment process involves asserting one's presence, making one's needs known, evaluating progress toward meeting one's goals, adjusting one's performance or expectations, and creating unique approaches to solve problems (Martin & Huber Marshall, 1995; Martin, Huber Marshall, & Maxson, 1993). Individuals who are self-determined establish goals, set a time line, develop specific plans to attain their goals, determine the benefits that reaching the goals will bring, block out discouraging influences and thoughts, and build coalitions with others who share similar goals (Mithaug, 1991).

211

SELF-DETERMINATION AND STUDENTS WITH AN INDIVIDUALIZED EDUCATION PROGRAM

The importance of self-determination skills to postschool success for students with individualized education programs (IEPs) is without question (Gerber, Ginsberg, & Reiff, 1992; Wehmeyer & Schwartz, 1997). Unfortunately, students with IEPs possess fewer self-determination skills than do secondary school general education students who do not have IEPs (Wolman, Campeau, DuBois, Mithaug, & Stolarski, 1994). If students are to learn and use self-determination behaviors in their everyday lives, self-determination beliefs and behaviors must become part of their daily routines. To make this happen, IEP teams need to strongly consider students' self-determination needs and then infuse self-determination goals into students' IEPs (Sale & Martin, 1997).

THE INDIVIDUALS WITH DISABILITIES EDUCATION ACT AND SELF-DETERMINATION

Educational policy leaders are saying that the ultimate goal for students with IEPs is the acquisition and use of self-determination skills (Ward & Halloran, 1993; Ward & Kohler, 1996). Axiomatically, self-determination is a critical outcome of the transition process (Halloran, 1993). In support, federal special education legislation has created two revolutionary opportunities to teach students crucial self-determination skills. First, the Individuals with Disabilities Education Act (IDEA) Amendments of 1997 (PL 105-17) mandate that students ages 14 and older be invited to attend their IEP meetings. Second, IEP transition goals and activities must be based on *students'* interests and preferences. The spirit of these new rules requires that students of transition age determine, when they are able and with support from the IEP team, their own goals, objectives, and activities based on the students' needs, preferences, and interests as *they* perceive them, not based simply on those expressed by parents and educators.

TEACHING SELF-DETERMINATION THROUGH THE IEP PROCESS

The *ChoiceMaker Series* self-determination materials teach students how to choose where they are going, determine how they will get there and how long it will take, and how all will know when they have arrived there. From learning to be aware of school, postsecondary activities, employment, personal, and housing and daily living needs, students learn to choose goals based on an understanding of their interests, skills, and limits. Through the use of the *Choice-Maker Series* materials, students learn how to express their needs and goals and how to obtain support for them. Students also learn how to take action on their goals by planning, using self-management strategies, acting on the plan, self-evaluating progress, and making adjustments (Martin & Huber Marshall, 1995). The *ChoiceMaker Series* is one of a growing number of lesson packages designed to teach these critical skills through student self-management of the IEP and transition processes (Field, Martin, Miller, Ward, & Wehmeyer, 1998).

CHOICEMAKER CONCEPTS AND CURRICULUM

I don't see how you can scoff at curriculum—you have to know what to teach—I think what people in the field scoff at is when curriculum is designed in a way that is inflexible, rigid, and when it is presented in environments that are not where the skills are typically used. (M.L. Wehmeyer, personal communication, May 21, 1996)

Thirty-seven self-determination concepts provide the foundation for the flexible *ChoiceMaker Curriculum.* The 37 concepts are grouped into seven areas (see Table 1). These areas are

1. Self-awareness
2. Self-advocacy
3. Self-efficacy
4. Decision making
5. Independent performance
6. Self-evaluation
7. Adjustment

Using a detailed social validity process that included interviews with adults with disabilities and their families, a multidisciplinary literature review, and a national survey, these concepts were merged into a curriculum (Martin & Huber Marshall, 1996b).

The *ChoiceMaker Curriculum* (see Figure 1) consists of three sections

1. Choosing Goals
2. Expressing Goals
3. Taking Action

Each section contains from two to four teaching goals and several teaching objectives addressing four transition domains. These transition domains are education; employment; personal; and daily living, housing, and community participation. Students learn to manage their goal attainment processes by making decisions and taking action on their plans.

Table 1.   *ChoiceMaker* self-determination concepts

Self-awareness	Identify needs	Identify interests	Identify and understand strengths
	Identify and understand limitations	Identify own values	
Self-advocacy	Assertively state wants and needs	Assertively state rights	Determine needed supports
	Pursue needed support	Obtain and evaluate needed support	Conduct own affairs
Self-efficacy	Expect to obtain goals		
Decision making	Assess situation demands	Set goals	Set standards
	Identify information to make decisions	Consider past solutions for new situations	Generate new, creative solutions
	Consider options	Choose best option	Develop plan
Independent performance	Initiate tasks on time	Complete tasks on time	Use self-management strategies
	Perform tasks to standard	Follow through on own plan	
Self-evaluation	Monitor task performance	Compare performance to standard	Evaluate effectiveness of self-management strategies
	Determine if plan completed and goal met		
Adjustment	Change goals	Change standards	Change plan
	Change strategies	Change support	Persistently adjust
	Use environmental feedback to aid adjustment		

From Martin, J.E., Huber Marshall, L., Maxson, L.L., & Jerman, P.A. (1996). *Self-Directed IEP.* Longmont, CO: Sopris West; adapted with permission from University Technology Corporation. Copyright ©1997 by University Technology Corporation.

THE *CHOICEMAKER SERIES*

The *ChoiceMaker Series* consists of an assessment tool and several instructional packages designed to teach the goals and objectives of the *ChoiceMaker Curriculum* (see Figure 2). Each lesson package is designed to be infused into existing school coursework and programs.

Because the *Choosing Goals* and *Taking Action* materials are compatible with middle and high school content area courses, they can be used for general education students and with students who have IEPs. The *Self-Directed IEP* materials, which support teaching the Expressing Goals section of the curriculum, are designed for students with IEPs.

The development of each lesson package followed the same process. A team of University of Colorado faculty, public school special educators and administrators, parents, students with IEPs, and adults with disabilities jointly worked on conceptualizing, writing, and field testing the materials. Using *ChoiceMaker Curriculum* objectives as the guideposts, the development teams spent many months crafting the lessons. Then the lessons were used in middle and high school programs, where they were tested, revised, and then tested again. Rigorous studies were then conducted to demonstrate the programs' effectiveness. Additional studies were still in progress at the time of this writing.

ChoiceMaker Assessment

Self-determination is a function both of students' skills and of the opportunity to learn and practice those skills (Wolman et al., 1994). Assessment of self-determination skills and the opportunities schools provide to teach and practice these skills need to be completed before instruction begins and also as a follow-up to instruction. Measurement of student self-determination skills and opportunities is primarily done through the use of teacher- or parent-administered assessment tools or student self-report approaches (Sitlington, Neubert, Begun, Lombard, & Laconte, 1996).

ChoiceMaker Assessment (Martin & Huber Marshall, 1996a) is a curriculum-referenced, teacher-completed tool that measures student skills and the opportunities the school provides for students to learn and practice each objective of *ChoiceMaker Curriculum*. This tool is unique in that it is one of the few curriculum-referenced self-determination assessment tools available (Field et al., 1998). *ChoiceMaker Assessment* is designed for middle and high school students who have mild to moderate learning disabilities, mental retardation, and behavior problems.

ChoiceMaker Assessment, like *ChoiceMaker Curriculum*, consists of three sections: Choosing Goals, Expressing Goals, and Taking Action. The Choosing Goals section measures skills and opportunities for goal setting, expression of transition interest across school, employment, post–high school education, and other curriculum areas. The Expressing Goals section measures students' participation; leadership; and expression of their interests, skills, and limits at their IEP meetings. The Taking Action section measures planning, action taking, self-evaluation, and adjustment, which are all used in the goal attainment process. Figure 3 presents the Expressing Goals section as an example of what the *ChoiceMaker Assessment* looks like.

A teacher completes the *ChoiceMaker Assessment* by circling a 5-point Likert scale response for each of the 54 items across the student skills and opportunities at school areas. The raw scores are summed, graphed, and then compared with the total points available to find the percentage of curriculum objectives performed across the three sections of *ChoiceMaker Curriculum*

Section	Teaching goals	Teaching objectives							
1. Choosing Goals (through school and community experience)	A. Student interests	A1. Express education interests	A2. Express employment interests	A3. Express personal interests	A4. Express daily living, housing, and community interests				
	B. Student skills and limits	B1. Express education skills and limits	B2. Express employment skills and limits	B3. Express personal skills and limits	B4. Express daily living, housing, and community skills and limits				
	C. Student goals	C1. Indicate options and choose education goals	C2. Indicate options and choose employment goals	C3. Indicate options and choose personal goals	C4. Indicate options and choose daily living, housing, and community goals				
2. Expressing Goals	D. Student leading meeting	D1. Begin meeting by stating purpose	D2. Introduce participants	D3. Review past goals and performance	D4. Ask for feedback	D5. Ask questions if do not understand	D6. Cope with differences in opinion	D7. State needed support	D8. Close meeting by summarizing decisions
	E. Student reporting	E1. Express interests (from A1–A4)	E2. Express skills and limits (from B1–B4)	E3. Express options and goals (from C1–C4)					

3. Taking Action		F1. Break general goals into specific goals that can be completed now	F2. Establish standard for specific goals	F3. Determine how to get feedback from environment	F4. Determine motivation to complete specific goals	F5. Determine strategies for completing specific goals	F6. Determine support needed to complete specific goals	F7. Prioritize and schedule to complete specific goals	F8. Express belief that goals can be obtained
	F. Student plan								
	G. Student action	G1. Record or report performance	G2. Perform specific goals to standard	G3. Obtain feedback on performance	G4. Motivate self to complete specific goals	G5. Use strategies to perform specific goals	G6. Obtain support needed	G7. Follow schedule	
	H. Student evaluation	H1. Determine whether goals are achieved	H2. Compare performance to standards	H3. Evaluate feedback	H4. Evaluate motivation	H5. Evaluate effectiveness of strategies	H6. Evaluate support used	H7. Evaluate schedule	H8. Evaluate belief
	I. Student adjustment	I1. Adjust goals if necessary	I2. Adjust or repeat goal standards	I3. Adjust or repeat method for feedback	I4. Adjust or repeat motivation	I5. Adjust or repeat strategies	I6. Adjust or repeat support	I7. Adjust or repeat schedule	I8. Adjust or repeat belief that goals can be obtained

Figure 1. ChoiceMaker self-determination curriculum matrix. (Copyright © 1997 by University Technology Corporation; reprinted by permission.)

Section	Goals	Lessons	Students
Choosing Goals	Student interests Student skills and limits Student goals	Choosing Employment Goals Choosing Personal Goals Choosing Education Goals Choosing Housing, Daily Living, and Community Participation Goals	Middle and high school general education students Middle and high school students with an IEP and mild to moderate learning and behavior problems
Expressing Goals	Student leading meeting Student reporting	Self-Directed IEP	Middle and high school students with an IEP and mild to moderate learning and behavior problems
Taking Action	Student plan Student action Student evaluation Student adjustment	Taking Action	Middle and high school general education students Middle and high school students with an IEP and mild to moderate learning and behavior problems

Figure 2.   *ChoiceMaker* lesson unit matrix. (Adapted from Martin, Huber Marshall, Maxson, & Jerman, 1996. Copyright © 1997 by University Technology Corporation.)

(see Figure 4). A 2-week test–retest reliability study of *ChoiceMaker Assessment* was validated by using more than 300 students with learning disabilities, mental retardation, and behavior problems from four states. The test–retest reliability is within acceptable ranges for a scale of this type (Martin & Huber Marshall, 1998).

Sale and Martin (1997) suggested that the results of *ChoiceMaker Assessment* may be used to help establish IEP goals. Following is a section of their chapter that describes how this may be done.

Once Zeke's IEP team reviewed the Opportunity at School section [of the *ChoiceMaker Assessment*] they realized they needed to improve their curriculum to allow for more self-determined behaviors to occur at school. Con-

Section 2: Expressing Goals

	Student skills (Does the student do this?)					Opportunity at school (Does school provide structured time?)				
	(Not at all)				(100%)	(Not at all)				(100%)
E. Student leading meeting. Does the student:										
E1. Begin meeting and introduce participants?	0	1	2	3	4	0	1	2	3	4
E2. Review past goals and performance?	0	1	2	3	4	0	1	2	3	4
E3. Ask questions if student does not understand something?	0	1	2	3	4	0	1	2	3	4
E4. Ask for feedback from group members?	0	1	2	3	4	0	1	2	3	4
E5. Deal with differences in opinion?	0	1	2	3	4	0	1	2	3	4
E6. Close meeting by summarizing decisions?	0	1	2	3	4	0	1	2	3	4
	Subtotal ___					Subtotal ___				
F. Student reporting. Does the student:										
F1. Express interests?	0	1	2	3	4	0	1	2	3	4
F2. Express skills and limits?	0	1	2	3	4	0	1	2	3	4
F3. Express options and goals?	0	1	2	3	4	0	1	2	3	4
	Subtotal ___					Subtotal ___				
	Total (E + F) ___					Total (E + F) ___				

Figure 3. ChoiceMaker Assessment Expressing Goals section. (From Martin, J.E., & Huber Marshall, L. [1996a]. ChoiceMaker Self-Determination Assessment [p. 3]. Longmont, CO: Sopris West, Inc. Copyright © 1997 by University Technology Corporation; reprinted by permission.)

Part II: *ChoiceMaker Self-Determination Transition Assessment Profile*

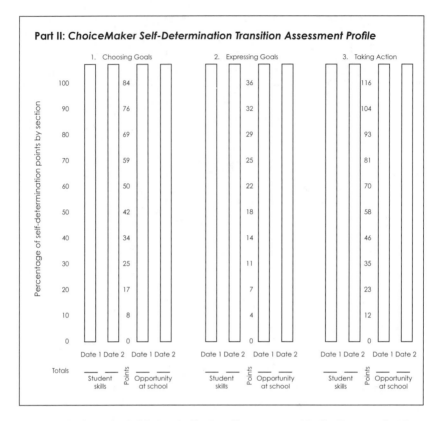

Figure 4. *ChoiceMaker* Self-Determination Transition Assessment Profile. (From Martin, J.E., & Huber Marshall, L. [1996b]. *ChoiceMaker Self-Determination Assessment* [p. 5]. Longmont, CO: Sopris West, Inc. Copyright © 1997 by University Technology Corporation; reprinted by permission.)

currently, Zeke and his IEP team set goals and discussed activities to achieve these goals based upon the *ChoiceMaker* assessment results. The IEP team used the goals and objectives from the ChoiceMaker Transition Curriculum Guide to assist them in this process.

Annual Goal

1. Zeke will express his employment and post-high school education interests, skills, limits, and goals at his next IEP meeting.

Sample Activities:

a. In his transition class and community work experiences, Zeke completes the Choosing Employment Goals lessons. These lessons provide Zeke the opportunity to learn the job characteristics he likes and whether they match different community job sites.

b.   In his learning strategies class, Zeke will complete the Choosing Education Goals lessons. Among other skills, Zeke will learn to identify the classroom characteristics he likes best (e.g., lecture or hands-on, small group activities) and compare them with available next semester classes.
2.   To increase Zeke's leadership of his IEP process.

Sample Activities:

a.   Zeke will complete the Self-Directed IEP lessons. For example, Zeke will learn the 11 steps needed for him to lead his own IEP meeting.
b.   Prior to his IEP meeting, Zeke will videotape a role play using the 11 steps needed to lead his own IEP meeting. Students and his teacher will each assume varying roles. After the role play, Zeke will review his performance with assistance from his peers and teacher. (Sale & Martin, 1997, pp. 62, 66)

Choosing Goals

The Choosing Goals section of *ChoiceMaker Curriculum* provides students with the necessary skills and personal information to articulate their interests, skills, limits, and goals across four transition areas. A videotape entitled *Choosing Goals to Plan Your Life* introduces the goal-choosing process by showing actual high school students learning and using the steps across four different transition areas. The Choosing Goals materials consist of four lesson packages:

* *Choosing Employment Goals* (Huber Marshall, Martin, Maxson, & Jerman, 1997)
* *Choosing Education Goals* (Martin, Huber Marshall, Hughes, Jerman, & Maxson, 1998)
* *Choosing Personal Goals* (Huber Marshall, Martin, Jerman, Hughes, & Maxson, 1998)
* *Choosing Housing, Daily Living, and Community Participation Goals* (Huber Marshall, Martin, Hughes, Jerman, & Maxson, 1998)

Each of these four instructional packages uses the same general Choosing Goals format with lessons, activities, and forms unique to the particular domain. In the remainder of this section, the general Choosing Goals process is reviewed and then *Choosing Employment Goals* is discussed as representative of the other Choosing Goals lesson packages.

Choosing General Goals Process   Each of the Choosing Goals lesson packages includes the Choosing General Goals process, lesson materials, and student instructional videotape. The lessons and activities within each of the four Choosing Goals lesson sets teach students the information that they need to complete the Choosing General Goals process within that domain.

After watching the videotape and completing the Choosing Goals lessons, students complete a Choosing General Goals worksheet. Figure 5 presents a sample Choosing General Goals worksheet from the *Choosing Employment Goals* lesson package for Thomas, a high school student who wants to work as a guitar player in a band. After the student knows how to complete the form, he simply reads each question and writes in his answer. If he does not know the answer, then that becomes his goal. In the Figure 5 example, Thomas does not know how to read sheet music, so learning to read sheet music becomes his goal. Once completed, students may take this form with them to their IEP meetings or use it for discussions in their school to work or transition class.

Choosing Employment Goals   The *Choosing Employment Goals* instructional package includes a videotape entitled *Choosing Goals to Plan Your Life*, teacher lesson plans, and reproducible student worksheets. The *ChoiceMaker Curriculum* objectives (see Figure 1) addressed by *Choosing Employment Goals* are

- *Objective A2:* Express employment interests
- *Objective B2:* Express employment skills and limits
- *Objective C2:* Indicate options and choose employment goals

The *Choosing Employment Goals* lesson sequence is flexible and is designed to be mixed and matched with the content and opportunities of existing school curricula, classes, and schedules.

The lesson activities, which take place in the community and in the classroom, are designed to help students reflect on their experiences, draw conclusions about themselves, and learn about community opportunities. Students collect and assimilate this information over time so that they can make informed life decisions. The *Choosing Employment Goals* lessons packet consists of three parts: 1) Choosing General Goals lessons (described previously), 2) Experience-Based lessons, and 3) Dream Job lessons.

Experience-Based Lessons   Experience-Based lessons are used with students who are participating in a job experience such as work-study, on-the-job training, volunteering, or an after-school job. The purpose is to help students draw meaningful conclusions about their interests, skills, and limits based on their own work experiences.

There are four main student worksheets used in the experience-based section. To help students learn their interests, they complete the Job Characteristics I Like (see Figure 6) and Job Duties I Like forms. To examine their on-the-job skills and limits, they complete a Work, Social, and Personal Skills form (see Figure 7) and a Job Duties—How I Did form. These worksheets are to be used repeatedly (see Figure 8). Students can summarize the information and display it in a graphic format to share with others (see Figure 9). Students can archive these forms to develop their own vocational portfolios, which they can show at their IEP meetings or to their state rehabilitation counselors. By using these

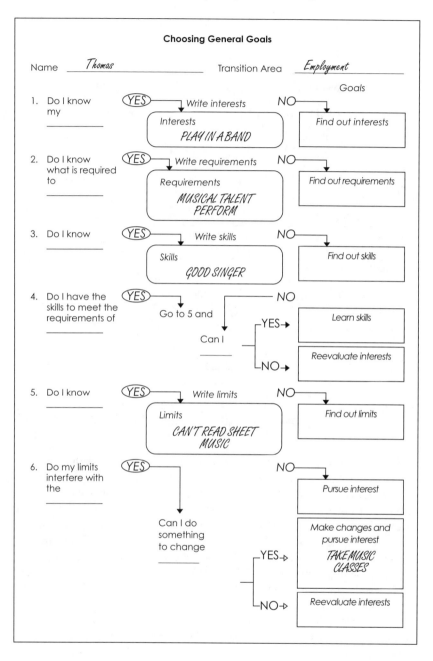

Figure 5.   Sample *ChoiceMaker* Choosing General Goals form. (From Martin, J.E., & Huber Marshall, L. [1996b]. *ChoiceMaker Self-Determination Assessment* [p. 91]. Longmont, CO: Sopris West, Inc. Copyright © 1997 by University Technology Corporation; reprinted by permission.)

Job Characteristics I Like Worksheet

Name: _____   Jobsite: _____   Date: _____

Directions: **What I Like** column: Circle the job characteristic that you like
best in each box.
What Is Here column: Circle the job characteristic in each box
that best describes what is at this job.
Matches column: Circle Yes if the first two columns are the
same. Circle No if they are not.

What I Like	What Is Here	Matches	
Work alone Lots of people around	Work alone Lots of people around	Yes	No
Quiet workplace Noisy workplace	Quiet workplace Noisy workplace	Yes	No

Work close to home
Distance to job does
    not matter
	Work close to home
	Distance to job does
	    not matter
		Yes	No

Weekdays only Weekends too	Weekdays only Weekends too	Yes	No
Easy job Challenging job	Easy job Challenging job	Yes	No

Figure 6.   Sample Job Characteristics I Like Worksheet (partial). (From Huber Marshall, L., Martin, J.E., Maxson, L., & Jerman, P.A. [1997]. *Choosing Employment Goals* [p. 117]. Long-mont, CO: Sopris West, Inc. Copyright © 1997 by University Technology Corporation; reprinted by permission.)

measures repeatedly, a more reliable assessment than what is obtained by using a single interest or aptitude inventory is achieved (Menchetti & Flynn, 1990).

Dream Job Lessons   With the dream job lessons, students gather information about a variety of jobs and then research those that they think they would like. Students determine how their interests, skills, and limits match those jobs. The lessons may be used sequentially or separately. There are four lessons in the dream job section: 1) job clusters, 2) dream job research, 3) dream job interviews (Figure 10), and 4) dream job shadowing (see Figure 11). These lessons are often taught in general education English, social studies, or transition classes.

Applied Examples   The *Choosing Employment Goals* package is used in a variety of settings, as illustrated in the vignettes that follow.

Experiences of One Colorado High School

Freshmen and sophomores with IEPs enroll in 2-hour-per-day career education class. In the class, students shadow several job-

Work, Social, and Personal Skills Student Worksheet

How I did column: Circle 3, 2, or 1, whichever best describes your performance.
Supervisor thinks column: From the Work, Social, and Personal Skills Supervisor Worksheet, copy the numbers that your supervisor chose to describe your performance.
Matches column: Circle Yes if your and your supervisor's evaluations are the same. If they are not the same, circle No.

Skills	How I did		Supervisor thinks		Comments	Matches	
Work							
1. Follows company rules	Very good Okay Needs improvement	3 2 1	Very good Okay Needs improvement	3 2 1		Yes	No
2. Comes to work on time or calls if late or absent	Very good Okay Needs improvement	3 2 1	Very good Okay Needs improvement	3 2 1		Yes	No
Social							
8. Talks the right amount	Very good Okay Needs improvement	3 2 1	Very good Okay Needs improvement	3 2 1		Yes	No
9. Behaves appropriately	Very good Okay Needs improvement	3 2 1	Very good Okay Needs improvement	3 2 1		Yes	No
Personal							
12. Works independently	Very good Okay Needs improvement	3 2 1	Very good Okay Needs improvement	3 2 1		Yes	No
13. Good grooming	Very good Okay Needs improvement	3 2 1	Very good Okay Needs improvement	3 2 1		Yes	No

Figure 7. Work, Social, and Personal Skills sample student worksheet (partial). (From Huber Marshall, L., Martin, J.E., Maxson, L., & Jerman, P.A. [1997]. *Choosing Employment Goals* [p. 157]. Longmont, CO: Sopris West, Inc. Copyright © 1997 by University Technology Corporation; reprinted by permission.)

Recommended Schedule for Using Experience-Based Worksheet

Below is a chart showing examples of when the five main worksheets and summaries may be used. The worksheets do not need to be used in a specific order, but they need to be completed at certain intervals. The "X" on the chart suggests when to complete each worksheet during short-term and extended work periods.

Category	Worksheets	Short-term (month or ??)			Extended (more than a month)			At end of a quarter or ??
		First	Middle	Last week	First	Intervals	Last week	
Interests	Job Duties I Like worksheet		X		X		X	
Interests	Job Characteristics I Like worksheet	X		X		Every 2–3 months ?? X		
Interests	Job characteristics I like							X
Skills and limits	Job Duties: How I Did		X		X		X	
Skills and limits	Work, Social, and Personal Skills worksheet	X	X			Every week for first 4–5 months X		
Skills and limits	Work, social, and personal skills							X
Skills and limits	Self-determination skills		X (Replaces work, social, and personal skills)			Every 2–3 months X (Replaces work, social, personal skills)		
Skills and limits	Site							X

Figure 8.   Recommended schedule for using experience-based worksheet. (From Huber Marshall, L., Martin, J.E., Maxson, L., & Jerman, P.A. [1997]. *Choosing Employment Goals* [p. 22]. Longmont, CO: Sopris West, Inc. Copyright © 1997 by University Technology Corporation; reprinted by permission.)

sites and then pick one job for the quarter. They work at the job for 3 days per week during classtime. At midquarter, students complete two interest worksheets—Job Characteristics I Like and Job Duties I Like—and two skills and limits worksheets—

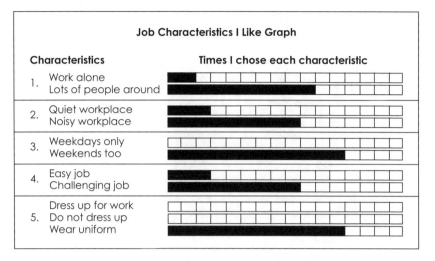

Figure 9. Sample Job Characteristics I Like Graph. (From Huber Marshall, L., Martin, J.E., Maxson, L., & Jerman, P.A. [1997]. *Choosing Employment Goals* [p. 125]. Longmont, CO: Sopris West, Inc. Copyright © 1997 by University Technology Corporation; reprinted by permission.)

Work, Social, and Personal Student Skills Worksheet and Job Duties—How I Did. Students receive feedback from their supervisors on the Work, Social, and Personal Skills Supervisor Evaluation. Students set goals based on the evaluations. Students record their choices on the Job Characteristics I Like and Work, Social, and Personal Skills Student Worksheets. At the end of the quarter, students complete the Site Summary for their jobs. By the end of the 2-year period, students will have worked at eight jobsites and completed a worksheet for each one. Juniors and seniors work in the community through the work-study program. They attend a 1-hour careers class each day, during which class they complete the Dream Job lesson.

Experiences of a District Transition Team

The school district's transition team has been exploring curriculum options for use in three junior high schools and two high schools. Each building has a different service delivery system. Employment-related, experience-based, and dream job lessons are conducive to meeting their unique needs. For example, the special education teacher and the civics teacher team-teach students in general and special education classes at a middle school. They use *Choosing Goals* and *Dream Job Series* for their career awareness units. The students complete the Job Clusters lesson; choose their dream jobs; and identify their interests, skills, and limits relating to the job. They research the job and then interview someone currently doing that job.

Sample Informational Interview Worksheet

Questions	Answers	Would I like this?	Could I do this?	Teacher's comments
Requirement Questions				
1. What are the job duties?		Yes No	Yes No	
2. What are the training or educational requirements of the job?		Yes No	Yes No	
3. What experience must people have to start here?		Yes No	Yes No	
Work Skills Questions				
1. How important are speed and accuracy in this job?		Yes No	Yes No	
2. What are the company's safety practices?		Yes No	Yes No	
3. What is the daily routine of the job?		Yes No	Yes No	
Social Skills Questions				
1. Do workers have contact with customers? If yes, what is the policy for customer interaction?		Yes No	Yes No	
2. Is there time for co-workers to talk to each other?		Yes No	Yes No	
Personal Skills Questions				
1. What is the dress code?		Yes No	Yes No	

Figure 10.   Sample Informational Interview Worksheet. (From Huber Marshall, L., Martin, J.E., Maxson, L., & Jerman, P.A. [1997]. *Choosing Employment Goals* [p. 255]. Longmont, CO: Sopris West, Inc. Copyright © 1997 by University Technology Corporation; reprinted by permission.)

Expressing Goals:
The Self-Directed Individualized Education Program

The William T. Grant Foundation (1988), in *The Forgotten Half: Pathways to Success for America's Youth and Young Families,* reported that teaching leadership skills to non–college-bound high school students prepares them for postschool success. The report stated that youth "become leaders when adults share their leadership opportunities with them" (p. 12). Students with IEPs need opportunities to learn leadership skills, too, as a means by which to facilitate their success. There are few opportunities better than the IEP process to learn these skills. This is affirmed by IDEA, which requires students with IEPs to be involved in their education and transition planning. In fact, these laws

---

DREAM JOB SHADOWING

Name: _____   Date: _____

Jobsite: _____   Job title: _____

Work   What is the daily routine of this job?

Social   Is this person required to talk to supervisors, co-workers, customers?

Personal   How does this person present him- or herself (e.g., dress, attitude)?

Requirements   What experience, education, or training is required for this job?

Can I do this job?   Yes   No   Why or why not?

Do I like this job?   Yes   No   Why or why not?

Figure 11.   Sample Dream Job Shadowing questions. (From Huber Marshall, L., Martin, J.E., Maxson, L., & Jerman, P.A. [1997]. *Choosing Employment Goals* [p. 269]. Longmont, CO: Sopris West, Inc. Copyright © 1997 by University Technology Corporation; reprinted by permission.)

mandate that students' individualized transition plans (ITPs) must be based on their needs, preferences, and interests, not just on the preferences or interests of parents or educators.

Being There Helps, but it Is Not Enough   Martin and Huber Marshall (1998) conducted a survey of 1,660 participants who attended middle and high school IEP meetings over a 3-year period. They found that when students simply attended their meetings, the students talked less and understood less about the reason for the meeting than did the other participants. Powers (1997) found, too, that if students are asked to attend their meetings without having received prior instruction in what to do, participants in the IEP meetings did not talk to the student, did not ask for student input, and the student did not understand what was being discussed or the meeting's purpose.

Martin and Huber Marshall (1998) found that students' presence at IEP meetings increases the likelihood of students' interests being discussed. Sweeney (1997) expanded on this finding. Her study found that students completing the *Self-Directed IEP* lessons were more likely to have their interests discussed by the meeting's participants than those students who did not receive *Self-Directed IEP* lesson package instruction.

Clearly, to make student-directed IEPs a meaningful educational experience, students need to learn their roles in the IEP process and what they can do to become a meaningful part of that process. Their presence alone achieves very little without their knowledge of the process and skills in what to do.

Purpose of* Self-Directed IEP   The Expressing Goals section of the *ChoiceMaker Series* identifies two teaching goals and 11 objectives crucial for student involvement in their own IEP planning process (see Figure 1). *Self-Directed IEP* is a lesson package designed to enable students to attain these goals and objectives. *Self-Directed IEP* is the only part of the *Choice-Maker Series* designed specifically for middle and high students with IEPs.

Self-Directed IEP *Lessons*   *Self-Directed IEP* teaches students to become active participants in their IEP meetings and to chair the meetings to the greatest extent of their ability. By using a model-lead-test approach, *Self-Directed IEP* lessons teach students 11 steps for leading their own IEP meetings (see Table 2). Through the use of *Self-Directed IEP* materials, role-play practice prior to the meeting, and participation in their actual meeting, students learn the leadership skills necessary to manage their IEP meetings. *Self-Directed IEP* contains several different instructional materials, including the following:

- Self-Directed IEP in Action *videotape* (7 minutes): This videotape shows students with disabilities using *Self-Directed IEP* lessons in their classes and talking about their experiences in using the steps in the lesson plans. This videotape is used to introduce *Self-Directed IEP* to students, parents, teachers, and administrators.
- Self-Directed IEP *videotape* (17 minutes): This videotape shows a student named Zeke using each of the 11 steps to lead his IEP meeting while describing the process to a younger, reluctant friend. Zeke's meeting provides a model for each of the 11 steps (see Table 2). After watching the videotape, students complete a lesson for each of the steps. A role-played meeting summarizes what the student learned and provides the teacher with information about how to help coach the student through the actual meeting. The meeting depicted in the videotape shows an ideal meeting in which the student viewers focus on the 11 steps, not on the content or on the interactions of Zeke's meeting.

Table 2.   The 11 steps of the *Self-Directed IEP*

1. Begin meeting by stating its purpose.
2. Introduce everyone.
3. Review past goals and performance.
4. Ask for others' feedback.
5. State your school and transition goals.
6. Ask questions if you do not understand.
7. Address differences in opinion.
8. State what supports you will need.
9. Summarize your goals.
10. Close meeting by thanking everyone.
11. Work on IEP goals all year.

From Martin, J.E., Huber Marshall, L., Maxson, L., & Jerman, P.A. (1996). *Self-Directed IEP* (p. 10). Longmont, CO: Sopris West, Inc. Copyright © 1997 by University Technology Corporation; reprinted by permission.

- *Teacher's manual:* This book provides background information, detailed lesson plans, and an answer key. Lessons include a variety of activities to teach each step, including a mnemonic learning strategy, vocabulary-building exercises (see Figure 12), role-playing (see Figure 13), discussion, and brief reading and writing activities. The lessons are presented in a model-lead-test format.
- *Student's workbook:* This workbook provides students with an opportunity to apply each step to their own IEPs. A script summarizing all the steps is completed at the ends of the lessons for students to use at their IEP meetings.
- ChoiceMaker Assessment: *ChoiceMaker Assessment* is a curriculum-based assessment and planning tool that measures student skills in performing *ChoiceMaker Curriculum* objectives and the opportunities that the school provides for students to learn and practice these skills. Teachers complete this assessment based on the behavior of their students and the school environment as the teachers observe them.

Students and Prerequisite Skills

Self-Directed IEP is designed for use by middle and high school students who have mild to moderate learning disabilities, mental retardation, or emotional or behavior problems. The lessons involve some reading and writing activities. Illustrations are provided in the teacher's manual to assist those students who cannot read the material.

Instructional Considerations

The IEP is a unique aspect of special education. If educators and families are serious about involving students in the IEP process, then students must be

---

Self-Directed IEP Vocabulary Quiz

Name: _____   Date: _____

Part 1

Directions: Fill in each blank with the correct word from the box below:

| Vocation   IEP   Goals   Staffing |

1. _____ are what you want to accomplish.
2. _____ is a meeting in which people write the IEP.
3. _____ is the individualized education program that contains your goals and how you are going to accomplish them.
4. _____ is the type of work a person does.

Figure 12.   Sample Self-Directed IEP Vocabulary Quiz (partial). (From Martin, J.E., Huber Marshall, L., Maxson, L., & Jerman, P.A. [1996]. *Self-Directed IEP* [p. 47]. Longmont, CO: Sopris West, Inc. Copyright © 1997 by University Technology Corporation; reprinted by permission.)

Self-Directed IEP Role-Play Recording Worksheet

Put a checkmark in the Completed step box next to each step if the student is able to provide the necessary information for each step.

Write any comments that you would like to make about how the student completed each step in the Comments box next to each step.

Self-Directed IEP Steps	Completed step	Comments
1. Begin meeting by stating the purpose.		
2. Introduce everyone.		
3. Review past goals and performance.		
4. Ask for others' feedback.		
5. State your school and transition goals.		
6. Ask questions if you do not understand.		
7. Deal with differences in opinion.		
8. State what support you will need.		
9. Summarize your goals.		
10. Close meeting by thanking everyone.		
Total number of +'s		
Percentage completed		

Eye contact
Mark the box below that best describes what the student did during the role-play.

	Most of the time	Some of the time	Not very much of the time
Looked at other people			

Tone of voice
Mark the box below that best describes the student's tone of voice during the role-play.

	Good	OK	Needs improvement
Tone of voice			

Figure 13.   Self-Directed IEP Role-Play Recording Worksheet. (From Martin, J.E., Huber Marshall, L., Maxson, L., & Jerman, P.A. [1997]. *Choosing Employment Goals* [p. 107]. Longmont, CO: Sopris West, Inc. Copyright © 1997 by University Technology Corporation; reprinted by permission.)

taught their roles. Even in fully included schools, students who have IEPs must receive instruction about the IEP process and their roles in it.

Self-Directed IEP contains 11 sequential lessons that can be taught in six to ten 45-minute sessions. The lessons may be taught in a resource room, study skills class, or other setting. Teaching students with disabilities who are fully included in general education classes may involve meeting with these students individually or with a group of these students during study hall or at other convenient times. The lessons may also be also taught in an elective class.

Sweeney (1997) undertook a pre–post controlled-group study to measure the impact of *Self-Directed IEP* on Florida high school students with learning disabilities and mental retardation. In comparison with the students in the control group who did not receive instruction, Sweeney found that the students who completed *Self-Directed IEP* lessons

- Attended IEP meetings more often
- Were more likely to have their parents attend their IEP meetings
- Talked more about their interests
- Shared more of their dreams for the future
- Talked more about the job that they wanted
- Felt like they were the boss of their IEP meetings
- Felt more confident in reaching their IEP goals

Other studies are under way to replicate and extend these findings.

Taking Action

Some view choice as the most important self-determination component. It is fun for students to choose and to dream what they would like to do at some point in the future. But goals are the engine that drives self-determined behavior; they are what makes the dream happen. Self-determination is the "attitudes and abilities that facilitate an individual's identification and *pursuit of goals*" (Powers et al., 1996, p. 292). It is self-directed action to attain goals that marks self-determined behaviors (Field & Hoffman, 1995). Self-determined individuals doggedly pursue their goals until the goals are attained (Martin et al., 1993).

Goal attainment begins with goal setting. Goal setting by itself is a powerful and extremely effective tool for bringing about changes in behavior (Johnson & Graham, 1990). Without goals, a person has nothing to strive toward. The goal attainment process makes the dream happen. To this end, Wehmeyer (1994) believed that goal attainment behavior is a critical self-determination instructional area. *ChoiceMaker Curriculum* (see Figure 1) emphasizes teaching goals and objectives in the *Taking Action* section. The four goals discussed there are

1. Student plan
2. Student action
3. Student evaluation
4. Student adjustment

The *Taking Action* lessons teach students a systematic method of attaining their own IEP or personal goals.

Taking Action *Dream*   Special education teachers believe it is their responsibility to make sure their students' IEP goals are attained, but is this really a recommended secondary-level educational practice? Something is wrong with a practice in which the student is absolved of any goal attainment responsibility. After all, whose goals are on the IEP? Whose education is it? If goal attainment is the most important part of being self-determined, then why are students not more responsible for their own goals? Are educators really acting in the students' best interest if teachers bear the entire responsibility for students' goal attainment?

We do not think so. We believe that students need to have at least an equal responsibility with teachers for achieving their own IEP goals, if not a greater responsibility. Our dream is that once the IEP meeting is concluded, the *Taking Action* process begins. Our dream finds students being systematically taught the *Taking Action* goal attainment strategy. Once the lessons are completed, students systematically apply, with teacher support, the *Taking Action* process to their own IEP goals. Our dream is to have students meet weekly throughout the year with their teachers to develop a plan to achieve their own IEP goals after evaluating the progress made during the previous week toward achieving that week's plan. We cannot think of a better way to make the IEP process a living student-centered document.

Taking Action *Overview*   The *Taking Action* lesson package (Huber Marshall et al., in press) teaches students to use a simple yet effective goal attainment process. As with the other *ChoiceMaker* lesson packages, this lesson package is introduced with a student-oriented videotape demonstrating the *Taking Action* concepts. *Taking Action* lessons teach students to plan how they will attain their goals by helping them decide

- A standard for goal performance
- A means by which to get performance feedback
- What motivates them
- Which strategies they will use
- What supports they need
- Schedules

This lesson package leads to student action, evaluation, and adjustment. It can be applied to any goal or project and thus is an excellent tool for use in content classes.

Taking Action *Lessons*   The *Taking Action* lessons systematically teach students an easy and effective goal attainment process. The lessons use a model-lead-test approach. In the remainder of this section, the lessons are discussed and sample instructional procedures are provided to demonstrate the major concepts.

Lesson 1   Lesson 1 introduces the *Taking Action* process for accomplishing goals and the four major parts of the *Taking Action* process: plan, act, evaluate, and adjust. Lesson 1 continues with the process of teaching students how to break long-term goals into short-term goals.

Lessons 2 and 3   Students watch the 10-minute *Taking Action* videotape, which shows students developing plans and working on attaining their own goals. The students in the videotape assisted in writing and creating the videotape; thus, the goals on which they are working in the videotape are goals from their own lives. Students are introduced to plan making in Lessons 2 and 3. Here they learn the parts of a plan needed to attain their short-term goals. Hands-on activities are used to demonstrate each plan part. One of the concluding activities is for students to match the question being asked to the correct part of the plan (see Figure 14).

Lesson 4   Using a criteria format, students in Lesson 4 examine three plans and predict whether each part of the plan will work (see Figure 15).

Lesson 5   Students develop a plan to accomplish a common goal.

Lesson 6   Students learn the importance of evaluation and adjustment to goal attainment (see Figure 16). They examine the evaluations and adjustments of earlier plans they examined.

Remaining Lessons   The remaining lessons teach students how to develop their own plans for sample goals and then for their own goals. The last lesson teaches students how to use the *Taking Action* goal attainment process in other settings and with a wide range of goals.

Impact of *Taking Action* Lessons

To examine the effectiveness of the *Taking Action* process with high school students, German, Marshall, and Martin (1997) completed a multiple-baseline study of six students with mental retardation to determine whether there were increases in goal attainment. The results showed that all students had significant increases in the attainment of specific daily goals. The students went from 0%–25% achievement of their daily goals during baseline to 80%–100% achievement after instruction in the *Taking Action* lessons.

CONCLUSIONS

The *ChoiceMaker Series* is our attempt to help teach students the 37 self-determination concepts. We combined these concepts to create the *Choice-Maker Curriculum.* From the curriculum emerged the *Choosing Goals* lesson packages, *Self-Directed IEP,* and *Taking Action* lessons. Together, these lesson packages teach the self-determination concepts. The *ChoiceMaker Curriculum* teaches students to

- Set goals based on an understanding of their interests, skills, and limits
- Express goals and gain support for them
- Develop a plan, implement it, evaluate the results, and make needed adjustments to attain the goal

Taking Action Review: Plan-Matching Exercise Worksheet

Name: _____   Date: _____

Find the question that explains each part of a plan. Write it under the correct part of the plan.

Questions			
How will I get information on my performance?	What help do I need?	When will I do it?	What will I be satisfied with?	What methods should I use?	Why do I want to do this?

Parts of a Plan			
Standard	Motivation	Strategy	Schedule	Support	Feedback

Figure 14. Taking Action Review: Plan-Matching Exercise Worksheet (partial). (From Huber Marshall, L., et al. [in press]. *Taking Action*. Longmont, CO: Sopris West, Inc. Copyright © 1997 by University Technology Corporation; reprinted by permission.)

Sample Plan: Taking Action Lesson 4

Name: _Michelle Pass_ Date: _March 15_

Long-term goal: _Pass the class_

Short-term goal: _Get a B on the unit test_

1. Student Plan

Standard What will I be satisfied with?	Motivation Why do I want to do this?	Strategy What methods should I use?	Schedule When will I do this?	Support What help do I need?	Feedback How will I get information on my performance?
Get a "B" on the test.	See what my grade is on the test.	Get better insurance rates.	Study with a friend.	Study with Joe.	Study with Joe all day Sunday before the test.

Figure 15. Sample plan used with Taking Action Lesson 4 (partial). (From Huber Marshall, L., et al. [in press]. *Taking Action.* Longmont, CO: Sopris West, Inc. Copyright © 1997 by University Technology Corporation; reprinted by permission.)

237

Sample Taking Action Evaluation and Adjustment Worksheet

2. Action

Did I meet my short-term goal?   YES   (NO)

Standard	Motivation	Strategy	Schedule	Support	Feedback
Did I meet the standard? Yes (No)	Was I motivated? (Yes) No	Did I use the strategy? (Yes) No	Did I follow the schedule? (Yes) No	Did I use support? (Yes) No	Did I get feedback? (Yes) No

3. Evaluate

Standard	Motivation	Strategy	Schedule	Support	Feedback
Was it the right standard? (Yes) No Why or why not? *Because I need to be in class on time at least 4 days to get a better grade*	Did it work? Yes (No) Why or why not? *I want better grades, but at 6:30 in the morning I want to sleep more*	Did it work? Yes (No) Why or why not? *I did not get up at 6:30 on 3 days*	Did it work? Yes (No) Why or why not? *I set the alarm each night, but I did not get up when it went off*	Did it work? Yes (No) Why or why not? *I kept hitting the snooze button on the alarm clock*	Was the feedback helpful? Yes (No) Why or why not? *Keeping track in my assignment notebook let me know that I did not meet my standard*

What were the reasons why you got these results? Look at the Action and Evaluate sections. If you met your short-term goal, consider the parts of the plan for which you answered Yes. If you did not meet the short-term goal, consider the parts for which you answered No.

I kept on hitting the snooze button and did not get up when the alarm went off.

4. Adjust

Short-term goal okay, or change? If change, new short-term goal: _____

Standard	Motivation	Strategy	Schedule	Support	Feedback
If standard was not right, what will change?	If I was not motivated, what will change?	If my strategy did not work, what will change?	If I did not follow my schedule, what will change?	If my support did not work, what will change?	If feedback was not helpful, what will change?

Figure 16.   Sample Taking Action Evaluation and Adjustment Worksheet. (From Huber Marshall, L., et al. [in press]. *Taking Action.* Longmont, CO: Sopris West, Inc. Copyright © 1997 by University Technology Corporation; reprinted by permission.)

238

The IEP process is truly a metaphor for self-determination (McAlonan & Longo, 1995). If educators want their students to learn critical self-determination skills, there is no better place to teach them than within the IEP planning process. No other part of the educational process is as uniform as IEP planning. Wherever students go, they can slip into the same self-determination–oriented program guided by a student-centered IEP process. A student-centered IEP process turns what so often has become a burdensome administrative hassle into one that is inclusive, meaningful, and provides a rich student educational experience.

REFERENCES

Field, S., & Hoffman, A. (1995). *Steps to self-determination.* Austin, TX: PRO-ED.

Field, S.S., Martin, J.E., Miller, R.J., Ward, M., & Wehmeyer, M.L. (1998). *Student self-determination guide.* Reston, VA: Council for Exceptional Children.

Gerber, P.J., Ginsberg, R., & Reiff, H.B. (1992). Identifying alterable patterns in employment success for highly successful adults with learning disabilities. *Journal of Learning Disabilities, 25,* 475–487.

German, S.L., Huber Marshall, L., & Martin, J.E. (1997). *Goal attainment through using the Take Action curriculum.* Colorado Springs: University of Colorado, Center for Self-Determination.

Halloran, W.D. (1993). Transition services requirement: Issues, implications, challenge. In R.C. Eaves & P.J. McLaughlin (Eds.), *Recent advances in special education and rehabilitation* (pp. 210–224). Boston: Andover Medical Publishers.

Huber Marshall, L., Martin, J.E., Hughes, W.M., Jerman, P.A., & Maxson, L.L. (1998). *Choosing Housing, Daily Living, and Community Participation.* Lesson package in preparation.

Huber Marshall, L., Martin, J.E., Jerman, P.A., Hughes, W.M., & Maxson, L.L. (1998). *Choosing Personal Goals.* Lesson package in preparation.

Huber Marshall, L., Martin, J.E., Maxson, L.L., & Jerman, P.A. (1997). *Choosing Employment Goals.* Longmont, CO: Sopris West.

Huber Marshall, L., Martin, J.E., Maxson, L.M., Miller, T.L., McGill, T., Hughes, W.M., & Jerman, P.A. (in press). *Taking Action* (videotape, assessment tool, and instructional material). Longmont, CO: Sopris West.

Individuals with Disabilities Education Act (IDEA) Amendments of 1997, PL 105-17, 20 U.S.C. §§ 1400 *et seq.*

Johnson, L.A., & Graham, S. (1990). Goal setting and its application with exceptional learners. *Preventing School Failure, 34,* 4–8.

Martin, J.E., & Huber Marshall, L. (1995). ChoiceMaker: A comprehensive self-determination transition program. *Intervention in School and Clinic, 30*(3), 147–156.

Martin, J.E., & Huber Marshall, L. (1996a). ChoiceMaker: Infusing self-determination instruction into the IEP and transition process. In D.J. Sands & M.L. Wehmeyer (Eds.), *Self-determination across the life span: Independence and choice for people with disabilities* (pp. 215–236). Baltimore: Paul H. Brookes Publishing Co.

Martin, J.E., & Huber Marshall, L. (1996b). *ChoiceMaker Self-Determination Assessment.* Longmont, CO: Sopris West.

Martin, J.E., & Huber Marshall, L. (1998). *Three-year survey of IEP participants.* Unpublished manuscript, University of Colorado at Colorado Springs.

Martin, J.E., Huber Marshall, L., Hughes, W.M., Jerman, P.A., & Maxson, L.L. (1998). *Choosing Educational Goals.* Lesson package in preparation.

Martin, J.E., Huber Marshall, L., & Maxson, L.L. (1993). Transition policy: Infusing self-determination and self-advocacy into transition programs. *Career Development for Exceptional Individuals, 16*(1), 53–61.

Martin, J.E., Huber Marshall, L., Maxson, L.L., & Jerman, P.A. (1996). *Self-Directed IEP.* Longmont, CO: Sopris West.

McAlonan, S.J., & Longo, P.A. (1995). *KEDS: Kids empowerment drives the system.* Paper presentation at the Seventh Collaborative Conference for Special Education, Colorado Springs, CO.

Menchetti, B.M., & Flynn, C.C. (1990). Vocational evaluation. In F.R. Rusch (Ed.), *Supported employment: Models, methods, and issues* (pp. 111–130). Sycamore, IL: Sycamore Publishing Co.

Mithaug, D.E. (1991). *Self-determined kids: Raising satisfied and successful children.* Lexington, MA: D.C. Heath & Co.

Powers, L.E. (1997). *Self-determination research results.* Paper presentation at University of Colorado self-determination meeting, Colorado Springs.

Powers, L.E., Sowers, J.-A., Turner, A., Nesbitt, M., Knowles, E., & Ellison, R. (1996). Take charge: A model for promoting self-determination among adolescents with challenges. In L.E. Powers, G.H.S. Singer, & J.-A. Sowers (Eds.), *On the road to autonomy: Promoting self-competence in children and youth with disabilities* (pp. 291–322). Baltimore: Paul H. Brookes Publishing Co.

Sale, P., & Martin, J.E. (1997). Self-determination. In P. Wehman & J. Kregel (Eds.), *Functional curriculum for elementary, middle, and secondary age students with special needs* (pp. 43–67). Austin, TX: PRO-ED.

Sitlington, P.L., Neubert, D.A., Begun, W., Lombard, R.C., & Laconte, P.J. (1996). *Assess for success: Handbook on transition assessment.* Reston, VA: Council for Exceptional Children.

Sweeney, M. (1997). *Effectiveness of the Self-Directed IEP.* Tallahassee: Florida State University.

Ward, M.J., & Halloran, W.D. (1993). Transition issues for the 1990's. *OSERS News in Print, VI*(1), 4–5.

Ward, M.J., & Kohler, P.J. (1996). Teaching self-determination: Content and process. In L.E. Powers, G.H.S. Singer, & J.-A. Sowers (Eds.), *On the road to autonomy: Promoting self-competence in children and youth with disabilities* (pp. 275–290). Baltimore: Paul H. Brookes Publishing Co.

Wehmeyer, M.L. (1994). Perceptions of self-determination and psychological empowerment of adolescents with mental retardation. *Education and Training in Mental Retardation and Developmental Disabilities, 29,* 9–21.

Wehmeyer, M.L., & Schwartz, M. (1997). Self-determination and positive adult outcomes: A follow-up of youth with mental retardation or learning disabilities. *Exceptional Children, 63*(2), 245–255.

William T. Grant Foundation. (1988). *The Forgotten half: Pathways to success for America's youth and young families.* Washington, DC: Author.

Wolman, M., Campeau, P.L., DuBois, P.A., Mithaug, D.E., & Stolarski, V.S. (1994). *AIR self-determination scale and user guide.* Palo Alto, CA: American Institutes for Research.

12

It's My Life

Preference-Based Planning for Self-Directed Goals

Emilee Curtis

Self-direction is difficult to teach. Educators and researchers continue to search for ways to instruct people on how to become self-directed. New Hats, Inc., is an organization that develops methods and materials to support self-determination and provide students with learning experiences that lead to improved opportunities in adulthood. New Hats, Inc., has developed *It's My Life* (Curtis & Dezelsky, 1996a), a curriculum that enables students to assume greater responsibility for their learning and educational planning. Through *It's My Life*, roles traditionally within the teacher's domain, including goal planner, organizer, decision maker, record keeper, and pace setter, are gradually assumed by the student. This chapter explores the benefits of self-directed planning, specific methods for facilitating student involvement in the goal

The *It's My Life* curriculum facilitator training and resource materials are available from New Hats, Inc., HC 64 Box 2509, Castle Valley, Utah 84532; (435) 259-9400 (telephone), (435) 259-2209 (fax), nhats@timp.net (email).

241

process, and the importance of including a focus on life dreams as part of the individualized education program (IEP) process.

THE QUEST FOR SELF-DETERMINATION

The challenge is a familiar one—to provide individuals experiencing disabilities with quality support services, resulting in full community participation, meaningful relationships, successful careers, and the fulfillment of dreams. Since the late 1980s, there have been numerous advances in special education and adult services that have provided increased opportunities for people with disabilities to participate in the mainstream of society and learn skills related to self-determination (Ward, 1996; Ward & Kohler, 1996). The common theme across these efforts has been that no one is better equipped than the individuals themselves, regardless of their abilities, to make choices, express preferences, and shape their lives. As people with disabilities gain confidence in their capacity to let others know what they want, and, as significant others begin to listen more closely, teams can work together to support individuals in reaching their goals and fulfilling their dreams.

Service providers and educators use a wide variety of planning methods to develop services and supports, including the IEP for students receiving special education services, the individualized program plan (IPP) or individualized service plan (ISP) for persons involved in adult services, and the individualized work rehabilitation plan (IWRP) for recipients of Vocational Rehabilitation services. These processes emerged based on the recognition that each person receiving services has unique needs and capacities, and they were implemented to ensure that service agencies and educational entities would provide supports based on these unique needs and capacities. However, despite the best intentions, many goals in planning documents reflected the needs and ideas of the program or service provider and failed to include the preferences and interests of the individual who was receiving services.

The self-determination movement began, in part, through the efforts of individuals committed to bridging this gap. In the mid-1980s, recipients of disability-related services began to articulate desires and goals that went beyond the opportunities typically provided to them. They stretched the limits of the status quo by saying, "I want to go to college!" "I want to get married!" "I want a career!" "I want to own a home!" It became clear that individuals experiencing disabilities wanted the same things that everyone else wanted. They wanted freedom from labels. They wanted jobs instead of placements. They wanted to graduate from the challenges of disability to the opportunities and challenges of real life. Services, supports, and planning began to take on new forms as professionals, individuals, and their families sought creative and innovative ways of moving toward self-determination and the fulfillment of their dreams. For many people with disabilities, *self-determination* means "the chance to live the American Dream" (Williams, 1989, p. 16), including meaningful work, a comfortable place to live, and rewarding leisure time. Self-determined individuals are aware of their own capacities, limitations, preferences, and interests; they pursue self-defined goals through their own initiative and motivation (Martin, Huber Marshall, Maxson, & Jerman, 1996). They make choices in their lives, have control over decision-making processes, and take responsibility for outcomes (Lovett, 1991). They have opportunities to develop meaningful relationships, network with others, and make their contributions to society (O'Brien, 1987).

Until the emergence of the self-determination movement, people experiencing disabilities were not encouraged to dream, express their preferences, or exert control over their decisions and choices. Debilitating stereotypes, low expectations, and learned helplessness limited opportunities for individuals to learn and practice self-direction. The advent of the self-determination movement has illuminated the fact that individuals with disabilities have both the right and the capacity to assert their preferences, shape their futures, and have input and control regarding the services they receive and, through that process, gain or regain power over their own lives (Bannerman, Sheldon, Sherman, & Harchik, 1990; Lovett, 1991; Ward, 1988). Federal initiatives have supported this movement and encouraged individuals who experience disabilities to raise their expectations and be confident that some of their dreams can be realized. Among these initiatives were a series of model demonstration projects funded by the U.S. Department of Education, Office of Special Education Programs (OSEP), to identify and teach the skills necessary for self-determination. *It's My Life* was developed through one of these projects and uses a preference-based planning process to enable students to achieve self-direction and self-determination through their IEPs.

OVERVIEW OF THE PREFERENCE-BASED PLANNING PROCESS

Successful individuals pursue outcomes that are meaningful to them through purposeful action and decision making designed to bring about a desired result. The IEP provides one of the best means of providing opportunities for self-determination and of developing capacities and effective skills for self-direction. The IEP planning process provides an opportunity for students to learn invaluable goal-setting and planning skills that they can use for managing their lives and achieving their goals and dreams beyond their school years and into adulthood.

Many teachers do not expect that students will or can play a major role in educational planning, decision making, and instruction (West & Parent, 1992). Time constraints and the need for structure and control of the classroom may limit opportunities for students to take control over learning and educational decision making (Wehmeyer, 1992, 1996). Because the IEP is a legal document with implications for accountability, educators have assumed primary responsibility for IEP development, meetings, implementation, and evaluation. In too many cases, the process has become a required annual activity, producing a document that is filed away until the next IEP is due (Smith, 1990).

The IEP process must be revitalized and charged with renewed meaning if students, teachers, and parents are to actively engage in the process with excitement, creativity, and energy. In the Preference-Based Planning Model (Figure 1), students assume a leadership role in all phases of the planning and implementation process and consequently learn valuable skills for working toward desired outcomes. Goals and objectives generated by such a process are related to outcomes that the student wants to achieve. This provides a reason for the student to invest in the process.

Preference-based planning begins with activities to discover personal interests, capacities, preferences, wants, and dreams that, in turn, are examined within the context of a person's desired lifestyle. Relevant options are examined to gauge how to achieve the desired outcomes. After careful consideration of personal capacities, resources, and motivation, decisions are made regarding what to pursue as long-range or short-term activities. With these priorities in mind, goals are developed and task-oriented steps are outlined, describing how each goal will be accomplished. Target dates, resource people, and achievement criteria are identified. Then the tasks and activities that lead to the fulfillment of goals (and therefore lifestyle dreams) go into a planner or onto a calendar. These tools guide daily activities and future schedules.

The Preference-Based Planning Model is based on the following principles:

1. Each individual has unique needs, interests, and preferences and is the best judge of his or her own needs.
2. To the maximum extent possible, people should direct their own lives and make their own decisions.
3. Every person deserves a fair opportunity to develop capacities in pursuit of self-defined goals.
4. Education has the responsibility and capacity to provide opportunities for individuals to take action and to regulate their efforts toward outcomes that are important to them.
5. Goal-setting skills build a capacity for self-direction and self-determination in adulthood.
6. Opportunities to evaluate progress, understand evaluation information, adjust performance or expectations, and celebrate results sustain an individual's engagement in working toward a desired outcome.
7. Goal implementation is an ongoing activity rather than a separate, yearly event.

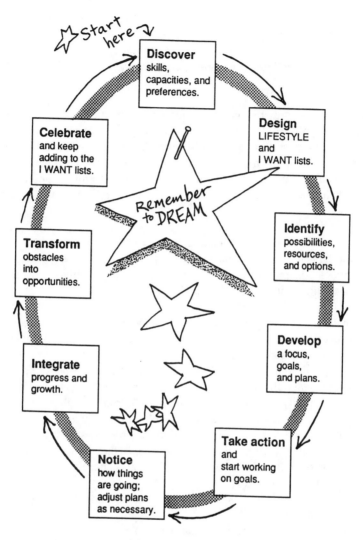

Figure 1.   The Preference-Based Planning Model.

8. Self-determination skills develop over a lifetime through a person's accumulated experience; by understanding the result of decisions and actions, individuals develop skills for pursuing successful future outcomes.

9. Knowledge about goals and participation in goal setting enhances motivation to learn.

10. Motivation to continue an effort depends on successfully predicting which strategies will bring about the desired result.

11. The most effective support people see themselves as facilitators and mentors.
12. Independence does not mean doing things alone; enhanced quality of life involves interdependence, community, relationships, and feeling connected.

The IEP process provides a unique opportunity for students to learn and apply vital skills applicable to any situation—identifying a potential outcome, evaluating activities and variables to achieve the desired result, estimating the likelihood of attaining the outcome, and developing goals and plans. Furthermore, students learn to make modifications as needed, enlist support, communicate their needs, identify their capacities, and evaluate their performance.

Facilitation Skills

The major role of the facilitator (e.g., teacher) in the Preference-Based Planning Model is to assist students in becoming self-directed, which involves encouraging students in their pursuit of self-selected goals that move them toward the fulfillment of their lifestyle dreams. Facilitators

1. Enable students to gather information about their capacities and limitations and to identify the steps involved in achieving desired outcomes
2. Provide a mirror for individuals to reflect on their capacities and preferences, understand how they learn, and predict consequences of decisions
3. Acknowledge that there are many different ways to learn and grow and that the ability to make effective decisions improves with practice
4. Encourage students to speak for themselves, listen attentively to what students say, and communicate a belief in students' capacities and values
5. Provide support while students do as much as they can on their own
6. Provide options and assistance as individuals choose attainable goals and develop plans to achieve them
7. Support students by acknowledging progress and attributing it to their effort and actions
8. Assist individuals in keeping their plans current with their evolving needs by evaluating results and making modifications

Table 1 provides some samples of the types of communications that facilitators might employ in the preference-based planning process.

The Importance of Dreams

All people have preferences about how they would like their lives to be. Some people know their lifestyle dreams, others need assistance in identifying their dreams, and some need permission and support to dream at all. Preference-based planning defines a *dream* as something that has not yet happened that a

Table 1.   Samples of facilitative communication

"I'm wondering if you have considered . . ."
"I'm interested in hearing your ideas about . . ."
"I'm wondering if you could give me a little more information about . . ."
"I'd like to hear about things you are doing now to get some of the things you mentioned you want to have . . . or to do . . ."
"I have some ideas about. . . . If you would like to hear them, let me know."
"I'm curious about how you feel things are going right now. What are you pleased with? What would you like to change?"
"I'm wondering how soon you would like to see this change happen? How would you feel if it took longer than this? Can you see a change happening sooner than this?"
"I'm curious about any ways that you see yourself getting in the way of your own progress. Are you aware of any patterns in the past when you made things more difficult for yourself?"
"I'm wondering what resources you have available to make this happen for yourself, in regard to finances, personal support from others, people who believe in you and your dreams, and so forth?"
"What kind of help do you think you need?"
"If I can be of assistance in your problem solving about this, let me know."

person really wants to happen. In this process, the dream comes first, followed by a goal, a plan, and a calendar entry. Dreams are the driving forces behind goals. The more powerful the list of dreams, the more likely that the necessary effort, motivation, and self-discipline can be sustained by an individual to accomplish goals and create the desired lifestyle. Through this process, individuals learn to think ahead and become self-directed, self-reinforcing, and self-determined. Dreams provide a motive and a rationale for answering questions such as the following:

- Why should I do the activities that are on my calendar for today?
- Why should I stick to a budget?
- Why should I get a job or a diploma?
- Why should I take good care of myself?
- Why do I want this goal?
- What can I look forward to?

Dreams provide the impetus for students to engage in the goal process. Motivation is sustained by the benefits that students receive by performing an activity that is immediately useful and satisfying and by making visible progress toward a desired outcome (Mithaug, 1996). The desire to repeat a task is fueled by an individual's recognition of his or her capacity to create change in his or her life and environment. West and Parent suggested that "the transfer of power and control over values, decisions, choices, and directions from external entities to the individual results in increased motivation to participate and succeed and a greater degree of dignity" (1992, p. 48).

The facilitator is the catalyst for the student's discovery of dreams and lifestyle preferences. The facilitator begins with the following questions: "What have you always dreamed of being or doing?" "What do you want?" Goals and plans are then formulated that become the steps toward making the person's dreams become reality. While working toward the dream, the person learns functional skills that are relevant and immediately useful in his or her life. When others listen to these dreams, both the dream and the dreamer are recognized as important and worthwhile. What follows is a discovery of individual potential and possibilities for contributing to community and relationships. First, a person feels valued; second, a person begins to see that his or her contribution will be of value. Sharing one's dreams and preferences opens the door to hope, change, and growth. Table 2 lists sample questions that facilitate the identification of dreams.

ACHIEVING STUDENT INVOLVEMENT IN THE IEP PROCESS

Questionnaires completed by teachers and students participating in the development of the *It's My Life* curriculum indicated that there was little active student involvement in the IEP process prior to the use of the preference-based planning materials. The overall results indicated that 85% of the students did very little talking at their meetings, 84% of the students did not know their IEP goals, 72% of the students did not know the purpose of their meetings, 92% of the students were not involved in evaluating their progress toward their IEP goals, and 88% of the students did not have any input in deciding who to invite to their IEP meetings (Curtis, 1995).

When project personnel and teachers first asked students if they wanted to become actively involved in planning their IEPs, many were unsure, stating that, for the most part, IEP meetings had not been positive experiences for them or that such planning was something that their teachers and parents did. Prior to their active involvement, many students believed that the meetings

Table 2.   Samples of questions to identify dreams

"Are there goals you're working on now?"

"What do you want for your future? What are your future dreams, hopes, or plans?"

"Is there any kind of change you would like to make?"

"Is there anything you've wanted to learn about? Any skills you would like to gain?"

"Is there anything about yourself that you'd like to change? Any kind of improvement? Anything that would make your life easier or more enjoyable?"

"Is there anywhere you would like to go where you've never been? Or anywhere you'd like to go again?"

"Is there anything you'd like to save your money for?"

"What are some things you've always thought would be really fun to do?"

were required rather than being occasions to which they looked forward. They reported that the focus seemed to be on their deficits and activities that they could not do well rather than on their preferences and capacities and the fulfillment of their dreams. Most students believed that the IEP process meant only the meetings because they had little ongoing interaction or experience with goal development and implementation. One student, while doing a presentation for teachers about goals during the course of the project, suddenly burst into tears and expressed how difficult it had been to be a passive participant in a process that she now uses to direct her life.

Because the potential value of the planning process has been underestimated, students have been denied access to the development of vital skills for shaping and directing their meeting and their lives. Directing one's own IEP meeting, however, is only one benefit of preference-based planning. The meeting itself is a public confirmation of roles, responsibilities, goals, and plans. The real heart of the process lies in two areas—the planning that precedes the meeting and the implementation of actual goals. IEP development occurs in eight stages: assessment, IEP development, identification of goals, development of plans, conference participation, monitoring of progress, evaluation of effectiveness, and modifications (Wilson, Caselia, & Wilson, 1989). For students to benefit fully, opportunities for involvement in each stage of the process must be available. Although partial involvement in each stage is an alternative, total and active participation in each stage should be the ultimate goal.

IT'S MY LIFE: A PREFERENCE-BASED PLANNING MODEL

The *It's My Life* curriculum and resource materials were developed over 3 years and included the development of 11 products and resources to facilitate self-determination and student direction. Through mentoring and workshops, students, teachers, and families were trained in methods that facilitate decision making, self-directed learning, and self-regulation. As part of the project, New Hats, Inc., also developed an innovative transition model that supported students ages 18–22 in living independently and acquiring meaningful employment while still in school. A combination of natural and formal supports continued to benefit students after they exited the school system. The curriculum and associated materials were evaluated through preliminary and main field tests involving teachers from four school districts. Students completed a Likert scale pretest of their knowledge and involvement in the IEP process. At the end of the school year, the scale was readministered and showed significant gains in all areas of knowledge and involvement.

Although the *It's My Life* materials were developed primarily for high school students, they have also been used by people working with younger students. In addition, because the materials use the term *goal planner* rather than *student,* these materials have been used extensively by human services professionals and adults with disabilities. They have also been used by teachers, parents, and agency staff to examine their own dreams and goals. *It's My Life* materials can be used separately or as a total unit. Each resource adds insight to the development of self-determination skills and provides specific tools for facilitators and goal planners in a ready-to-use format. The following is a description of resources and tools that compose the *It's My Life* curriculum.

Self-Determination Profile

The *Self-Determination Profile* (Curtis & Coffey, 1996) is an assessment package that includes

1. A set of five decks of cards (324 cards in all) showing potential goals and self-determining outcomes in the categories of Places, People and Relationships, Decisions, Skills, and Personal Respect
2. A facilitator's guide
3. Recording sheets in both long- and short-form versions

The *Self-Determination Profile* assists people in gettting to know themselves better, evaluating their skills, and setting goals for improvement. The information gathered in the profile examines how personal preferences and capacities can be better realized and identifies positive changes in self-image, relationships, environments, skills, and supports that enhance an individual's control over his or her life. Priorities are identified on the recording sheets as possible goals or are added to the person's "I Want" lists. These tools can be used by goal planners to determine a baseline of current skill levels, to set goals, and to define plans. The profile can be implemented individually or in groups.

The 324 cards are numbered and color coded so that they can be matched with specific recording sheets. The People and Relationships profile stimulates consideration about a person's relationships: what activities are shared with others and what personal needs are or are not met in various relationships. The Places profile identifies where individuals go currently and places they would like to go in the future. The Decisions profile identifies preferences, activities, and routines as they are currently, and any changes that participants want to make. The Skills profile identifies capacities in life management, employment, and living skills. The Personal Respect profile enables a person to examine how he or she views and/or feels about him- or herself and to identify personal characteristics, feelings, and attributes that he or she would like to develop.

A Self-Determined Life Guidebook

A Self-Determined Life Guidebook is a facilitator's guidebook containing information about the model, *It's My Life*, and its life-planning tools. The guidebook describes the essential elements of self-determination and dignity-based support services. It explores the fine-tuning of specific facilitation skills, new professional roles, and strategies for encouraging greater self-reliance and personal responsibility. The last third of the book contains lifestyle design activities, tools, and worksheets that assist individuals in identifying goals that move toward the fulfillment of their dreams.

Preference-Based Planning and Self-Directed Goal Meetings

Preference-Based Planning and Self-Directed Goal Meetings (Curtis & Dezelsky, 1994) is a facilitator's guide and goal planner's workbook (e.g., student, participant). This resource was designed to accompany a 1- to 2-day facilitator's workshop, or it can be used on its own. The facilitator's guide includes materials about self-directed learning, self-reinforcement strategies, facilitation skills, goal planning, and implementation. It also provides facilitation instructions for each activity in the goal planner's workbook. The workbook is divided into the following parts:

- Organizing My Planner
- Hopes, Dreams, Preferences
- Possibilities, Priorities, Goals
- My Meeting

Elementary and secondary versions of this material are available and the goal planner workbook is packaged as a set of reproducible masters. Facilitators choose appropriate material from the goal planner workbook and support individuals in creating their own goal notebooks. The training and materials show how individuals, with the support of a facilitator, can take an active role in all aspects of the planning process, including

- Making their preferences known
- Identifying possibilities and opportunities for creating desired outcomes
- Deciding on potential goals
- Prioritizing these goals and estimating the effort, skills, and time involved in achieving them
- Selecting achievable goals
- Enlisting others for support
- Leading their own planning meetings
- Working on their goals
- Crediting themselves for their progress
- Celebrating their accomplishments

This model helps students to make the connection between daily decisions and realizing their dreams.

My Life Planner Series

The *Life Planner Series* (Curtis & Dezlesky, 1996b) is a curriculum guide containing six workbooks:

• Organizing My Life
• People, Places, and Fun
• Living on My Own
• Jobs and My Career
• Speaking for Myself, Solving Problems, and Making Decisions
• My Dreams and Plans

The *Life Planner* workbooks are available as separate, spiral-bound workbooks or as a set of reproducible masters. The workbooks contain activities and recording sheets that guide individuals in making important decisions related to work, leisure time pursuits, friendships and social life, moving into their own place, independent living, self-advocacy, and getting around in the community. Selected pages can be used as worksheets or to create *Life Planner* notebooks for keeping an up-to-date record of important events, learning activities, and most cherished dreams. The workbook provides tools for identifying a person's desired lifestyle and offers life management, planning, and organizational tools.

The *Life Planner Series* curriculum has been used by students and teachers in a variety of settings: resource classes, career classes, psychology classes, English classes, life skills classes, adult services, and others. Each life planner provides tools that teach self-direction through the acquisition of life skills. The life skills areas include life and time management, employment, transportation, friendships and relationships, legal rights and protections, assertive communication, money management, leisure time planning, consumer awareness, nutrition, independent living, and self-advocacy.

The Fulfillment of Dreams

The Fulfillment of Dreams is a parents' workbook that enables parents to support their sons and daughters in creating a successful and meaningful adult life and in attaining the highest possible level of independence. The delicate issues of independence and self-determination are addressed through the major life decisions that coincide with transition: employment, living situations, long-term relationships, and the freedoms associated with adulthood. The parents' workbook is a companion book to *Preference-Based Planning*.

I Want My Dream Deck

The 148 illustrated *I Want My Dream Deck* cards (Curtis, Coffey, & Dezelsky, 1991) offer lively, concrete pictures of ways to have fun, contribute, grow, and celebrate. Blank cards are included to allow for creation of additional cards. The cards may suggest a dream exactly or free the imagination to recall forgotten hopes and memories. *I Want My Dream Deck* is used to discover ideas for "I Want" statements that generate goals and ideas for celebrations of progress toward a goal and goal accomplishment.

I Want My Dream Deck can be used with a partner or facilitator or in groups. The partner contributes as listener, witness, clarifier, and supporter as the individual embarks on the adventure of discovering exciting, intriguing dreams. It is important to use the deck gradually over time rather than to go through the entire deck at one sitting. For example, one card or idea is examined at a time and, when the person finds something he or she wants, the next step is to detail the specifics of the dream. The dream comes first and is followed by the goals and the plans for attaining these goals.

Hat Cards

Hat Cards (Curtis, Coffey, & Dezelsky, 1987) is used to assist people in identifying several of the "hats" (i.e., skills, roles, activities of daily living) that individuals wear or would like to wear. It is a tool for identifying talents, personal gifts, and capacities and can also be used to identify areas for learning and improvement. The *Preference-Based Planning* and *My Life Planner* workbooks provide recording sheets to use with the cards.

The concept of hats is useful in supporting change and risk taking. If an individual goes into a store and tries on a hat that does not fit, he or she does not leave the store. More likely, he or she continues to try on the hats until one is found that fits his or her preferences at that time. Life itself is like this experience: Individuals continue to try on different roles and ways of doing things until they find what fits best for them at the time.

The hat cards can be used in a variety of ways. They are useful for exploring career ideas, jobs, skills, and roles the person has already developed or would like to achieve. Hat cards can be used to identify skills individuals have or want to improve. Students can use selected cards to discuss their strengths and limitations in IEP meetings when present levels of performance are addressed. The *My Life Planner, A Self-Determined Life,* and *Preference-Based Planning* workbooks provide activities for using the *Hat Cards, I Want My Dream Deck,* and *Self-Determination Profile* card decks.

It's My Life Videotape

The *It's My Life* videotape describes the model, explores self-determination, and introduces the preference-based planning process.

USING THE MATERIALS FOR STUDENT-DIRECTED INDIVIDUALIZED EDUCATION PROGRAMS

The *It's My Life* materials, specifically the facilitator's guide and the *Preference-Based Planning and Self-Directed Goal Meetings* workbook, provide resources for students to participate in each phase of the IEP planning process and direct their learning activities. The facilitator's guide contains four sections: Introduction, A Choice for Facilitation, Self-Directed Learning, and Overview of the Preference-Based Goal Planning Workbook.

IEP goals are based on a student's desire to achieve a personal dream and a lifestyle that is unique to him or her. Materials from Section 1 of the *Preference-Based Planning* workbook, entitled *Organizing My Planner,* and the *My Life Planner Series* are used by individuals to assemble life management tools in a day planner to keep track of their activities, schedules, and assignments. Students begin the goal process by developing and clarifying a list of what they want and outcomes they want to achieve, using materials from Section 2 of *Preference-Based Planning* goal planner's workbook, entitled Hopes, Dreams, Preferences. Students prioritize and select outcomes (i.e., dreams) significant enough to them that they are willing and ready to do whatever they can to make the dreams come true. The *I Want My Dream Deck, A Self-Determined Life,* and *Self-Determination Profile* card decks provide tools to enhance the process. The *Self-Determination Profile* and *Hat Cards* are used in conjunction with other assessment procedures to measure present capacities and identify needed skills and actions for making dreams become reality. Section 3 of the goal planner workbook, entitled Possibilities, Priorities, Goals, provides materials that individuals can use to assess the potential for achievement of their selected dreams by developing goals and plans that relate in some way to the desired outcomes. Goal planning and progress sheets simplify the process and prompt the student to identify measurable steps, activities, and time lines for achieving each goal. Using materials from Section 4 of the workbook, students plan and facilitate their own IEP meetings.

When teachers adopt a more facilitative or consultative role, many learning activities become student directed. Students track progress toward the accomplishment of their goals by creating a goal notebook with goal documentation and material from the *Preference-Based Planning* workbook, *Life Planner Series,* and other curricular resources. Each person uses a customized planning book to keep a daily record of schedules, achievements, and events to keep track of and control his or her life's details. The teacher uses the facilitator's guidebooks, A *Self-Determined Life, Preference-Based Planning, Self-Determination Profile,* and *Life Planner Series* to implement the *It's My Life* curriculum. These guidebooks contain instruction for supporting self-determination and also support teachers in their new role of facilitator.

Using a facilitative approach, teachers provide experiences and communicate in ways that result in students' learning to think for themselves and direct their own activities. Everyday educational experiences provide countless learning opportunities for students to plan and manage their time, acquire resources, initiate activities, request and specify desired assistance, communicate their preferences, make decisions, and identify and solve problems.

The *Preference-Based Planning* Goal Process

Getting Organized   The first section of the *Preference-Based Planning* goal planner workbook contains materials for making a planner (or information about using one that is commercially produced). The planner is used to keep track of goal and planning activities, schedules, assignments, and important telephone numbers.

Assessment   Formal assessment information is reviewed, as well as information from the *Self-Determination Profile,* to examine present capacities and improvement areas. Four sheets are completed listing outcomes the person wants to achieve. The categories on the "I Want" lists are: 1) what I want to do, 2) places I want to go, 3) things I want to have, and 4) how I want to be. The "I Want" lists begin the process and continue to grow and change as individuals become more knowledgeable about themselves, what they want, and what it takes to achieve their lifestyle dreams. A worksheet is provided to enable students to review the previous year's goals to determine which ones were accomplished so that they can be discussed at the planning meeting and also to make decisions about whether to continue trying to accomplish previously set goals or revising them to create new ones.

IEP Development   A worksheet entitled *Possible Goals* collects ideas for goals to be considered during the coming year. To identify priorities, individuals review their "I Want" lists, previous year's goals, and assessment information. Individuals also meet with parents and teachers to prioritize and select their IEP goals for the current year. Goals are selected by examining the following questions:

- Do I want this goal?
- Will achieving this goal make my life better?
- Is this the right time for this goal?
- Am I ready to devote my time and effort to this goal?
- Do I think my plan will work?
- Will I know when I have completed my goal?
- Can I measure my progress?
- Do I have the support, skills, and resources that I need?
- Do I believe this goal can really happen?
- Will my dreams come true?

Achievable goals are determined by figuring out what it will take to make a desired outcome happen. This requires gathering accurate information, selecting from among various options, estimating the amount of effort required, predicting possible results, and assessing whether the opportunity exists to execute the plan. Present skills, capacities, and limitations, as well as time and environmental factors, are evaluated to determine the potential for goal achievement and the degree of risk for failure. When a suggested idea seems difficult to achieve, delving into why the outcome is important to the individual can prompt ideas for new, attainable goals.

Identification of Goals and Plans　　Once goals are identified, plans can be made to achieve them. The third section of the *Preference-Based Planning* workbook provides goal-planning sheets that contain the following information:

1. I want . . . (something I want to have, to do, or to be)
2. My goal is . . . (an achievable outcome that is connected with an outcome I want)
3. My plan is . . . (the steps I will take to reach my goal)
4. How often I plan to work on this goal and when I will start
5. Resource people . . . (those who will assist me in working on this goal)
6. How I plan to keep track of my progress
7. I know I will have completed this goal when . . . (criteria for accomplishment)
8. I will reward myself by . . . (a final celebration or celebrations along the way)

Students identify the action steps for each goal and establish criteria for accomplishment. The goals are written in students' own words whenever possible. Sometimes students identify personal goals that do not become part of the IEP document. These goals can receive equal attention and be discussed at the IEP meeting, even though they may not become IEP goals.

Preparation for the Meeting　　The *Preference-Based Planning* workbook provides materials for developing an invitation or announcement of the meeting and tips for leading the meeting. It is recommended that individuals practice ahead of time if they are facilitating their first meeting. Individuals can add personal touches to a suggested agenda. Students gain valuable experience by practicing with each other; those with previous experience can be mentors for individuals who are facilitating a meeting for the first time. Figure 2 provides a sample agenda for an IEP meeting.

Meeting Participation　　Students prepare, plan, and facilitate their own IEP meetings. In the meeting, the IEP document can be completed as the student reviews his or her goals, and it can then be signed by the IEP team. When the goals are rewritten in education terminology, the student should be reassured that the words on the formal paper mean the same thing, and care must be taken to make sure that this is true.

Implementation　　Implementing successful goal-directed behavior is a skill that develops over a lifetime. Such implementation involves a process of trial and error, learning from mistakes, and adjusting expectations as limitations are discovered and experiences are integrated. It requires that

Sample IEP Meeting Agenda

Give welcome and opening speech.
Discuss my dreams.
Focus on what I'm good at doing.
Discuss what I want to learn.
Review last year's goals.
Determine my new goals.
Answer any questions and discuss any ideas.
Sign IEP forms.
Review my rights.
Thank people for coming.

Figure 2.   Sample IEP meeting agenda.

individuals learn to delay immediate gratification for the long-term benefits of focused action toward their goals. Individuals become more willing to risk and increase the goal's complexity or level of challenge as they gain experience—creating higher expectations for themselves over time.

Monitoring Progress   Accomplishment of a goal depends on ongoing evaluation of progress, adjustments of plans and efforts, and the ability to incorporate new information gained along the way. Evaluation efforts are directed toward the effectiveness of the plan and toward the individual's implementation of it. Materials and charts are provided in the goal planner workbook for students to keep track of their progress. Following the meeting, students' "I Want" sheets and goals are put in a binder, which becomes their goal notebook. Documentation related to each goal can be added behind the progress charts or journal entries describing work done on their goals. Students review and chart their progress at regular intervals of at least once a month.

Modifications   Good plans predict the amount of time and energy required for results to accumulate with consistent effort, given that adequate resources and opportunities are available. When life circumstances or environmental factors change, modifications to goals, plans, and criteria for accomplishment can be established.

INNOVATIONS IN THE PLANNING PROCESS

It is indicated that the IEP process needs to be infused with new life and new energy. The *It's My Life* curriculum and materials provide such innovation and support such vigor and energy. Teachers and students using the *It's My Life* curriculum and materials have successfully identified creative ways (and adequate time) to focus on the self-directed IEP process. Teaching students to take an active role in their planning initially takes time. Subsequent IEPs require less of the teacher's time because students develop skills and gain experience. Once the process is started, students can mentor other students in becoming more involved in their IEPs. Many of the students who became actively involved in the self-directed planning process 3 years ago are directing much of it themselves in their fourth year. One desired outcome often produces several goals, and larger dreams may take several years to accomplish through a series of goals and activities. Rather than developing new material and preference lists each year, previous information is revisited and updated. When elementary school–age students and older students have the opportunity to increase their involvement in the IEP process, they develop skills that enable them to confront major life-planning issues arising in adult life.

FACILITATOR TRAINING FOR
TEACHERS, PARENTS, AND STUDENTS

Although the *It's My Life* materials provide instructional materials and resources for implementing preference-based planning, additional benefits can be achieved through training workshops. Such workshops provide students, along with parents and teachers, the opportunity to network and discuss the implementation of the model specific to their needs and interests. In workshops for teachers, hands-on activities provide the opportunity to practice facilitation skills and to directly experience the process, thus renewing their commitment and vitality by bringing their personal philosophies and work into greater alignment. The developers of the *It's My Life* materials present specific techniques and examples, which they have found successful in empowering individuals to express their preferences, identify capacities, and make their contribution. Participants become familiar with all of the various New Hats materials and develop a toolbox of resources to select from and use with specific individuals.

Workshops with parents and their sons and/or daughters expedite the goal development process by providing time for individuals to identify their lifestyle dreams and potential goals. Also provided are valuable networking opportunities as individuals exchange ideas about potential plans and strategies for creating their lives of choice. The workshops facilitate parents' dreams as they support their sons or daughters in identifying their own dreams. Self-determination is most likely to occur with the support and involvement of parents and families (Wilcox & Bellamy, 1987). Individuals with disabilities who succeed often have parents who expect them to aspire, achieve, and go out to meet the world (Harrison & Rousso, 1989). Self-determination is viewed as a long-range goal by most parents (Cook, Brotherson, Weigel-Garrey, & Mize, 1996); however, although parents and professionals may be aware of the need to provide opportunities for self-direction, decision making, and problem solving, many do not know how to facilitate the acquisition of these skills (Fredericks, 1988).

Because of their familiarity with their sons' or daughters' preferences and routines, parents may unknowingly miss valuable opportunities to promote choice and decision making. A first step for increasing opportunity and self-determination capacities involves parents' developing an awareness of the types of cues they provide that influence their sons' or daughters' independence, as well as their ability to

1. Initiate tasks
2. Think for themselves
3. Express their preferences
4. Request assistance
5. Anticipate events, activities, and consequences

There is a natural tendency for parents to help by providing direction or offering a reminder or an answer. By becoming aware of the subtle cues that they provide, parents can consciously redirect their influence and communication to instead foster self-direction, self-regulation, and self-reliance in their sons and daughters. Through training, parents learn methods for guiding their sons and daughters toward thinking for themselves, developing their own strategies, solving their own problems, and finding their own solutions.

CONCLUSIONS

Through involvement in the IEP process, students learn valuable goal-setting skills that they can apply throughout their lives. Many teachers, parents, and students have discovered that planning can be exciting, hopeful, fun, and meaningful for everyone involved. Preference-based planning supports the development of skills that will be invaluable for individuals as they pursue their dreams, opportunities, and goals in adult life. These planning skills form a complete thought process that applies to any situation: Determine a desired outcome, assess skill performance and needs, identify opportunities and resources, set a goal, determine a plan, execute the plan, evaluate progress, self-reward one's efforts along the way, adjust plans and performance as needed, and celebrate the results. These skills are the core of a self-determined life.

After experiencing the impact of the self-directed IEP, teachers and students reported that they could not consider planning without active student involvement (Curtis, 1995). This is an idea whose time has come; the IEP has been a "diamond in the rough" and a resource whose full potential has yet to be utilized. It is a viable tool for teaching students how to apply the skills and information they have learned in school by empowering them to plan, control, and direct their own lives. Everyone has the potential to create a self-directed life. Ultimately, this is the goal of education.

REFERENCES

Bannerman, D.J., Sheldon, J.B., Sherman, J.A., & Harchik, A.E. (1990). Balancing the right to habilitation with the right to personal liberties: The rights of people with developmental disabilities to eat too many doughnuts and take a nap. *Journal of Applied Behavior Analysis, 23*, 79–89.

Cook, C.C., Brotherson, M.J., Weigel-Garrey, C., & Mize, I. (1996). Homes to support the self-determination of children. In D.J. Sands & M.L. Wehmeyer (Eds.), *Self-determination across the life span: Independence and choice for people with disabilities* (pp. 91–110). Baltimore: Paul H. Brookes Publishing Co.

Curtis, E. (1995). *It's My Life: Final report for Office of Special Education and Rehabilitation Services.* Salt Lake City, UT: Author.

Curtis, E., & Coffey, C. (1996). *Self-determination profile.* Salt Lake City, UT: New Hats, Inc.

Curtis, E., Coffey, C., & Dezelsky, M. (1987). *Hat cards.* Salt Lake City, UT: New Hats, Inc.

Curtis, E., Coffey, C., & Dezelsky, M. (1991). *I want my dream deck.* Salt Lake City, UT: New Hats, Inc.

Curtis, E., & Dezelsky, M. (1994). *Preference-based planning and self-directed goal meetings.* Salt Lake City, UT: New Hats, Inc.

Curtis, E., & Dezelsky, M. (1996a). *A self-determined life: Tools to support dignity, diversity, community, and dreams.* Salt Lake City, UT: New Hats, Inc.

Curtis, E., & Dezelsky, M. (1996b). *Life planner series.* Salt Lake City, UT: New Hats, Inc.

Fredericks, H.D.B. (1988). Tim becomes an eagle scout. *Transition Summary: National Information Center for Handicapped Children and Youth, 5,* 8–10.

Harrison, J., & Rousso, H. (1989). *Positive images: Portraits of women with disabilities.* New York: Networking Project for Disabled Women and Girls.

Lovett, H. (1991). Empowerment and choices. In L.H. Meyer, C.A. Peck, & L. Brown (Eds.), *Critical issues in the lives of people with severe disabilities* (pp. 625–626). Baltimore: Paul H. Brookes Publishing Co.

Martin, J.E., Huber Marshall, L., Maxson, L., & Jerman, P.A. (1996). *Self-Directed IEP.* Longmont, CO: Sopris West, Inc.

Mithaug, D.E. (1996). The optimal prospects principle: A theoretical basis for rethinking instructional practices for self-determination. In D.J. Sands & M.L. Wehmeyer (Eds.), *Self-determination across the life span: Independence and choice for people with disabilities* (pp. 147–165). Baltimore: Paul H. Brookes Publishing Co.

O'Brien, J. (1987). A guide to life-style planning: Using *The Activities Catalog* to integrate services and natural support systems. In B. Wilcox & G.T. Bellamy (Eds.), *A comprehensive guide to the* Activities Catalog (pp. 175–190). Baltimore: Paul H. Brookes Publishing Co.

Smith, S. (1990). Individualized education programs (IEPs) in special education: From intent to acquiescence. *Exceptional Children, 57,* 6–14.

Ward, M.J. (1988). The many facets of self-determination. *Transition Summary: National Information Center for Handicapped Children and Youth, 5,* 2–5.

Ward, M.J. (1996). Coming of age in the age of self-determination: A historical and personal perspective. In D.J. Sands & M.L. Wehmeyer (Eds.), *Self-determination across the life span: Independence and choice for people with disabilities* (pp. 1–22). Baltimore: Paul H. Brookes Publishing Co.

Ward, M.J., & Kohler, P. (1996). *Teaching self-determination: Content and process.* In L.E. Powers, G.H.S. Singer, & J.-A. Sowers (Eds.), *On the road to autonomy: Pro-*

moting self-competence in children and youth with disabilities (pp. 275–290). Baltimore: Paul H. Brookes Publishing Co.

Wehmeyer, M.L. (1992). Self-determination and the education of students with mental retardation. *Education and Training in Mental Retardation, 27,* 303–314.

Wehmeyer, M.L. (1996). Self-determination for youth with significant cognitive disabilities: From theory to practice. In L.E. Powers, G.H.S. Singer, & J.-A. Sowers (Eds.), *On the road to autonomy: Promoting self-competence in children and youth with disabilities* (pp. 115–133). Baltimore: Paul H. Brookes Publishing Co.

West, M., & Parent, W. (1992). Consumer choice and empowerment in supported employment services: Issues and strategies. *Journal of The Association for Persons with Severe Handicaps, 17,* 47–52.

Wilcox, B., & Bellamy, G.T. (Eds.). (1987). *A comprehensive guide to* The Activities Catalog. Baltimore: Paul H. Brookes Publishing Co.

Williams, R.R. (1989, January). *Creating a new world of opportunity: Expanding choice and self-determination in the lives of Americans with severe disability by 1992 and beyond.* Paper presented at the National Conference on Self-Determination, Arlington, VA.

Wilson, P.B., Caselia, V.R., & Wilson, W.C. (1989). Microcomputers and new technologies. In R. Gaylord-Ross (Ed.), *Integration strategies for students with handicaps* (pp. 249–280). Baltimore: Paul H. Brookes Publishing Co.

13

Become Your Own Expert!

A Self-Advocacy Curriculum for Secondary School–Age Students with Learning Disabilities

Winnelle D. Carpenter

There is a significant need for students with learning disabilities to learn self-advocacy skills. Researchers have emphasized this need, suggesting that all people with disabilities should have the opportunity to develop skills that maximize their potential and enable them to succeed (Bursuck & Rose, 1991;

The development of *Become Your Own Expert!* was funded in part by the Minnesota Departments of Education and Economic Security through a cooperative agreement with the U.S. Department of Education, Office of Special Education and Rehabilitative Services (OSERS), under Grant HI5810040, Statewide Strategies for Improving the Delivery of Transition Services for Youth with Disabilities and Families in Minnesota. *Become Your Own Expert!* can be purchased from Minnesota Educational Services, Capitol View Center, 70 West County Road B2, Little Canada, Minnesota 55117-1402; (612) 415-5379. The curriculum's author, Winnelle D. Carpenter, M.A., is available to train people how to use the curriculum. She can be reached at Cognitive Learning Consultants, Post Office Box 202065, Bloomington, Minnesota 55420; (612) 854-4935.

Durlak, Rose, & Bursuck, 1994; Mangrum & Strichart, 1988; Phillips, 1990; Shaw, Norlander, McGuire, Byron, & Anderson, 1988; Ward, 1988).

To become effective self-advocates, students need to learn about their specific disabilities and begin to understand their individual strengths and challenges. Students also need to learn how to 1) identify barriers to effective learning and ultimately to outcomes such as employment, 2) acquire coping skills, and 3) obtain appropriate accommodations. In addition, students should learn, through careful guidance, to communicate this knowledge when speaking on their own behalf. Because individuals with disabilities differ widely in their needs, interests, and abilities, no single program or curriculum can adequately address every area. *Become Your Own Expert!* was designed to teach core self-advocacy skills to secondary school–age students with learning disabilities, which in turn enables students to address their unique needs. Effective implementation of the curriculum provides a process involving self-, peer-, and teacher-directed strategies through which students can learn and apply self-advocacy skills.

Become Your Own Expert! was developed to be used in the context of a one-semester class. An initial draft of the curriculum was pilot tested with students with learning disabilities who were attending a community college and subsequently field tested with students attending a high school in Minnesota. The pilot test, conducted at Minneapolis Community College in Minneapolis, Minnesota, helped students to gain an overview of self-advocacy needs. Based on this pilot test, the curriculum was revised and field tested with secondary school–age students with learning disabilities who completed *Become Your Own Expert!* in a one-semester course. Both before and after the course, these students completed the Piers–Harris Self-Concept Scale (Piers, 1969), filled out a self-advocacy questionnaire, and were videotaped answering the following questions:

1. What is a learning disability?
2. What is your learning disability, and how does it affect you in school and on the job?
3. What kind of accommodations do you need? Do you ask for them regularly?
4. What is the difference between an advocate and a self-advocate?
5. What is the purpose of an individualized education program (IEP) or an individualized transition plan (ITP)?
6. Describe your participation in your IEP/ITP planning process. What prevents you from asking for help? How do you learn best? What transition goals are listed on your IEP?

Students participating in *Become Your Own Expert!* learn to identify academic strengths, challenges, and learning styles; set goals for completing high school and continuing postsecondary education and training; and identify classroom and workplace accommodations that can enable them to succeed. They also study laws that provide protection that will support them in their efforts. When they have completed the curriculum, students should be able to define *learning disability* and identify their own disabilities.

CURRICULUM OBJECTIVES

The lessons, activities, and materials that compose *Become Your Own Expert!* were developed to support students to achieve the following objectives:

1. Describe their specific learning disabilities and how these disabilities affect
    a. Educational outcomes
    b. Employment options
    c. Social interactions
2. Describe any other disabilities they may have and relate the impact that these disabilities have on learning and employment
3. Understand their strengths and challenges when learning difficult or unfamiliar information in school and on the job
4. List specific compensations and accommodations related to their learning disabilities, learning styles, or other disabilities that are needed for academic and employment success
5. Monitor and recognize challenges and use effective problem-solving tools to meet individual needs
6. Identify two assistive technology resources they can use
7. Identify two or more useful community resources
8. Learn the disability-related laws and protections that apply to secondary education, postsecondary education, and employment settings
9. Develop individual self-advocacy folders containing
    a. A list of compensations and accommodations that they need in school and at work
    b. Fact sheets about learning disabilities; disability-related and civil rights laws; learning styles; famous people with learning disabilities; and additional resources, articles, and pertinent materials for effective self-advocacy
10. Discuss their roles in the IEP/ITP planning process, as well as their IEP/ITP goals and their progress toward achieving them
11. Define transition from school to adult life, identify five components of transition, and cite examples of each component
12. Become more active in planning their futures
13. Take greater responsibility for their lives and make more of their own choices

CURRICULUM OVERVIEW

Become Your Own Expert! addresses topics in the following seven units:

1. Self-Awareness
2. Modality
3. Learning Styles
4. Accommodations
5. Practice, Rehearse, Role-Play
6. Becoming the Expert
7. Postassessment/Closure

There are a total of 43 lesson plans, each of which includes student objectives, a list of instructional materials needed to complete the lesson, and teaching activities. Table 1 provides the list of lessons by topic for each unit. Many of the lessons also include vocabulary words, a classroom warmup activity, teacher notes, discussion questions, and homework assignments. Figure 1 provides a sample lesson from the curriculum that addresses the topic of asking for accommodations. The curriculum includes both teacher lesson plans and a student workbook. An accompanying program assists parents in learning how to help their sons or daughters to acquire the skills targeted by the curriculum.

As indicated previously, the curriculum is designed to be implemented within the context of a semester-long course. For example, field test participants completed the materials in one semester in which they met 4 days per week for 50 minutes per meeting. To counter the negative experiences that many students with learning disabilities have within the special education context, the course is designed to be taught in a general education classroom. This is not, however, a read-the-book, do-the-worksheet, and take-the-test class. The curriculum provides students with hands-on activities and experiences and enables teachers to employ multiple instructional strategies, including 1) structured group problem solving, 2) videotaped self-evaluations, 3) visits to postsecondary programs, 4) interactions with postsecondary education students and adults with learning disabilities, 5) cognitive coaching, 6) trial-and-error learning, and 7) role playing. The curriculum also directs teachers to a variety of support materials, including pamphlets, articles, games, resource books, educational videotapes, and students' IEPs/ITPs.

Effective implementation of *Become Your Own Expert!* requires participation by both teachers and students. It is important for the teacher (referred to as the *facilitator* in the curriculum) to have experience in teaching students with learning disabilities and to be creative in identifying and using strategies that enable students to recognize the value of learning self-advocacy skills. It is also important for the facilitator to be supportive, sensitive, and genuinely interested in each student to gain his or her trust and to enable the student to

Table 1.   Table of contents for *Become Your Own Expert!*

Unit	Lesson and topic

Unit 1: Self-Awareness	1. Introduction of Curriculum
	      Self-Advocacy Defined
	2. Speaker Presentation
	3. Time Management and Organization
	4. Panel Presentation of College Students
	      with Learning Disabilities
	5. Preassessment—Written
	6. Preassessment—Videotape
	7. Disability Awareness
	      Celebrities with Disabilities
	8. Introduction of Transition and Federal Laws
	9. Preparation of Group Presentations on
	      Learning Disabilities
	10. Group Presentation of Learning
	      Disability Definition
	11. Knowledge Check (test)
	      Booklet (*Yes You Can!*)
	12. IEP/ITP
	      Famous People with Learning Disabilities
	13. Postsecondary Site Visit
	      Section 504, Rehabilitation Act of 1973
	14. Postsecondary Site Visit
	15. Student and Parent Completion of
	      "Definition: Learning Disabilities Unit"
	16. Knowledge Check (test)
	      Telephone Script for College Screening
	17. Individual Student Interviews
	18. Students Practice Defining "Learning
	      Disability"

Unit 2: Modality	1a. Introduction of Modality Channels:
	      Visual, Auditory, and Haptic
	1b. Student and Parent Completion of
	      "Modality Unit"
	1c. Modality Challenges Can Impede
	      Learning and Job Performance
	1d. Modality Knowledge Check (test)
	1e. Comparison of Parent and Student
	      Completion of "Modality Unit"
	2. F.A.T. City Videotape

Unit 3: Learning Styles	1. Learning Styles Assessment/Interpretation

Unit 4: Accommodations	1. Diagnostic Interpretation
	2. Organization of Student Information
	      Job Performance Evaluation
	3. Postsecondary Site Visit
	4. Academic and Employment
	      Accommodations
	      Americans with Disabilities Act (ADA) of
	      1990
	5. Asking for Accommodations

(continued)

Table 1. (continued)

Unit	Lesson and topic
	6. Personal Goals/Problem Solving 7. Individual Student Conferences with Parents 8. Completion of Academic Accommodation Form Reevaluation of IEP/ITP "HELP" Videotape
Unit 5: Practice, Rehearse, Role-Play	1. Practice and Rehearse 2. Labeling and Disclosure 3. Self-Advocacy: Teacher Tips Self-Advocacy: Student Scripts 4. Communication Skills: Passive, Assertive, Aggressive Role Playing: Problem Solving 5. Successful Self-Advocacy: Qualities and Traits Monitoring Self-Advocacy 6. Role Playing: Regular Education Teachers
Unit 6: Becoming the Expert	1. Develop Personal History Profiles Prepare Ninth-Grade Presentation 2. Ninth-Grade Presentation 3. Self-Advocacy Folders 4. Steps for Self-Directed IEP/ITP Conference
Unit 7: Postassessment/ Closure	Postintervention Videotape and Written Self-Evaluation

overcome discrimination toward, and ignorance about, people with learning disabilities.

Curriculum Synopsis

The table of contents for the *Become Your Own Expert!* curriculum presented in Table 1 provides an overview of the instructional sequence of the curriculum, whereas this section provides a synopsis of major activities in the curriculum. In the first week of the course, students learn about the curriculum and explore a definition of *self-advocacy*. They then hear from adults and college students with learning disabilities who are invited to describe how they have managed to accommodate for their disabilities. Examples of questions that students have asked guest speakers include the following:

1. Did you find yourself struggling more than other students?
2. In high school, did you feel different from others? If so, how?
3. Do you also have attention-deficit/hyperactivity disorder?
4. Did the teachers treat you as though you were not very smart?
5. How did you feel when you were told that you had a learning disability?
6. How did your parents help or treat you?

7. Have you ever been fired from a job because of your learning disability?
8. How did your friends react when you told them about your learning disability?
9. Is it difficult to get through college if you have a learning disability?

Next, students learn about transition and transition planning and how to run their own IEP meetings. Students are then taught how to choose an appropriate postsecondary institution and learn the types of questions that are important to ask during visits to postsecondary institutions. The curriculum recommends two such trips. It is not uncommon for students to be anxious and afraid during these visits and to worry about not fitting in in a postsecondary education setting. Many students are intimidated, embarrassed, and shy when asking questions about disability services, or they think that if they enter the office for students with disabilities, observers will stereotype them. Some students simply do not know how to behave on a college campus. Through visits to postsecondary institutions, the curriculum offers opportunities for students to learn how to deal with these feelings and emotions. After each visit, students can address their questions and concerns about having learning disabilities through the course. Some common questions that are asked include the following:

1. Will I get over or outgrow my learning disability?
2. Does having a learning disability mean I am slow?
3. What are the advantages of having a disability?

An aspect of the curriculum that is intended to improve student motivation and responsibility for learning involves the area of learning styles. Students involved in the course complete several learning-style assessments. Gaining an understanding of how they learn best enables students to recognize poor matches between their unique learning styles and the classroom, communicate personal learning style knowledge to classroom teachers and employers, receive validation and understanding about their own natural abilities, and become self-directed learners.

Become Your Own Expert! also enables the facilitator to increase students' understanding of the term *accommodation* as it relates to school and employment settings. Students learn about a variety of accommodations and their rights to request such supports. Students then identify academic and employment accommodations appropriate to their unique learning and employment needs.

Although most academic accommodations are listed on the IEP/ITP under typical education modifications and accommodations, students often have difficulty communicating this information to teachers. Students participating in *Become Your Own Expert!* prepare organizational outlines listing their aca-

Sample Lesson Plan

Unit 4   **Accommodations**

Lesson 5   (to be completed in three to four class periods)

Objectives

1. Teacher will complete the "Student Fact Sheet."
2. Help students develop a plan for deciding how and when to ask for an accommodation.
3. Students will practice identifying and asking for accommodations.
4. Increase student understanding of how one's level of self-awareness increases the ability to ask for and receive appropriate accommodations.
5. Help students understand that practice and rehearsal build confidence.
6. Learn the value of planning ahead.
7. Learn the importance of having a backup plan when accommodation requests are denied.

Materials

1. Student three-ring binder pp. 87–90, "A Successful Self-Advocate"
2. Student rough draft of Academic Accommodation Form
3. Student three-ring binder p. 108, "Academic Accommodations—Basic Facts"
4. Student IEP/ITP
5. Student three-ring binder p. 109, "Academic Accommodations— Becoming the Expert!"
6. Student three-ring binder p. 110, "What if . . ."
7. Student three-ring binder p. 111, "Student Interview"

Warm-up

Students' rough draft of Academic Accommodation Form should be placed on their desks. Ask students to pair up and share the kinds of accommodations they will request and list on their Academic Accommodation Form. After a few minutes, have students switch pairs and share with another classmate.

Activity I: Complete Section 5 of "A Successful Self-Advocate"

Students will use their Academic Accommodation Form to complete Section 5 of "A Successful Self-Advocate." Today they will list specific academic accommodations in areas that are a challenge. Some students may want to work in pairs. In Section 5, encourage students to write, "This area is a strength," when a challenge is *not* identified.

When this activity is completed, encourage students to share their thoughts about the kinds of accommodations or compensations they will use. This will help them learn from each other.

Activity II: Academic Accommodations (Practice and Rehearse)

Have students turn to p. 108, "Academic Accommodations—Basic Facts." Read and discuss this handout. Tell students that they will practice and rehearse using the Academic Accommodation Form.

(continued)

Figure 1.   Sample lesson plan.

Figure 1. *(continued)*

Ask them to remove from their three-ring binders p. 109, "Academic Accommodations—Becoming the Expert!" Help students to develop responses to these questions.

Teacher note: You have a choice. You can "role-model" suggested responses first and let the group role-model responses *or* let them jump right in and practice (through investigation and trial and error). In either case, divide them later into pairs to practice and rehearse with each other. Then continue to switch pairs so they can learn from many classmates. Encourage students to write notes.

Activity III: Role-Play

Direct students to p. 110, "What if . . ." Explain that self-advocates plan ahead and anticipate what could happen when advocating for themselves. This strategy allows students to plan a number of alternatives or backup plans in case things do not happen as they would like. Explain that role playing allows individuals to practice alternative responses. Develop the ideas listed in "What if . . ." into role playing. Ask the students to brainstorm other situations where planning could be wise.

Activity IV: Employment Accommodations

Explain that asking for accommodations on the job is just as important as seeking them in school. However, one needs to carefully plan how and when to make requests. (In a future unit, employment disclosure will be discussed at length.) At this time, have students focus on stating the employment accommodations that they think they will need. Help them explore ways to state their needs. They can refer to "Evaluate Job Performance" for their notes.

Activity V: Student Interview

Ask students to remove p. 111, "Student Interview," from their three-ring binders and find a partner who is wearing the same color or a portion of the same color clothing that they are wearing. When they have finished interviewing each other, ask them to share their partners' responses with the class, if the partner agrees.

Teacher note: a. Complete the "Student Fact Sheet" in "Employment Areas Affected" and "Important Job Compensations and/or Accommodations the Student Will Need." Use their "Evaluate Job Performance" handouts for student information.
   b. Let students know the upcoming schedule for parent conferences.

demic accommodations. At the same time, they are encouraged to experiment to determine which accommodations will help them meet their goals. Students are then grouped in pairs to practice asking for academic accommodations. The following are some of the questions they rehearse:

1. Why would you ask for academic accommodations?
2. How would you explain that your accommodation requests are necessary?

3. How would you begin asking for an accommodation?
4. What might prevent you from asking for a specific accommodation?
5. Do you get angry easily?
6. What are some ways in which you might cope with anger so that it does not interfere with your requests for accommodations?
7. How do you know when you need an accommodation?
8. What kind of backup plan should you have in case an academic accommodation request is denied?
9. Under what conditions would you negotiate an accommodation, and when would you compromise?

Through these role-playing activities, students learn that self-advocates anticipate what can happen when self-advocating. Consequently, students learn to prepare backup plans in case their initial requests are not honored.

The curriculum also suggests that role-play strategies be used to prepare students to answer the following questions:

1. What is a learning disability?
2. What type of learning disability do you have?
3. How does your learning disability have the potential to interfere with academic learning and/or job performance?
4. How would you define *accommodation*?
5. List four accommodations you currently use or will eventually use.
6. What are your strengths?
7. Briefly explain three important federal disability rights laws.
8. What does *transition* mean?
9. What is the purpose of the IEP/ITP?
10. What does *self-advocacy* mean?

When students can respond effectively to each question, they invite general education teachers into the classroom for further role playing. This is also a good opportunity for the teachers to learn more about learning disabilities and educational accommodations. Classroom teachers who participate are given a Student Fact Sheet (Figure 2) that provides information on each student, thus allowing for individualized role-play activities. The teachers are also given a list of possible questions to ask students.

Practicing self-advocacy with general and special education teachers, counselors, social workers, and other adults allows the student to gain poise and self-confidence and to receive constructive feedback in a supportive environment. As students become more able to confidently request accommodations, lessons in *Become Your Own Expert!* enable them to deal with hurtful or unfavorable responses. As a class activity, students compile common unpleas-

Sample Student Fact Sheet

The following student fact sheet is to be completed prior to the student–parent meeting. This sheet, used during role-playing activities, will provide information about students' strengths, challenges, learning disabilities, and compensations and accommodations they will need.

Student: _____*Sarah*_____   Date: _____*3-15-97*_____
Teacher: _____*Ms. Johnson*_____
Case manager: _*Mr. Smith*_____

Identify the processing channels (visual, auditory, haptic) affected by student's learning disability:

1. _____*Sarah*_____'s learning disability is: _*in both the visual/auditory*_ _*channel. She has sequential and memory challenges. Sarah also has significant*_ _*challenges in written language.*_

2. a. Academic areas affected: (Comment on how learning disability challenges in the following areas affect student learning.)
   _X_ Reading _*outlining key points is difficult*_
   _X_ Arithmetic _*trouble remembering sequences*_
   _X_ Language _*superior verbal expression; inadequate sentence and grammatical structure*_
      _X_ a. Written   ___ b. Receptive   ___ c. Expressive
   _X_ Spelling _____
   _X_ Memory _*poor "rote" memory—forgets test information*_
   _X_ Test taking _*high test anxiety; allow for performance-based assessments*_
   _X_ Concentration and attention _*excellent attendance and focusing on tasks*_
   ___ Impulsiveness _*None*_
   _X_ Organization/time management _*difficulty developing outline sequences*_ _*for papers*_
   _X_ Social perceptions and interactions _*excellent social skills*_

   Comments: _*Sarah's memory improves significantly when new information is per-*_ _*sonalized and interpreted. She does not perform well when "rote" memory is required.*_ _*Her memory also improves when she is allowed to reason and become involved in "hands-*_ _*on" activities. Sarah learns best through activities that are meaningful and that allow*_ _*for movement.*_

   b. List three or more important academic accommodations that the student will need: (Attach a copy of the completed student Academic Accommodation Form to this fact sheet.) _*Proofreaders, note*_ _*takers in difficult classes, Franklin Speller, weekly meetings with instructor of diffi-*_ _*cult classes to have her notes reviewed, practice test questions, and essay answers on*_ _*tests need to be recorded rather than written*_

3. a. Employment areas affected: _*Remembering sequences—Sarah currently is*_ _*being trained as a cashier. She has made visual organizational outlines listing the steps in*_ _*operating the cash register. She laminated the information on small cards and brings*_ _*them to work.*_

(continued)

Figure 2.   Sample Student Fact Sheet.

Figure 2. (*continued*)

> b. List three or more important job compensations and/or accommo-
> dations the student will need: *Sarah will require visual organizational
> outlines listing specific job responsibilities, organizational procedures, a supervisor
> available to answer immediate questions, and additional time when learning equipment
> procedures.*

4. Overall strengths: *Sarah has excellent reasoning, verbal, and gross motor skills.
She is mature and responsible. Sarah has kept an assignment notebook for 3 years.
She is determined and is not afraid to ask for help.*

5. To develop and strengthen _____*Sarah's*_____ self-advocacy skills, it
    is suggested that he or she role-play the following situations:
    a. *Rehearse asking a supervisor for an outline of responsibilities.*
    b. *Practice defining a learning disability.*
    c. *Practice making a request to record her essay answers onto a tape recorder.*
    d. *Rehearse telling an instructor about her learning disability.*
    e. _____

6. Other disabilities and health or other personal issues that may affect
    academic learning and/or job performance: *None*

7. Final comments: *Sarah would like to attend college. Provide extra encouragement
    because she really does not believe she could handle college.*

ant comments that they have heard directed toward them and then write assertive responses to use in such situations. Examples of unfavorable comments that students have listed are:

1. "If you just came to class . . ."
2. "Everybody has problems learning."
3. "If you just try harder . . ."
4. "That would be unfair to others."
5. "You don't look like you have problems."
6. "It's a thin book. Why *can't* you read it?"

As students practice verbal skills, learn effective communication strategies, and build confidence, the following discussion questions (posed in the
curriculum) help them to apply their new knowledge, evaluate themselves,
and revise their personal goals:

1. What was something that you had in common with your classmates that you did not know about?
2. What did you have in common with your classmates as you rehearsed and role-played?
3. In what area do you need more practice?
4. How easy or difficult was it to reverse roles?
5. In what ways was this activity painful or frightening?
6. What did you learn about your partner?
7. How have you improved your self-advocacy skills through role-playing activities?
8. What would you like to remember that you keep forgetting?
9. What new technique have you tried that you learned from a classmate when advocating for yourself?
10. What else did you learn through role playing?

This curriculum also has students examine the issues of disclosure (e.g., whether to tell someone about their disability) and labeling (e.g., being identified or labeled as having a specific disability) and the feelings associated with each. Students learn that deciding whether to disclose information about their disabilities is a personal decision. They explore the fear and anxiety associated with disclosing such information to a teacher, employer, or friend. Although sensitivity to and awareness of learning disabilities have increased in the 1990s, individuals with learning disabilities still must exercise caution in deciding who they tell because, unfortunately, it is still too common to be misunderstood, regarded with suspicion, or perceived as less than equal based on stereotypes about disabilities.

Toward the end of the course, students plan and deliver a 1-hour self-advocacy presentation to middle school students. This encourages them to recognize that, by practicing self-advocacy skills, they become mentors for other students with learning disabilities.

Efficacy of Curriculum

Our impressions and conclusions from the field and pilot tests of *Become Your Own Expert!*, based on videotapes and written pre- and postintervention assessments and on anecdotal information, were as follows:

1. As a result of the one-semester self-advocacy course, students
   a. Were able to ask for help in many situations in which they would not have done so previously
   b. Appeared more confident and comfortable in applying and using self-advocacy skills
   c. Appeared to have greater confidence in disclosing their disability to their boyfriends or girlfriends, teachers, and some employers

    d.   Were willing to negotiate to get accommodations they needed

    e.   Were willing to accompany and support each other in joint self-advocacy ventures

    f.   Became more willing to ask for what they needed

2.   There was a tremendous sense of empowerment as students learned about their disabilities, determined how they learned best, and recognized that, with appropriate accommodations, compensations, and effective instructional strategies, they could learn.

3.   Local college students with learning disabilities were powerful role models. Listening to and openly and honestly interacting with older students with learning disabilities offered comfort and encouragement. Participants learned that, with determination, perseverance, and self-advocacy skills, they can achieve in spite of challenges.

4.   The students' presentations on learning disabilities at middle schools were thrilling to witness. The high school students received a great deal of positive feedback from staff and students as they taught the very skills that they had learned.

5.   Role-playing and rehearsing activities with general education teachers and other adults were vital to learning to explain one's learning disability and making accommodation requests of general education teachers and/or employers.

6.   A great amount of time and energy was needed to address emotional responses to the course content and with the emotions and feelings that students have held for many years.

7.   Visits to postsecondary institutions helped students to see how self-advocacy worked.

8.   Because students' friends and families also completed the learning-style assessments, students realized that they were not the only ones who were experiencing learning challenges.

9.   Despite concerns to the contrary, involvement in the course did not simply heighten already existing negative feelings.

10.   The development of self-advocacy skills through the *Become Your Own Expert!* curriculum was positively correlated with improved self-concept as measured by the Piers–Harris Self-Concept Scale (Piers, 1969).

11.   With adequate time, interest, support of the school district, an appropriate environment, and an experiential and interactive curriculum, students can become responsible for their learning and self-advocacy needs. Momentum peaked when students learned from each other during role-playing and rehearsing activities. It was common for students to praise each other for their helpful ideas and suggestions. They freely adopted each other's strategies when they observed their usefulness.

CONCLUSIONS

The fact that students who were involved with *Become Your Own Expert!* improved their self-advocacy skills and increased their self-esteem confirmed the proposition that self-advocacy skills can and should be explicitly taught. Such skills can become the driving force in helping students to become involved in their IEPs/ITPs. *Become Your Own Expert!* provides a proven means to achieve this outcome.

REFERENCES

Bursuck, W., & Rose, E. (1991). Community college options for students with mild disabilities. In F.R. Rusch, L. DeStefano, J. Chadsey-Rusch, L. Phelps, & E. Szymanski (Eds.), *Transitions from school to adult life* (pp. 71–92). Sycamore, IL: Sycamore Publishing Co.

Durlak, C., Rose, E., & Bursuck, W. (1994). Preparing high school students with learning disabilities for the transition to post-secondary education: Teaching the skills of self-determination. *Journal of Learning Disabilities, 27,* 51–59.

Mangrum, C., & Strichart, S. (Eds.). (1988). *College and the learning disabled student* (2nd ed.). New York: Grune & Stratton.

Phillips, P. (1990). A self-advocacy plan for high school students with learning disabilities: A comparative case study analysis of students', teachers', and parents' perceptions of program effects. *Journal of Learning Disabilities, 23,* 466–471.

Piers, E. (1969). *The Piers–Harris Self-Concept Scale.* Nashville, TN: Counselor Recordings and Tapes.

Shaw, S., Norlander, K., McGuire, J., Byron, J., & Anderson, P. (1988, May). *Preparation of students with learning disabilities for post-secondary education: Issues in transition planning.* Paper presented at the annual conference of the Council for Exceptional Children, Washington, DC.

Ward, M. (1988). *The many facets of self determination: Transition summary* (pp. 2–3). Washington, DC: National Information Center for Children and Youth with Handicaps.

14

Putting Feet on My Dreams

Involving Students with Autism in Life Planning

Ann Fullerton

To become self-determined, students need to learn to develop and implement a realistic plan for their lives. This requires that they integrate awareness of their strengths and challenges with the knowledge and skills needed for adulthood. This process takes time, and most students need teachers, family members, and other people to provide them with opportunities to become

This chapter was supported by Grant H158K20019 from the U.S. Department of Education, Office of Special Education Programs (OSEP), to Portland State University, Portland, Oregon. This chapter does not necessarily represent the policy of the U.S. Department of Education, and no endorsement by the federal government should be inferred.

The *Putting Feet on My Dreams: A Program in Self-Determination* curriculum is available from the author: Ann Fullerton, Ph.D., Department of Special and Counselor Education, Portland State University, Box 751, Portland, Oregon 97207.

The author would like to thank Dr. Amy Driscoll of Portland State University, Portland, Oregon, for use of the term *advancework*, which Dr. Driscoll uses in teacher preparation.

Figures 3 and 4 in this chapter were created and provided by artist Georgianne Thomas of Corvallis, Oregon, and are used herein with her permission.

self-determined (Abery, Rudrud, Arndt, Schauben, & Eggebeen, 1995). This chapter describes a program, *Putting Feet on My Dreams: A Program in Self-Determination* (Fullerton, 1994), that enables students with autism to develop life-planning and self-determination skills.

The first step in the development of this program was to identify the life-planning needs of students with autism. To achieve this goal, an advisory group of specialists in the area of autism and young adults with autism and their parents was formed, and, through this process, two primary instructional needs were identified. The first need was to develop instructional materials and strategies that would enable students with autism to understand and participate in self-directed life-planning activities. Advisory group members stressed that such materials needed to take into account the unique learning needs of students with autism. *Putting Feet on My Dreams* was subsequently developed to meet this need.

The second need was for materials to educate other people about the experiences of adolescents and young adults with autism and to provide strategies for assisting students with autism. Advisory group members with autism reported being frequently misunderstood by teachers, peers, and employers. Specialists indicated that assistance provided to students with autism too often promotes dependence instead of self-directed performance. Although not described in this chapter, a second publication, *Higher Functioning Adolescents and Young Adults with Autism: A Teacher's Guide* (Fullerton, Stratton, Coyne, & Gray, 1996) was developed to address this need.

The purpose of this chapter is threefold. In the first section of the chapter, the experiences of people with autism are described to provide readers with an understanding of the instructional focus used in this program. The second section of the chapter describes *Putting Feet on My Dreams* and its development, field testing, and use. An evaluation study of the curriculum is discussed in the final section.

UNDERSTANDING THE EXPERIENCES OF PEOPLE WITH AUTISM

Donna Williams, a young woman with autism, stated, "Autism is just an information processing problem that controls who I appear to be" (1994, p. 238). The way in which children with autism process information is neurologically based and can be seen within the first 3 years of the child's life. Autism is associated with differences in 1) responses to sensory stimuli; 2) the rate of development of social and language skills; 3) pragmatic communication; and 4) ways of relating to people, objects, and events (Autism Society of America, 1996). People with autism are considered to be *higher functioning* when they use functional, expressive verbal language and have average to above average intelligence (Schopler & Mesibov, 1992). Included in this group are people with Asperger syndrome, a subtype of higher-functioning autism (Dawson &

Castelloe, 1992). Among people with autism, the severity of autistic characteristics varies greatly.

Since 1987, much has been learned about autism through new research
and through the writings of individuals with autism. The following section
summarizes current information in three overlapping areas: sensory, cognitive, and social experiences. It is important to remember that each individual
with autism is unique and may or may not experience all of the sensory, cognitive, and social challenges described here.

Sensory Experiences

All individuals perceive and learn about the world through their sensory systems.
People with autism often have hyper- or hyposensitivities in hearing, sight, touch,
or other senses. Grandin described her auditory experiences as follows:

> My hearing is like having a hearing aid with the volume control stuck on
> "super loud." It is like an open microphone that picks up everything. I have
> two choices; turn the mike on and get deluged with sound, or shut it off. . . . I
> can't modulate incoming auditory stimulation. (1992, p. 107)

Visual hypersensitivity to light and to specific colors has also been reported
(Edelson, 1994). Some individuals with autism avoid direct eye contact (Rimland, 1964; Slavik, 1983; Volkmar & Mayes, 1990) and instead use their
peripheral vision to observe others. One man, when asked why he looked at
people using his peripheral vision, replied that looking directly at a person "is
like looking through jelly" (G. Marcus, personal communication, June 1992).
For others, visual perception may be fragmented such that the parts and the
whole of an object, person, or scene are not viewed as one integrated perception (Williams, 1994).

Some people with autism experience hyper- and hyposensitivities to tactile stimuli. For example, it may take a person with autism several days to adjust to the feel and fit of different clothes. Adults with autism have reported
that, as children, physical contact with others, such as a light touch or hug,
was physically unpleasant, and thus they avoided such contact (Edelson,
1994). Grandin described her tactile experiences as "an approach–avoid situation. I wanted to feel the good feeling of being hugged, but when people
hugged me the stimuli washed over me like a tidal wave" (1992, p. 108).

The result of these sensory differences can be sensory overload, a tempo-
rary shutdown in the ability to process incoming visual, auditory, or tactile information because of too much sensory input or problems shifting attention
from one sensory modality to another (Grandin, 1992; Williams, 1994). To
cope with these sensory challenges, people with autism sometimes behave in
ways that are misinterpreted by others. They may appear to withdraw or to
avoid social situations when in fact they are experiencing sensory overload.

Cognitive Experiences

Cognitively, individuals with autism have strengths and challenges, as all people do. People with autism are usually able to attend to stimuli but may have difficulty in controlling and shifting the focus of their attention (Rumsey, 1992). Many individuals with autism have excellent long-term memory and can learn new factual information after it is presented to them only one time (Janzen, 1993). However, such information may be processed without the same kind of analysis or integration employed by people without autism. As a result, individuals with autism may remember all aspects of an experience as equally significant and may later have difficulty in extracting the information that others would describe as most relevant from that situation (Frith, 1989; Prizant, 1983; Rumsey, 1992).

This cognitive condition has implications for the problem-solving skills of the person with autism because the person may not identify the information that is needed to solve a problem (Frith, 1989). For example, Carpenter described her experience as an indexer of newspaper articles:

> I started indexing the *Chicago Times* at home on a part-time basis. However, I was unable to deal with the subtle nuances of the work: Which subject heading should I use? Should I index this editorial? I could not figure out the answers. This was a problem I had had in other jobs as well. I could not generalize from one situation to another and could not deal with the many complexities involved in any one task—a typical problem in autistic people. I was let go from this job primarily for that reason, although my supervisor greatly admired my work and wanted me to continue. (1992, p. 292)

Some people with autism describe themselves as and are observed to be strong visual thinkers (Lissner, 1992). Grandin, a professor in animal husbandry and an international consultant on the design of livestock-processing plants, noted that

> visual thinking is an asset for an equipment designer. I am able to "see" how all the parts of a project will fit together and see potential problems. . . . I am able to visualize a motion picture of the finished facility in my imagination. (1992, pp. 116–117)

Janzen (1996) noted that although some people with autism have difficulty organizing information, if it is organized visually to highlight meanings, relationships, and sequences, they learn remarkably quickly. These cognitive strengths and challenges have important implications for the design of instruction methods.

Social Experiences

For people with autism, communication and social interaction are often the most challenging aspects of living with autism (Grandin, 1992; Sinclair, 1992; Williams, 1992, 1994). Coordinating the language, physical, and cognitive components of social interactions comes naturally to most people without autism, but individuals with autism describe themselves as lacking the "basic instincts which make communication a natural process" (Cesaroni & Garber, 1991, p. 311). Grandin (1992) indicated that she had to learn social interaction skills by using her intellect.

Higher-functioning individuals with autism may have difficulty in understanding situations that they have not experienced directly (Janzen, 1993) or the meaning of words when that meaning depends on the context in which the word is used. Humor and sarcasm (Dewey, 1980) and expressions such as "save your breath" (Moreno, 1991) can be confusing for these people. Williams indicated that "the words 'know' and 'feel' were like 'it' and 'of' and 'by'—you couldn't see them or touch them, so the meaning wasn't significant" (1994, p. 68).

Rumsey suggested that some individuals with autism may have difficulty controlling "their own vocal intonation and facial expression to convey the emotions they feel, leading others to misperceive him or her as unfeeling or aloof" (1992, p. 42). The pace of social interactions can make it difficult for people with autism to catch everything that happens (Williams, 1994), possibly because the person needs more time to shift between auditory and visual cues (Grandin, 1992).

Critical components of social interaction include "knowing" what to do in social situations, inferring the intentions of others, empathizing, and taking another's point of view. These aspects of social cognition, referred to as *metarepresentational capacities* (e.g., thinking about what others know or are thinking about), can be difficult for people with autism to learn and understand. One young man with autism commented that "people give each other messages with their eyes but I don't know what they are saying" (Wing, 1992, p. 131). Carpenter explained that "it is very difficult for even a higher functioning autistic adult to know exactly when to say something, when to ask for help, or when to remain quiet. To such a person, life is a game in which the rules are constantly changing without rhyme or reason" (1992, p. 291).

Social experiences change during adolescence, when the social cues and contexts of peer interactions become more abstract, subtle, and multifaceted (Eisenberg & Harris, 1984). Youth with autism may find it more difficult to interact with people and consequently experience miscommunications with peers. Adolescence is also a time of increasing self-awareness, which, for adolescents with autism, can involve realizing that others know something that they do not know. Williams stated that what she wanted were "rules I could carry around with me that applied to all situations, regardless of context. I wanted rules without exceptions" (1994, p. 65). It is not possible or advisable to provide ironclad rules for social situations, but it is important to provide students who have autism with social information that other people take for granted but of which they may not be aware. *Putting Feet on My Dreams*, including the teacher's guide and instructional strategies described in the next section, were developed to teach students with autism life-planning and self-determination skills while taking into account the unique needs and abilities of individuals with autism.

CURRICULUM DEVELOPMENT AND FIELD TESTING

Identifying Content and Instructional Strategies

Many student involvement and self-determination strategies and materials contain content and practice in life skills, goal setting, and decision making (Abery et al., 1995; Hoffman & Field, 1995; Ludi & Martin, 1995; Martin & Huber Marshall, 1995; Wehmeyer, 1995), and these areas were identified as equally important for students with autism. In addition, the instructional areas of communication, learning strategies (e.g., metacognitive and metarepresentational skills), and organizational skills were identified as critical areas in which students with autism needed to gain increased understanding, self-awareness, and skills.

Field Testing the Program

Because autism is a low-prevalence disability (Schopler & Mesibov, 1992), few students with autism attend a high school at any one time. This fact contributed to the need to design a program that could be used in inclusive classroom environments and that could be implemented with all students while still including instructional methods that facilitate the participation of a student with autism in the class. To ensure that the curriculum reflected the needs of students with autism, young adults with autism were hired as participant evaluators. During the course of 2 years, three different groups of young adults with autism (a total of 26 individuals) met as a college class and completed the program. The classes were taught by the author of *Putting Feet on My Dreams* and specialists in autism. Specific content and instructional methods were field tested, critiqued, and revised accordingly.

To determine its usefulness with high school students, *Putting Feet on My Dreams* was then field tested by high school teachers in 10 different high school classes. The field tests were performed with more than 100 students over the course of 3 years. These classes were arranged for students without disabilities and students with disabilities, and each class included one or two students with autism. Input from the high school teachers and students was also incorporated into the program. This series of field tests was used to ensure that the content and teaching strategies were effective with a range of high school students in a classroom setting.

Curricular Themes and Major Activities

The title of the program, *Putting Feet on My Dreams*, was suggested by one of the individuals participating in the field test. When asked what *self-*

determination meant to him, he said that it meant "putting feet on my dreams so that my dreams can go somewhere." This is a visual metaphor for self-determination. Through the curriculum, self-determination concepts and student involvement skills are addressed in three theme areas: self-knowledge, life knowledge, and life planning (Figure 1).

Self-knowledge includes identifying one's interests, strengths, and challenges. *Life knowledge* is becoming aware of and learning about the information and skills one needs for independent adulthood. Self-knowledge and life knowledge are also explored in the areas of communication, learning, and organizing. The third theme, *life planning*, involves the process of identifying one's goals, developing plans for reaching one's goals, and implementing those plans.

There are two major activities that span the entire program and organize the student's work within the framework of the themes just described. The first is the creation of a *self-folio*, which is a portfolio of resources organized by a student for his or her own personal use in life planning. The use of portfolios has become popular in transition and school-to-work programs. Although it contains information similar to that in a portfolio, the self-folio is created and organized by the student in a way that makes sense and is useful to him or her so that he or she can retrieve and use information in the future. Teachers can use the development of a self-folio to teach the value of using a personal organizer and personal resource file to facilitate independence in adulthood. Students begin compiling the self-folio in the first unit, and it is organized for continued personal use after the program during the last unit.

The second activity is called *advancework*. Advancework projects are self-directed learning projects that students can do in advance to prepare for their adult lives. The idea of advancework is introduced after students have identified the information and skills that they will need to become more independent as adults. For example, finding a place to live and evaluating the costs and responsibilities involved is an advancework project. The teacher introduces the idea that, although students may not be ready to find, afford, and maintain a personal residence today, they can learn much now, in advance, about this life task for use at a later time.

Both small-group projects in life domains and individual projects based on personal goals are completed. Advancework projects are introduced early in *Putting Feet on My Dreams*, and teachers schedule time each week for students to work on these projects. To explore their topics thoroughly, students start with a visual organizer (Figure 2), which organizes and details the information that they need. Then students gather information from community resources, interview knowledgeable adults, and write a how-to manual that contains resources. During the final unit of the program, students teach each other what they have learned about the life tasks they studied, and all students include the manuals in their own self-folios.

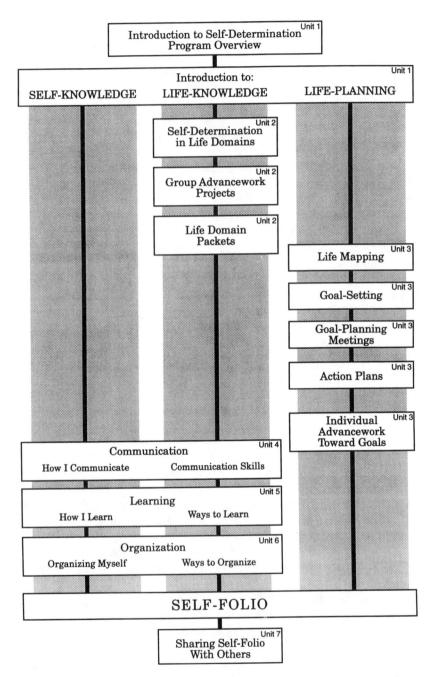

Figure 1. Overview of *Putting Feet on My Dreams: A Program in Self-Determination.* Copyright © 1994 by Ann Fullerton.

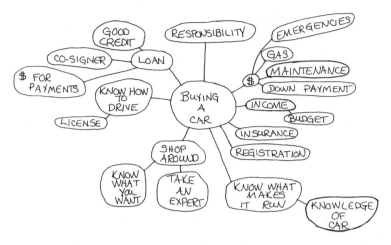

Figure 2.   Example of a student's visual organizer to begin an *advancework* project.

Curriculum Units

Putting Feet on My Dreams is divided into seven units. The relationship of these units to the curricular themes, advance work, and the self-folio is depicted in Figure 1.

Unit 1: Introduction to Self-Determination   In Unit 1, the program goals, sequence, and major activities are introduced. Students develop a collective definition of *self-determination* and establish ground rules so that they feel safe in sharing their experiences and learning about themselves in the presence of their peers. These ground rules are posted during all class sessions, and students can revise and revisit them as needed to maintain a supportive learning community.

Visual organizers are introduced during this unit and are used throughout the curriculum to assist students in understanding the progression of program activities. Program maps show students where they are within the curriculum sequence. Teachers prepare and post an agenda for each session. As each activity is completed, it is crossed off the agenda and the next activity is highlighted.

Unit 2: Life Knowledge for Self-Determination   In Unit 2, students identify, through discussions with peers and independent study, life domains (e.g., a place of residence) and life tasks (e.g., finding an apartment) required for independence in adulthood. Through small-group activities, students determine what they know and still need to know about these life tasks. This activity then becomes the basis for the advancework projects.

One effective way to use Unit 2 is to integrate it with the life skills, vocational skills, and community skills training experiences already in use in the classroom. The intent of Unit 2 is to motivate students by creating an opportunity to discover the relationship between developing life and work skills now and the extent of control one will achieve over life decisions and outcomes in the future.

Unit 3: Life Planning   Unit 3 contains a series of activities designed to enable students to engage in life planning, set personal goals, and participate in their own advancework projects aimed at achieving personal goals. Students first develop a *life map* (see Figure 3). Within a square drawn in the center of a large sheet of paper, students use pictures and words to depict the important aspects of their lives. Then, outside of the square, students depict what they want their lives to look like in about 5 years. All life domains, such as work and leisure, are included in the life map, which students work on for several days. Once completed, each student shares his or her life map with classmates.

The life map becomes a self-created visual organizer that assists students in seeing how the parts of their lives fit together and enabling them to elaborate on and communicate their understanding of their lives to others. As students share their life maps, teachers and peers can ask questions that help students to clarify and elaborate their views of their lives in the present and in the future. The map is then used to visually illustrate the concept of a goal and to identify each student's personal long-term goals. The teacher points out that getting from where students are to where they want to be in 5 years is what is called a *long-term goal*.

The life-mapping process has been expanded by teachers and students using *Putting Feet on My Dreams*. For example, one student added the concept of a *dream box*, in which a person draws something that he or she wants in the future but that may not actually be achieved. The dream box is a useful strategy for distinguishing more realistic goals from less realistic ones. In some classes, students drew a life map each year because it served as a useful chronicle of the development of personal goals and life domains over time. Other teachers had students develop a life map and then used it as a visual organizer for students to use as they self-directed their transition-planning meetings.

Once personal goals are identified, a *goal-planning meeting* is conducted for each student to discuss one of his or her goals. These meetings are structured with specific roles and rules so that the teacher and peers can suggest possible steps a student can take to attain a goal while the final choice of which steps to take is left to the student. Students receive assistance as needed, organizing the steps into an overall action plan. Subsequently, the initial steps in student's plans are formulated into an individual advancework project.

Unit 4: Communication   Unit 4 focuses on communicating with others. Students first discuss why effective communicators have more control over their lives. They then examine the verbal and nonverbal actions of listeners and speakers associated with effective communication using role playing and

Figure 3.   Example of a student's life map developed in Unit 3: Life Planning of *Putting Feet on My Dreams: A Program in Self-Determination*.

videotaped conversations with each other. Students and teachers view the video-taped conversations and use them to identify and discuss communication skills. The videotapes also provide a vehicle for students to self-assess and practice conversation skills. Visual images are used to illustrate communication concepts. For example, the drawing in Figure 4 illustrates the difference between a conversation in which each person talks for about the same amount of time and a conversation in which one person talks far more than the other person.

Unit 5: Learning   In Unit 5, students examine different ways that people learn and how to self-direct learning. The unit begins with a visual model of how people take in new information, use it, and retain it (Figure 5). Students explore how they use their visual, auditory, and kinesthetic senses to learn. Next, teachers model (e.g., "thinking aloud") the use of various learning strategies. Students then use these strategies to solve academic and everyday problems. As students become aware of how they take in, process, and retain information, they determine how they can enhance their ability to learn desired information and skills in school and work situations. This unit can be used in conjunction with more extensive strategy instruction programs (e.g., Deshler, Ellis, & Lenz, 1996).

Unit 6: Organizing   In Unit 6, students explore ways in which people organize themselves and examine their own existing and needed organizational strategies. Teachers and students discuss three aspects of life that can be organized—tasks, materials, and time. Students identify what aspects of life self-determined adults must organize and then list who in their lives is performing these organizational tasks for them. Students' realization that teachers and family members are organizing important parts of their lives can motivate them to learn self-organization skills. Students then learn and apply methods

Figure 4.   Which depicts a balanced conversation? Illustration used to discuss balanced conversations from Unit 4: Communication of *Putting Feet on My Dreams: A Program in Self-Determination.*

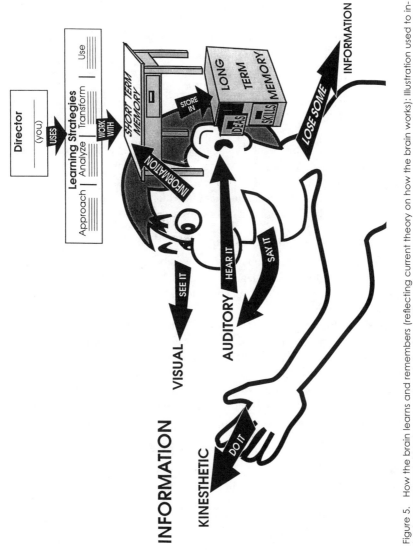

Figure 5. How the brain learns and remembers (reflecting current theory on how the brain works): Illustration used to introduce concepts in Unit 5: Learning of *Putting Feet on My Dreams: A Program in Self-Determination.* (Copyright © 1994 by Ann Fullerton.)

291

for organizing tasks and materials. Time management is also explored through activities that help students become aware of how they use their time. For example, students record and analyze their activities for 1 week. Students then plan and schedule their time to accomplish one project. Finally, students develop a weekly schedule for multiple tasks.

Unit 7: Sharing Self-Folio with Others   As depicted in Figure 2, information learned in each of the instructional units is stored in the student's self-folio. In Unit 7, the self-folio is the catalyst for teaching the concept of using a personal resource file for life planning and self-direction. Students teach their classmates what they have learned through their advancework projects, and each student receives a manual from each group or individual project for their self-folio. Students review and organize their self-folios, and they generate examples of when they might use the information in the future and what kind of information they might add later as they continue to work toward their goals. Students also decide what aspects of their self-folio, such as their life map, they want to share with family members. As a means of closure and review, students plan and prepare an event in which they share what they have learned with family members and other guests.

How to Implement the Program

Teachers can implement all units as sequenced or choose between the various units based on individual student's needs. Each lesson contains detailed instructional scripts that teachers can revise to fit their teaching styles. Each unit also contains teacher preparations, vocabulary, and master copies of transparencies and handouts ready for duplication. If implemented as described, the program can be taught for 3–4 hours per week over the course of a semester. When integrated with other life skills and vocational learning experiences the program has been taught throughout the school year. Teachers have found that certain activities (e.g., life mapping, advancework) and topics (e.g., communication, organization) are useful to repeat because students' interests and concerns change as they get closer to the transition from school to adulthood.

Instruction Strategies for Students with Autism

Embedded in the units and activities just described are two instruction strategies designed to maximize the meaningful participation of students with autism. Often, these strategies help other students as well. Teachers using *Putting Feet on My Dreams* have commented that they have become more effective as teachers by incorporating these strategies into their teaching.

The first strategy is to provide information visually. Visual organizers and drawings help students with autism to understand time periods, sequences, concepts, where and how materials are arranged, and social situations. For example, when a teacher refers to the program map and daily agenda, students with autism can see the sequence in which events will occur and when events will begin and end. When the teacher creates semantic webs as he or she talks about new concepts or as the class discusses ideas, students with autism can see how others are organizing and understanding these spoken words. In Unit 2, students also visually organize and communicate their own ideas through a life-planning process. Visual information helps students to organize concepts when they are introduced as well as provide a permanent record for retention.

The second instructional strategy is to provide students who have autism with information about social situations. For example, the ground rules that students create during Unit 1 and that are posted during program sessions help students to understand and remember shared expectations. Small-group activities are structured; a written description of roles and procedures, as well as their purpose, is provided; and these roles and procedures are demonstrated before students engage in the activity. Students who have difficulty interpreting implicit social cues have indicated that this information is very useful. One student said, "This is great information! Everybody in class should be told this!", when provided with written information about a group activity beforehand. Social information is also provided in the communication unit when drawings are used to define and discuss social concepts, and communication skills are identified as they occur during videotaped conversations. Descriptions and explanations of social situations enable students with autism to participate in and contribute to the classroom.

These and other instructional methods are fully described in the teacher's guide (Fullerton et al., 1996) developed during this project. This guide contains strategies for providing individualized academic, organizational, and social assistance to students with autism in ways that promote the development of self-directed performance.

Program Evaluation by Parents

Parents of high school students involved in the curriculum completed the *Self-Determination Descriptors Scale* (SDDS) (Fullerton, 1992) before and after their child participated in the program. The SDDS is a 39-item, five-point behavior rating scale designed to assess the degree to which raters have observed various skills and attitudes related to self-determination during a 2-week period. The items in the SDDS were constructed to reflect skills and attitudes viewed as correlates of self-determination in the literature. Field testing of the SDDS indicated adequate short-term test–retest reliability ($r = .86$). A total of 19 parents completed and returned both scales. A matched t-test was conducted to examine differences between pre- and postintervention scores. Parents reported significant improvement in their children's skills and attitudes related to self-determination after participation in the program [$t(18) = 2.03, p = .033$].

Parents of higher-functioning students with autism who participated in the program as a college class were asked to participate in pre- and postintervention telephone interviews. Six parents were interviewed before and after their son or daughter attended the class. Parents' open-ended responses were recorded verbatim. The interview consisted of a series of questions about what students were doing in areas related to the curriculum. These areas were 1) self-awareness of one's experiences and challenges related to autism, 2) actions toward stated short- and long-term goals, 3) communication skills, and 4) organization skills.

For each curricular area, parents' pre- and postintervention responses were compared by raters who knew the students. These raters judged whether the parents' postintervention responses, when compared with the parents' preintervention responses, indicated that the students had initiated and self-directed additional changes in their behavior after completing the program. Parents' postintervention responses were scored as either 1, defined as "describes an increase in self-directed behavior in this area," or 0, defined as "describes no change in self-directed behavior in this area" (interrater agreement higher than .80 for all areas). All parents (100%) reported student behaviors that the raters categorized as reflecting an increase in self-awareness of one's experiences and challenges related to autism. Three of the parents (50%) reported student behaviors that the raters viewed as actions toward stated goals. Three of the parents (50%) reported student behaviors that the raters viewed as an increase in self-directed use of communication skills. Finally, four parents (66%) reported student behaviors that the raters viewed as self-directed use of organization skills.

The results of the field test in high schools with a variety of students suggested that students gained knowledge and skills related to self-determination that were observable by parents. The field test of small classes conducted with higher-functioning students with autism suggested that parents observed some increases in self-awareness and self-directed behavior that were considered important for these students' self-determination.

CONCLUSIONS

As one man with autism noted, "Even if an autistic person has the same goals as a non-autistic person, he or she might need to follow a different procedure to get there" (Sinclair, 1992, p. 15). Students with autism need instruction that takes into account their unique learning styles, visually based thinking, and need for social information in order to pursue life planning and become more self-determined adults.

REFERENCES

Abery, B., Rudrud, L., Arndt, K., Schauben, L., & Eggebeen, A. (1995). Evaluating a multicomponent program for enhancing the self-determination of youth with disabilities. *Intervention in School and Clinic, 30,* 170–179.

Autism Society of America. (1996). Definition of autism. *Advocate: Newsletter of the Autism Society of America, 28*(5), 3.

Carpenter, A. (1992). Personal essays. In E. Schopler & G.B. Mesibov (Eds.), *High-functioning individuals with autism* (pp. 289–294). New York: Plenum.

Cesaroni, L., & Garber, M. (1991). Exploring the experience of autism through first-hand accounts. *Journal of Autism and Developmental Disorders, 21,* 303–313.

Dawson, G., & Castelloe, P. (1992). Autism. In C.E. Walker & M.C. Roberts (Eds.), *Handbook of clinical child psychology* (pp. 375–397). New York: John Wiley & Sons.

Deshler, D.D., Ellis, E.S., & Lenz, B.K. (1996). *Teaching adolescents with learning disabilities: Strategies and methods.* Denver: Love Publishing Co.

Dewey, M.A. (1980). *The socially aware autistic adult and child.* Paper presented at the Warwick Conference, Nottingham University, Nottingham, England.

Edelson, S. (1994). *Sensory dysfunction in autism.* Unpublished manuscript, Willamette University, Salem, Oregon.

Eisenberg, N., & Harris, J.D. (1984). Social competence: A developmental perspective. *School Psychology Review, 13,* 278–291.

Frith, U. (1989). *Autism: Explaining the enigma.* Oxford, England: Blackwell Publishers.

Fullerton, A. (1992). *The Self-Determination Descriptors Scale.* Portland, OR: Portland State University.

Fullerton, A. (1994). *Putting Feet on My Dreams: A Program in Self-Determination.* Portland, OR: Portland State University.

Fullerton, A., Stratton, J., Coyne, P., & Gray, C. (1996). *Higher functioning adolescents and young adults with autism: A teacher's guide.* Austin, TX: PRO-ED.

Grandin, T. (1992). An inside view of autism. In E. Schopler & G.B. Mesibov (Eds.), *High-functioning individuals with autism* (pp. 105–126). New York: Plenum.

Hoffman, A., & Field, S. (1995). Promoting self-determination through effective curriculum development. *Intervention in School and Clinic, 30,* 134–141.

Janzen, J.E. (1993). *Understanding autism in the young child: Practical intervention strategies.* Portland, OR: Portland State University, Rapsource Access Project, School of Extended Studies.

Janzen, J.E. (1996). *Understanding the nature of autism: A practical guide.* San Antonio, TX: Communication Skill Builders.

Lissner, K. (1992). Personal essays. In E. Schopler & G.B. Mesibov (Eds.), *High-functioning individuals with autism* (pp. 289–294). New York: Plenum.

Ludi, D., & Martin, L. (1995). The road to personal freedom: Self-determination. *Intervention in School and Clinic, 30,* 164–169.

Martin, J.E., & Huber Marshall, L. (1995). ChoiceMaker: A comprehensive self-determination transition program. *Intervention in School and Clinic, 30,* 147–156.

Moreno, S. (1991). *High-functioning individuals with autism: Advice and information for parents and others who care.* Crown Point, IN: MAAP Services.

Prizant, B.M. (1983). Language acquisition and communicative behavior in autism: Toward an understanding of the "whole" of it. *Journal of Speech and Hearing Disorders, 48,* 296–307.

Rimland, B. (1964). *Infantile autism.* New York: Appleton-Century-Crofts.

Rumsey, J.M. (1992). Neuropsychological studies of high-level autism. In E. Schopler & G.B. Mesibov (Eds.), *High-functioning individuals with autism* (pp. 41–64). New York: Plenum.

Schopler, E., & Mesibov, G.B. (Eds.). (1992). *High-functioning individuals with autism.* New York: Plenum.

Sinclair, J. (1992). Editorial: What does being different mean? *Our Voice: The Newsletter of the Autism International Network, 1*, 14–16.

Slavik, B.A. (1983). Vestibular stimulation and eye contact in autistic children. *American Journal of Occupational Therapy, 37*, 17.

Volkmar, F.R., & Mayes, L.C. (1990). Gaze behavior in autism. *Development and Psychopathology, 2*, 61–69.

Wehmeyer, M. (1995). A career approach: Self-determination for youth with mild cognitive disabilities. *Intervention in School and Clinic, 30*, 157–163.

Williams, D. (1992). *Nobody nowhere*. New York: Avon Books.

Williams, D. (1994). *Somebody somewhere*. New York: Avon Books.

Wing, L. (1992). Manifestations of social problems in high-functioning autistic people. In E. Schopler & G.B. Mesibov (Eds.), *High-functioning individuals with autism* (pp. 129–142). New York: Plenum.

III

STUDENT INVOLVEMENT IN PROGRAM IMPLEMENTATION AND EVALUATION

15

The Self-Determined
Learning Model of Instruction

*Engaging Students to Solve
Their Learning Problems*

Dennis E. Mithaug, Michael L. Wehmeyer,
Martin Agran, James E. Martin, and Susan Palmer

A model of teaching, according to Joyce and Weil, is "a plan or pattern that can be used to shape curriculums (long term courses of study), to design instructional materials, and to guide instruction in the classroom and other settings" (1980, p. 1). Such models are typically derived from theories about human behavior, learning, or cognition. Effective teachers employ multiple models of teaching, taking into account the unique characteristics of the learner and types of learning.

Like all educators, teachers working with students who receive special education services have an arsenal of teaching models that they deploy according to the students' learning characteristics and the content under consideration. A teacher may use the role-playing model to teach social behaviors, social simulation and social inquiry models to examine social problems and solutions, assertiveness training to teach self-advocacy skills, or a training model to teach vocational skills. Likewise, special educators employ more traditional, cognitively based models of teaching, such as the concept attainment model to teach thinking skills, the memory model for increasing the retention of facts, or inductive thinking and inquiry training models to teach reasoning and academic skills. The teaching model most frequently adopted by special educators is probably the contingency management model, which draws on principles contained in operant conditioning psychology.

The common theme across these models of teaching is that they are, by and large, teacher directed. As discussed in Chapter 1, however, there are numerous benefits to employing student-directed models of instruction. This chapter introduces an instructional model, the Self-Determined Learning Model of Instruction, that was derived from an earlier instructional model, the Adaptability Instruction Model, and that is based on the component elements of self-determination, the process of self-regulated problem solving, and research on student-directed learning. The model is appropriate for students with and without disabilities across a wide range of content areas and enables teachers to engage students in the totality of their educational programs by increasing opportunities to self-direct learning and, in the process, to improve students' prospects for success after they leave school.

THE ADAPTABILITY INSTRUCTION MODEL

The Self-Determined Learning Model of Instruction was derived from the Adaptability Instruction Model put forth by Mithaug, Martin, and Agran (1987) and Mithaug, Martin, Agran, and Rusch (1988), which drew extensively from theory and research on self-management and self-control (Agran & Martin, 1987; Bandura, 1986; Kanfer & Goldstein, 1986; Martin, Burger, Elias-Burger, & Mithaug, 1988). Its purpose was to teach students with disabilities generic adaptability skills for use during school-to-work transitions. Its rationale, according to Mithaug et al., was that "clearly, programs are needed that enhance self-direction and that teach problem-solving skills in classrooms, community sites, and work settings" (1987, p. 501). Mithaug and colleagues suggested that, by learning decision making, independent performance, self-evaluation, and adjustment, students will make better adjustments in postschool settings. The skills and the sequence of their use as proposed by the model were as follows:

- *Decision making*: First, students learn to identify their needs, interests, and abilities; consider alternatives; and select their goals.
- *Independent performance:* Second, students learn independent performance by following through on their action plans. They perform tasks independently by using self-management and self-control strategies. These

may include self-instructional and other antecedent procedures (e.g., picture cues, written prompts, verbal labeling) to remind them what to do, when to do it, and where.

- *Self-evaluation:* Third, while working on the tasks identified in their plans, students also learn to self-evaluate by monitoring and recording performance outcomes and then compare their results with goals and performance expectations that they set for themselves during decision making. In classroom and work situations, their self-evaluations may focus, for example, on being on time, task selections, productivity, accuracy, and earnings. These self-evaluations are used in the next phase, when they decide what to do for their next adjustment episode.

- *Adjustments:* In the last phase, students learn to adjust by connecting their future actions with past performance. Before beginning another task or project, they review feedback from previous decisions and performance outcomes and select goals, plans, and performance objectives accordingly.

The appeal of the preceding model was its focus on two processes everyone experiences in life: problem solving and adjustment. Because many students with disabilities seemed to lack the skills to perform these actions after leaving school, teaching them seemed to be a practical solution to reported postschool adjustment problems. Mithaug et al. (1987) identified a body of research on self-management and self-control that offered an array of instructional tactics and procedures that could be used to teach the skills identified by the model. All that remained was to implement the model. The assumption was that if adaptability skills were taught, the school-to-work transition problem would be solved and students with disabilities would adjust to their postschool circumstances as well as students without disabilities did.

THE SELF-DETERMINED LEARNING MODEL OF INSTRUCTION

Since publication of the Adaptability Instruction Model in 1987 (Mithaug et al., 1987), the authors of this chapter have learned that the obstacles facing students with disabilities who are entering community life are more complex than originally understood. This understanding led us to challenge the assumption of that model that students with disabilities fail to get what they need and want in life only or primarily because they cannot adjust to their circumstances. We considered the possibilities that individuals with disabilities contend with circumstances that are less favorable than those experienced by their peers without disabilities and that in a society stressing personal initiative to improve one's situation, simply adjusting to the ways of society does not accomplish much. Being adaptable to an unfavorable and perhaps unfair circumstance in life does little to alter the fairness or optimality of that circumstance. Extending this reasoning further, we considered the argument that if students with disabilities are to improve their prospects for living the good life after school, they must learn more than adaptability skills. Students with disabilities must also learn self-determination skills, and they must learn how to advocate for their own needs and interests by taking action to change circumstances that pose obstacles to their pursuits. Their simply adjusting to existing circumstances does not accomplish these goals.

The Self-Determined Learning Model of Instruction reflects this new thinking. It recognizes that success in life requires more than adjustment to present circumstances. It also requires altering those circumstances to make them more favorable for a self-selected pursuit. Accounts of how famous people have overcome formidable obstacles attest to the necessity of acting *on* one's circumstances rather than simply reacting *to* one's circumstances and illustrate the importance of acting as a causal agent in one's life (see Chapter 1). Such stories highlight the difference between fitting into a niche created by someone else and fitting into a niche created by one's own actions. The latter mode of adjustment is not a salient feature of the Adaptability Instruction Model. The Self-Determined Learning Model of Instruction corrects this deficiency by identifying the skills that are necessary to act on the environment to achieve goals that satisfy one's self-defined needs and interests.

The Adaptability Instruction Model failed to stress that self-determined people persistently regulate their problem solving to meet their own goals in life. Hill (1939/1960) was the first person to describe these problem-solving strategies in his best-selling book entitled *Think and Grow Rich,* in which he identified a five-step problem-solving strategy that he claimed all successful people use to get what they need and want. That five-step sequence was 1) to identify a definite goal to be obtained, 2) to develop sufficient power to attain that goal, 3) to perfect a practical plan for attaining that goal, 4) to accumulate specialized knowledge necessary for the attainment of that goal, and 5) to persist in carrying out the plan (Mithaug, 1991). These steps can be restated as six questions that any child or adult can ask to achieve goal-directed problem solving (Mithaug, 1991). They can also be used to assess self-determination among students with and without disabilities (Wolman, Campeau, DuBois, Mithaug, & Stolarski, 1994).

1. What do I need and want?
2. What goal will satisfy my needs and wants?
3. What plan will enable me to reach that goal?
4. What actions will complete my plan?
5. What results did I get?
6. What do I need to do next time?

What is learned from this reconstruction of Hill's formula is that there is a sequence of thoughts and actions that must be followed for any person's actions to produce results that satisfy his or her needs and interests. To understand the logic inherent in these six questions, the reader should trace his or her own thinking while moving down the list of six questions. First, identify needs and interests; then construct a goal based on those needs and interests, formulate a plan of action to meet that goal, identify actions that will complete that plan, and compare results with expectations identified in the goal; and finally compare progress toward the goal with the satisfaction of needs and interests. Now skip one of those questions and see what happens: The chain of logic breaks, as does the causal sequence it depicts.

This demonstration should convince the reader that the six questions are linked in a means–ends problem-solving sequence. Solving the problem identified by Question 2 (reaching my goal) is the means of solving the problem identified by Question 1 (getting what I need and want), solving the problem identified by Question 3 (constructing a plan) is the means of solving the problem identified by Question 2 (reaching my goal), solving the problem identified by Question 4 (taking actions on my plan) is the means of solving the problem identified by Question 3 (constructing a plan), solving the problem identified by Question 5 (evaluating my results) is the means of solving the problem identified by Question 4 (taking actions on my plan), and solving the problem of Question 6 (planning for next time) is the means of solving the problem identified by Question 1 (getting what I need and want).

This illustrates what is meant when we say that self-determination involves self-regulated problem solving to get what you need and want in life. Self-determination involves solving a sequence of problems to construct a means–ends chain—a causal sequence—that moves people from where they are, an actual state of not having needs and interests satisfied, to where they want to be, a goal state of having those needs and interests satisfied. It is problem solving to reduce or eliminate this discrepancy between what people want and what they have. This means–ends sequence is constructed by answering the six self-determination questions that connect needs and interests to actions and results via goals and plans. The six questions are used to guide or regulate our problem solving toward the construction of this means–ends chain between what one has, one's actual state or present situation, and what one wants, one's goal state or expected situation.

According to this analysis, self-directed learning and, for that matter, much of self-determination is more than solving one problem to get what one needs and wants in life; it entails solving many problems that are connected in a means–ends chain or chains. Consequently, self-directed learning requires the regulation of many problem-solving activities to connect needs and wants with actions and results. The basic strategy that we have identified to teach students is reflected in the six questions. To answer the questions in this sequence, students must regulate their own problem solving 1) to construct goals to meet needs, 2) to formulate plans to meet goals, and 3) to adjust actions to complete plans. Moreover, students must repeat this goal–plan–action problem-solving sequence until they satisfy their needs and interests.

Self-regulation theory explains this process of self-regulated problem solving. It is based in part on research on human problem solving conducted by Newell and Simon (1972), who identified the three-step process in which all humans engage when solving complex problems. They verified their findings on human problem solving by developing a computer program called the *General Problem Solver* (GPS) to demonstrate how this generic problem strategy simulates human problem solving of complex everyday problems. In the following passage, Simon described this three-step strategy that corresponded to human problem solving:

> A problem is defined for GPS by giving it a starting situation and a goal situation (or a test for determining whether the goal has been reached), together with a set of operators that may be used, separately or severally, to transform the starting situation into the goal situation by a sequence of successive applications. Means–ends analysis is the technique used by GPS to decide which operator to apply next:
>
> 1. It compares current situation with goal situation to detect one or more differences between them.
> 2. It retrieves from memory an operator that is associated with a difference it has found (i.e., an operator that has the usual effect of reducing differences of this kind).
> 3. It applies the operator or, if it is not applicable in the current situation, sets up the new goal of creating the conditions that will make it applicable. (1989, p. 53)

Simon also illustrated this three-step problem-solving strategy in the following example, which illustrates means–ends problem solving at work on a practical discrepancy problem:

> I want to take my son to nursery school. What's the difference between what I have and what I want? Distance. What changes distance? My automobile. My automobile won't work. What is needed to make it work? A new battery. What has new batteries? An auto repair shop. I want the repair shop to put in a new battery but the shop doesn't know I need one. What is the difficulty? One of communication. What allows communication? Telephone . . . and so on. (1989, p. 54)

Simon (1989) wanted to eliminate the discrepancy between the *goal state* of his child being at preschool and the *actual state* of his child being at home. To eliminate the discrepancy, he solved a series of interconnected problems in which the solution to one problem constituted the means of solving another. The following reconstruction of that reasoning clarifies this means–ends sequence, ending at the goal state, in which his son is at nursery school:

My goal state: Son at nursery school
My actual state: Son at home
Problem: Discrepancy between goal state and actual state

1. *Problem:* Reduce distance from home to nursery school.
   Solution: Use car to take son to nursery school.
2. *Problem:* Car will not start; battery is dead.
   Solution: Get new battery to start car.
3. *Problem:* Do not have new battery at home.
   Solution: Get new battery at repair shop.
4. *Problem:* Repair shop does not know I need a new battery.
   Solution: Telephone repair shop to bring new battery and install it.
5. *Action:* Telephone repair shop.
6. *Result:* Auto repairman comes and installs new battery.
7. *Action:* Drive son to nursery school.
8. *Result:* Son is at nursery school. (Mithaug, 1993, p. 54)

This is self-regulated problem solving to meet a goal. People engage in it to reach any goal in life. The language we use to describe the process is different from that used by Newell and Simon (1972), but the process is the same. Terms such as *expectations, choices, actions,* and *results* are used. Expectations to reduce differences between what we have and what we want are created. We choose the means that we believe will reduce the difference, we take action on our choices, and then we check to see if the results of our actions match our expectations. If they do, then we are satisfied because the problem is solved. This process is self-regulated problem solving and is explained by self-regulation theory, which describes how we regulate our expectations, choices, actions, and results to solve the problem of getting from Point A to Point B (Mithaug, 1993). The theory explains why some patterns of self-regulated problem solving are more efficient (i.e., optimal) than others.

The Self-Determined Learning Model of Instruction is a variant of the self-regulation process in that it describes the problem solving in which people engage to satisfy their needs and interests, as contrasted with the problem solving in which people engage to reach goals that others expect them to meet. Of the two types, the latter is perhaps more difficult because it requires people to solve the problem of knowing what they need and want and then translating that understanding of themselves into goals that will get them what they need and want. This problem is not present when people regulate their problem solving to meet goals that others assign to them, because then all they must do is solve problems related to constructing a plan and then acting on it.

The Self-Determined Learning Model of Instruction reflects changes in the understanding of what students must learn to improve their long-term outcomes in life. It incorporates the six self-determination questions listed previously as well as self-regulated problem solving to answer those questions. The model defines the problem of self-directed learning as comprising three self-determination–related questions that can be answered through means–ends problem solving: What is my goal? What is my plan? and What are my adjustments? Figure 1 is a matrix showing how these three questions guided our additions and adjustments to the Adaptability Instruction Model in Column 2 during the construction of the Self-Determined Learning Model of Instruction in Column 5. We took into account the six questions listed in Column 1 and the self-regulated problem-solving steps in Column 4 to construct the Self-Determined Learning Model of Instruction in Column 5.

The Self-Determined Learning Model of Instruction identifies the three problems that self-determined students solve when they direct their own learning. They solve the problems of knowing 1) what goals to set, 2) what plans to construct, and 3) what behaviors to adjust. The general problem-solving skills that students use to accomplish these tasks are presented in Column 3. For each problem of knowing what to do, they set expectations, make choices, take actions, and produce results. To set a goal, students define their problem as the difference between what they have and what they want and, to reduce that difference, they set expectations, make choices, take actions, and produce a result that is a goal. To construct a plan, students define their problem as the difference between a goal and the present situation and, to reduce that difference, they set expectations, make choices, take action, and produce a result that is a plan. To adjust their behaviors, students define their problem as the difference between their plan and their actions and, to reduce that difference, they set expectations, make choices, take actions, and produce a result that is a change in their behavior.

Column 5 shows how these three types of problem-solving activities function during student-directed learning. To solve the first problem, self-determined students decide what to learn. To make that decision, they determine 1) what they want to learn, 2) what they know about that topic or skill, 3) what must change to learn what they do not know, and 4) what they can do to produce that change. The first two questions constitute the discrepancy problem. They determine what will reduce the difference between what they want to know and what they know. The answer is their expectation for changing what they do not know. Next, they consider different ways of meeting their expectation for changing what they do not know. They consider different areas of what they do not know. These are their options for reducing what they do not know. Then they act by choosing a specific area that they want to know. Finally, they ask themselves if their action—the selection of this learning goal—meets their expectation of knowing something that they do not currently know. If it does, then they have solved the first problem of identifying a learning goal: They have identified specifically what they do not know and that they want to change this circumstance so that they know what they want to know.

Question	The Adaptability Instruction Model (1987)	Self-determination (self-regulated problem solving to get what you need and want)	Self-regulation (problem solving to set goals, make plans, and adjust)	The Self-Determined Learning Model of Instruction
What is my goal?	• Decision making	• What do I need and want? • What goal will satisfy my needs and wants?	• *Expectations:* What results do I expect will reduce the difference between what I want and what I have? • *Choices:* What goals can I choose to produce those results? • *Actions:* Did I choose a goal? • *Results:* What is the result of reaching my goal?	• What do I want to learn? • What do I know about it now? • What must change to learn that which I do not know? • What can I do to produce that change?
What is my plan?	• Independent performance	• What plan will enable me to reach that goal?	• *Expectations:* What result can I expect to reduce the difference between my goal and my present situation?	• What can I do now to change what I do not know? • What will prevent me from taking action now to produce that change?

(continued)

Figure 1. Matrix comparing adaptability, self-determination, self-regulation, and self-determined learning.

Figure 1. (continued)

Question	The Adaptability Instruction Model (1987)	Self-determination (self-regulated problem solving to get what you need and want)	Self-regulation (problem solving to set goals, make plans, and adjust)	The Self-Determined Learning Model of Instruction
What are my adjustments?	• Self-evaluation • Self-adjustment	• What actions will complete my plan? • What results did I get? • What do I need to do next time?	• *Choices:* What plans can I construct to produce those results? • *Actions:* What plan did I construct? • *Results:* Will completing my plan reduce the difference between my goal and my present situation? • *Expectations:* What do I expect will reduce the difference between my plan to act and what I am doing?	• What can I do to remove these obstacles? • When will I take action and remove these obstacles? • What actions have I taken? • What obstacles have been removed? • What has changed about what I do not know?

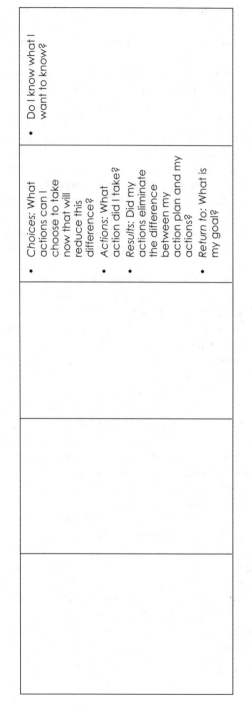

- *Choices:* What actions can I choose to take now that will reduce this difference?
- *Actions:* What action did I take?
- *Results:* Did my actions eliminate the difference between my action plan and my actions?
- *Return to:* What is my goal?

- Do I know what I want to know?

The second problem that self-determined learners solve is how to achieve their learning goals. They solve this problem by addressing Questions 5–7, which focus their attention on deciding what they can do now to change what they do not know, what will prevent them from taking action to produce this change, what they can to do remove those obstacles, and when they will take action to remove obstacles. Questions 5 and 6 describe the discrepancy problem. Students solve it by determining what will reduce the difference between what they can do now to change what they do not know and the present circumstances that prevent them from taking action to make this change. The solution is their expectation for what actions they can take to change what they do not know. Next, they consider different ways of taking those actions to produce this change. They consider their options for acting and removing obstacles to learning. Then they act by constructing a plan to take action and remove obstacles. Finally, they ask themselves if their plan will meet their expectation to change what they do not know. If it does, they have solved the second problem by constructing a plan to learn that which they do not currently know.

The third problem that self-determined learners solve is how to take action to change what they do not know and to learn that which they want to know. They solve this problem by asking Questions 9–12 about what actions they have taken, what obstacles have been removed, what has changed about what they do not know, and whether they know what they want to know. Here, Questions 9 and 10 define the discrepancy problem. Students solve it by deciding what will reduce the difference between their action plan and actions taken now. The solution is their expectation to monitor their behaviors and to motivate their action to change what they do not know. Next, they consider different ways of meeting this expectation to monitor and motivate their behaviors: They consider their options for self-engagement in learning what they do not know. Then they act by choosing one of those methods that ensures action and the removal of obstacles. Finally, they ask themselves if their actions have completed their plan to know what they do not know; if so, they have solved the problem of adjusting their behavior.

Finally, they ask whether the results of their plan have changed what they do not know (i.e., whether they have met their learning goal) and have satisfied what they want to know (i.e., whether they have met their need). If they have met their learning goals and satisfied their needs, they are finished directing their own learning for this topic. However, if they did not meet their learning goals, they repeat the second problem episode by constructing another plan. If they met their learning goals but not their learning needs, they repeat the three-part problem-solving sequence again, and they persist in this process of setting learning goals, constructing learning plans, and adjusting their behavior until they fully know what they want to know.

Implementing the
Self-Determined Learning Model of Instruction

As can be seen in Tables 1–3, the Self-Determined Learning Model of Instruction is described by providing 1) *student questions*, derived from the questions discussed previously; 2) *teacher objectives*; and 3) *instructional strategies* that can be used by teachers. The model is based on a universal problem-

Table 1.   Self-Determined Learning Model of Instruction, Phase 1: Setting a learning goal

Student questions	Teacher objectives	Instruction strategies
• What do I want to learn? • What do I know about it now? • What must change to learn what I do not know? • What can I do to produce that change?	• Enable student to identify specific strengths (capabilities) and instructional needs in a specific area. • Enable student to evaluate and communicate preferences, interests, beliefs, and values that relate to this area. • Assist student to gather information about opportunities and barriers in physical and social environments. • Enable student to decide if action will be focused toward individual capacity building, physical/social environment modification, or both. • Teach student to prioritize needs. • Support student in choosing a need to address from a prioritized list. • Teach student to state a goal and identify criteria for achieving that goal.	• Student self-assessment of interests, abilities, and instructional needs • Nondirective teaching model • Awareness training • Choice-making instruction • Problem-solving instruction • Decision-making instruction • Goal-setting instruction

Table 2.   Self-Determined Learning Model of Instruction, Phase 2: Constructing a learning plan

Student questions	Teacher objectives	Instruction strategies
• What can I do now to change what I do not know? • What will prevent me from taking action now to produce that change? • What can I do to remove these obstacles? • When will I take action and remove these obstacles?	• Enable student to self-evaluate progress toward goal achievement. • Enable student to determine plan of action to bridge gap between self-evaluated current status and self-identified goal status. • Collaborate with student to identify most appropriate instruction strategies. • Enable student to self-evaluate barriers and obstacles to implementing an action plan. • Enable student to identify and implement strategies to overcome barriers and obstacles. • Teach student the needed student-directed learning strategies. • Support student to implement student-directed learning strategies. • Provide mutually agreed-on teacher-directed instruction. • Enable student to determine schedule for action plan. • Enable student to self-monitor progress on implementing action plan (not evaluating success of plan).	• Self-scheduling • Self-instruction • Antecedent cue regulation • Choice-making instruction • Goal attainment strategies • Problem-solving instruction • Decision-making instruction • Self-advocacy instruction • Assertiveness training • Communication skills training • Self-monitoring

Table 3. Self-Determined Learning Model of Instruction, Phase 3: Adjusting behaviors

Student questions	Teacher objectives	Instruction strategies
• What actions have I taken? • What obstacles have been removed? • What has changed about what I do not know? • Do I know what I want to know?	• Enable student to self-evaluate progress toward goal achievement. • Collaborate with student to compare progress with desired outcomes. • Enable student to decide if progress is adequate, inadequate, or if goal has been achieved. • Support student to reevaluate goal if progress is insufficient. • Assist student in deciding if goal remains the same or changes. • Collaborate with student to identify if action plan is adequate or inadequate given revised or retained goal. • Assist student to change action plan if necessary. • Enable student to determine if he or she has met goal criterion or if there is more work to complete.	• Self-evaluation strategies • Goal setting • Choice-making instruction • Problem-solving instruction • Decision-making instruction • Goal-setting instruction

solving strategy and can be applied to a large number of instructional content areas. The basic flow of instruction for the model is depicted in Figure 2. As depicted in Figure 2, the model consists of three primary phases. In each phase, the student is the primary agent for choices, decisions, and actions, even when actions are teacher directed.

Phase 1: Setting a Learning Goal

The purpose of the first phase of the Self-Determined Learning Model of Instruction is to enable students to set a goal based on an understanding of their interests, preferences, and needs; their opportunities to learn or practice skills

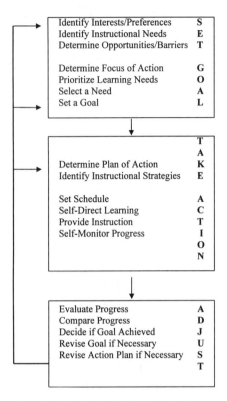

Identify Interests/Preferences	S
Identify Instructional Needs	E
Determine Opportunities/Barriers	T
Determine Focus of Action	G
Prioritize Learning Needs	O
Select a Need	A
Set a Goal	L

	T
	A
Determine Plan of Action	K
Identify Instructional Strategies	E
Set Schedule	A
Self-Direct Learning	C
Provide Instruction	T
Self-Monitor Progress	I
	O
	N

Evaluate Progress	A
Compare Progress	D
Decide if Goal Achieved	J
Revise Goal if Necessary	U
Revise Action Plan if Necessary	S
	T

Figure 2.   Flowchart of Self-Determined Learning Model of Instruction.

in a given area; and the priority of this goal when compared with their other educational needs. Such a process enables students and teachers to generate goals that are based on student preferences and interests and that take into account students' needs.

Student Questions   Across all phases of the model, student questions serve to communicate to both the student and his or her teacher what will result from the process. The questions are written as self-instruction statements and enable students to self-direct learning to the greatest possible extent. Self-instruction is a self-management strategy that has been shown to be effective across multiple domains and instructional areas and with a wide range of students. Chapter 16 provides detailed information about self-instruction statements, including research supporting their efficacy and usefulness, and thus this topic is not discussed further in this chapter.

In the first phase, student questions focus on students by identifying what they do well and where they need assistance and by stating their interests and preferences. Students then change from evaluating their capacity to evaluating the opportunities that they have to learn or perform the behavior. This recognizes that instructional needs not only are student based but also involve environmental modifications. There is considerable evidence that the environments in which students with disabilities live, learn, work, and play do not support but in fact hinder self-determination (Brotherson, Cook, Cunconan-Lahr, & Wehmeyer, 1995; Cook, Brotherson, Weigel-Garrey, & Mize, 1996; Wehmeyer, Kelchner, & Richards, 1996). Brotherson and colleagues (1995) identified ways in which the environments of children have an impact on self-determination. They noted that interaction with the physical environment is a critical way in which children acquire and develop self-determination skills and establish beliefs about themselves and their impact on the world that enable them to act in a self-determined manner. They stressed the importance of modifying environments to ensure that children have frequent opportunities to make choices about what they wear and the activities in which they engage. There are numerous features of any environment that can either support or hinder the development and expression of self-determination, including "signage, circulation pathways, storage placement and height, furnishings and equipment selection, and room arrangement" (Brotherson et al., 1995, p. 5).

Brotherson and colleagues identified actions in home, school, and community environments that can promote self-determination, suggesting that actions in the home should

- Give children a sense of control in their home environment
- Expand daily activities to encourage independence and choice
- Balance the need for protections/safety with risk taking and decision making
- Offer suggestions to schools regarding accommodations to meet child's need
- Expand accessible housing and supported living options in the community
- Provide families a greater voice in retrofitting communities
- Support children with disabilities to voice their choices (1995, p. 11)

Brotherson et al. also offered the following suggestions with regard to school-related activities:

- Teach choice, decision-making, and self-advocacy skills
- Structure school environment to ensure opportunities for choice
- Serve as a resource for both home and community environments
- Be advocates for community change and support parent advocacy
- Support community in accommodating to the needs of children
- Build partnerships with business and community leaders (1995, p. 11)

Futhermore, community-related activities that Brotherson et al. suggested to build self-determination across multiple environments included

- Retrofitting community to accommodate children with disabilities
- Providing accessible stores, theaters, offices, and community programs
- Educating community planners, architects, designers, and developers
- Expanding housing options in the community
- Supporting landlords and builders to create supported living options in the community
- Working with schools and vocational rehabilitation to expand employment opportunities (1995, p. 11)

These suggestions were forwarded to promote an awareness of the role of multiple environments in promoting self-determination. Unfortunately, the limited data that exist indicate that, too frequently, these environments do not support self-determination. For example, Cook and colleagues (1996) found that despite the fact that family members viewed self-determination as an important long-term goal for their sons or daughters with disabilities, the home environment was often not organized in a manner to support this outcome and instead promoted dependency. A survey of home environments found that children had limited access to their clothing and limited choices about clothes selection, often because drawers were too high or too heavy and not because the parents restricted access. Assistive technology, including wheelchairs, that increased student autonomy often were not available in the home. In some cases, the family could not afford a second wheelchair and had to keep the first one at school. In other cases, the house was not wheelchair accessible (e.g., carpet too deep, doors not wide enough) or the family was concerned about damage to the house from the wheelchair. No such data exist to evaluate school environments; but it seems likely that, just as in homes, many classrooms are arranged in such a manner as to limit student access to materials and to hinder opportunities to make choices and learn self-determination.

The physical environment is not, however, the only barrier to self-determination that students need to consider when examining external factors. There are also social barriers that create an atmosphere in which student self-determination is suppressed. Such barriers include the attitudes and beliefs of teachers and other school personnel and opportunities, or the lack thereof, to interact with peers with and peers without disabilities. Chapter 2 provides evidence that student variables related to time spent with peers without disabilities in the general education classroom were significant predictors of student self-determination. Wehmeyer, Kelchner, and Richards (1996) found that students with mental retardation were more likely than their peers without disabilities to perceive their classroom environment as highly controlling. Houghton, Bronicki, and Guess (1987) determined that classroom staff responded at very low rates to student-initiated expressions of preference or choice during the school day. In short, students need to be supported not only to identify any instructional needs that they might have related to skills capacity building but also to explore their physical and social environments to determine whether those environments should be the focus of intervention.

After students evaluate their current capacity and opportunity to do the skill or learn the concept, they prioritize the need for such action with other needs that arise through the process. Finally, the student develops a goal to meet the need.

Teacher Objectives   Teacher objectives are just that, the objectives that a teacher tries to accomplish. In each phase, the objectives are based on student questions. These objectives can be met by using strategies provided in the following section of the model. In Phase 1, the primary objectives of the teacher are to enable students to identify their own strengths and instructional needs; to assist students in gathering information about their environment and coming to a decision about the opportunities they have to learn and practice the given skill; to enable students to communicate their preferences, interests, beliefs, and values; to enable students to decide whether any instruction will focus on capacity building or environmental modification (or both); to teach and enable students to prioritize their needs; to support students in choosing a need from that list; and to teach students to state a goal and identify criteria for the achievement of that goal.

Instruction Strategies   Teachers can use instruction strategies to achieve teacher objectives and to enable students to achieve the outcomes listed. For Phase 1, such strategies include the use of awareness training, choice-making instruction, problem-solving and decision-making strategies, and goal-setting instruction. The model draws heavily on self-management and student-directed learning strategies to enable students to learn skills. Many such strategies are discussed in Chapters 16 and 17 and in other resources (e.g., Agran, 1997). As discussed briefly in Chapter 1, student-directed learning strategies involve the student as the primary change agent in the educational process. Agran suggested that student-directed learning "involves the students' use of one or more instructional strategies that allows them to plan, perform, or monitor a learning task" (1997, p. 4). According to Agran (1997), such strategies have been shown to have educational efficacy and have the added benefit of saving teachers' time and promoting generalization. Strategies typically employed include

1. Self-instruction strategies
   a. Overt verbalizations
   b. Covert instructions
2. Self-scheduling strategies
3. Self-monitoring strategies
   a. Self-observation
   b. Self-recording
   c. Self-evaluation
   d. Graphing or charting

4. Self-reinforcement strategies
   a. Self-determination of reinforcers
   b. Self-delivery of consequences
5. Self-managed antecedent cues
   a. Visual cues
   b. Sequencing of tasks
   c. Scheduling
6. Goal-setting strategies
7. Problem-solving strategies
8. Decision-making strategies
9. Choice-making strategies

These strategies are used across all phases, and, in some cases, the same strategy can be employed in multiple phases.

Phase 2: Constructing a Learning Plan

The second phase of the Self-Determined Learning Model of Instruction focuses on enabling the student to use self-directed learning strategies to achieve the goal identified and articulated in Phase 1.

   Student Objectives   Students begin the student objectives phase by creating an action plan that enables them to bridge the gap between their current status and their goal status. Students work collaboratively with the teacher to create and implement this plan of action. As students work through the plan, they perform periodic checks to ensure that they are on track (i.e., sticking to their plan).

   Teacher Objectives   In Phase 2, teachers are challenged to enable the student to perform many of the activities that were previously teacher directed. Using a host of student-directed learning strategies, teachers work to enable students to build a plan of action; identify appropriate and effective instructional strategies; and schedule and implement the action plan, provide direct instruction when necessary, and enable students to self-monitor their progress in implementing the plan.

   Instruction Strategies   The instruction strategies in Phase 2 are primarily student-directed learning strategies from the self-management and self-regulation literature. These include self-scheduling, self-instruction, antecedent cue regulation, problem solving, and self-monitoring. Using such strategies, teachers can enable most students to self-direct learning. In addition, teachers may employ self-advocacy instruction, assertiveness training, or communication skills training. Several strategies are applicable in all phases, including choice-making instruction or decision-making instruction.

Phase 3: Adjusting Behaviors

One of the unique aspects of both the Adaptability Instruction Model and the Self-Determined Learning Model of Instruction is the inclusion of a means of adjusting one's actions or goals to achieve outcomes. Adjustment is key to self-regulation, yet many instructional models do not include an adjustment component. In this phase, students examine their progress toward achieving their goals and determine whether they have met their goals, need to change their goals, or need to change their action plans.

Student Objectives   Students examine what may have changed in their situation based on the action they took toward achieving their goal. They compare such changes to see if they are closer or further away from the goal and decide whether they need to change their goal or their plan. There are several courses of action from this point, including deciding that the goal has been met and ending instruction; deciding that the goal has not been met but that progress is sufficient and returning to the action plan; deciding that the goal has not been met and needs to be rewritten; or deciding that the goal has not been met but is fine and that a new action plan is needed.

Teacher Objectives   Teachers work to enable students to self-evaluate their progress, to compare their progress with their desired outcomes, and to determine which course of action to follow based on these comparisons.

Instruction Strategies   Strategies important to this phase include self-evaluation strategies, goal attainment strategies, choice- and decision-making strategies, and problem solving.

USING THE SELF-DETERMINED
LEARNING MODEL OF INSTRUCTION

Using this model to teach students to direct their own learning requires a substantially different perspective on instruction than that to which we are accustomed or what we may have experienced as teachers or as students in elementary and secondary schools. The reason this approach is different is that its goal is to engage students in their own learning by provoking them to solve their learning problems. Table 1 identifies the three types of problem solving that the model directs us to encourage. The model directs us to provoke students 1) to solve the problem of setting their own goal to change what they do not know, 2) to solve the problem of planning how they will learn what they do not know, and 3) to solve the problem of adjusting their own behavior to match their plan to learn what they do not know. When we are successful in getting students to solve these three problems, we have provoked them to learn on their own. We have arranged conditions to motivate students to discover for themselves what will satisfy their own need to know that which they do not currently know. When we have helped students in this way, we have encouraged them to be self-determined learners.

This is how the model of instruction is different from those designed to direct students to produce x or y learning outcome. Self-determined learning focuses on helping students to solve their own problems of knowing what to learn, how to construct a strategy to learn it, and how to manage behaviors to follow that strategy for learning. Consequently, its success depends on student engagement in these problem-solving activities. This method of teaching has engaged them to learn on their own because they want to know something they do not currently know or they want to know how to do something that they cannot do.

With this model of teaching, success is less a function of who the teacher is or what the teacher does than a function of the type of problem in which the student engages while learning new information and skills. The marker of success of the Self-Determined Learning Model of Instruction is engagement in self-directed learning; it is not the use of a particular methodology or procedure that singularly promises an x, y, or z outcome. Consequently, what works to produce engagement for one student may be less teacher assistance than what will produce the same level of engagement for another student. Moreover, the engagement produced by these different tactics has less to do with the student's ability than with the student's interest in and need to know that which he or she does not know.

Although there is obviously no single formula that engages students to solve their learning problems, there is a guiding principle to use in provoking engagement in problem solving for learning. This is the *discrepancy condition*—the difference between wanting to know something and knowing something. When we present this circumstance so that students understand the difference between what they want to know and what they actually know, this recognition of what they do not know will motivate them to change it. It will provoke them into problem solving for self-determined learning.

It is important to keep in mind that the Self-Determined Learning Model of Instruction is not a curriculum or a program. It is a model of instruction or teaching that can be used by teachers to develop curricular materials, to identify and develop effective instructional strategies, and to drive other instructional activities. The following examples from the lead author's work with teachers to promote self-regulated learning illustrate two different approaches to constructing the discrepancy conditions to promote self-determined learning. Both examples served as real-world tests of issues pertaining to self-directed and self-determined learning as we developed the model. Although neither example used the exact phases described in the Self-Determined Learning Model of Instruction, teachers who want to apply this model to their situations may find it useful to explore how other teachers have structured the classroom experience to achieve a similar outcome.

In the first example, a dissertation study conducted by DeRobertis (1997), 50 secondary school students from ethnically diverse backgrounds who were enrolled in a special education program in New York City were provoked into solving the problem of not knowing how successful people get what they need and want in life. In the process of finding out what they did not know about how people succeed, these students learned how to meet their own goals. In the second example, a dissertation study conducted by Mithaug (1998), six elementary school special education students from ethnically diverse backgrounds who were enrolled in a New York City school were provoked into learning how to solve the problem of not knowing how to plan or to follow through on their plans for independent learning. These students learned a set of self-determined planning skills that solved the problem of not knowing how to decide what to do during unsupervised periods of independent work. In both examples, students were provoked into solving problems of learning something that they wanted to know. This discrepancy condition provoked them to solve these problems and, in the process, engaged them as self-determined learners. Details of these two studies are discussed in the next two sections.

An Example of Self-Determined
Learning at the Secondary School–Age Level

DeRobertis (1997) provided self-determined learning instruction to 50 students during a period of several months. Her general approach included an introduction to self-determined learning that provoked student interest in the process, followed by three problem-solving phases that taught goal setting, planning, and adjusting. In the introduction, DeRobertis (1997) discussed the problem of not knowing how successful people meet their goals. During the next three phases of instruction, she presented problems of not knowing how to choose goals, not knowing how to construct a plan to meet goals, and not knowing how to adjust behaviors to act on a plan. Throughout these teaching sessions, DeRobertis (1997) presented problems as discrepancies between what the students wanted to know and what they already knew. Then she led various types of group discussions while helping students to construct their own solutions to solve those problems and eliminate the discrepancies.

During the introductory sessions, DeRobertis (1997) constructed a discrepancy condition by presenting stories of famous people whom the students admired. She provided descriptions of famous people at the peak of their careers and during their high school years before they became successful. She described the early failures they experienced, which posed a discrepancy problem that engaged the students who *wanted to know* how these people got from high school, a time when they were not widely known, to be where they are, with everyone knowing them. Solving this problem led to discussions of the goals–plans–actions strategies that successful people use to get what they need and want in life.

During goal-setting sessions, she asked students to identify what they wanted compared with what they had. Some students said they wanted money; others said that to get money, one needs a job; and others said to get a job, one needs to be able to read. These means–ends problem-solving discussions helped students to identify a goal that would move them from their current state of not knowing how to "get money" to a goal state of knowing how to earn it. If they improved their grades, they reasoned, they would earn more money by getting a better job.

During planning sessions, DeRobertis (1997) presented another discrepancy condition—the difference between the activities in which students usually engage during school and the activities likely to produce good grades. She introduced this problem by asking what students can do to get good grades. During brainstorming sessions, students generated possibilities and then considered the likely consequences of each. Then they selected one that was best for them. This selection was their plan to improve their grades.

During adjustment sessions, DeRobertis (1997) introduced a self-monitoring method that students could use to define their own discrepancies between their plans to improve their grades and actions taken on those plans. She showed them how to monitor their own behaviors by recording when they would study, for how long, and how they were going to adjust their plans when they discovered a discrepancy between their plan of action on a particular day and what they actually did.

Evaluation of the effects of the program indicated that mean levels of self-determination increased significantly between pre- and posttest measures of students' own reports of goal-setting, planning, and adjustment skills and between pre- and posttest measures of teachers' assessments of those skills. Self-determination assessments of a comparison group of 27 students at the same school who did not receive self-determined learning instruction did not show significant gains between pre- and posttest measures. Finally, teachers also reported to DeRobertis that her students were engaged in pursuing their goals outside of her class. For example, some students requested increased amounts of assigned homework.

An Example of Self-Determined Learning at the Elementary School–Age Level

Mithaug (1998) focused on provoking elementary school–age students to solve two of the three problems of self-determined learning, how to plan what to do, and how to adjust behavior based on that plan. The purpose of this study was to increase students' engagement in self-directed learning during unsupervised periods in the afternoon, when there were no consequences for not working. The six children who participated in the study were 6–8 years of age, and they spent an average of 56% of their time engaged in independent work during those unsupervised periods during the afternoon.

Following 4 weeks of baseline, the students received self-management instruction during daily morning sessions. Instruction was delivered in a multiple-baseline schedule, with the first two students receiving the instructional package first, the second two students receiving the package several weeks later, and the third group of two students receiving the package several weeks after that. Two weeks after instruction commenced for the last group, instruction on the three skills was discontinued during the daily morning sessions. Throughout the study, students were free to use their self-management skills to complete their assignment folder during daily 20-minute unsupervised work sessions in the afternoon.

The instructional package was divided into two parts. During the teacher choice part, Mithaug (1998) sat with each student and completed the self-planning sheet for the student. She assigned each student subjects on which to work by circling the picture of the subject area on the assignment sheet. The sheet displayed a picture for math, a picture for reading, a picture for science, and a picture for social studies. Next, she printed the number of tasks the student was to complete during that morning work session. After the student completed that work, Mithaug sat with the student again and completed the record sheet by printing the number of assignments that the student completed for each subject assigned and then circling "yes" on the record sheet if the student had completed exactly the number of tasks that were assigned or "no" if the student had completed more or less than the assigned number. At the end of the session, the student selected a prize from a reward bag for every "yes" circled on the record sheet.

The same record sheet was used during the student choice procedure, which was introduced several weeks after the teacher choice procedure. During student choice, Mithaug (1998) gave the students the self-planning sheet and instructed them to 1) circle the subjects on which they wanted to work, 2) record the number of tasks they planned to complete for each subject they chose, 3) complete their self-assigned tasks, 4) record the number of tasks that they actually completed after finishing their work, and 5) circle "yes" or "no" for each subject to indicate whether they had done exactly what they planned to do for that subject. At the end of the morning session, students selected a prize from a reward bag for each "yes" correctly circled on their self-planning sheets.

All instruction took place in the morning, and all unsupervised independent work occurred in the afternoon. During the afternoon sessions, students sat at their assigned workstations, where their work, assignment folders, and planning sheet were located. They were free to work as they wished. They received no approval or disapproval for their behavior or for their work, nor did they receive any prizes for tasks completed. Mithaug (1998) used a momentary time-sampling procedure to record students' on-task behavior during those sessions. She also collected the student folders and their work to determine their use of the self-planning sheet to assign themselves work and to record and evaluate work completed.

Results indicated that students increased their engagement in self-directed learning during the unsupervised periods in the afternoon as a result of the instruction they received during the morning sessions. During the baseline periods, the amount of time spent on task during unsupervised periods was 56% for all six students. During the last week of the morning training sessions, the amount of time spent on task increased to 96%. When the morning instruction was discontinued, the amount of time spent on task during afternoon sessions decreased to 67%. It was clear that encouraging students to manage their own work in the morning increased their self-directed engagement in the afternoon. Data on the use of these skills during unsupervised periods also reflected this dramatic change. During the baseline period, the average percentage of the sessions in which the students performed the four self-planning skills correctly was 0%; during the last week of instruction, the percentage of correct use of self-planning skills was 95%. When instruction was discontinued in the morning, the students' use of these self-planning skills during afternoon unsupervised work periods decreased to 39%.

Solving the Discrepancy Problem

The DeRobertis (1997) and Mithaug (1998) studies illustrated how two very different instructional approaches increased student engagement in problem solving for self-determined learning. The DeRobertis study employed various methods of group discussion to encourage secondary school students with disabilities to solve all three types of problems of self-determined learning—setting a goal, constructing a plan, and adjusting behaviors to match that plan. The Mithaug study, in contrast, employed direct instruction to encourage elementary school–age students to solve two of the self-determined learning problems: constructing a plan and adjusting behaviors to match that plan. Both approaches increased engagement in self-determined learning, the ultimate objective of the Self-Determined Learning Model of Instruction. Students in the DeRobertis study were engaged in discussions about how to set goals, make plans, and adjust their behaviors, and this engagement extended beyond those class sessions. Students in the Mithaug study were engaged during morning instructional sessions with the teacher present and then during unsupervised sessions in which they were free to work on and use their self-determined planning skills as they pleased.

Also, both methods of instruction produced new learning. Students in the DeRobertis (1997) study increased their knowledge and use of self-determination strategies as evidenced by written answers to the six questions of self-determination discussed earlier in the chapter: What do I need and want? What is my goal? What is my plan? What are my actions? What will be my results? How can I plan better next time? Students in the Mithaug (1998) study learned the self-determined planning skills of choosing subjects and tasks to complete, the self-evaluation skills of recording what they did and determining whether they met their plan, and the self-adjustment skills of increasing the correspondence between their plans and their actions over time.

Finally, and most important, both studies provoked students to solve discrepancy problems. DeRobertis (1997) encouraged group discussions that revealed discrepancies between what students expected and their actual situations. Mithaug (1998) taught students to use a self-determined planning sheet that revealed their own discrepancy problems, which occurred when students assigned themselves subjects and tasks that they did not complete. The sheet allowed them to compare what they did with what they planned to do. Moreover, the only way they could resolve those discrepancies was to change the noes to yeses. This was possible the next day, when they made new plans and took new actions. Over the course of the study, students improved this correspondence. They adjusted their behaviors to match their plans during unsupervised sessions in the afternoons.

THE OPTIMAL CHALLENGE: WHY CHOICE MOTIVATES

There are several strong arguments in favor of adopting the Self-Determined Learning Model of Instruction to guide the approach to teaching *all* children and youth, both students with and without disabilities. One argument is that it encourages students to think and act on their own, which is important if they are to take charge of their lives after they leave school. Another argument is that giving students a say in their own learning means giving them a choice, which is good in itself. Because freedom of choice is a founding value of the United States, the more that opportunities for choice can be expanded, the more often children and youth will experience what it means to be free to think and act according to one's own needs and interests. This circumstance is consistent with any educational goal in the United States. Applying this reasoning in reverse, it can be argued that denying choice without good reason is equally undesirable and perhaps even wrong. Unless we can demonstrate that limiting opportunities to choose is in a child's long-term best interest, we should not do so.

A third argument for considering choice making as fundamental to the sound education of all children is that the opportunity to choose is often intrinsically rewarding in the sense that it motivates students to act on their own. A growing body of research describes this intuitive sense that acting on circumstances people have selected to change is more enjoyable for them than acting on circumstances that another person has decided they should change. It may well be that the mere act of choosing is reinforcing in some fundamental sense. A moment's reflection suggests why this might be so. When we have a choice, we are free to set our own expectations for what we can accomplish. When we add to this opportunity extensive experience in setting expectations for that circumstance, we know what is reasonable for us to accomplish in that situation. We know what expectations are just beyond what we have achieved in the past and thus that we have a good chance of meeting them. In other words, when we have experience in making choices and are free to do so, we can judge that just-right distance between where we are and what we want that offers the right amount of risk to motivate us to act. The just-right challenge engages our minds and motivates us to act to produce the most pleasurable experience of being in control of our circumstances.

Moreover, when we have frequent experiences of this nature, we experience cycles of self-regulated problem solving that accumulate these experiences of control and empowerment. In the language of problem solving, the individual sets expectations that are just right, chooses the best option from those available, acts on that option with her best performance, and produces results that he or she expects. Moreover, the positive experience of one self-regulation episode affects the next, enabling a

> person to repeat the cycle, each time being encouraged to repeat the previous success by setting slightly higher expectations that provide the just-right challenge to motivate her to enhance her capacity further. She feels empowered and perfectly matched with the opportunity [in which] she is engaged. (Mithaug, 1996a, pp. 74–75)

Csikszentmihalyi called this experience the *optimal experience flow*:

> The optimal state of inner experience is one in which there is *order in consciousness*. This happens when psychic energy—or attention—is invested in realistic goals, and when skills match the opportunities for action. The pursuit of a goal brings order in awareness because a person must concentrate attention on the task at hand and momentarily forget everything else. These periods of struggling to overcome challenges are what people find to be the most enjoyable times of their lives. . . . A person who has achieved control over psychic energy and has invested it in consciously chosen goals cannot help but grow into a more complex being. By stretching skills, by reaching toward higher challenges, such a person becomes an increasingly extraordinary individual. (1990, p. 6)

The problem with traditional methods of instruction is that they prevent students from making choices that give them this sense of control over their own learning. Consequently, they never become self-determined learners, and they never experience the feeling of empowerment and fulfillment that comes from this type of learning. Mithaug (1996b) argued that knowing how to solve the types of problems that affect goal attainment is what distinguishes students who are self-determined from students who are not. Students who are self-determined

> fulfill their potential by setting expectations slightly higher than they think they are capable of achieving and then choosing behaviors and strategies that produce results that match those expectations. . . . Students who do not act in

self-determined ways do not know how to conduct means–ends problem solving to get what they want at school or in other areas of their lives. Their deficits in ends management show up when 1) they fail to set goals; 2) they have set goals, but have failed to select standards for judging when they have met those goals; or 3) they fail to specify their expectations for producing incremental gain toward goal attainment. Their deficits in means management show up when they fail to 1) consider different options and then choose the most profitable one for producing incremental gain, 2) produce results that move them toward their goals, or 3) compare results of their choices with their expectations for incremental gain and then adjust subsequent choices and performances accordingly. Lacking both sets of skills and experiences, they have little chance of connecting a given end [i.e., goal] with an available mean [i.e., plan of action] successfully. As a consequence, they depend upon others to not only set goals for them but to tell them what strategies to use to reach those goals as well. (Mithaug, 1996b, pp. 148–149)

The Self-Determined Learning Model of Instruction challenges teachers to establish the motivational condition that provokes this type of self-regulated problem solving: the discrepancy between what the student wants to know and what the student knows. When students recognize this condition and when they have experience in setting their own expectations, making choices, and then taking action to reduce the feeling of dissatisfaction produced by this discrepancy condition, they engage themselves in determining the content and direction of their own learning. Then they will be self-determined learners.

REFERENCES

Agran, M. (1997). *Student-directed learning: Teaching self-determination skills.* Pacific Grove, CA: Brooks/Cole.

Agran, M., & Martin, J.E. (1987). Applying a technology of self-control in community environments for individuals who are mentally retarded. In M. Hersen, R.M. Eisler, & P.M. Miller (Eds.), *Progress in behavior modification* (pp. 108–151). Beverly Hills: Sage Publications.

Bandura, A. (1986). *Social foundations of thought and action: A social cognitive theory.* Englewood Cliffs, NJ: Prentice-Hall.

Brotherson, M.J., Cook, C.C., Cunconan-Lahr, R., & Wehmeyer, M.L. (1995). Policy supporting self-determination in the environments of persons with disabilities. *Education and Training in Mental Retardation and Developmental Disabilities, 30,* 3–14.

Cook, C.C., Brotherson, M.J., Weigel-Garrey, C., & Mize, I. (1996). Homes to support the self-determination of children. In D.J. Sands & M.L. Wehmeyer (Eds.), *Self-determination across the life span: Independence and choice for people with disabilities* (pp. 91–110). Baltimore: Paul H. Brookes Publishing Co.

Csikszentmihalyi, M. (1990). *Flow: The psychology of optimal experience.* New York: Harper & Row.

DeRobertis, M. (1997). *The effects of problem-solving instruction on the self-determination of high school students with mild disabilities.* Unpublished doctoral dissertation, Teachers College, Columbia University, New York.

Hill, N. (1960). *Think and grow rich.* New York: Fawcett Crest. (Original work published 1939)

Houghton, J., Bronicki, G.J.B., & Guess, D. (1987). Opportunities to express preferences and make choices among students with severe disabilities in classroom settings. *Journal of The Association for Persons with Severe Handicaps, 10,* 79–86.

Joyce, B., & Weil, M. (1980). *Models of teaching* (2nd ed.). Englewood Cliffs, NJ: Prentice-Hall.

Kanfer, F.H., & Goldstein, A.P. (1986). *Helping people change: A textbook of methods* (3rd ed.). New York: Pergamon Press.

Martin, J.E., Burger, D.L., Elias-Burger, S., & Mithaug, D.E. (1988). Applications of self-control strategies to facilitate independence in vocational and instructional settings. In N. Bray (Ed.), *International review of research in mental retardation* (pp. 155–193). San Diego: Academic Press.

Mithaug, D.E. (1991). *Self-determined kids: Raising satisfied and successful children.* San Francisco: Lexington Books.

Mithaug, D.E. (1993). *Self-regulation theory: How optimal adjustment maximizes gain.* Westport, CT: Praeger.

Mithaug, D.E. (1996a). *Equal opportunity theory.* Thousand Oaks, CA: Sage Publications.

Mithaug, D.E. (1996b). The optimal prospects principle: A theoretical basis for rethinking instructional practices for self-determination. In D.J. Sands & M.L. Wehmeyer (Eds.), *Self-determination across the life span: Independence and choice for people with disabilities* (pp. 147–165). Baltimore: Paul H. Brookes Publishing Co.

Mithaug, D.E., Martin, J.E., & Agran, M. (1987). Adaptability instruction: The goal of transitional programming. *Exceptional Children, 53,* 500–505.

Mithaug, D.E., Martin, J.E., Agran, M., & Rusch, F.R. (1988). *Why special education graduates fail: How to teach them to succeed.* Colorado Springs, CO: Ascent.

Mithaug, D.K. (1998). *The effects of instruction on the levels of independence and self-determination in young children with disabilities.* Unpublished doctoral dissertation, Teachers College, Columbia University, New York.

Newell, A., & Simon, H.H. (1972). *Human problem solving.* Englewood Cliffs, NJ: Prentice-Hall.

Simon, H.A. (1989). *Models of thought.* New Haven, CT: Yale University Press.

Wehmeyer, M.L., Kelchner, K., & Richards, S. (1996). Essential characteristics of self-determined behaviors of adults with mental retardation and developmental disabilities. *American Journal on Mental Retardation, 100,* 632–642.

Wolman, J., Campeau, P.L., DuBois, P.A., Mithaug, D.E., & Stolarski, V.S. (1994). *AIR self-determination scale and user guide.* Palo Alto, CA: American Institutes for Research.

16

Self-Management and Self-Instruction

The Benefits of Student Involvement in
Individualized Education Program Implementation

Carolyn Hughes and Judith A. Presley

A busy undergraduate student in biology retrieves her calendar from her backpack. As her professor announces the date for the midterm exam, she jots it down. With so many dates, tests, and assignments to remember for all her classes, she knows she will never keep them straight unless she puts them in her calendar. A first grader walks home from school for the first time without his mother. As he approaches the traffic light at an intersection, he tells himself what his mother has told him over and over, "Cross at the green, not in between," as he waits for the light to turn green to indicate that it is safe to cross the street. A high school student working as a waitress in a trendy Italian restaurant waits for a table of customers to motion to her that they are ready to order before she approaches their table. She has noticed that she gets bigger tips when she attends immediately to her customers' needs and does not hover around them while they eat. Although the situations and tasks vary across these scenarios, one similarity is that a self-management strategy is being used in each case to help guide the individual's performance. Writing a note to oneself, repeating a verbal instruction, and waiting for an environmental cue are all examples of self-management techniques that people may use to manage their own behavior when the assistance of others is not available. This chapter discusses the benefits of involving students in their own educational programming through the use of self-management and self-instruction strategies.

TRADITIONAL INSTRUCTION STRATEGIES

Using direct instruction methods, teachers and transition specialists have been successful at teaching high school students with disabilities myriad skills, including academic tasks (Gilbert, Williams, & McLaughlin, 1996), social skills (Minskoff & Demoss, 1994), packaging tasks (Smith, 1994), food preparation (Davis, Williams, Brady, & Burta, 1992), housekeeping and custodial tasks (Winking, O'Reilly, & Moon, 1993), laundry skills (Inge, Moon, & Parent, 1993), and safety skills (Agran, Fodor-Davis, Moore, & Martella, 1992). However, teachers have been less effective at teaching students strategies that they need to adapt and maintain their performance when conditions are different from those encountered during instruction (Rusch, Hughes, & Wilson, 1995). Failure to regulate their own behavior may limit students' employability when entering adult life (Kregel, Wehman, Revell, & Hill, 1990). For example, a high school student may not get a job if she fails to speak up at her job interview, or she may lose her job as an office custodian if she forgets to knock before entering offices to clean them.

Direct instructional methods (e.g., prompting, modeling, corrective feedback) represent a powerful technique for teaching acquisition of new skills. For example, Cuvo, Leaf, and Borakove (1978) used task analysis to teach secondary students with mental retardation to perform a series of 181 steps for cleaning high school restrooms. Used exclusively, however, direct instructional methods often fail to take into account the role of individual students in implementing and evaluating their own individualized education programs (IEPs). Unless responsibility for self-regulation and behavior change is assumed by students themselves, they are not likely to generalize and maintain newly acquired skills in the absence of their teachers, transition specialists, or job coaches (Hughes & Agran, 1993). At the same time, however, teachers and related services personnel typically assume responsibility for their students rather than teaching students strategies to direct their own behavior (Wehmeyer & Metzler, 1995). To be consistent with the Individuals with Disabilities Education Act (IDEA) of 1990 (PL 101-476), the Rehabilitation Act Amendments of 1992 (PL 102-569), and the Individuals with Disabilities Education Act Amendments of 1997 (PL 105-17), teachers should include students with disabilities as active participants in their IEPs. Lack of training in self-determination and self-management strategies and lack of opportunity to exercise personal choice may relate to the poor out-comes (e.g., economic dependence, disengagement, segregation) faced by many young adults as they leave their secondary special education programs (Wagner, 1995).

SELF-MANAGEMENT STRATEGIES

To address the shortcomings of traditional instructional methods, interven-tionists have recommended teaching students to use self-management strate-gies to increase their self-directed behavior and independent performance (Agran, 1997; Hughes & Scott, 1997; Whitman, 1987). Self-management can promote independent performance in the absence of a teacher or transi-tion specialist by allowing students to serve as their own change agents. When teachers instruct students to self-manage, students learn to generate the necessary responses to prompt and maintain their own desired behavior (Lagomarcino, Hughes, & Rusch, 1989). In using self-management, students apply to their own behavior the same behavior change strategies that teach-ers use to facilitate learning, such as positive reinforcement or antecedent cue regulation (Agran, 1997).

Definition of *Self-Management*

Two theoretical explanations of self-management as a strategy dominate the literature: 1) the operant conditioning explanation (e.g., Brigham, 1978; Skin-ner, 1953) and 2) the cognitive interpretation (e.g., Bandura, 1969; Kanfer, 1971). Skinner (1953) may have been the first theorist to propose an operant conditioning view of the self-management paradigm. He theorized that indi-viduals control their behavior as they would control the behavior of anyone else: through manipulation of the variables of which their own behavior is a function. For example, to avoid responding impulsively on a math test, a stu-dent could make the behavior less probable by altering functionally related variables (e.g., by reminding him- or herself to count to 3 before responding). Skinner's paradigm involved two separate responses: the *controlling re-sponse*, or the behavior that affects the variables (e.g., counting to 3) in such a way as to change the probability of the *controlled response*, or the behavior to be increased or decreased (e.g., responding impulsively) (Hughes & Lloyd, 1993). An individual's behavior ultimately is accounted for by environmental variables external to the individual (e.g., behavioral consequences) (Skinner, 1953). However, Kazdin (1978) suggested that individuals are in the best position to observe occurrences of their own behavior and administer conse-quences for their control.

The cognitive explanation of self-management suggests the occurrence of two steps: 1) the assessment of and decision to control one's behavior fol-lowed by 2) the actual self-controlling response (e.g., Bandura, 1969). Emphasis is placed on the first step, which is assumed to begin when individuals evaluate their own behavior and subsequently decide to change that behavior. For example, Premack (1970) argued that individuals' observations of deficiencies in their own performance and their resulting decision to address these deficiencies are the critical components of self-management. Bandura (1971) concurred that self-management is a process that begins with monitoring and evaluating one's behavior followed by reinforcing improvements in one's performance. For example, a student may infer from deteriorating grades that his or her study behavior is ineffective, prompting him or her to modify this behavior, which is reinforced ultimately by improved test scores.

According to the cognitive view of self-management, discrimination of one's behavior is followed by a decision to control or to change one's performance to achieve a self-determined outcome. Kanfer (1971) claimed that this decision resulted from individuals' observations of a discrepancy between their behavior and their self-established standard of performance. Similarly, Bandura argued that the

> selection of well-defined objectives . . . is an essential aspect of any self-directed program of change. The goals that individuals choose for themselves must be specified sufficiently . . . to provide adequate guidance for the actions that must be taken daily to attain desired outcomes. (1969, p. 255)

Goldfried and Merbaum concurred that self-management "represents a personal decision arrived at through conscious deliberation for the purpose of integrating action which is designed to achieve certain desired outcomes or goals as determined by the individual himself" (1973, p. 12). They acknowledged that their viewpoint, as does Bandura's and Kanfer's, stresses

> the importance of mediating variables in dealing with the process of self-control. All of these [cognitive] conceptions lean heavily on the importance of thought and language in delaying impulsive action, and for introducing a competing cognitive alternative into the self-regulatory sequence. (Goldfried & Merbaum, 1973, p. 12)

Although there are differences between the operant and cognitive perspectives on self-management, they share characteristics (Hughes & Lloyd, 1993). Indeed, both views arose from a behavioral perspective rather than a psychoanalytic or nonempirical tradition. Furthermore, according to both views, self-management is not a trait. Whereas people might refer to general concepts such as willpower or other psychological qualities, neither the cognitive nor the operant view of self-management requires recourse to personality attributes. In addition, according to both views, individuals can be taught to acquire greater skill in exercising self-management strategies and directing their own behavior.

How to Teach Self-Management

According to the paradigm presented in this chapter, *self-management* refers to instances in which individuals control their own behavior by manipulating the variables of which their behavior is a function. In addition, the environment has been described as the ultimate source of behavioral control, a view that may seem to limit one's personal responsibility with respect to self-regulation (Skinner, 1971). A focus on the environmental influences on self-management processes, however, has the benefit of making these processes more amenable to educational influences because we can manipulate environmental variables. In this section, we discuss how to teach self-management.

Because investigators have analyzed the variables of which behavior is a function, it should be possible to teach individuals to manipulate variables that influence their own behavior (Skinner, 1953). Baer (1984) and Rachlin (1978) suggested that it is possible to make people more aware of the contingencies that are in effect in their lives by increasing the saliency of the antecedents and consequences of environmental events. For example, through the use of direct instructional principles such as prompting, modeling, practice, and corrective feedback, people have been taught to observe instances of their undesired behavior and the environmental consequences of their behavior (e.g., a student learns that his angry outbursts are causing his friends to avoid him). The use of recording devices such as golf shot counters, tally marks, or checklists may help to make these events and their consequences more salient to the individual. In addition, an individual's behavior initially may be brought into conformity with long-term consequences by using techniques such as 1) commitment strategies (e.g., arranging to receive a wake-up call to catch the bus on time for school; Rachlin, 1978), 2) rules and verbal behavior (e.g., raising one's hand before speaking in class, to avoid loss of privileges; Malott, 1984), or 3) antecedent cue regulation (e.g., eating only when sitting at a table, to avoid snacking between meals; Skinner, 1953).

Brigham (1978) proposed that, through direct instruction, individuals can be taught to analyze their environments to identify functional variables that influence their behavior. The next step, therefore, is to teach people to modify the variables that control the behavior they want to change. For example, a student who responds impulsively on written tests could be taught to monitor his or her behavior and the resulting frequency of errors it produces. He or she then could be taught to pause before responding by first identifying the key elements of each question before writing an answer. Brigham (1978) and Skinner (1953) suggested that, because many of the variables of which the target behavior is a function may be manipulated, many self-management strategies are available, and one can be chosen that is appropriate for a particular environmental context. The next section discusses effective applications of self-management strategies.

Types of Self-Management Strategies

Various taxonomies of self-management strategies have been proposed in the literature (e.g., Kanfer, 1970; Kazdin, 1984; Skinner, 1953). Four strategies have been particularly effective with secondary students with disabilities. These strategies are antecedent cue regulation (including picture prompts and self-scheduling), self-monitoring, self-reinforcement, and self-instruction (Lagomarcino et al., 1989). Briefly, *antecedent cue regulation* refers to arranging stimulus conditions to prompt the occurrence of a desired behavior. *Self-monitoring* involves individuals observing their own behavior and then systematically reporting or recording their performance. *Self-reinforcement* typically is used in combination with self-monitoring and provides an opportunity for individuals to reinforce their own behavior contingent on performance of a target behavior. *Self-instruction* teaches individuals to use their own verbal behavior to guide their performance. We next discuss specific applications of these strategies, with particular emphasis on the use of self-instruction.

Antecedent Cue Regulation   Applications of antecedent cue regulation are based on the principles of stimulus control and discrimination training. These principles imply that behavior can be controlled by antecedent stimuli that signal the probability that reinforcement will occur after the performance of a specific behavior. Discrimination training establishes an antecedent stimulus as a cue for the availability of a reinforcer, increasing the probability that a behavior will occur in the presence of the stimulus (Kazdin, 1978). Two antecedent cue regulation strategies that have been used effectively with individuals with disabilities are picture prompts and self-scheduling.

Picture prompts are visual cues that are prearranged to increase the likelihood of the occurrence of a desired behavior. Stromer, Mackay, Howell, McVay, and Flusser (1996) used picture prompts as antecedent cues to improve the spelling performance of students with mental retardation and hearing impairments. The students, who had delays in spelling, were taught to use computer-generated pictures of objects to prompt their independent performance on a series of computer, object manipulation, and handwritten spelling tasks. Findings indicated that the use of picture prompts resulted in increased accuracy and generalization of spelling performance across a variety of tasks.

Self-scheduling is a variation of antecedent cue regulation that allows individuals to independently select, schedule, and perform daily events. Bambara and Ager (1992) taught individuals with mental retardation who were living in the community to use self-scheduling to engage in daily leisure activities. Participants were taught to choose picture cards depicting leisure and recreational activities and then to place the cards in a sequenced activity book for each day of the week. Using the sequenced pictures as prompts, participants substantially increased the frequency and diversity of the self-directed leisure activities in which they engaged, and they maintained these increases over time.

Self-Monitoring   Self-monitoring, which involves the systematic observation and recording of one's own behavior, has been used extensively to modify a variety of behaviors such as social skills, academic skills, work performance, and independent living skills (see Chapter 17). Students typically are taught to self-monitor through direct instruction (Agran, 1997). For example, Maag, Reid, and DiGangi (1993) used modeling and verbal rehearsal to teach students with learning disabilities to monitor their rate, accuracy, and attention to task when completing mathematics worksheets. Students were taught to discriminate their behavior and record occurrences of target behaviors on recording sheets. Self-monitoring resulted in increases in target behaviors for the students when they were engaged in mathematics tasks in both general and special education classes.

Self-Reinforcement   Self-reinforcement consists of administering to oneself a reinforcer upon the occurrence of a target behavior (see Chapter 17). Self-reinforcement typically is used in combination with other self-management strategies such as self-monitoring or self-instruction. For example, Jackson and Altman (1996) used self-reinforcement in combination with self-monitoring and social skills training to decrease the aggressive behavior of a young man with mental retardation, mental illness, and a history of verbal and physical aggression. The young man was taught to complete a self-management schedule log in which half-hour periods were designated throughout a 16-hour day. Each half hour, the participant would reinforce targeted behaviors by recording and assigning himself points based on the occurrence of these targeted behaviors. The points were exchangeable for reinforcers such as privileges or activities. Implementation of the self-management program resulted in immediate and substantial decreases in the young man's verbal and physical aggression as well as increases in appropriate social interaction behavior.

Summary   We have briefly discussed applications of self-management strategies including antecedent cue regulation (e.g., picture prompts, self-scheduling), self-monitoring, self-reinforcement, and combinations of these strategies. The remainder of this chapter focuses in depth on applications of an additional self-management strategy, self-instruction, with secondary school students who have disabilities.

APPLICATIONS OF SELF-INSTRUCTION

Self-instruction is a powerful strategy that is available to teachers to help them support secondary school students in taking control of and directing their own lives. When students are taught self-instruction, they learn to use their own verbal behavior to guide their performance (Hughes & Agran, 1993). *Self-instruction* is a critical self-management strategy that contributes to an individual's self-determination skills.

Definition of *Self-Instruction*

How does self-instruction work? How does verbal behavior guide one's performance? For years, the field has speculated on the role of self-instruction in directing performance (Skinner, 1957; Whitman, 1990). Possibly, a self-delivered instruction acts as an antecedent cue that increases the probability that a targeted behavior will follow (Hughes, 1997). That is, an individual's self-instruction may be explained by a traditional behavioral paradigm in which an *antecedent* or environmental cue prompts an individual's *behavior* to occur, which is followed by a *consequence* that reinforces the behavior and makes it more likely to occur again (Skinner, 1957). In other words, a student may self-instruct by 1) stating a problem situation that serves as an antecedent, 2) stating a possible response, 3) performing that response or behavior, and 4) evaluating the response and verbally reinforcing him- or herself as a consequence.

For example, a high school student may be home alone after school and want to go to a movie with her friends. However, she may know that her grades have not been good and that she should get her homework done first. If the student had been taught to self-instruct, she could have first verbalized the problem (e.g., "I gotta do my homework first"), which may have served as a cue for an appropriate response (e.g., "I'm going to start it right now before I go anywhere"). As she began to work, the student could have evaluated her progress and reinforced herself (e.g., by saying, "Good. I'm getting my work done. Algebra's finished, and I'm ready to start on French"). In the preceding example, the verbal sequence appears to promote an individual's targeted responses by prompting performance and following the performance with consequences that are intended to strengthen and maintain the behavior.

Self-instruction also may serve as a self-regulation strategy in which language mediates behavior (Hughes & Agran, 1993; Whitman, 1987). Terms such as *cognitive processing* (Park & Gaylord-Ross, 1989), *verbal mediation* (Kanfer, 1971), and *correspondence training* (Crouch, Rusch, & Karlan, 1984) have been used to describe the process by which language may affect one's behavior. Bandura (1971) suggested that verbal mediation, language, and thought are critical variables in the self-regulation process. Similarly, Whitman (1990) argued that language is a tool that may be used to label, monitor, analyze, and control one's behavior.

For example, a high school vocational student may observe that he has already been late to his first period auto body class eight times in the first semester of his sophomore year. He knows that if he is late to class two more times, he will not get credit for the semester. The student realizes that being late would not be good, because if he does not pass all of his classes, he will not graduate and go to trade school. Consequently, he may decide that it is more important to pass his classes than to go to parties every night and wake up late as he has been doing all semester long. This decision may prompt him to decide to change his behavior. For example, the student could decide to get to bed every night by 11 P.M. He then could tell himself to set the alarm clock for 6 A.M. and get out of bed in the morning as soon as he hears it ring. When he gets to auto body class on time, he can congratulate himself and, in his notebook, keep track of how many times he has made it to class on time. As a result of his self-instruction program, the student might make it through the school year without being tardy again, and pass his auto body class. He might also observe how much more comfortable he is in class now that he knows what is going on and can participate without being afraid that he is doing something wrong.

Self-Instruction in Practice

In a general sense, *self-instruction* simply means that a person tells him- or herself to do something and then does it. This process would be infallible if one's motor performance were always under the control of one's verbal behavior. For example, if a student tells herself every morning that she will come home from school and complete her homework before hanging out with her friends, she might increase her likelihood of passing her classes for the semester if her behavior actually matched her verbal instructions. However, the process of self-instruction becomes less effective if verbal instructions have little influence over actual behavior. In this student's case, if, despite her self-instructions, she comes home, throws her books on the table, parties until 1 A.M. with her friends, and consequently wakes up late for school without getting her work done, her chances of passing her classes for the semester will likely be minimized.

Because people sometimes fail to use their verbal instructions effectively, the process of self-instruction may require systematic teaching. Direct instruction methods are often used to teach people to self-instruct. These methods typically include modeling, providing opportunities for practice, providing corrective feedback, and presenting reinforcement during brief instructional periods (e.g., one or two 2-hour sessions, four or five 30-minute sessions). Extended instruction time may be required for students with significant or multiple disabilities before they learn to self-instruct. For example, Hughes (1992) reported that one man with mental retardation in her study required twenty 30-minute training sessions to learn to self-instruct to solve task-related problems associated with completing household chores.

Meichenbaum and Goodman (1971) developed a sequence for teaching self-instruction that has become the prototype for many teaching applications.

Their sequence consisted of five steps, including 1) teacher performs task, instructing aloud while student observes; 2) student performs task while teacher instructs aloud; 3) student performs task while self-instructing aloud; 4) student performs task while whispering; and 5) student performs task while self-instructing covertly. Contemporary empirical investigations of Meichenbaum and Goodman's (1971) teaching sequence typically omit the final two steps because of research requirements for measuring self-instructions verbalized by individuals during observation of performance. Attempts are made by researchers to have individuals talk aloud as unobtrusively as possible, for example, in the presence of the researchers alone. When a functional relationship has been demonstrated between self-instructing and correct responding, students no longer are required to self-instruct overtly. The goal for teachers is to provide students with a powerful, self-regulating tool, but not to have students draw attention to themselves by using the tool in an obtrusive fashion, such as talking loudly.

Advantages of Self-Instruction

Self-instruction has potential as a valuable instruction strategy to promote self-determination. Most students can learn to use their verbal behavior to guide their own performance even when no one else is around; therefore, self-instruction may be an appropriate strategy to teach people to use when they are on their own, outside an instructional setting. Because one's verbal behavior is always available to him- or herself, self-instruction may allow people to live more self-determined lives in settings in which instructional support typically is unavailable, such as on the bus, interacting at work, or at a movie theater with friends. Self-instruction may be especially appropriate among students with disabilities, who frequently need support when learning to independently direct their own behavior. For example, for the high school students mentioned previously, self-instruction could have been useful in helping them schedule their studying time at home and restricting the amount of time they spent visiting with friends at night. By using self-instruction, the students could have helped to direct themselves to wake up in time for school each day and thereby increase the likelihood that they would improve their grades in school.

Self-Instruction Teaching Models

Teachers may choose from several models of self-instruction when teaching students to guide their own behavior. The traditional teaching model is based on Meichenbaum and Goodman's (1971) original sequence and comprises four basic steps: 1) stating a problem (e.g., "I've got to get up on time tomorrow so that I don't miss first period"), 2) stating a possible response to the problem (e.g., "I'm going to set the alarm tonight and put it across the room so that I have to get out of bed to shut it off"), 3) evaluating the response (e.g., "Hey, I did it. I got up on time. I'm gonna make it to class" or "Well, I just slept right through that alarm. Guess I'll have to turn up the radio with some really loud rock music so that it blasts me out of bed. I'll do better tomorrow"), and 4) verbally reinforcing oneself (e.g., "Good for me. I got up. I can't wait to see the auto body teacher's face when he sees me on time"). Some or all of these statements are taught to students in variations of self-instructional models.

One adaptation of the traditional self-instruction model (Meichenbaum & Goodman, 1971) was designed for use with people who have severe disabilities and limited verbal skills. Hughes and Rusch (1989) taught two individuals with mental retardation who were working in a soap-packaging plant to verbalize statements such as those in Table 1 while solving job-related problems. In comparison with the statements described previously, these statements were designed to be considerably shorter and simpler in response to the participants' limited verbal skills. However, the four statements are functionally the same as those in the lengthier, more traditional version (i.e., identifying the problem, stating the correct response, evaluating the response, self-reinforcing). Teachers should adapt the length and complexity of self-instructional statements to accommodate a student's needs and skills.

Other models for teaching self-instruction have been investigated by Agran and colleagues (Agran, Fodor-Davis, & Moore, 1986; Agran, Fodor-Davis, Moore, & Deer, 1989; Agran et al., 1992). These models include Did-Next-Now, What/Where, and Interactive self-instruction strategies, which may be adapted for students with mild or severe disabilities. Did-Next-Now is especially useful for teaching students to perform a series of tasks in a sequence (e.g., loading a commercial dishwasher). This model involves teaching an individual to state the response just completed ("Did") and the next response to be performed ("Next") and then to direct him- or herself to perform that response ("Now"). A strategy script for designing a Did-Next-Now self-instruction program is provided in Figure 1. The script prompts the teacher to identify a preceding response (e.g., sweeping the floor), a Did-Next-Now verbal sequence (e.g., "I swept the floor. I gotta empty the trash. I gotta do it now"), a subsequent target response (e.g., emptying the trash), a reinforcer to follow and maintain the target response (e.g., "Good job. Look at that floor"), and a correction procedure to use in case of error (e.g., "Oops. I was supposed to empty the trash next. Guess I better do that now"). Using this strategy, Agran et al. (1986) taught job-sequencing skills to four students with mental retardation enrolled in a hospital work skills program. The students stated the

Table 1.   Self-instructional statements for job-related problems

---

- "Not plugged in" (Identifying the problem)
- "Got to plug in" (Stating the correct response)
- "Fixed it" (Evaluating the response)
- "Good" (Self-reinforcing)

Adapted from Wehmeyer, Agran, and Hughes (1998).

Did-Next-Now Strategy Script

Student: _____   Setting: _____

Instructional Target: _____   Task: _____

Preceding Response	Verbalization (What student says)	Target Response (What student should do)	Reinforcer	Correction Procedure
	Did: Next: Now:			
	Did: Next: Now:			
	Did: Next: Now:			

Figure 1. Did-Next-Now strategy script. (From Wehmeyer, M.L., Agran, M., & Hughes, C. [1998]. *Teaching self-determination to students with disabilities: Basic skills for successful transition* [p. 163]. Baltimore: Paul H. Brookes Publishing Co.; reprinted by permission.)

Did-Next-Now verbal sequence when performing a 21-step task sequence for cleaning patient rooms, which included tasks such as dusting and cleaning restrooms. The sequence was repeated each time the students began a new step of the sequence (e.g., "I just brought the bucket to the room. I need to fill the bucket. I'm going to fill the bucket now").

The What/Where self-instructional model is used to help guide a student's performance in response to an instruction. Students are taught to select key words from a verbal or written instruction and determine what they are to do and where to do it. For example, a student worker in a large department store may be told by a supervisor, "These are the juniors' dresses. They go on the sales rack." Using the What/Where strategy, the student would repeat "juniors' dresses, sales rack" while beginning to hang the dresses on the correct rack in the juniors' department. For students who have difficulty following instructions, the What/Where strategy provides them with a procedure to identify the relevant information in an instruction that will serve to guide their performance.

The Interactive self-instruction model teaches students to state their self-instructions as questions that are embedded in conversation. This strategy is particularly useful for a student who is interacting with customers in public, when self-instructing aloud would draw unwanted attention to the student. Agran et al. (1992) taught this strategy to three students with moderate to severe disabilities who were learning to work as kitchen assistants. The students were responsible for taking sandwich orders from customers. Agran et al. (1992) taught the students to repeat the step just completed ("Did") and then remind themselves that they needed to ask the customer what to do next ("Next"). Then the students asked the customer for the next ingredient to be included in the sandwich ("Ask"). For example, one set of interactive self-instructions might be "Did meat" (after placing meat on bread), "Cheese next" (reminding oneself to ask the customer), and then "What kind of cheese?" (asking the customer for the next step in the order).

HOW TO TEACH SELF-INSTRUCTION

This section of the chapter presents an overview of empirical studies in which self-instruction has been taught to people with disabilities in school, work, and residential environments. Studies are grouped according to skill areas specific to each environment. Variations in methods of teaching self-instruction skills are compared to guide teachers in instructing their students to apply recommended strategies.

Teaching Self-Instruction in School Environments

Self-instruction skills that have been taught in school environments have addressed a variety of student behaviors. Targeted behaviors have included academic skills, community living and work skills, and social and interpersonal skills.

Academic Skills   Applications of self-instruction to academic skills typically have targeted performance of traditional academic tasks characteristic of curricula for students with mild disabilities. In addition, most investigations have used the traditional Meichenbaum and Goodman (1971) sequence (i.e., stating a problem, stating a response, evaluating the response, verbally reinforcing oneself) to guide student performance (see Table 1). For example, the effects of self-instruction on mathematics performance were investigated in a series of studies. Using the traditional Meichenbaum and Goodman (1971) training sequence, Johnston, Whitman, and Johnson (1980) and Whitman and Johnston (1983) taught students with mental retardation to add and subtract numbers with regrouping. Self-instructions comprised a series of questions based on a task analysis of the computational process. An example of the self-instructions that students used when adding with regrouping using a number line is shown in Figure 2.

Using the same self-instruction format as in Figure 2, Keogh, Whitman, and Maxwell (1988) compared the effects of self-instruction and teacher-delivered instruction on rate and accuracy of adding with regrouping by students with and students without mental retardation. Students without mental retardation improved their accuracy following both instructional conditions and their rate following teacher-delivered instruction only. Only the self-instruction condition resulted in improvements in rate and accuracy for students with mental retardation. Keogh et al. argued that these findings suggest that self-instruction may provide individuals who have mental retardation with the strategies they need to attend to and accurately solve problems.

Community Living and Work Skills   Wacker and colleagues (Wacker, Carroll, & Moe, 1980; Wacker & Greenebaum, 1984) adapted the original Meichenbaum and Goodman (1971) self-instructional sequence to teach sorting and assembly skills to students with mental retardation. Their abbreviated self-instructional method (i.e., self-labeling) required that students say aloud only the color or shape of cards as they sorted or assembled them in sequence.

As in the Meichenbaum and Goodman (1971) training sequence, the teacher demonstrated the correct performance of the required task sequence while stating aloud the colors or shapes of the cards being sorted or assembled. During subsequent instructional sessions, the students were taught to self-label (i.e., verbalize the names of the colors or shapes without prompting) while independently completing the assembly steps. Students in both studies improved their accuracy on required tasks following training and generalized their skills from the instructional setting to the regular classroom. In addition, using a group comparison design, Wacker and Greenebaum (1984) demonstrated that self-labeling was more effective than direct instruction at producing task acquisition and that only self-labeling produced generalization across related responses. Wacker and colleagues (1988) concluded that self-labeling

Q. What kind of a problem is this?   36
                                       +47

A. It's an add problem. I can tell by the sign.

Q. Now what do I do?

A. I start with the top number in the ones column and I add. Six plus 7 (the child points to the 6 on the number line and counts down 7 spaces) is 13. Thirteen has two digits. That means I have to carry. This is hard, so I go slowly. I put the 3 in the ones column (the child writes the 3 in the ones column in the answer) and the 1 in the tens column (the child writes the 1 above the top number in the tens column in the problem).

Q. Now what do I do?

A. I start with the top number in the tens column. One plus 3 (the child points to the 1 on the number line and counts down 3 spaces) is 4. Four plus 4 (the child counts down 4 more spaces) is 8 (the child writes the 8 in the tens column in the answer).

Q. I want to get it right, so I check it. How do I check it?

A. I cover up my answer (the child covers the answer with a small piece of paper) and add again, starting with the bottom number in the ones column. Seven plus 6 (the child points to the 7 on the number line and counts down 6 spaces) is 13 (the child slides the piece of paper to the left and uncovers the 3; the child sees the 1 that he or she has written over the top number in the tens column in the problem). Got it right. Four plus 3 (the child points to the 4 on the number line and counts down 3 spaces) is 7. Seven plus 1 (the child counts down 1 more space) is 8 (the child removes the small piece of paper so that the entire answer is visible). I got it right, so I'm doing well. (If, by checking his or her work, the child determines that he or she has made an error, he or she says, "I got it wrong. I can fix it if I go slowly"). The child then repeats the self-instruction sequence, starting from the beginning.

Figure 2. Example of self-instruction training sequence for addition with regrouping. (Reprinted from *Applied Research in Mental Retardation, 1*, M.B. Johnston, T.L. Whitman, & M. Johnson. Teaching addition and subtraction to mentally retarded children: A self-instruction program, pp. 141–160, copyright © 1980, with kind permission from Elsevier Science Ltd., The Boulevard, Langford Lane, Kidlington 0X5 1GB, U.K.)

may prompt individuals with mental retardation to focus on the relevant features of a task, thereby improving overall task performance.

Hughes, Hugo, and Blatt (1996) combined the Meichenbaum and Goodman (1971) sequence with the teaching of multiple examples of targeted responses to teach a domestic skill (i.e., making toast) to five high school students with mental retardation. The toast-making sequence was divided into 10 tasks. Five problem-solving tasks were used as training examples (i.e., multiple exemplars), and the remaining five served as generalization probes. The students were initially taught to self-instruct in response to one of the five training examples (e.g., toaster unplugged when making toast), using statements similar to those in Table 1. When the students were proficient at self-instructing with one example, the remaining four training examples were introduced. All five students learned to self-instruct while performing the training tasks and to generalize their use of the strategy to the untrained tasks, performing all steps of the toast-making task in sequence. In addition, performance across both trained and untrained tasks maintained after instructional support was withdrawn.

Social and Interpersonal Skills   Presley and Hughes (1998) used a self-instruction strategy called *cognitive processing* (Collet-Klingenberg & Chadsey-Rusch, 1991) in combination with an adaptation of the "Assess, Amend, and Act" strategy developed by Walker, Todis, Holmes, and Horton (1988) to teach appropriate expression of anger to two high school students with behavior disorders. The students were taught to verbalize three different types of statements (i.e., assessing, amending, and acting) in response to written scenarios in which students were involved in anger-provoking social situations with high school peers. For example, a student's belongings may have been taken or destroyed or a peer may have been spreading false rumors about the student. The students and a general education peer buddy role-played the verbal statements in response to the scenarios. An example of a scenario and the statements role-played by the students are provided in Table 2. Findings indicated that the students learned to self-instruct and generalize the use of the assess, amend, and act strategy to new role-play scenes involving anger-provoking situations.

Hughes, Harmer, Killian, and Niarhos (1995) adapted the Meichenbaum and Goodman (1971) self-instruction training sequence to teach four high school students with mental retardation to initiate and respond to conversation with a variety of familiar and unfamiliar peers, some of whom had disabilities and some of whom did not. Peers without disabilities taught the students to self-instruct during conversational skills training using the statements provided in Table 3. In addition, the peers modeled interactive conversations characteristic of typical high school students and provided corrective feedback and reinforcement to the students as the students learned their new conversational skills. Following self-instruction training by peers, all four students learned to initiate and maintain conversation with new conversation partners in a variety of high school settings. In addition, the students' conversational skills compared favorably to that of a group of typical high school students without disabilities.

Teaching Self-Instruction in Work Environments

Teaching self-instruction skills has been extended to settings in which people with disabilities are employed. Areas of focus include work skills, productivity, and social and interpersonal skills.

Work Skills   Wacker et al. (1988) adapted the self-labeling strategy used in school settings (e.g., Wacker et al., 1980) for students with mental re-

Table 2.   Steps in expressing anger

Assess

Student will not speak aloud for at least 3 seconds to assess the situation.

Student will ask and answer aloud, "What is going on?"

Student will ask and answer aloud, "Why did he or she do or say what he or she did?"

Student will ask and answer aloud, "Did he or she do this on purpose, or is it something that just happened?"

Student will ask and answer aloud, "How does he or she feel about the situation?"

Student will ask and answer aloud, "Is he or she upset or just kidding?"

Amend

Student chooses an appropriate alternative response to anger. Example: Not responding verbally or nonverbally to the situation, initiating another topic for discussion, or walking away from the problem.

Student asks the other person to explain why he or she said or did this. Example: "Why did you take my notebook from my desk? Did you not have paper or were you looking for the homework we had to turn in for class?"

Student tells the other person how this situation makes him or her feel. Example: "I am upset that you would not just ask me for paper or to see my homework. I considered you my friend and thought that you considered me your friend. Therefore, I am surprised that you took my notebook without asking me."

Student asks the other person to tell him or her how this makes him or her feel. Example: "How do you feel just taking my notebook without asking me?"

Act

Student responds to the situation, using the Assess and Amend steps. Example: Student follows steps in the Assess and Amend components in responding to the role-play situation.

Student evaluates his or her initial response to the situation and makes changes, if necessary, in his or her response by using the Assess and Amend steps. Example: Student speaks aloud that he or she has not followed the steps in the Assess and Amend components. Student speaks aloud the steps to assess the situation using the steps in the Assess component and amends the situation using these steps.

tardation who were receiving vocational evaluations in a university-based work setting. When entering data into a computer, calculator, or checkbook, the students were taught to self-label each letter, number, or character as it was entered. Following self-labeling training, all students increased their accuracy

Table 3.   Self-instructional statements for conversational skills training

- "I want to talk." (Identifying the problem)
- "I need to look and talk." (Stating the response)
- "I did it. I talked." (Self-evaluating)
- "I did a good job." (Self-reinforcing)

Adapted from Wehmeyer, Agran, and Hughes (1998).

in data entry across trained and untrained data entry tasks. In addition, when asked if they found self-labeling disruptive, the students' co-workers responded that they were not aware that the students were talking aloud.

Agran et al. (1989) used a What/Where self-instruction strategy script similar to that in Figure 3 to teach instruction-following skills to five students with mental retardation enrolled in a janitorial skills training program. The students were taught to say to themselves what they were supposed to do and where they were supposed to do it after they were given an instruction. For example, the students were taught to say "Vacuum under table" when they were told to vacuum the carpet under the table or to say "Wipe front stove" when given an instruction to wipe the front of a stove. All students improved their instruction-following skills across trained and untrained instructions when they used their self-instructions.

Hughes and Rusch (1989) combined self-instruction with multiple exemplars of targeted responses to teach two workers with mental retardation employed in a soap-packaging company to solve work-related problems. First, the work supervisor identified problem situations that were likely to occur during the workday, such as a puddle of soap on a table on which work was to be completed or a paper towel plugging the drain of a sink. Next, the employees were taught to self-instruct in response to five of the identified problem situations using statements similar to those in Table 1. Acquisition of the problem-solving strategy was demonstrated in addition to generalized use of the strategy to untrained problem situations.

Productivity   An adaptation of self-instruction called *verbal correspondence* was used by Crouch et al. (1984) to improve kitchen workers' start times, productivity, and supervisor ratings when performing kitchen tasks such as sweeping, mopping, and setting up food on a lunch line. Using this procedure, the employees were taught to say the times at which they would start and complete their work (i.e., the second step [stating the response] of Meichenbaum and Goodman's [1971] self-instructional sequence). They were initially reinforced for stating the correct times. Next, they were reinforced each time their stated times and actual start and completion times were the same. Stating their start and completion times increased the rate of production of all employees and improved their supervisors' ratings of their performance as well.

Rusch, Martin, Lagomarcino, and White (1987) used an adaptation of self-instruction correspondence called *verbal mediation* to teach a woman with mental retardation employed in a fast-food restaurant to state her required job sequences (i.e., 23 setup and cleanup tasks) before performing the tasks. Tasks included clearing tables, taking out trash, wiping tables and counters, and sweeping and mopping the dining area. The verbal mediation strategy required the employee to state in detail each step of the job sequence (i.e., the second step of the Meichenbaum and Goodman [1971] sequence) before performing the required responses. Using verbal mediation, the employee

What/Where Strategy Script

Student: _____   Setting: _____

Instructional Target: _____   Task: _____

Target Response (What student should do)	Antecedent Stimuli	Verbalization (What student says)	Reinforcer	Correction Procedure
	What: Where:			
	What: Where:			
	What: Where:			

Figure 3. What/Where strategy script. (From Wehmeyer, M.L., Agran, M., & Hughes, C. [1998]. *Teaching self-determination to students with disabilities: Basic skills for successful transition* [p. 172]. Baltimore: Paul H. Brookes Publishing Co; reprinted by permission.)

347

learned to perform tasks in sequence as well as to generalize her skills across scheduled changes in task demands.

Moore, Agran, and Fodor-Davis (1989) examined the effects of a self-management program involving self-instruction, goal setting, and self-reinforcement on the production rates of four employees with mental retardation employed in a sheltered workshop. The participants were responsible for a packaging task. They were instructed to set performance goals for themselves (i.e., set timers to specified periods of time), to tell themselves to work faster, and to reinforce themselves with coins when they met their criteria. After training, all participants increased and maintained their production rates at criterion levels for up to 3 months.

Social and Interpersonal Skills   Adaptations of self-instruction procedures have been applied to teaching employees with disabilities to seek assistance when needed to complete tasks. Agran, Salzberg, and Stowitschek (1987) taught five employees with moderate to severe disabilities in a vocational training setting to initiate requests when they were out of materials or in need of assistance. The employees were taught to state two steps of the Meichenbaum and Goodman (1971) training sequence (i.e., stating the problem and stating the correct response) when they needed help to complete tasks involved with unpackaging cheese, assembling recliner chairs and irrigation wheels, and making candles. For example, employees would say "I am out of —" (stating the problem) and "I need to get more —. I'll ask for —" (stating the response). Next, the employees would ask a supervisor for assistance. After self-instruction training, participants increased their requests for assistance in both the training and work setting.

Using a teaching format similar to that reported in Agran et al. (1987) (i.e., stating the problem and stating the correct response), Rusch, McKee, Chadsey-Rusch, and Renzaglia (1988) taught a young man with mental retardation employed in a university-operated film center to make appropriate requests when materials were not available and when materials ran out. The employee's job was to receive, fill, and deliver orders for desk supplies to clerical workers. When materials were unavailable or ran out, the young man was taught to state "Can't [complete order]." He then would tap a picture of a teacher's aide that was taped to his wheelchair and say "Tell [the aide]." Next, he was taught to approach the aide, establish eye contact, say "Excuse me," and request the missing items by saying, "I need more [name of item]." Following completion of all self-instruction steps, the employee was taught to reinforce himself with a nickel. Requests for assistance were found to increase when the young man performed his self-instruction steps.

The traditional Meichenbaum and Goodman (1971) teaching sequence has been used in employment settings to increase time on task among employees with mental retardation. Hughes and Petersen (1989) and Rusch, Morgan, Martin, Riva, and Agran (1985) taught employees with mental retardation to increase their time on task while performing required job-related tasks. Employees in these studies were taught to ask, "What does [the supervisor] want me to do?" (stating the problem); "I am supposed to wipe the counter and restock the supplies" (stating the response); "Okay, I wiped the counter" (self-evaluating); and "Good, I did that right" (self-reinforcing). To prompt self-instruction, Hughes and Petersen (1989) placed photographs on the employees' work tables that showed the employees busily working. Following self-instruction training, increases in time spent working generalized from the training to the work situation for employees across both studies.

Teaching Self-Instruction in Residential Environments

Two studies investigated the effects of self-instruction in residential environments among people with severe disabilities. These studies addressed community living skills and recreation and leisure skills.

Community Living Skills Hughes (1992) combined traditional self-instruction (Meichenbaum & Goodman, 1971) with multiple exemplars to teach four residents who had mental retardation in a group home to solve task-related problems. Four problem situations served as training tasks (i.e., multiple exemplars), and four served as generalization probes. The combined strategy was associated with generalization to untrained problems for all residents, as well as maintenance of the problem-solving strategy (i.e., responding to multiple exemplars and self-instruction). Because an analysis of instructional components was not conducted, however, it is not clear which component was responsible for generalization.

Recreation and Leisure Skills Keogh, Faw, Whitman, and Reid (1984) used self-instruction to teach two adolescent boys with behavior problems who lived in a community residence to play board games. The boys were taught to state the second step of the Meichenbaum and Goodman (1971) sequence (states correct response) by verbalizing individual game steps as they played. Both boys increased performance and verbalization of game steps when instruction was introduced sequentially across games. Prompts and additional instruction were required before generalization occurred in dyad and free-play situations; generalization to three untrained games did not occur. Game skills maintained although occasional instruction sessions were required.

Summary of Empirical Studies

As indicated in the previous review, investigations of the effects of self-instruction among people with disabilities have been conducted across school, work, and residential settings. Self-instruction was effective in increasing proficiency in the areas of academics, daily living skills, social skills, productivity, and employment skills. Applications of self-instruction included replications of the original Meichenbaum and Goodman (1971) teaching sequence as well as variations of the procedure. In addition, self-instruction was found to be effective in producing generalization and maintenance of target behaviors to varying degrees across studies.

CONCLUSIONS

Self-management strategies have several advantages over traditional instructional strategies. Although direct instruction strategies such as positive reinforcement are powerful strategies for teaching skill acquisition, using them exclusively may teach students to be dependent on teachers or transition specialists to prompt desired behaviors. A benefit of self-management procedures is that they allow students to take responsibility for their own behavior management and self-regulation. Furthermore, self-management is consistent with IDEA because its use allows students to be included as active participants in their own education programs. In using self-management, students apply to their own behavior the same instruction strategies that teachers use to facilitate learning, such as prompting or positive reinforcement. Because students are in the best position to observe and monitor occurrences of their own behavior across time and situations, it is logical that they may learn to become effective managers of their behavior.

In this chapter, we have discussed major explanations of the self-management process, including operant and cognitive interpretations. In addition, we have addressed how to teach self-management and have illustrated, with examples, the major types of self-management techniques that have been used with secondary students with disabilities (i.e., antecedent cue regulation, self-monitoring, self-reinforcement, self-instruction). Self-instruction has been described in detail, both in theory and in practice. Models for teaching self-instruction have been presented and applications of self-instruction models across school, work, and residential environments have been illustrated with examples from the empirical literature.

Self-management and self-instruction have much to offer secondary education in actively involving students in their own IEPs. Self-management strategies appear to appeal to teachers and other practitioners and to be applicable and robust across a variety of settings, behaviors, and students. Furthermore, they have benefits for students because they offer a potential means of changing behaviors that are important and socially valuable to the students themselves. We recommend an expanded use of self-management among secondary students to include critical behaviors related to choice, preferences, personal satisfaction, and quality of life.

REFERENCES

Agran, M. (1997). Teaching self-management. In M. Agran (Ed.), *Student-directed learning: Teaching self-determination skills* (pp. 1–27). Belmont, CA: Wadsworth.

Agran, M., Fodor-Davis, J., & Moore, S. (1986). The effects of self-instructional training on job-task sequencing: Suggesting a problem-solving strategy. *Education and Training of the Mentally Retarded, 21,* 273–281.

Agran, M., Fodor-Davis, J., Moore, S., & Deer, M. (1989). The application of a self-management program on instruction-following skills. *Journal of The Association for Persons with Severe Handicaps, 14,* 147–154.

Agran, M., Fodor-Davis, J., Moore, S., & Martella, R. (1992). The effects of peer-delivered self-instructional training on a lunch-making work task for students with severe handicaps. *Education and Training in Mental Retardation, 27,* 230–240.

Agran, M., Salzberg, C.L., & Stowitschek, J.J. (1987). An analysis of the effects of a social skills training program using self-instructions on the acquisition and generalization of two social behaviors in a working setting. *Journal of The Association for Persons with Severe Handicaps, 12,* 131–139.

Baer, D.M. (1984). Does research on self-control need more control? *Analysis and Intervention in Developmental Disabilities, 4,* 211–218.

Bambara, L.M., & Ager, C. (1992). Using self-scheduling to promote self-directed leisure activity in home and community settings. *Journal of The Association for Persons with Severe Handicaps, 17,* 67–76.

Bandura, A. (1969). *Principles of behavior modification.* New York: Holt, Rinehart & Winston.

Bandura, A. (1971). Vicarious and self-reinforcement processes. In R. Glaser (Ed.), *The nature of reinforcement* (pp. 228–279). New York: Academic Press.

Brigham, T.A. (1978). Self-control: Part II. In A.C. Catania & T.A. Brigham (Eds.), *Handbook of applied behavior analysis: Social and instructional processes* (pp. 259–274). New York: Irvington.

Collet-Klingenberg, L., & Chadsey-Rusch, J. (1991). Using a cognitive-process approach to teach social skills. *Education and Training in Mental Retardation, 26,* 258–270.

Crouch, K.P., Rusch, F.R., & Karlan, G.R. (1984). Competitive employment utilizing the correspondence training paradigm to enhance productivity. *Education and Training of the Mentally Retarded, 19,* 268–275.

Cuvo, A.J., Leaf, R.B., & Borakove, L.S. (1978). Teaching janitorial skills to the mentally retarded: Acquisition, generalization, and maintenance. *Journal of Applied Behavior Analysis, 11,* 345–355.

Davis, C.A., Williams, R.E., Brady, M.P., & Burta, M. (1992). The effects of self-operated auditory prompting tapes on the performance fluency of persons with severe mental retardation. *Education and Training in Mental Retardation, 27,* 39–50.

Gilbert, L.M., Williams, R.L., & McLaughlin, T.F. (1996). Use of assisted reading to increase correct reading rates and decrease error rates of students with learning disabilities. *Journal of Applied Behavior Analysis, 29,* 255–257.

Goldfried, M.R., & Merbaum, M. (1973). A perspective on self-control. In M.R. Goldfried & M. Merbaum (Eds.), *Behavior change through self-control* (pp. 3–34). New York: Holt, Rinehart & Winston.

Hughes, C. (1992). Teaching self-instruction utilizing multiple exemplars to produce generalized problem-solving by individuals with severe mental retardation. *American Journal on Mental Retardation, 97,* 302–314.

Hughes, C. (1997). Self-instruction. In M. Agran (Ed.), *Student directed learning: Teaching self-determination skills* (pp. 144–170). Pacific Grove, CA: Brooks/Cole.

Hughes, C., & Agran, M. (1993). Teaching persons with severe disabilities to use self-instruction in community settings: An analysis of applications. *Journal of The Association for Persons with Severe Handicaps, 18,* 261–274.

Hughes, C., Harmer, M.L., Killian, D.J., & Niarhos, F. (1995). The effects of multiple-exemplar self-instructional training on high school students' generalized conversational interactions. *Journal of Applied Behavior Analysis, 28*, 201–218.

Hughes, C., Hugo, K., & Blatt, J. (1996). A self-instructional intervention for teaching generalized problem solving within a functional task sequence. *American Journal on Mental Retardation, 100*, 565–579.

Hughes, C., & Lloyd, J.W. (1993). An analysis of self-management. *Journal of Behavioral Education, 3*, 405–425.

Hughes, C., & Petersen, D. (1989). Utilizing a self-instructional training package to increase on-task behavior and work performance. *Education and Training in Mental Retardation, 24*, 114–120.

Hughes, C., & Rusch, F.R. (1989). Teaching supported employees with severe mental retardation to solve problems. *Journal of Applied Behavior Analysis, 22*, 365–372.

Hughes, C., & Scott, S.V. (1997). Teaching self-management in employment settings. *Journal of Vocational Rehabilitation, 8*, 43–53.

Individuals with Disabilities Education Act (IDEA) of 1990, PL 101-476, 20 U.S.C. §§ 1400 *et seq.*

Individuals with Disabilities Education Act Amendments of 1997, PL 105-17, 20 U.S.C. §§ 1400 *et seq.*

Inge, K.J., Moon, M.S., & Parent, W. (1993). Applied behavior analysis in supported employment settings. *Journal of Vocational Rehabilitation, 3*, 53–60.

Jackson, T.L., & Altman, R. (1996). Self-management of aggression in an adult male with mental retardation and severe behavior disorders. *Education and Training in Mental Retardation and Developmental Disabilities, 31*, 55–65.

Johnston, M.B., Whitman, T.L., & Johnson, M. (1980). Teaching addition and subtraction to mentally retarded children: A self-instruction program. *Applied Research in Mental Retardation, 1*, 141–160.

Kanfer, F.H. (1970). Self-monitoring: Methodological issues and clinical applications. *Journal of Consulting and Clinical Psychology, 35*, 143–152.

Kanfer, F.H. (1971). The maintenance of behavior by self-generated stimuli and reinforcement. In A. Jacobs & L.B. Sachs (Eds.), *The psychology of private events: Perspectives on covert response systems* (pp. 39–59). New York: Academic Press.

Kazdin, A.E. (1978). *History of behavior modification: Experimental foundations of contemporary research.* Baltimore: University Park Press.

Kazdin, A.E. (1984). *Behavior modification in applied settings* (3rd ed.). Homewood, IL: Dorsey.

Keogh, D.A., Faw, G.D., Whitman, T.L., & Reid, D. (1984). Enhancing leisure skills in severely retarded adolescents through a self-instructional treatment package. *Analysis and Intervention in Developmental Disabilities, 4*, 333–351.

Keogh, D.A., Whitman, T.L., & Maxwell, S.E. (1988). Self-instruction versus external instruction: Individual differences and training effectiveness. *Cognitive Therapy and Research, 12*, 591–610.

Kregel, J., Wehman, P., Revell, W.G., & Hill, M. (1990). Supported employment in Virginia. In F.R. Rusch (Ed.), *Supported employment: Models, methods, and issues* (pp. 15–29). Sycamore, IL: Sycamore Publishing Co.

Lagomarcino, T.R., Hughes, C., & Rusch, F.R. (1989). Utilizing self-management to teach independence on the job. *Education and Training in Mental Retardation, 24*, 139–148.

Maag, J.W., Reid, R., & DiGangi, S.A. (1993). Differential effects of self-monitoring attention, accuracy, and productivity. *Journal of Applied Behavior Analysis, 26*, 329–344.

Malott, R.W. (1984). Rule-governed behavior, self-management, and the developmentally disabled: A theoretical analysis. *Analysis and Intervention in Developmental Disabilities, 4,* 199–209.

Meichenbaum, D., & Goodman, J. (1971). Training impulsive children to talk to themselves: A means of developing self-control. *Journal of Abnormal Psychology, 77,* 115–126.

Minskoff, E.H., & Demoss, S. (1994). Workplace social skills and individuals with learning disabilities. *Journal of Vocational Rehabilitation, 4,* 113–121.

Moore, S.C., Agran, M., & Fodor-Davis, J. (1989). Using self-management strategies to increase the production rates of workers with severe handicaps. *Education and Training in Mental Retardation, 24,* 324–332.

Park, H., & Gaylord-Ross, R. (1989). A problem-solving approach to social skills training in employment settings with mentally retarded youth. *Journal of Applied Behavior Analysis, 22,* 373–380.

Premack, D. (1970). Mechanisms of self-control. In W. Hunt (Ed.), *Learning and mechanisms of control in smoking* (pp. 107–123). Chicago: Aldine.

Presley, J.A., & Hughes, C. (1998). *Teaching high school students with behavior disorders to express anger appropriately.* Manuscript submitted for publication.

Rachlin, H. (1978). Self-control: Part I. In A.C. Catania & T.A. Brigham (Eds.), *Handbook of applied behavior analysis: Social and instructional processes* (pp. 246–258). New York: Irvington.

Rehabilitation Act Amendments of 1992, PL 102-569, 29 U.S.C. §§ 701 *et seq.*

Rusch, F.R., Hughes, C., & Wilson, P.G. (1995). Utilizing cognitive strategies in the acquisition of employment skills. In W. O'Donohue & L. Krasner (Eds.), *Handbook of skills training with adults* (pp. 363–382). Needham Heights, MA: Allyn & Bacon.

Rusch, F.R., Martin, J.E., Lagomarcino, T.R., & White, D.M. (1987). Teaching task sequencing via verbal mediation. *Education and Training in Mental Retardation, 22,* 229–235.

Rusch, F.R., McKee, M., Chadsey-Rusch, J., & Renzaglia, A. (1988). Teaching a student with severe handicaps to self-instruct: A brief report. *Education and Training in Mental Retardation, 23,* 51–58.

Rusch, F.R., Morgan, T.K., Martin, J.E., Riva, M., & Agran, M. (1985). Competitive employment: Teaching mentally retarded employees self-instructional strategies. *Applied Research in Mental Retardation, 6,* 389–407.

Skinner, B.F. (1953). *Science and human behavior.* New York: Free Press.

Skinner, B.F. (1957). *Verbal behavior.* New York: Appleton-Century-Crofts.

Skinner, B.F. (1971). *Beyond freedom and dignity.* New York: Alfred A. Knopf.

Smith, M.D. (1994). Increasing work productivity of employees disabled by autism. *Journal of Vocational Rehabilitation, 4,* 60–65.

Stromer, R., Mackay, H.A., Howell, S.R., McVay, A.A., & Flusser, D. (1996). Teaching computer-based spelling to individuals with developmental and hearing disabilities: Transfer of stimulus control to writing tasks. *Journal of Applied Behavior Analysis, 29,* 25–42.

Wacker, D.P., Berg, W.K., McMahon, C., Templeman, M., McKinney, J., Swarts, V., Visser, M., & Marquardt, P. (1988). An evaluation of labeling-then-doing with moderately handicapped persons: Acquisition and generalization with complex tasks. *Journal of Applied Behavior Analysis, 21,* 369–380.

Wacker, D.P., Carroll, J.L., & Moe, G.L. (1980). Acquisition, generalization, and maintenance of an assembly task by mentally retarded children. *American Journal of Mental Deficiency, 85,* 286–290.

Wacker, D.P., & Greenebaum, F.T. (1984). Efficacy of a verbal training sequence on the sorting performance of moderately and severely mentally retarded adolescents. *American Journal of Mental Deficiency, 88,* 653–660.

Wagner, M. (1995). *Transition from high school to employment and post-secondary education: Interdisciplinary implications for youths with mental retardation.* Paper presented at the 119th annual meeting of the American Association on Mental Retardation, San Francisco.

Walker, H.M., Todis, B., Holmes, D., & Horton, G. (1988). *The Walker social skills curriculum: The ACCESS program adolescent curriculum for communication and effective social skills.* Austin, TX: PRO-ED.

Wehmeyer, M.L., Agran, M., & Hughes, C. (1998). *Teaching self-determination to students with disabilities: Basic skills for successful transition.* Baltimore: Paul H. Brookes Publishing Co.

Wehmeyer, M.L., & Metzler, C.A. (1995). How self-determined are people with mental retardation? The National Consumer Survey. *Mental Retardation, 33,* 111–119.

Whitman, T.L. (1987). Self-instruction, individual differences, and mental retardation. *American Journal on Mental Retardation, 92,* 213–223.

Whitman, T.L. (1990). Self-regulation and mental retardation. *American Journal on Mental Retardation, 94,* 347–362.

Whitman, T.L., & Johnston, M.B. (1983). Teaching addition and subtraction with regrouping to educable mentally retarded children: A group self-instructional training program. *Behavior Therapy, 14,* 127–143.

Winking, D.L., O'Reilly, M.F., & Moon, M.S. (1993). Preference: The missing link in the job match process for individuals without functional communication skills. *Journal of Vocational Rehabilitation, 3,* 27–42.

17

Student-Directed Learning Strategies

Martin Agran

Throughout this book, various rationales are offered in support of the importance of fostering self-directed behaviors among students in schools. Simply
put, successful people engage in self-directed behaviors. Mithaug, Martin,
Agran, and Rusch (1988) conducted a comprehensive literature review on
success behaviors (i.e., behaviors considered critical to success) reported by a
sample of notable individuals. Although terms differed across the various reports, more than 40 skills were identified, and four major activities or skill
clusters were evident. First, successful individuals set goals for themselves.
They selected goals that were clearly feasible to achieve. Second, successful
individuals engaged in independent performance. They initiated actions based
on their goals and used a variety of self-directed strategies (e.g., problem solving) to achieve their aims. Third, successful people engaged in meaningful
self-evaluation. They were able to evaluate their performance, either self-
imposed or externally imposed. Finally, successful individuals have adaptability skills that allow them to learn from their mistakes and to change or adjust
their goals or the actions they take. In a similar study, Garfield (1986) interviewed 1,500 people and reported that successful people are adept at making
decisions, managing their behavior, and adapting to change. They start with a

goal, follow an action plan, and then evaluate and modify their behavior as needed. Garfield (1986) suggested that such skills serve as the keys to success and can be taught systematically.

It is becoming increasingly clear that, to promote student involvement in learning, it is essential to teach students to regulate their own behavior (Agran, 1997; Mithaug, Martin, Agran, et al., 1988), in other words, to use the success strategies mentioned before. Without this set of skills, students will not know whether they are achieving desired levels of performance, and they will remain dependent on other people for this information. These skills are particularly important for secondary school students who are preparing for successful transitions into work and home environments and community living, but they are also of great value for all students with disabilities who are seeking to enhance their independence, competence, and self-determination. Unfortunately, as Martin and Huber Marshall (1997) indicated, students with disabilities often do not know what to do to achieve success. Rather than making choices that will have a direct impact on their lives, setting their own goals, and having high expectations for themselves, they fail to take control over their learning and development. They have low expectations for themselves and little motivation. Clearly, the characteristics of successful people suggest that self-regulated or self-directed behavior is a critical component of success for all students. Therefore, teaching self-regulated behaviors is of critical importance to students with disabilities.

Based on results of research and recognizing the need for active student involvement, Mithaug, Martin, Agran, et al. (1988) developed the Adaptability Instruction Model (described in detail in Chapter 15), which was used to teach students with disabilities the previously mentioned success-related behaviors. Crucial to the Adaptability Instruction Model is the student's accurate appraisal of his or her skills and abilities and interests and preferences. To set appropriate goals, the student needs to know whether he or she has the capacity to achieve those goals. Likewise, the selection of a performance strategy involves an assessment of the student's skill repertoire and the feasibility of acquiring a new strategy. In addition, adjusting to change (determining a better course of action to achieve a goal) involves an evaluative analysis of all components of the model—goals selected, action plans, performance strategies, performance data, and adjustments made. Finally, rather than waiting for a teacher to deliver a positive consequence, students can be taught to provide their own reinforcement for performing a target behavior. In the Adaptability Instruction Model, the evaluation and adjustment components allow the student to assess his or her performance and provide an opportunity for the student to reinforce him- or herself if the goals set have been met. Such reinforcement is immediate; effective; and, most important, student directed. Self-reinforcement represents a major component of most conceptualizations of self-management (Brigham, 1989) and is considered by some researchers to be an important component of self-regulation (Harter, 1982; Wehmeyer, Agran, & Hughes, 1998). If we are committed to promoting students' involvement and investment in their own learning, self-reinforcement can be most helpful in achieving this outcome (Agran, 1997).

This chapter describes the importance of self-regulation or student-directed learning strategies (i.e., goal setting, self-monitoring, self-evaluation, self-reinforcement) in promoting student involvement in learning. The value of self-directed or self-regulated behavior is initially discussed. Then the theoretical basis for self-regulation and self-reinforcement is presented. Next, operational information about implementing such strategies is provided, along with a description of the effects of these strategies in promoting behavior change. Finally, recommendations on teaching students how to direct their own learning are presented.

SELF-REGULATION

Critical to an individual's success in learning and task performance is the ability to self-regulate his or her performance (Watson & Tharp, 1989). To achieve goals, standards (e.g., desired levels of performance) must be present. With these standards, the individual can determine whether there is a discrepancy between the existing level of performance and the desired level of performance. With this information, an appropriate action can be taken to modify the situation and a consequent evaluation of the appropriateness of the action can be conducted. Lack of these skills represents one of the greatest problems for students who are receiving special education services (Agran, Martin, & Mithaug, 1989; Mithaug, Martin, Agran, & Rusch, 1988). Such skills empower students (Graham, Harris, & Reid, 1992) and encourage them to truly take responsibility for their learning (Schuler & Perez, 1987). Self-regulation has been suggested as the central concept in self-management (Karoly & Kanfer, 1977) and ultimately in self-determination (Agran, 1997).

Typically, the following strategies are associated with self-regulation: goal setting, self-monitoring, and self-evaluation (Smith & Nelson, 1997), with self-reinforcement also being included. *Goal setting* refers to setting a performance goal to achieve for oneself. *Self-monitoring* refers to observing and recording one's performance. *Self-evaluation* involves comparing these recordings with a known performance standard. *Self-reinforcement* involves the student's selection and delivery of a reinforcer to him- or herself. Each of these may be used alone or in combination with the others.

Clearly, all people self-regulate; but, for several reasons, they do not do so with equal success (Mithaug, 1993). Standards may be lacking; if they are present, students may not be aware of them. Also, students may not know how to observe their own behavior or how to compare their behavior with these standards (Watson & Tharp, 1989). Furthermore, they may lack the strategies needed to achieve their goals, even if they have been able to compare their performance with known standards. Last, reinforcers may be too distant or too delayed to have much functional value. For example, quitting when only half of the problems are completed on a math worksheet may be more reinforcing for a student than finishing the sheet if the student has great difficulty with the calculations and will not be reinforced until the teacher's aide completes his or her rotation among all the students in the class.

It is not surprising that the success behaviors discussed previously function as self-regulation strategies. These strategies allow individuals to pursue self-selected goals, initiate and follow through on a course of action, adjust their performance as needed, and reinforce appropriate responding. Without self-regulated performance, the likelihood of a student achieving success is minimized appreciably. Our dependence on a teacher-directed instructional model in which the teacher has full responsibility for determining what a student will learn, how it will be taught, and how it will be evaluated and provided with a consequence has helped to create a situation in which the student has been denied any meaningful role in his or her education except for passively responding (Agran, 1997). Clearly, self-regulation creates a very different situation—one in which the student will have increased responsibility and learning power.

Whitman (1990) suggested that self-regulation involves a system of responses that enables individuals to examine their environments and their responses in these environments so that they can determine how to make the best decisions on how they should act, how to evaluate the adequacy of their actions, and how to revise their plans as necessary. But what causes individuals to engage in self-regulation?

Mithaug (1993) suggested that individuals are often in flux between actual or existing states and goal or desired states (see Chapter 14 for more detail). When a discrepancy exists between what one has and what one wants, an incentive for self-regulation and subsequent action may be operative. With the realization that a problem or discrepancy exists, the individual may set out to achieve the goal or desired state. Because of a history of failure or a sense of powerlessness or learned helplessness, these individuals may do little to change their situations. They may set expectations that are too low or, in some cases, too high. As Mithaug (1993) noted, negative feelings produce low expectations. Inaccurate self-assessments may produce unrealistic or infeasible expectations.

To promote success, individuals need to enhance or increase their expectations. The ability to set appropriate expectations is based on the individual's success in matching his or her capacity with present opportunity. *Capacity* is the individual's assessment of existing resources (e.g., skills, interests, motivation), and *opportunity* refers to the aspects of the existing situation that will allow the individual to achieve the desired gain. Mithaug (1996) referred to optimal prospects as just-right matches in which individuals are able to correctly match their capacity (i.e., skills, interests) with existing opportunities (e.g., potential jobs). The experience generated during self-regulation "is a function of repeated interaction between capacity and opportunity over time" (Mithaug, 1996, p. 159). As Mithaug noted, "the more competent we are, the fewer errors we make, and the less time we take, the greater the gain we produce" (1996, p. 156). With additional experience in self-regulation, students can gain expertise in identifying both short- and long-term goals, the resources and actions needed to achieve these goals, and self-corrective procedures to use if success eludes them.

Students also need to use strategies to optimize opportunity for gain, such as those that allow them to monitor, evaluate, and reinforce their own behavior. For example, a student has expressed a strong interest in enrolling in a biology class, but the teacher is reluctant to admit him because of past negative experiences. At the time, the student would not stay seated and attend to the lectures, would never contribute to class discussion, and would rarely complete a homework assignment. To accommodate the student's interest, the student's resource and biology teachers developed a plan to enable the student to manage his own behavior. A monitoring sheet was developed, and the student was taught to record whether he was in his seat and attending to the lecture for a specified period of time (the teachers and student agreed on the time). Also, each time he contributed to class discussion, he was instructed to record a tally mark. As with on-task behavior, the student and his teacher would determine the minimum number of contributions he needed to make each day. After completing his homework, he checked off a line indicating that he had done so. The plan allows the student to optimize gain.

Evaluating the effectiveness of the strategy and adjusting one's actions until the goal is achieved represents an important component of self-regulation. For the student in the previous example, a failure to behave appropriately may be due to any of a number of factors (e.g., failure to record on-task behavior). Thus, the student may be instructed to verbally remind him- or herself to monitor his or her own behavior. As noted before, students with disabilities often do not know how to direct their own learning or correct their own behavior. Self-regulation is most valuable in this respect.

Self-regulation represents a dynamic process in which all of the components interact with and influence each other. With increased experience in regulating their behavior, students will become more adept at setting appropriate goals, monitoring their behavior, and making necessary adjustments. Two important components of self-determination are self-efficacy and efficacy expectations (see Chapter 1). *Self-efficacy* refers to the individual's knowledge and confidence that he or she can perform a specific behavior to produce a desired outcome, and *efficacy expectations* refer to the belief that performance of this behavior will produce the desired or anticipated outcome. These perceptions are critical for self-determination, and use of the self-regulation strategies will be of great assistance to the student in developing these attributes. For example, Tollefson, Tracy, Johnson, and Chatman (1986) taught students with learning disabilities to set performance goals; evaluate their performance; and verbally attribute the quality of their performance to ability, effort, or luck. Tollefson et al. (1986) reported that gains in the target behaviors were achieved by all students and that they attributed their success to personal effort.

VALUE OF SELF-REINFORCEMENT

As noted previously, self-reinforcement also serves an important function in self-regulation. The value of self-reinforcement, either separate from or as part of a self-regulation instructional package, in facilitating behavior change is appreciable in itself. Self-reinforcement involves teaching students to select and administer reinforcers to themselves as if they were being delivered by teachers or other instructional agents. Under certain conditions, there are multiple benefits of self-reinforcement.

First, it is crucial that reinforcement is provided immediately after a target behavior is executed. Unfortunately, teachers may not be available to perform this function. If this occurs repeatedly, opportunities to establish a desired behavior may be compromised. By teaching the student to administer his or her own consequences, such problems are averted. The student is always around to self-administer consequences, and immediate delivery is guaranteed. No opportunities will be lost as long as the student attends to the target behavior and delivers the reinforcer.

Second, successful reinforcement is contingent on the delivery of the reinforcer only after the target behavior is exhibited. Repeated delivery of a reinforcer to a nontarget behavior may serve to establish that behavior instead of the target behavior. As long as the student can discriminate the response and has been reinforced to make this discrimination, the behavior will be reinforced after it has occurred. This may also prompt the student to attend more to the target behavior.

Third, as a target behavior becomes more established (i.e., as it occurs more frequently at a predicted time), the reinforcement schedule (i.e., how often the reinforcer is presented) needs to be changed from a fixed or continuous schedule to an intermittent or variable schedule. This schedule change is recommended because it allows the response to be maintained with less reinforcement and allows the behavior to be under the control of natural reinforcers (e.g., teacher praise). Lovitt and Curtis (1969) reported that not only could students determine their own reinforcement schedules but also their performance was better in conditions in which they determined their own schedule. Consequently, students can be taught to select and administer consequences and to do so according to varying schedules.

Also, self-reinforcement is considered of great value because it not only provides the student with immediate consequences but also serves to access long-term or delayed reinforcers; that is, it brings the behavior into contact with more powerful reinforcers (Hughes & Lloyd, 1993). Rachlin (1974) indicated that self-reinforcement does not function according to conditioning principles. The consequences serve instead as feedback. Consequently, its stimulus properties may have greater effect than its reinforcing properties (Hughes & Lloyd, 1993; Rachlin, 1978). Also, Catania (1976) noted that self-reinforcement may be peripheral. What is important is not that individuals reinforce themselves but that individuals learn to discern that the response is good enough to be reinforced by others. Self-reinforcement permits students to observe and evaluate their own behavior and receive an immediate and short-term consequence for a delayed or indirect contingency. This contingency serves as the ultimate control.

Last, Bandura (1977) suggested that the development of behavior is based on an individual's observation of others' behavior. These observations serve as models for later imitation and help individuals set standards for themselves. Meeting these standards serves as the basis for self-reinforcement.

Because of the benefits, several researchers have suggested that self-reinforcement is at least as effective as, if not superior to, teacher-administered reinforcement (Deutsch Smith, 1989; Kurtz & Neisworth, 1976; Schloss & Smith, 1994). The available research indicates that students using self-reinforcement are just as successful in changing their behaviors as are students receiving teacher-administered reinforcement. Self-reinforcement represents one of the most powerful self-management strategies that is effective alone or in combination with other procedures (O'Leary & Dubey, 1979).

SELF-REGULATION STRATEGIES

This section describes the effects of self-regulation strategies in promoting learning. As indicated previously, these include goal setting, self-monitoring, self-evaluation, and self-reinforcement.

Goal Setting

Chapter 3 provides a comprehensive overview of goal setting and decision making. However, because goal setting is essential to self-regulation, it is worth revisiting this topic within this context. Goal setting is a critical component of self-regulation because it provides the student with a clear illustration of the discrepancy between an existing level of performance and a desired level of performance and what he or she needs to do to reduce that discrepancy. In this respect, goal setting is analogous to Mithaug's (1993) just-right match theory. That is, individuals engage in self-regulation when there is a discrepancy between what they have and what they want (or what someone else convinces them they should want). Goal setting has been used to improve a variety of academic skills (Fuchs, Bahr, & Rieth, 1989; Schunk, 1985), homework completion (Trammel, Schloss, & Alper, 1994), transition and work skills (Flexer, Newbery, & Martin, 1979; Mithaug, Martin, Husch, Agran, & Rusch, 1988; Moore, Agran, & Fodor-Davis, 1989), and conversational skills (Hughes, Killian, & Fischer, 1996).

For example, out of a pool of 30 middle school students with learning disabilities, Schunk (1985) taught 10 randomly assigned students to set math goals in subtraction for themselves; of the 20 remaining students, 10 were randomly assigned to a group in which the teacher set goals and 10 were assigned to a group in which goals were not set. An analysis of covariance revealed statistically significant differences among the three groups, with the greatest skill gains demonstrated by the students who had set their own goals. That is, students showed more improvement when they set their own goals compared to having either no goals or teacher-set goals. Also, Dickerson and Creedon (1981) and Farnum, Brigham, and Johnson (1977) found that students did better on academic tasks when they set their own performance goals. Thus, self-selected goals may be as effective as teacher-selected goals in enhancing student performance, if not more so (Hughes, 1997; Rosenbaum & Drabman, 1979). Most important, goal setting allows students to achieve self-determination. If they have not set their goals or at least participated in the decision-making process regarding the selection of goals, they may not engage actively in their own behavior change (Agran, 1997). Students are more likely to engage in self-directed behavior change if they believe the behavior to be changed is important to them (Smith & Nelson, 1997). As Schunk (1985) indicated, goal setting promotes self-efficacy and active task involvement.

Goal setting is believed to have an impact on behavior change because it uses some degree of self-monitoring and self-evaluation. Goals are set and later changed based on the student's monitoring and evaluation of his or her own performance. If a student easily meets a goal (e.g., the number of math problems to be completed), then it is likely that, based on the student's self-evaluation of his or her productivity, a higher goal will be set. If the student has great difficulty meeting a goal, then a lower expectation will be set. In either case, goal setting is directly contingent on the student's evaluation of his or her own behavior. Without this information, reasonable goals could not be set.

As Wehmeyer et al. (1998) indicated, goal setting involves several different dimensions. Besides selecting a desired outcome (e.g., new skill, enhanced level of performance of an existing skill), the student also needs to be aware of the actions that need to be taken to achieve the goal, the consequences that may occur if the goal is not achieved, and the contingencies present in the environment that will either facilitate or hinder the student's success in achieving the goal. For example, if Ruth wants to improve her keyboarding skills, she may decide to have this goal included in her individualized education program (IEP). Before she decides what is needed to improve her skills, however, it is also important that she consider how she will improve (e.g., taking a class, more practice), what will occur if she does not (e.g., failing grade, less employable in the future), and the operative contingencies in the environment (e.g., encouragement from parents and teacher, available time to work on goal). Also, because her improvement may take a considerable period of time, she may consider some way in which she can stay motivated (e.g., drawing a smiley face on a monitoring form every time she completes a typing assignment). This situation illustrates an important issue regarding goal setting and self-regulation. As indicated previously, self-regulation strategies may be used independently or in combination. For Ruth, the effectiveness of her goal setting depends on the appropriateness of the goal she sets, self-monitoring of assignment completion, self-evaluation of her performance, and self-reinforcement. Goal setting may be the first part of self-regulation, but it depends on, and is integrally locked to, the other procedures that comprise self-regulation. Critical to self-regulation is the individual's accurate evaluation of his or her own behavior, and goal setting is an invaluable process to achieve this outcome.

Self-Monitoring

Self-monitoring involves teaching a student to observe and record the frequency of occurrences of his or her own behavior. It has been used to teach a number of academic, classroom behavior, and social skills (see Smith & Nelson, 1997). For example, Stecker, Whinnery, and Fuchs (1996) taught five students with mild disabilities to reduce the length of time spent making the transition from one classroom to another by recording their time in minutes and seconds. Reduction in time out of class was evident for all participants. Also, self-monitoring has been used in transition programs to teach a variety of work skills, including task completion (Agran et al., 1989), job task changes (Sowers, Verdi, Bourbeau, & Sheehan, 1985), and increased productivity (Ackerman & Shapiro, 1984). Sowers et al. (1985) taught four high school students with severe disabilities to improve their job task changes by self-monitoring. The students were instructed to refer to picture cues that illustrated the job sequence. After completing a task, they were taught to find the picture, mark that it was completed, and then proceed to the next task. The instruction produced successful outcomes for all participants.

Self-monitoring involves two activities. First, the student must discern that the target behavior did or did not occur within a specified period of time. Second, the student must accurately record its occurrence. Inaccurate monitoring may result in positive consequation even though the behavior was not performed or in lack of consequation even though the behavior was performed. However, there are ample demonstrations in the research literature that self-monitoring appears to have a reactive effect (Agran & Martin, 1987; Goetz & Etzel, 1978); that is, the self-monitoring procedure will produce and maintain a desired change without any other intervention. Furthermore, the procedure will produce such an effect even if the student's recordings are not accurate. For example, although all students in the Stecker et al. (1996) investigation demonstrated positive behavior change (i.e., reductions in time spent out of class), the accuracy of recordings varied, thus indicating that accuracy is not essential to producing change. It is suggested that self-monitoring has a reactive effect because it functions as a discriminative stimulus to cue desired responses (Baer, 1984) or because it mediates or strengthens weak contingencies (Malott, 1984). For example, as part of his individualized transition plan (ITP), Juán works several hours a week at a local cheese-processing factory packaging cheese for shipping. He is paid on a piecework basis. Although Juán likes the job, he remains unsure of how much money he is earning. Thus, Juán was taught to self-monitor the number of boxes he packages. This enabled him to track how much extra money he earned and potentially increase his productivity.

Self-monitoring is also recommended because it promotes generalization and maintenance. It has been amply demonstrated that self-management or self-directed learning strategies have greatly enhanced generalized responding (Agran, 1997; Fantuzzo, Polite, Cook, & Quinn, 1988). Self-monitoring provides students with increased opportunities to attend to and discriminate target behaviors. Consequently, the relationship between the stimulus (i.e., the cue to observe one's behavior, a counting device) and the target behavior is strengthened, and stimulus control is enhanced. Also, since the stimulus is transportable, its presence in another environment provides common stimuli across settings. For example, Misra (1992) taught three individuals with mental retardation several social behaviors, such as using amenities and asking questions. These individuals were provided with counters and taught to monitor their performance; specifically, they were taught to count the number of times they initiated a conversation or appropriately used amenities. Also, they were taught to use the counters across a variety of settings. The results indicated that gains were achieved for all participants, and generalized responding was observed. The counter may have served as a common stimulus across settings.

Self-Evaluation

Self-evaluation involves the comparison of a self-monitored behavior with a standard or set performance goal (Smith & Nelson, 1997). It represents a critical component in the self-regulation process because it informs the student whether he or she is meeting the goal. Having students evaluate their own performance allows them to discern the extent to which they have achieved their goals and to experience a potentially reinforcing event (Agran & Hughes, 1997). Of particular value is the fact that self-evaluation allows the students to obtain immediate feedback on their own performance without having to rely on a teacher for feedback. Self-evaluation facilitates behavior change because it provides the student with a constant measure or standard against which to assess his or her behavior. If the student is meeting the standard, the comparison may prove to be reinforcing. If the standard is not being met, the comparison may serve a corrective function. In this respect, self-evaluation functions as a feedback system in which the student can proceed to apply positive consequences to appropriate responding or correct the lack thereof (Agran, 1997).

Self-evaluation has been used to modify a variety of adaptive behaviors. For example, Clark and McKenzie (1989) taught three students with behavior disorders to evaluate their classroom behavior. Target behaviors included being on task, following directions, and not engaging in disruptive behavior. The results revealed that rates of appropriate behavior increased for all participants, with strong generalized effects across settings.

Smith, Young, West, Morgan, and Rhode (1988) taught four students with behavior disorders to decrease their disruptive and off-task behaviors by using self-evaluation. A three-phase training program was used. The students were initially taught to evaluate their behavior every 10 minutes. They recorded their evaluations on a self-evaluation card on which they circled 5 if they followed the classroom rules and stayed on task for the entire interval, 4 if they stayed on task but had one violation, 3 if they needed to be reminded twice to stay on task, 2 if they were on task for only half of the interval, and 1 if they were off task and their behavior was unacceptable. After conducting their self-evaluations, the students matched their evaluations to those of their teacher and received reinforcers based on the number of accurate matches. In the second phase of training, the interval was increased to 15 minutes, and, in the third phase, it was increased to 30 minutes. The findings revealed that the procedure was effective in reducing the target behavior for all participants.

Mithaug, Martin, Agran, et al. (1988) taught students with varying disabilities to evaluate their work skills. Using the Adaptability Instruction Model (see Chapter 14), the students were taught to 1) select performance goals and develop action plans to meet these goals; 2) use one or more self-management strategies in the execution of these action plans; 3) evaluate their performance in terms of whether they met their goals, the level of assistance they needed, and the number of steps they completed; and 4) adjust their behavior by determining what they needed to do to meet their goals the next time. With the Adaptability Instruction Model, achieving success is directly contingent on the evaluation data obtained. Once a student can discriminate a target behavior, teaching the student to record its occurrence and then evaluate his or her performance is feasible. Most important, the Adaptability Instruction Model provides students with a practical, motivating, and reinforcing means by which to promote their involvement and self-regulation.

Self-Reinforcement

Self-reinforcement represents the major theoretical and procedural component of most conceptualizations of self-management and self-regulation (Brigham, 1989). Unlike teacher-delivered reinforcement systems, self-reinforcement allows students to immediately reinforce their own behavior. The possibility of lost reinforcement opportunities is minimized, and immediate feedback is essentially guaranteed. As mentioned previously, students often have difficulty in acquiring desired responses because the natural consequences are too delayed or are perceived as being too small or not achievable (Malott, 1984). In a situation in which feedback may not be frequently available, self-reinforcement serves as the invaluable link between response and outcome. The more often a student can discriminate a target behavior and be consistently reinforced for its occurrence, the more likely it is that it will occur in the future.

Functionally, self-reinforcement involves two operations: discrimination and delivery. Before the student can reinforce him- or herself, the student must discern that the target behavior occurred. Consequently, self-reinforcement serves a similar function to self-monitoring. Thus, a number of researchers have suggested that self-monitoring may be sufficient alone to change the behavior because it appears to involve a reinforcement function (Brigham, 1978; Catania, 1975). Likewise, self-reinforcement may assume stimulus properties and cue appropriate responding.

Self-reinforcement has been extensively studied, and numerous researchers have demonstrated the effectiveness of the procedure across different environments. For example, DiGangi, Maag, and Rutherford (1991) taught two students with learning disabilities to monitor and reinforce their on-task behavior and academic performance; specifically, the students were taught to monitor the number of math problems that they answered correctly. These students were taught to monitor whether they were on task by asking themselves "Was I paying attention?" when an audiotaped beeper sounded at specific intervals of 30–90 seconds. Also, the students were taught to evaluate their performance and to verbally self-reinforce at the end of the session ("I did okay"; "I did a great job"). For one student, the program increased both academic performance and on-task behavior; but, for the other student, only academic performance improved. An analysis of the differential effects of the strategies indicated that, although self-monitoring clearly produced positive effects, the effects were evident but difficult to determine.

Lloyd and Hilliard (1989) taught five students with emotional disturbances to monitor and reinforce their own on-task behavior. Students who recorded accurately that they were on task for 80% of the observation intervals (the intervals varied in length from 2 to 6 minutes) gave themselves a credit that could be used for free time or for a tangible reinforcer. Improvements in on-task behavior were reported.

Coleman and Whitman (1984) improved the physical fitness of 17 individuals with mental retardation through the use of self-monitoring and self-reinforcement procedures. The individuals were taught to self-monitor and self-reward their exercise activities. At the end of the session, participants were instructed to put a sticker on the exercise chart; the stickers were later converted into back-up reinforcers depending on the accuracy of their self-recordings. Increases in the number of exercises executed during unsupervised exercise improved physical fitness, and increased accuracy in recording rates of exercising was also reported. Furthermore, the skills were maintained across several weeks.

Stevenson and Fantuzzo (1984) taught two fifth-grade students who were having difficulty in completing math assignments and engaged in disruptive classroom behavior, reinforcing their academic performance. The students were taught to 1) set goals for the number of problems to complete accurately, 2) count the number completed, 3) compare this number with the predetermined goal, 4) award themselves gold stars if the goal was met, and 5) exchange the gold stars for back-up reinforcers. The findings suggested that the self-management program was effective in increasing accurate math performance and decreasing disruptive behavior.

Many investigations of self-reinforcement in transition programs or work settings have examined the effects of the strategy on work productivity. For example, Wehman and McLauglin (1980) reported that a self-reinforcement strategy was used to increase the production rate of an adult with mental retardation who worked on jump rope assembly and packing tasks. The effects of externally administered and self-administered reinforcement were compared, and, although both reinforcement procedures increased production, the mean production rate for self-administered production was higher.

Finally, using a multicomponent self-management program that comprised self-instruction, goal setting, and self-reinforcement, four employees with mental retardation were taught to increase their productivity rates (Moore et al., 1989). The employees were responsible for sorting various machine parts as part of a U.S. Air Force contract. While working, the employees were taught to say "I need to work faster" and set timers to specified periods of work time. In addition, they were instructed to reward themselves if they achieved specific levels when the timer bell rang. All employees dramatically increased their production work rates, and these increases were maintained for as long as 3 months.

In summary, self-reinforcement has been found to be an effective strategy for students with disabilities to use. Overall, the data suggest that self-reinforcement is as effective as, and in some cases is more effective than, externally administered reinforcement.

TEACHING SELF-REGULATION

There are numerous demonstrations in the research literature that students with disabilities can learn the self-regulatory procedures described in this chapter. Although many people routinely use self-regulatory skills, students with disabilities do not learn and incorporate these skills automatically. Students with disabilities must be taught these skills through the use of consistent, systematic, direct instruction methods (Hughes, 1997). Recommendations for teaching these procedures are presented next.

As Wehmeyer et al. (1998) indicated, incorporating goal setting into a student's IEP is relatively easy. Initially, it is recommended that achievable goals be set—goals that are easily reachable and potentially reinforcing. Unattainable or difficult-to-achieve goals only enhance failure. With increased experience in goal setting, more ambitious goals can be pursued.

Smith and Nelson (1997) recommended a seven-step process for goal setting (Table 1). First, a conference with the student, his or her parents, and relevant professionals is arranged. Second, a discussion is conducted with the student regarding identifying a goal and the importance of his or her input. Third, resolving differences regarding the identified discrepancy is discussed. This involves clarification of the nature and severity of the problem. Fourth, a solution to the problem—that is, setting a goal—is proposed. Such goals should be specific, proactive, and discussed in a positive tone. Fifth, the positive consequences for meeting the goal are determined. Sixth, a plan for monitoring the student's progress toward meeting this goal is developed. Last, it is recommended that a simple contract or agreement is developed and signed.

Martino (1993) recommended that goals be set on a weekly basis and determined privately. Also, the teacher and student need to meet regularly to discuss the student's progress. As Wehmeyer et al. (1998) indicated, if students are to be active participants in educational programming and decision making, they should be provided the opportunity not only to set their own goals but also to evaluate whether they are achieving them.

Table 1.   Goal-setting steps

Step	Description
1	Arrange a conference.
2	Identify a goal.
3	Clarify discrepancies with a positive, matter-of-fact attitude.
4	Identify a solution.
5	Identify positive consequences for meeting the goal.
6	Develop a monitoring plan.
7	Write a simple goal contract and have it signed.

From Smith, D.J., & Nelson, J.R. (1997). Goal setting, self-monitoring, and self-evaluation for students with disabilities. In M. Agran (Ed.), *Student-directed learning: Teaching self-determination skills* (p. 90). Belmont, CA: Wadsworth; reprinted by permission.

SELF-MONITORING

As mentioned previously, self-monitoring involves teaching the student to discriminate the target behavior and record its occurrence. Consequently, an easy-to-use self-monitoring procedure in which the behavior is clearly defined and represented on the monitoring form and a recording procedure that the student can easily perform are recommended.

In teaching students to monitor their behavior, the following procedure is recommended. After a goal is set, a monitoring form needs to be developed. Such forms should vary according to the student's instructional needs and capacity. They may range from pictorial representations of a target behavior to a verbal checklist of multiple target behaviors. Kunzelmann (1975) recommended the use of "countoons," which are stick figures performing the target behavior. Mithaug, Martin, Agran, et al. (1988) used both verbal and graphic representations on self-monitoring forms designed for students receiving adaptability instruction in ITPs (Figure 1). Next, the consequences for correct monitoring need to be determined (Smith & Nelson, 1997). First, the student is reinforced by a teacher for correctly discriminating the target behavior. Both examples and nonexamples of the behavior are presented via modeling, role-plays, videotape, or observation of other students displaying the behavior. Second, the student is taught how to use the monitoring form and is reinforced initially for using the form—discriminating the target behavior and recording its occurrence. Third, the student is taught to discriminate the target behavior, record its occurrence accurately, and reinforce him- or herself.

Mithaug (1993) suggested that the more frequently individuals can observe their gains, the more intelligent and competent they will be and the more likely it is that they will regard the self-regulation process as being useful. Self-monitoring can be invaluable in promoting this perception.

SELF-EVALUATION

Typically, competence in self-evaluation is achieved by having students evaluate their performance and then compare or match their self-ratings to those provided by teachers or other significant individuals (e.g., peers, job coaches). These coevaluators provide reinforcement or corrective feedback as needed. As the student achieves increased competence, the frequency of matching evaluations is reduced and eventually may be put on an intermittent schedule. To ensure successful self-evaluation, it is critical that the student be able to discriminate both the target behavior to be monitored and the standard or performance level that will be used to evaluate it. As indicated previously, this goal-setting activity should fully involve the student.

Next, an evaluation form with a built-in procedure to match the student's evaluation with that of his or her teacher's is needed. Smith, Nelson, and

Laundry Sorting

My Goal | **To Complete** | 0 1 2 3 4 5 6 | **Steps**

My Plan | **To Work With** | 0 1 2 3 4 5 6 | **Helps**

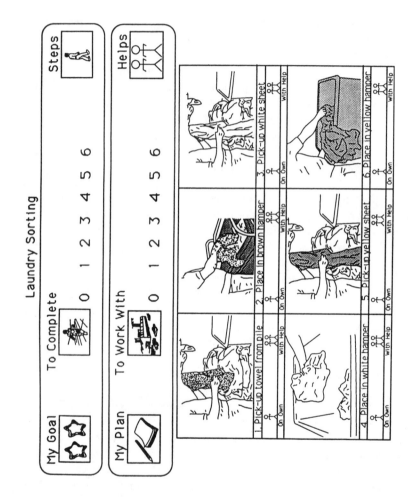

1. Pick-up towel from pile — On Own / With Help
2. Place in brown hamper — On Own / With Help
3. Pick-up white sheet — On Own / With Help
4. Place in white hamper — On Own / With Help
5. Pick-up yellow sheet — On Own / With Help
6. Place in yellow hamper — On Own / With Help

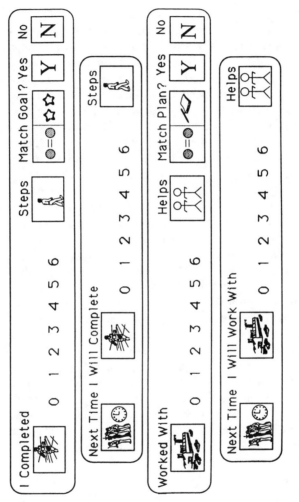

Figure 1. Pictorial self-evaluation form.

Ludwig (1993) recommended a numerical rating scale (e.g., 3 represents meeting all expectations; 2, meeting some expectations; 1, meeting one expectation; 0, meeting zero expectations) or a pictorial scale (e.g., a happy face represents meeting all expectations and a sad face represents meeting no expectations). Apart from the form, logistical decisions regarding when and where the form is to be used need to be determined.

After the form is developed, the student and his or her teacher need to determine the consequences of responding to the form. Although the long-term goal is to improve performance as specified in the goal statement, more immediate reinforcers are probably needed (e.g., tokens that can be redeemed for tangible reinforcers or increased free time). The goal is that over time these reinforcers can be eliminated and that natural reinforcers (e.g., improved performance, teacher attention) will eventually promote the desired change.

Self-evaluation is taught by essentially following the same sequence as self-monitoring, with one difference. Although students are actively encouraged to monitor their behavior accurately, the fact that self-monitoring has reactive effects, typically in a positive direction and without regard to whether the student records his or her behavior accurately, suggests that accuracy may ultimately be a secondary issue. Of primary concern is whether the student consistently uses the strategy and whether the desired change in behavior is evident. However, accuracy in monitoring is essential in self-evaluation because the students' assessment of their progress toward achieving a goal is contingent on an accurate evaluation of performance. Thus, efforts must be made to ensure that students find the use of these strategies reinforcing. A target behavior that is positive and occurs frequently needs to be selected. This allows students to have repeated practice in reinforcing their behavior.

Needless to say, the first and second steps involve identifying the target behavior and the desired criterion to achieve. Next, it is recommended that the student should determine the type and amount of reinforcer. Having the teacher select the reinforcer negates the benefits that may be realized by teaching students to be self-determined. The best reinforcers are those commonly used in the classroom (e.g., extra recess or free time, verbal praise). Ultimately, the reinforcer should be students' self-directed verbal praise. Also, students should determine the criteria or standard that must be met to warrant self-reinforcement.

A high level of accuracy that is based on frequent matches by student and teacher evaluations needs to be established. Inaccurate evaluations undoubtedly jeopardize students' acquisition of both short- and long-term consequences.

SELF-REINFORCEMENT

Self-reinforcement appears to be most effective when combined with self-monitoring. Although self-reinforcement is moderately effective by itself, it is most effective when combined with self-monitoring or self-evaluation. Before students can reinforce themselves, they need to be able to discern when the target behavior has occurred. Their inability to do so will result in erroneous self-reinforcement. Wolery, Bailey, and Sugai (1988) suggested that children should be fluent in accurate self-monitoring to ensure that self-reinforcement is effective. Students should be able to consistently and accurately discriminate the target behavior. Thus, it is recommended that, before being given instruction in self-reinforcement, students are taught to self-monitor.

It is safe to say that many students with disabilities have had limited experience in monitoring, evaluating, or reinforcing their own behavior. Indeed, it is the lack of these experiences that has resulted in their limited autonomy and self-determination (Wehmeyer et al., 1998). Next, as stated previously, a self-monitoring procedure needs to be developed. After that step, the student is taught to use the self-reinforcement procedure. The student is told that he or she needs to reinforce him- or herself after he or she has performed a desired behavior to a specified level. This is determined by responding to the self-monitoring form and determining whether he or she met the set goal. If so, the student is taught to deliver the reinforcer in the agreed-on quantity to him- or herself. The last step involves teaching the student to set new behavioral criteria as needed as competency is achieved.

The educational experiences of many students with disabilities have been controlled by teachers' and other professionals' consequating their behavior. Therefore, many students are uncomfortable with learning to evaluate and reinforce their own behavior. Indeed, if they performed these actions more often, they very well might be more successful learners (Agran, 1997). Thus, when teaching students to self-reinforce, attention should be directed to ensuring that the outcomes will be positive. Students need to become enthusiastic about reinforcing their behavior. When they realize that success (i.e., positive consequences) is literally in their hands, self-determination becomes more realizable and attainable.

CONCLUSIONS

The self-regulatory procedures described in this chapter are designed to promote the total involvement of students in their learning experiences. Many of the instructional activities done for them by teachers (e.g., selecting goals, monitoring performance, reinforcing correct responding) can be done by the students themselves instead. The benefits of using these procedures are easily apparent. As Agran (1997) noted, without active student involvement in the planning, monitoring, and reinforcing of desired behavior, teachers may be minimizing, in both quality and quantity, the educational outcomes of students. Successful individuals are those who consistently use self-regulatory strategies. Such individuals know not only what they want but also what to do to achieve these goals and what to do if the goals are not easily met. In addition, they know how to experience satisfaction at the achievement of their goals. With acquisition of these skills, students better realize the value of their involvement in learning and how much they can gain by doing so.

REFERENCES

Ackerman, A., & Shapiro, E. (1984). Self-monitoring and work productivity with mentally retarded adults. *Journal of Applied Behavior Analysis, 17,* 403–407.

Agran, M. (Ed.). (1997). *Student-directed learning: Teaching self-determination skills.* Pacific Grove, CA: Brooks/Cole.

Agran, M., & Hughes, C. (1997). Problem solving. In M. Agran (Ed.), *Student-directed learning: Teaching self-determination skills* (pp. 171–198). Pacific Grove, CA: Brooks/Cole.

Agran, M., & Martin, J.E. (1987). Applying a technology of self-control in community environments for individuals who are mentally retarded. In M. Hersen, R.M. Eisler, & P.M. Miller (Eds.), *Progress in behavior modification* (Vol. 21, pp. 108–151). Beverly Hills: Sage Publications.

Agran, M., Martin, J.E., & Mithaug, D.E. (1989). Achieving transition through adaptability instruction. *Teaching Exceptional Children, 21,* 4–7.

Baer, D.M. (1984). Does research on self-control need more control? *Analysis and Intervention in Developmental Disabilities, 4,* 211–218.

Bandura, A. (1977). *Social learning theory.* Englewood Cliffs, NJ: Prentice-Hall.

Brigham, T.A. (1978). Self-control: Part II. In A.C. Cantania & T.A. Brigham (Eds.), *Handbook of applied behavior analysis: Social and instructional processes.* New York: Irvington.

Brigham, T.A. (1989). *Self-management for adolescents: A skills training program.* New York: Guilford Press.

Catania, A.C. (1975). The myth of self-reinforcement. *Behaviorism, 3,* 192–199.

Catania, A.C. (1976). The myth of self-reinforcement. In T.A. Brigham, R. Hawkins, J. Scott, & T.F. McLaughlin (Eds.), *Behavior analysis in education: Self-control and reading.* Dubuque, IA: Kendall/Hunt.

Clark, L.A., & McKenzie, H.S. (1989). Effects of self-evaluation training of seriously emotionally disturbed children on the generalization of their classroom rule following and work behaviors across settings and teachers. *Behavioral Disorders, 14,* 89–98.

Coleman, R.S., & Whitman, T.L. (1984). Developing, generating, and maintaining physical fitness in mentally retarded adults: Toward a self-directed program. *Analysis and Intervention in Developmental Disabilities, 4,* 109–127.

Deutsch Smith, D. (1989). *Teaching students with learning and behavior problems.* Englewood Cliffs, NJ: Prentice-Hall.

Dickerson, E.A., & Creedon, C.F. (1981). Self-selection of standards by children: The relative effectiveness of pupil-selected and teacher-selected standards of performance. *Journal of Applied Behavior Analysis, 14,* 425–433.

DiGangi, S.A., Maag, J.W., & Rutherford, R.B., Jr. (1991). Self-graphing of on-task behavior: Enhancing the reactive effects of self-monitoring on on-task behavior and academic performance. *Learning Disability Quarterly, 14,* 221–230.

Fantuzzo, J.W., Polite, K., Cook, D.M., & Quinn, G. (1988). An evaluation of the effectiveness of teacher- vs. student-management classroom interventions. *Psychology in the Schools, 25,* 154–163.

Farnum, M., Brigham, T.A., & Johnson, G. (1977). *A comparison of the effects of teacher-determined and student-determined contingencies on arithmetic performance.* Unpublished manuscript, Department of Psychology, Washington State University, Pullman.

Flexer, R.W., Newbery, J.F., & Martin, A.S. (1979). Use of goal-setting procedures in increasing task assembly rate of severely retarded workers. *Education and Training of the Mentally Retarded, 14,* 177–184.

Fuchs, L.S., Bahr, C.M., & Rieth, H.J. (1989). Effects of goal structures and performance contingencies on the math performance of adolescents with learning disabilities. *Journal of Learning Disabilities, 22,* 554–560.

Garfield, G. (1986). *Peak performers: The new heroes of American business.* New York: Avon Books.

Goetz, E.M., & Etzel, B.C. (1978). A brief review of self-control procedures: Problems and solutions. *Behavior Therapists, 1,* 5–8.

Graham, S., Harris, K.R., & Reid, R. (1992). Developing self-regulated learners. *Focus on Exceptional Children, 24*(6), 1–16.

Harter, S. (1982). A developmental perspective on some parameters of self-regulation in children. In P. Karoly & F.H. Kanfer (Eds.), *Self-management and behavior change* (pp. 165–204). New York: Pergamon Press.

Hughes, C. (1997). Self-instruction. In M. Agran (Ed.), *Student-directed learning: Teaching self-determination skills* (pp. 144–170). Pacific Grove, CA: Brooks/Cole.

Hughes, C., Killian, D.J., & Fischer, G.M. (1996). Validation and assessment of a conversational interaction intervention. *American Journal on Mental Retardation, 100,* 493–509.

Hughes, C., & Lloyd, J.W. (1993). An analysis of self-management. *Journal of Behavioral Education, 4,* 405–425.

Karoly, P., & Kanfer, F.H. (Eds.). (1977). *Self-management and behavior change: From theory to practice.* New York: Pergamon Press.

Kunzelmann, H.D. (Ed.). (1975). *Precision teaching.* Seattle, WA: Special Child Publications.

Kurtz, P.D., & Neisworth, J.T. (1976). Self-control possibilities for exceptional children. *Exceptional Children, 42,* 212–217.

Lloyd, M.E., & Hilliard, A.M. (1989). Accuracy of self-recording as a function of repeated experience with different self-control contingencies. *Child and Family Behavior Therapy, 11*(2), 1–14.

Lovitt, T., & Curtis, K.A. (1969). Academic response rate as a function of teacher- and self-imposed contingencies. *Journal of Applied Behavior Analysis, 2,* 49–54.

Malott, R.W. (1984). Rule-governed behavior, self-management, and the developmentally disabled: A theoretical analysis. *Analysis and Intervention in Developmental Disabilities, 4,* 199–209.

Martin, J.E., & Huber Marshall, L. (1997). Choice making: Description of a model project. In M. Agran (Ed.), *Student-directed learning: Teaching self-determination skills* (pp. 224–248). Pacific Grove, CA: Brooks/Cole.

Martino, L.R. (1993). A goal-setting model for young adolescent at-risk students. *Middle School Journal, 24,* 19–22.

Misra, A. (1992). Generalization of social skills through self-monitoring by adults with mild mental retardation. *Exceptional Children, 58,* 495–507.

Mithaug, D., Martin, J.E., Husch, J.V., Agran, M., & Rusch, F.R. (1988). *When will persons in supported employment need less support?* Colorado Springs, CO: Ascent.

Mithaug, D.E. (1993). *Self-regulation theory: How optimal adjustment maximizes gain.* Westport, CT: Praeger.

Mithaug, D.E. (1996). The optimal prospects principle: A theoretical basis for rethinking instructional practices for self-determination. In D.J. Sands & M.L. Wehmeyer (Eds.), *Self-determination across the life span: Independence and choice for people with disabilities* (pp. 147–165). Baltimore: Paul H. Brookes Publishing Co.

Mithaug, D.E., Martin, J.E., Agran, M., & Rusch, F.R. (1988). *Why special education graduates fail: How to teach them to succeed.* Colorado Springs, CO: Ascent.

Moore, S.C., Agran, M., & Fodor-Davis, J. (1989). Using self-management strategies to increase the production rates of workers with severe handicaps. *Education and Training in Mental Retardation, 24,* 324–332.

O'Leary, S.G., & Dubey, D.R. (1979). Applications of self-control procedures by children: A review. *Journal of Applied Behavior Analysis, 12,* 449–465.

Rachlin, H. (1974). Self-control. *Behaviorism, 2,* 94–107.

Rachlin, H. (1978). Self-control: Part I. In A.C. Catania & T.A. Brigham (Eds.), *Handbook of applied behavior analysis: Social and instructional processes.* New York: Irvington.

Rosenbaum, M.S., & Drabman, R.S. (1979). Self-control training in the classroom: A review and critique. *Journal of Applied Behavior Analysis, 12,* 467–485.

Schloss, P.J., & Smith, M.A. (1994). *Applied behavior analysis in the classroom.* Needham Heights, MA: Allyn & Bacon.

Schuler, A.L., & Perez, L. (1987). The role of social interaction in the development of thinking skills. *Focus on Exceptional Children, 19*(7), 1–11.

Schunk, D.H. (1985). Participation in goal setting: Effects on self-efficacy and skills of learning-disabled children. *Journal of Special Education, 19,* 307–317.

Smith, D.J., & Nelson, J.R. (1997). Goal setting, self-monitoring, and self-evaluation for students with disabilities. In M. Agran (Ed.), *Student-directed learning: Teaching self-determination skills* (pp. 80–110). Belmont, CA: Wadsworth.

Smith, D.J., Nelson, J.R., & Ludwig, C. (1993, May). *The effects of self-management on the playground deportment of young children exhibiting aggressive behaviors.* Paper presented at the annual Association for Behavior Analysis conference, Chicago.

Smith, D.J., Young, K.R., West, R.P., Morgan, D., & Rhode, G. (1988). Reducing the disruptive behavior of junior high school students: A classroom self-management procedure. *Behavioral Disorders, 13*(4), 231–239.

Sowers, J., Verdi, M., Bourbeau, P., & Sheehan, M. (1985). Teaching job independence and flexibility to mentally retarded students through the use of a self-control package. *Journal of Applied Behavior Analysis, 18,* 81–85.

Stecker, P.M., Whinnery, K.W., & Fuchs, L.S. (1996). Self-recording during unsupervised academic activity: Effects on time spent out of class. *Exceptionality, 6*(3), 133–147.

Stevenson, H.C., & Fantuzzo, J.W. (1984). Application of the "generalization map" to a self-control intervention with school-aged children. *Journal of Applied Behavior Analysis, 17,* 203–212.

Tollefson, N., Tracy, D.B., Johnson, E.P., & Chatman, J. (1986). Teaching learning disabled students goal-implementation skills. *Psychology in the Schools, 23,* 194–204.

Trammel, D.L., Schloss, P.J., & Alper, S. (1994). Using self-recording, evaluation, and graphing to increase completion of homework assignments. *Journal of Learning Disabilities, 27,* 75–81.

Watson, D.L., & Tharp, R.G. (1989). *Self-directed behavior.* Pacific Grove, CA: Brooks/Cole.

Wehman, P., & McLaughlin, P.J. (1980). *Vocational curriculum for developmentally disabled persons.* Baltimore: University Park Press.

Wehmeyer, M.L., Agran, M., & Hughes, C. (1998). *Teaching self-determination to students with disabilities: Basic skills for successful transition.* Baltimore: Paul H. Brookes Publishing Co.

Whitman, T.L. (1990). Self-regulation and mental retardation. *American Journal on Mental Retardation, 94,* 347–362.

Wolery, M., Bailey, D.B., Jr., & Sugai, G.M. (1988). *Effective teaching: Principles and procedures of applied behavior analysis with exceptional students.* Needham Heights, MA: Allyn & Bacon.

IV

SUMMARY

Future Directions in Student Involvement

Education Planning, Decision Making, and Instruction

Michael L. Wehmeyer and Deanna J. Sands

This book has introduced numerous strategies, curricula, and programs to promote active student involvement in education planning, decision making, and instruction. The emphasis on student involvement in transition-related planning and decision making, first articulated in the Individuals with Disabilities Education Act (IDEA) of 1990 (PL 101-476), has resulted in considerable attention to and impetus for student involvement. However, as the authors and editors of this book readily corroborate, strategies, curricula, and programs are not enough, in and of themselves, to make real student involvement happen.

In this chapter, we pull the camera back from the focus on programs and strategies and broaden the frame to examine other ways of putting into practice the variables of valuing and providing opportunities for active student involvement. This includes looking at classroom-, building-, and district-level issues and factors. Next, we review a life-span approach to supporting active student involvement and self-determination. The chapter ends with a discussion of why it is also important to think about student involvement outside the context of special education, in the educational environments of all students.

TEACHER AND CLASSROOM VARIABLES AND STUDENT INVOLVEMENT

One way that teachers act on their values and beliefs about what is important in schools is to employ strategies, curricula, and programs that are in concert with their values and beliefs. For example, when teachers believe that literacy is an important tool for students to gain access to and communicate information, they target their materials and teaching strategies to support student acquisition of literacy skills and knowledge bases. However, the strategies, curricula, and programs that teachers employ constitute only one component of teacher-related variables that can have an impact on and uphold a value for student involvement in education planning, decision making, and instruction. In addition, educators need to consider their expectations for students with disabilities, their own control orientation and the power structure in their classroom, and the type of learning environment they create in their classroom. The next section examines each of these variables.

Teacher Expectations

Chapter 1 discusses the ways in which expectations based on stereotypes of disability have an impact on students and adults. In this chapter, we reiterate that it is critically important for teachers to examine how they view disability and how the biases and stereotypes associated with that view of disability influence their expectations for students to become actively involved in their education programs. Feldman, Saletsky, Sullivan, and Theiss pointed out that "one of the best supported findings in recent years demonstrates that the expectations that teachers hold about student performance are related to subsequent student outcomes" (1983, p. 27). Those outcomes include student perceptions about themselves and the control they have over their lives. By setting and communicating high expectations, teachers communicate to students that they believe the students are capable and competent. Such expectations should be established for students individually based on each student's abilities, and the importance of the student's making an effort to meet those expectations should be emphasized.

Research has also examined the effect on students' perceptions of control and efficacy when teachers treat students differently, as well as the relationship between teacher and student expectations. For example, Wigfield and Harold (1992) reviewed research on the latter and concluded that students' expectancies for themselves are strongly associated with teachers' expectations for them. As for the influence of teachers' responses to students on student perceptions, research by Weinstein (1985, 1989) showed that students perceive teachers as providing more negative feedback and more directed instruction to low-achieving students. They also perceive teachers as providing more choice and more messages of high expectations to high-achieving students. These types of interactions, in and of themselves, serve to shape students' expectations of their own abilities. Students believe that they must be low-achieving students when teacher interactions with them are overly directed, consist of negative feedback, or provide limited choice-making opportunities in the classroom.

Several conditions appear to make it difficult for teachers to monitor and control how their beliefs and values may inadvertently have an impact on students. Although most teachers are quite aware that their beliefs about students influence their performance, they are typically not cognizant that they are treating children differently. Wigfield and Harold (1992) pointed out that student–teacher interactions occur so frequently and so rapidly that teachers cannot realistically process such interactions and may be unaware of the kinds of messages that they are providing to different students. An additional problem is that it is neither preferable nor feasible to treat all students exactly the same, because students vary considerably in what they need to succeed. Wigfield and Harold (1992) also pointed out that part of the reason that teachers develop specific expectations about students is the emphasis in most classrooms on normative comparisons of student ability. They suggested that, by focusing attention on student progress and mastery instead of using comparative ability assessments, teachers can overcome the inherent biases and expectations built up by a constant emphasis on ability levels.

Wigfield and Harold (1992) provided several suggestions for educational practice to counter the negative impact of teacher expectations and differential treatment on student self-perceptions. First, teachers should not necessarily strive to treat all students the same but instead should strive to make sure that they are not treating children differently based on their own beliefs or expectations. Students should receive differential treatment based on their demonstrated needs and abilities, not on teachers' beliefs and expectations. Second, Wigfield and Harold (1992) suggested that, in addition to being aware that their expectancies can influence behavior, teachers should collaborate with colleagues, observe one another's interactions with students, and discuss ways in which their behavior might influence students' self-perceptions. If teachers have high expectations for and strong beliefs about active student involvement, we would expect to see classrooms operating in a manner consistent with many of the suggestions given in Chapter 3. Regardless of their individual abilities, students would have a high degree of involvement in classroom routines such as assessment, curriculum, instruction, classroom management, and establishment of a positive climate for all learners.

Teacher Control Orientation

In addition to examining their expectations for students, teachers need to consider their own control orientation, particularly as this orientation influences the power structure in the classroom. Student involvement and student-directed learning is fundamentally about *who* is in control and has power in the classroom. Teachers who want to promote active student involvement must balance the need to shift control to the student while retaining ultimate control over or, more appropriately, responsibility for the learning process. Research has linked excessive teacher control orientations with maladaptive student motivation and self-esteem (Deci, Spiegel, Ryan, Koestner, & Kauffman, 1982), lower academic achievement (Boggiano & Katz, 1991), and decrements in performance (Flink, Boggiano, & Barrett, 1990). This research suggests that students' perceptions of their classroom environments are linked with the teaching style and control orientation of the classroom teacher. Related research on social influences in classrooms and on the impact of instructional communication styles has also focused on the issue of teacher control, specifically on teachers' use of power in classrooms. Richmond and Roach noted that

> the role of a teacher, almost by definition, involves social influence. The tasks of a teacher are many-fold. An instructor is responsible for presenting subject content, explaining difficult concepts, modeling and stimulating problem-solving skills, promoting both cognitive and affective learning in students, motivating students toward academic achievement, and providing an environment conducive to learning. Simply stated, a teacher's job is to influence students. One can quickly see the importance and operation of power in the instructional setting. (1992, p. 58)

Richmond and Roach concluded that the use of power is an inherent part of the teaching process when that power is focused on influencing students toward educational achievements. There are different types or bases of power that come into play in the classroom. Barraclough and Stewert identified five types of classroom power:

1. *Reward power:* Based on the student's perception that the teacher has the ability to mediate reward for her or him
2. *Coercive power:* Based on the student's perceptions that the teacher has the ability to mediate punishments for her or him
3. *Legitimate power:* Based on the student's perception that the teacher has a legitimate right to prescribe and proscribe behavior for her or him
4. *Referent power:* Based on the student's identification with the teacher
5. *Expert power:* Based on the student's perception that the teacher has some special knowledge or expertise (1992, pp. 4–5)

Richmond and Roach (1992) pointed out that using these various types of powers to create an effective learning climate is a difficult tightrope for teachers to walk. This may be particularly so for teachers who work with students with disabilities, who frequently need more structure, guidance, and direction than other students. However, given the potential detrimental impact of teaching styles that are overly controlling, this is an area that warrants consideration. For example, using the application principles outlined in Chapter 3, teachers can provide a systematic manner of releasing control to students for their educational planning, decision making, and instruction as students are developmentally ready to handle this responsibility.

It is important to distinguish between excessive teacher control and effective classroom management, organization, and structure. There is a tendency to confuse issues of structure with control, and there is the belief on the part of many educators that promoting self-determination (and student involvement) is synonymous with giving up all structure in the classroom (Wehmeyer, Agran, & Hughes, 1998). This is simply not true and, in fact, could not be further from the truth. As Deci and Chandler (1986) noted, promoting self-determination is not the same as allowing chaos. In classrooms with little structure and no expectations for appropriate behavior, students cannot learn. However, special education environments are often too tightly structured and controlling (Ianacone & Stodden, 1987; Wehmeyer, 1992) and limit any meaningful opportunities to achieve self-determination or to promote students' positive perceptions of control. Within established structures and routines, students can assume greater control and responsibility.

Creating a Positive Classroom Environment

One means of successfully balancing teacher control and student involvement is to create classroom learning environments that focus on active student involvement. Book and Putnam identified a three-stage process in the development of the classroom as a learning community in which students are active participants, the first stage of which, "Beginnings," focuses on five primary tasks of the teacher:

1. Inform students about life in a classroom learning community, with the emphasis [being] on class members as a community.
2. Help students learn [their classmates'] names, [and] become acquainted [with] and begin to build trust among community members.
3. Foster appreciation of other students' multiple abilities.
4. Promote students' developing a voice in the learning community.
5. Assess what students know and can do and use [and then use that information] as a database for reflection. (1992, p. 23)

As Book and Putnam (1992) described it, life in a classroom learning community emphasizes the values of differences among students, participation, and open communication, as well as the importance of learning from mistakes and the need to learn from and respect others in the community. To foster an appreciation of other students' abilities, they recommend designing group projects in which each student contributes something unique to the completion of the project. In such circumstances, students learn that their own goals and objectives can be reached by working with others who have different talents and abilities. Teachers need to reinforce the importance of open communication and the value of students' opinions and input to the learning community. Students are encouraged to ask questions of themselves, their teachers, and their peers and are encouraged to show ongoing respect for themselves and others in the course of these interactions. Finally, this first stage of building a learning community focuses on determining what students know and do well and works from that vantage point, as opposed to identifying impairments and starting there.

The second stage in the process of building a learning community is to establish expectations. Book and Putnam described this stage as one

> in which the teacher and students build shared understanding through making norms, roles, rules and procedures explicit by providing students with
> (a) descriptions,
> (b) reasons for their existence,
> (c) illustrations of what they look like in the learning community,
> (d) practice opportunities,
> (e) feedback to individuals and groups, and
> (f) consequences to the individual and community when the norms, roles, rules, and procedures are not followed. (1992, p. 26)

At this stage, teachers work with students to establish appropriate behavioral norms for interactions within the community. Such norms include demonstrating respect for each other by listening, responding, questioning, and working cooperatively to solve problems and achieve mutually identified goals. The roles of each student within the community are defined and assigned. There are individual roles (e.g., small-group facilitator, timer, recorder) and group roles. Group roles involve those roles that all students are expected to fulfill, including contributing to discussions, providing information, or asking questions. Based on these established norms and roles, community rules and classroom procedures can be established.

The third stage in the process of building a community learning environment is to identify and resolve the inevitable conflicts that emerge in any group. A key feature of a learning community is that power is distributed among members of the class as well as among teachers. However, as emphasized in the discussion about power in the classroom, it is still the teacher's role to use power to facilitate learning. One such use of power will be to resolve students' behavior problems. Conflict resolution strategies become important ways to structure problem solving and support within a learning environment. The fourth stage of building a learning community is to expand the community. This stage involves the use of a wide variety of instructional strategies across different environments outside of the classroom. For example, students may engage in project-related activities in alternative learning environments, such as a museum.

By creating a classroom climate that focuses on building a learning community, teachers in essence redefine their role as the power broker and enable students to take greater ownership over the classroom and their learning. It seems evident that student involvement programs and self-directed learning strategies will thrive in such classrooms.

BUILDING- AND DISTRICT-LEVEL VARIABLES AND STUDENT INVOLVEMENT

Valuing and providing opportunities for increased student involvement in education planning, decision making, and instruction does not stop at the classroom door. In fact, to provide the types of learning opportunities and supports that students need to learn and practice these important skills, work must be done at the building and district levels, too.

In ways that might not be evident at first glance, a call for increased student involvement is, in fact, a call for teacher empowerment. Teachers do not operate in a vacuum, and although an effective classroom teacher can make a tremendous difference, he or she cannot act alone and expect to ultimately succeed. The call for student participation in education planning, decision making, and instruction is also a call for teacher participation in the decisions that have an impact on every classroom and every student in that district. There are several valid reasons why such teacher participation is important. For example, Sarason stated his acceptance of this principle based on the "belief that when a process makes people feel that they have a voice in matters that affect them, they will have a greater commitment to the overall enterprise and will take greater responsibility for what happens in the enterprise" (1990, p. 61). The author of Chapter 1 argues that students who are involved in their education programs are more likely to take ownership of and responsibility for their learning. This is as true for teachers and their relationships with the educational system as it is for students and their relationships to learning.

Sarason also pointed out that the absence of meaningful involvement by teachers "ensures that no one feels responsible, that blame will always be directed externally, [and] that adversarial interactions will be a notable feature of school life" (1990, p. 61). In most circumstances in the public schools today, Sarason (1990) argued, each teacher is responsible only for what happens in his or her classroom, at least partly because the power status in schools has not fundamentally changed since the mid-1940s. Just as power within the classroom is a basic element that has an impact on student involvement, so too are the power status of teachers and the power structure of the system basic features of and barriers to achieving meaningful, active student involvement. Sarason summarized this situation quite succinctly as follows:

> Whatever factors, variables, and ambiance are conducive for the growth, development, and self-regard of a school's staff are precisely those that are crucial to obtaining the same consequences for students in a classroom. To focus on the latter and ignore or gloss over the former is an invitation to disillusionment. (1990, p. 52)

To guarantee student involvement, we must ensure teacher participation. Ironically, it is apparent that this is true for student achievement, not just student involvement. Golarz and Golarz (1995), summarizing research examining effective schools, identified three overarching characteristics of successful schools:

1. High levels of parental involvement and support
2. Collaborative collegial instructional planning
3. Individual school autonomy and the resulting flexibility

Such schools adopt a *participatory governance,* which Golarz and Golarz defined as "the transfer of authority and responsibility from those who hold power by virtue of law, contract or organizational role to those not so empowered" (1995, p. 4). Schools that succeed are schools in which the power structure is not hierarchical, descending from school board member to administrator, then to the teacher, and finally to the student. Instead, the power structure of such schools actively involves all constituents, including parents, teachers, and students, in decision-making processes. Student involvement as such is as much a part of school reform as it is a component of transition planning. Thus, when individual schools and the district hold a positive value for student involvement, teachers are empowered to act in ways that facilitate this outcome.

A LIFE-SPAN APPROACH TO STUDENT INVOLVEMENT AND SELF-DETERMINATION

It is never too late to initiate efforts to actively involve students in education planning, decision making, and instruction or to promote student self-determination. However, when such efforts begin early, students are likely to experience greater ownership over the process and have greater opportunities to acquire the skills they need to take control of their learning and ultimately become more self-determined young people. Sands and colleagues (Doll, Sands, Wehmeyer, & Palmer, 1996; Sands & Doll, 1996; Wehmeyer, Sands, Doll, & Palmer, in press) described the development of self-determination by examining the development and acquisition of component elements of self-determination (see also Chapter 1).

Some of these component elements are in place early in life, whereas others are best addressed later in development. For example, the developmental antecedents to making choices, identifying preferences, and communicating such preferences to make choices are often in place before the child reaches 2 years of age. Consequently, efforts to promote choice making are focused on expanding opportunities for children to make choices and learn about consequences and options resulting from such choices. In addition, in the case of some students with more significant disabilities, these efforts are focused on providing alternative means by which to communicate preferences and thus make choices. However, teaching decision-making skills is more effective with older elementary school–age students and adolescents because these students have developed a better understanding of their strengths and limitations, the range of options available to them in a situation, the consequences of each option, and rudimentary problem-solving skills. Accordingly, student involvement in the early elementary school years takes a different form from student involvement in secondary education. The following section provides some suggestions for instructional activities that promote self-determination and ultimately student involvement.

Early Childhood Years

Even preschool children evidence some rudimentary elements of self-determined behavior. They can recognize their own preferences, express these clearly and unequivocally when provided the opportunity, and are typically aware of some though not all of the alternative options in a decision. Choice making among preschoolers is largely dependent on the quality of their caregiver relationships, in which control over the process is retained by caregivers and freedom to engage in the process is dependent on the level of trust that exists between child and caregiver. In addition, preschool children's growing mastery of language appears essential to choice making, increasing the ease with which choices can be offered and described to the child and the ease with which the child can identify preferences. Preschoolers appear to lack linkages to connect the choices and preferences they indicate to personal goals that describe what, ultimately, they might want to achieve. In large part, this may be because preschool children do not yet reflect purposefully on personal goals or aspirations, although their imaginary play does reflect a fascination with being grown up and some preconceptions about what that might entail. Thus, their choices appear to reflect their present wants unencumbered by the need to achieve some future goal or objective.

Even if preschoolers could voice their goals, however, it is unlikely that they would systematically shape their actions to achieve them because inaccurate or overoptimistic estimates of their own abilities limit their capacity to direct their own purposeful efforts. In addition, their egocentric social perspective precludes the skilled direction of others' behavior. Although they are aware of their own uniqueness and are sensitive to their own varying affect, they tend not to reflect on these features in others. Moreover, within the limits of a single task, preschool children do not spontaneously or systematically refine or revise their choice of actions in accordance with whether they lead to success or failure.

Adults can support elements of self-determination emergent in preschool children and promote student involvement by providing ample chances for them to exercise the choice-making and choice recognition capacities that they possess, particularly in relation to the education process (see Chapter 5 for examples of infusing choice into the daily classroom routine). Necessary supports might include 1) offering choices to the child whenever possible, 2) assisting the child in recognizing alternative choices, and 3) restricting the child from making choices that are detrimental to his or her future opportunities. Adults can encourage a preschooler's emergent understanding of the links between choices and outcomes by revisiting the choices that the child has made in the recent past, helping him or her to identify the consequences of those choices, and discussing plans for similar choices in the future. Education-planning meetings would be an opportune time to engage in such activities. Another opportunity for student involvement involves establishing linkages between the choices the students have made and later outcomes, which can be fostered by encouraging preschoolers to plan their daily activities and evaluate how close they were to being able to carry out their plan.

Early Elementary School Years

By the early elementary school years, students more actively direct their own thinking and reasoning. They identify increasingly varied solutions to problems that they encounter. Compared with preschoolers, these students are more likely to implement the solutions that they generate. Because they are better judges of their own strengths and weaknesses, these students are more likely to select strategies, solutions, and options that complement their abilities. Their concrete operations reasoning ability allows them to recognize generic rules that explain problems and solutions, which can be generalized and applied to new though similar problems in the future. Moreover, their improved perspective taking makes it possible for these students to shape the ways that others behave toward them, granting them some control over their social context as well. As such, students can begin to take a greater role in making decisions about their individualized education programs (IEPs) and in participating in self-directed instructional activities.

Still, once they have chosen a path or a plan, early elementary school–age students are slow to abandon it, persisting with their original approach even when faced with little or no success. Despite their initial responsiveness, they do not purposefully redirect their efforts in response to information about their plan's results. Although first graders can set goals and work to achieve them for brief intervals, they need the support of an adult to point out their incremental improvements and praise them liberally for these successes. Without such adult direction, early elementary school–age students do not spontaneously engage in goal-governed actions.

Adult support for self-determination and student involvement in the early elementary school years should reinforce a student's identification of multiple strategies and options for choice and decision making (see Chapter 3). Participation in IEP planning might focus more on identifying the range of instructional and programmatic options available and providing students the opportunity to discuss these options in the course of the meeting. Support should assist students in articulating and making explicit the match between the strategies that they select and their own unique abilities, another topic of potential discussion at IEP planning meetings and between students and teachers. More important, both in the meeting and during the course of the year, adults can assist the student in revisiting previously made decisions and choices, evaluate how well their actions and choices are helping them to achieve their goals, and shift or maintain their approach as necessary. Students should also be encouraged to practice their newly emerging understanding of rule-based decision making. Where rules that can guide decision making and problem solving exist, they should be encouraged to say the rule aloud, apply it to the problem, and decide whether the rule points to the best choice. Again, IEP meetings provide unique opportunities to do these activities.

Late Elementary School Years

It is during the late elementary school years that the first real evidence emerges to indicate that students spontaneously set personal goals that shape their subsequent actions. In part, this is because late elementary school–age students have acquired the capacity to systematically recognize when their problem-solving approach is and is not working and, if necessary, to adopt a new strategy more likely to be successful. They are able to recognize when they need assistance and ask for this assistance. They also recognize when additional effort is likely to improve their performance on a task. Moreover, they can anticipate the response that their behavior is likely to elicit from other people and select actions with those social consequences in mind. With these essential tools, students in late elementary school grades are able to selectively shape their actions so that these support, rather than subvert, their aspirations. It is not surprising, then, to find that late elementary school–age students can make medical treatment decisions that approximate those of adults even though they cannot systematically analyze the consequences of the various choices, and their preferences still reflect the most salient consequences of a choice. Given their increased capacities, students need to become actively involved as decision makers in their education programs and not just act as passive recipients.

What late elementary school–age students lack is the structure for systematic analysis of the consequences of the various options from which they can choose. Therefore, it is not always possible for them to verbalize a clear rationale for the decisions that they make, even though they are able to make decisions similar to those of adults. Moreover, these students are likely to disregard less salient or striking options of a decision, especially when a problem is new or unfamiliar.

Late elementary school–age students can benefit from adult support in structuring their decision-making activities, assisting them through the process of listing options, explicitly describing their consequences, and weighing the respective costs and benefits of each. Structuring activities helps them to arrange their list of decision options in a manner that is easier to compare systematically. Adults can assist students in systematically revisiting past decisions to recognize the impact that these have on their present lives and to make the cost–benefit decisions more concrete. These activities should be components of the supports available to students at this age to enable them to participate more in the decision-making process.

Next, late elementary school–age students can be assisted to generalize their decision-making skills to setting specific and achievable goals for their own personal and academic lives, determining whether current decisions advance or conflict with those goals, and monitoring their progress toward them. Most late elementary school–age students require adult guidance to formulate evaluations of their own strengths and weaknesses that are both accurate (so that students can advance their abilities to plan for realistic future goals) and accepting (so that students can acknowledge skill deficits and limitations without disrupting their sense of personal confidence and self-worth).

Secondary School Years

Secondary school students demonstrate a capacity for systematic decision making that is similar in most respects to that of adults. Their decisions incorporate an analysis of the consequences of each choice as well as a determination of the credibility of the information that they use. Similarly, their approach to task completion and problem solving is spontaneously strategic, and they systematically analyze and revise their strategies in the face of successful or unsuccessful experiences. They easily generalize successful problem-solving strategies from one task to other tasks. Moreover, their sophisticated perspective taking makes it possible for them to exert accurate and effective control over the social ecology that determines their destiny. Informed consent by adolescents approximates that of adults. In fact, the primary barrier to student involvement for adolescents tends to be their emotionality; individual differences in their perceptions of self-control have more to do with their emotional turbulence and their prior learning experiences than with their developmental potential.

The primary emphasis of adult support for students at this level is the provision of frequent and varied opportunities to practice self-directed and self-determined behaviors. So that adults do not inadvertently limit students' self-determination opportunities or unnecessarily protect students from the consequences of those decisions, it is often useful to plan in advance for ways to extend students' self-determination opportunities with the students and with other adults who support those students. Secondary students also continue to need assistance to analyze their decisions systematically and to critically evaluate the sources of knowledge they use to make decisions. Finally, adults can assist secondary school students with the emotional demands that self-determination requires by providing emotional support to assist the students in recognizing their strengths and limitations without obscuring the reality of their life decisions.

EXPANDING SELF-DETERMINATION AND STUDENT INVOLVEMENT BEYOND SPECIAL EDUCATION

Baron and Brown suggested that "teaching decision making in schools is a part of a larger movement to make schooling more thoughtful" (1991, p. 5). To a great degree, the emphasis on self-determination and student involvement that emerged in special education in the 1990s is also a part of such a larger movement. This broad school reform movement shares common themes around needs to 1) enable young people to become more effective decision makers and problem solvers so that they can cope more effectively with the demands of an increasingly complex society; and 2) prepare young people to become self-sufficient, self-reliant, and competent citizens (Apple & Beane, 1995; Harmin, 1994). These needs are not unique to students with disabilities, although they may be more urgent and more salient for them.

Although students with disabilities have been the focus of the discussions in this text, an exclusive focus on students with disabilities and on student involvement in the IEP planning process ultimately only further marginalizes students with disabilities. We have stressed that students with disabilities need to be involved in all aspects of their educational programs, from assessment and planning through instruction and program evaluation. The common themes shared by the chapters in this book have involved expanding students' opportunities for choices; promoting problem-solving, decision-making, and goal-setting skills, as well as opportunities to employ those skills; and involving students in self-directed learning experiences. These needs exist for many students, independent of the presence or absence of a disability. Kohn argued that "the key to transforming student apathy into student engagement may be as simple as allowing students to make decisions about their learning" (1993,

p. 9). Kohn was referring not to students with disabilities but instead to students in all U.S. schools. He provided two overarching ways to achieve this outcome:

1. Involve students in academic decisions about what, how, how well, and why they learn
2. Think about ways to help students to take an active part in decisions that are only indirectly related to academics, including the classroom rules, schedule, and the learning environment

These are, in essence, the fundamental beliefs and strategies emphasized throughout this book. It is evident that issues of self-determination and student involvement are areas in which students with and students without disabilities share common needs and where special educators can provide valuable direction, insight, and strategies. As previously suggested (Sands & Wehmeyer, 1996), the self-determination and student involvement movements need to be considered along with, and indeed as an integral component of, the broader movements toward inclusion and school reform.

MAKING IT HAPPEN

As with any significant change, there are barriers to achieving the goal of student involvement. Perhaps the most significant is the hesitancy on the part of many educators to turn greater control over to students. Kohn described this resistance as follows:

> A number of writers and teachers who resist giving children the chance to make decisions have justified their opposition by erecting an enormous straw man called "absolute freedom" and counter-posing it to the status quo. Since most of us do not relish the idea of children spending their time at school doing anything they please, deprived of structured or adult guidance, we are encouraged to settle for the controlling practices that now exist. (1993, p. 14)

As Kohn described it, this represents a false dichotomy. Student involvement and self-determination are not about giving students absolute freedom to create chaos and disorder, as discussed previously. As described here, the challenge for the teacher is to relinquish control of learning to the student while retaining responsibility for ensuring student learning and achievement. Done well, student involvement becomes the teacher's ally, providing a potentially powerful means by which to circumvent barriers to learning such as the lack of student motivation and discipline problems. Realistically, this presents a new challenge for teachers and, in many ways, redefines their role in the classroom. In many cases, teachers are not adequately prepared to assume such a role, and the former teacher-directed, controlling environments continue to prevail. Personnel preparation programs must begin to more adequately enable teachers to walk the tightrope between student control and teacher responsibility for learning.

There are also structural barriers to student involvement. Kohn (1993) pointed out that classroom teachers often indicate that they would provide more opportunities for students to participate in the decision-making process, except that they have limited control over who makes such decisions in the first place. We have addressed this in a previous section and again emphasize here that a call for student involvement is a call for teacher involvement and empowerment and for reexamining overly bureaucratic and structured systems that limit active involvement by all stakeholders—students, parents, and teachers.

There is yet another barrier to student involvement that warrants consideration—the students themselves. Student involvement and self-determination are not the magic solution to all educational woes. Our experience has been that students are often resistant to assuming greater control over their educational programs. If students were involved from the time they enter school, as described previously, we suggest that such resistance would disappear as a significant barrier. However, it remains a fact that many students are not ready or willing to take more responsibility for their learning process. Students have probably learned over the years that decisions are made by someone else other than themselves and that the educational process is largely unrelated to their interests and preferences. School is a place where they must go to do something that someone else has determined is important (Kohn, 1993). It takes time and effort to overcome this barrier, and teachers need to convince students that their efforts to relinquish control to students are sincere. Students need to be supported and encouraged as they make small steps toward their own involvement, supports need to be in place so that students can succeed, and student involvement needs to begin early.

CONCLUSIONS

This book provides an overview of student involvement and introduces programs, strategies, and materials that seek to actively involve students in their education planning, decision making, and instruction. In this chapter, we have illustrated that, in addition to programs, materials, and instructional strategies, teachers and building- and district-level administrators must hold values and beliefs in favor of, and must actively implement, opportunities for student involvement. As we have articulated, much of the impetus for such activities has sprung from the increased emphasis on self-determination and from the student involvement mandates in the IDEA. We believe, however, that as students with disabilities receive more of their education programs with peers without disabilities and as school reform efforts increase participatory governance and stakeholder participation, the need for student involvement will expand and take on increased importance. In addition, it seems evident that students with disabilities need an additional set of tools at their disposal if they are to succeed as adults—namely, self-determination skills; the opportunity to employ them; and the experience of active student involvement in education planning, decision making, and instruction. Making it happen will, these authors believe, move us closer to the outcome of all students with and students without disabilities becoming self-sufficient and self-reliant people.

REFERENCES

Apple, M.W., & Beane, J.A. (1995). *Democratic schools.* Alexandria, VA: Association for Supervision and Curriculum Development.

Baron, J., & Brown, R.V. (1991). Introduction. In J. Baron & R.V. Brown (Eds.), *Teaching decision making to adolescents* (pp. 1–6). Hillsdale, NJ: Lawrence Erlbaum Associates.

Barraclough, R.A., & Stewert, R.A. (1992). Power and control: Social science perspectives. In V.P. Richmond & J.C. McCroskey (Eds.), *Power in the classroom: Communication, control, and concern* (pp. 1–18). Hillsdale, NJ: Lawrence Erlbaum Associates.

Boggiano, A. K., & Katz, P. (1991). Maladaptive achievement patterns in students: The role of teachers' controlling strategies. *Journal of Social Issues, 47*(4), 35–51.

Book, C.L., & Putnam, J.G. (1992). Organization and management of a classroom as a learning community culture. In V.P. Richmond & J.C. McCroskey (Eds.), *Power in the classroom: Communication, control, and concern* (pp. 19–34). Hillsdale, NJ: Lawrence Erlbaum Associates.

Deci, E.L., & Chandler, C.L. (1986). The importance of motivation for the future of the LD field. *Journal of Learning Disabilities, 19,* 587–594.

Deci, E.L., Spiegel, N.H., Ryan, R.M., Koestner, R., & Kauffman, M. (1982). Effects of performance standards on teaching styles: Behavior of controlling teachers. *Journal of Educational Psychology, 74,* 852–859.

Doll, B., Sands, D.J., Wehmeyer, M.L., & Palmer, S. (1996). Promoting the development and acquisition of self-determined behavior. In D.J. Sands & M.L. Wehmeyer (Eds.), *Self-determination across the life span: Independence and choice for people with disabilities* (pp. 65–90). Baltimore: Paul H. Brookes Publishing Co.

Feldman, R.S., Saletsky, R.D., Sullivan, J., & Theiss, A. (1983). Student locus of control and response to expectations about self and teacher. *Journal of Educational Psychology, 75,* 27–32.

Flink, C., Boggiano, A.K., & Barrett, M. (1990). Controlling teaching strategies: Undermining children's self-determination and performance. *Journal of Personality and Social Psychology, 59,* 916–924.

Golarz, R.J., & Golarz, M.J. (1995). *The power of participation: Improving schools in a democratic society.* Champaign, IL: Research Press.

Harmin, M. (1994). *Inspiring active learning: A handbook for teachers.* Alexandria, VA: Association for Supervision and Curriculum Development.

Ianacone, R.N., & Stodden, R.A. (1987). Transition issues and directions for individuals who are mentally retarded. In R.N. Ianacone & R.A. Stodden (Eds.), *Transition issues and directions* (pp. 1–7). Reston, VA: Council for Exceptional Children.

Individuals with Disabilities Education Act (IDEA) of 1990, PL 101-476, 20 U.S.C. §§ 1400 *et seq.*

Kohn, A. (1993). Choices for children: Why and how to let students decide. *Phi Delta Kappan, 75*(1), 8–20.

Richmond, V.P., & Roach, K.D. (1992). Power in the classroom: Seminal studies. In V.P. Richmond & J.C. McCroskey (Eds.), *Power in the classroom: Communication, control, and concern* (pp. 47–66). Hillsdale, NJ: Lawrence Erlbaum Associates.

Sands, D.J., & Doll, B. (1996). Fostering self-determination is a developmental task. *Journal of Special Education, 30*, 58–76.

Sands, D.J., & Wehmeyer, M.L. (Eds.). (1996). *Self-determination across the life span: Independence and choice for people with disabilities.* Baltimore: Paul H. Brookes Publishing Co.

Sarason, S.B. (1990). *The predictable failure of educational reform: Can we change course before it's too late?* San Francisco: Jossey-Bass.

Wehmeyer, M.L. (1992). Self-determination and the education of students with mental retardation. *Education and Training in Mental Retardation, 27*, 303–314.

Wehmeyer, M.L., Agran, M., & Hughes, C. (1998). *Teaching self-determination to students with disabilities: Basic skills for successful transition.* Baltimore: Paul H. Brookes Publishing Co.

Wehmeyer, M.L., Sands, D.J., Doll, B., & Palmer, S. (in press). The development of self-determination and implications for educational interventions for students with disabilities. *International Journal on Development, Disability, and Education.*

Weinstein, R.S. (1985). Student mediation of classroom expectancy effects. In J.B. Dusek (Ed.), *Teacher expectancies* (pp. 329–350). Hillsdale, NJ: Lawrence Erlbaum Associates.

Weinstein, R.S. (1989). Perceptions of classroom processes and student motivation: Children's views of self-fulfilling prophecies. In C. Ames & R. Ames (Eds.), *Research on motivation in education* (Vol. 3, pp. 187–221). San Diego: Academic Press.

Wigfield, A., & Harold, R.D. (1992). Teacher beliefs and children's achievement self-perceptions: A developmental perspective. In D.H. Schunk & J.L. Meece (Eds.), *Student perceptions in the classroom* (pp. 95–121). Hillsdale, NJ: Lawrence Erlbaum Associates.

Index

Page numbers followed by "f" indicate figures; those followed by "t" indicate tables.